MEXICO:
IN SEARCH OF SECURITY

North·South Center
UNIVERSITY OF MIAMI

MEXICO:
IN SEARCH OF SECURITY

EDITED BY

BRUCE MICHAEL BAGLEY
AND
SERGIO AGUAYO QUEZADA

Transaction Publishers
New Brunswick (U.S.A.) and London (U.K.)

Library of Congress Cataloging-in-Publication Data

Mexico : in search of security / edited by Bruce Michael Bagley. Sergio Aguayo Quezada.

p.   cm.

"Revised product of a conference held at the Universidad Nacional Autónoma de México in Mexico City on February 22-24, 1989" — Introd.

Includes bibliographical references and index.

ISBN 1-56000-686-2 (paper.)

1. Mexico — Foreign relations — 1970- 2. National Security — Mexico. 3. Mexico — Foreign relations — United States. 4. United States — Foreign relations — Mexico. I. Bagley, Bruce Michael. II. Aguayo, Sergio. III. University of Miami. North-South Center.

F1236.M476 1993
327.72—dc20   93-527
                                                          CIP

ISBN-1-56000-686-2 (paper)
Printed in the United States of America

Contents

Part Three:
Economy, Environment, and National Security

Part Four:
Bilateral Issues and National Security

Part Five:
Rethinking Mexican National Security

Acknowledgments

The editors gratefully acknowledge the financial assistance of the Social Science Research Council, the MacArthur Foundation, and the facilities of the Latin American Institute for Transnational Studies (ILET-Mexico). At these institutions the contributions of Richard Rockwell, Richard Moss, Michael Gross, José Casar, and Guadalupe González were essential to the project.

This volume is a somewhat shorter and, in places, slightly revised English-language version of *En busca de la seguridad perdida: Aproximaciones a la seguridad nacional mexicana* published by Siglo Veintiuno Editores in Mexico City. In the handling of the text special thanks are due to Jeffrey Stark for editing, Claudio Alatorre for style editing of Spanish-language manuscripts, and Pilar Morales for project coordination in Mexico; Sallie Lee, Gabriela Lemus, and Tricia Juhn for translations; Karen Payne for copyediting; Diane Duys, Nancy Colón, Norma Laird, Shantell Lugo, and Valerie Collins for manuscript preparation; and Kathleen Hamman, editorial director of the North-South Center.

Prologue

Lorenzo Meyer

O ne of the main problems in social science is the definition of
concepts. Rarely, if ever, are the basic instruments for constructing theory or research so precise as to avoid error, ambiguity, or a
plurality of interpretation. National security is a paradigmatic example
of this phenomenon. On the one hand, it is a concept central to
international relations theory; on the other hand, it is a difficult term
to manage because there exists not even the remotest consensus on its
definition. Moreover, as is the case with almost all concepts in political
science, its importance is not only theoretical but also practical, since
it can grant or take away the legitimacy of basic national policies.

The concept of national security has a particularly difficult
practical history in Latin America. During the Cold War years, a number
of anti-democratic governments in the region — particularly those
headed by military officers — custom-tailored it so as to justify the
political and physical destruction of the so-called "internal enemy,"
which in practice turned out to be anyone who opposed the governments or authoritarian regimes. For a long period of time, in the name
of national security, democrats, unionists, and militant leftists were
labeled and persecuted as enemies of the nation at the service of
international forces. The political and physical eradication of the
enemy became indispensable for the preservation of the nation's
higher interests.[1]

Given its history in Latin America — a history of "dirty wars" from
which Mexico cannot completely extricate itself — the national
security concept has not, over the last half century, been favorably
viewed by Mexican social scientists. Nor has it easily entered into
official political discourse, which has sought to dissociate itself from

the schools of thought developed by the Southern Cone military regimes, in particular those of Brazil, Argentina, and Chile. For this reason, the term "national security" is relatively new in Mexico, and although much has changed in the panorama of Latin American politics, the concept still arouses suspicion since the Mexican authoritarian structure continues to have the potential for improper use of the national security concept; that is, to justify the state's repressive and illegal action against its opponents while claiming to defend the essence of the nation.

However, although late in arriving and not without problems, the controversial concept has established its presence in official documents and in Mexican academic analysis. One of the definitions of national security that explicitly appears in this work is the one proposed by Luis Herrera-Lasso and Guadalupe González: "the entirety of conditions — political, economic, military, social, and cultural — necessary to guarantee the sovereignty, independence, and promotion of the national interest...." Initially, the definition seems adequate. But as often happens while constructing concepts in the social sciences, the terms themselves require definition — in this case, three rather difficult ones: sovereignty, independence, and national interest. In the definition of these, the inevitable — and insurmountable — ambiguities appear.

Like the concept of security, that of national interest has no clear definition. Its empirical content is twofold: one, it emerges from geographic factors, the political-historic process, and the collective aspiration to which both give rise; and two, its substance depends on the practical objectives of the institutions, groups, and individuals in each country that make basic international policy decisions (Gori 1988, 860-61). In the specific case of Mexico, the substance of national interest depends to a large extent not just on national actors, but on the policy taken toward Mexico by the regional hegemonic leader, the United States. Internally, the fundamental role of defining the nation's direction belongs to the political institution that since the end of the last century has been at the center of Mexican politics — the presidency, axis of the principal political and social alliances that have subsequently directed the country.

The other two concepts, sovereignty and independence, suffer from the same weakness as national interest. Both are used frequently and interchangeably to refer to the capacity of the state to make basic internal and external policy decisions — to abolish or issue laws, and define its allies and its enemies, to use the terms employed by Jean Bodin — without subordinating them to the interests of one or another member or structure of the international community. In reality, the independence as well as the sovereignty of nation-states has always been relative, particularly, but not only in the case of, weak or peripheral states like Mexico.

The difference of degrees in the practice of states' sovereignty and independence has opened the way to a theoretical focus — interdependence — which seeks to explain and facilitate relationships among international political actors based on the assumption that the national interest of each state must occur within an international context where states, including industrialized ones, rarely, if ever, have the capacity to exercise full sovereignty, especially in economic terms.[2]

The difficulties presented by the application of the concept of national security in the Mexican case arise not only out of the country's political history or from the theoretical nature of the term itself, but also from the historic nature of Mexico's national formation. Our country, like many others of the Third World, but distinct from the original nation-states, emerged as an independent actor in the international arena at the beginning of the last century without the social attributes of a true nation. During a good part of the nineteenth century, the profound political, social, and racial divisions inherited from the colonial era — exemplified by the existence of one republic of Indians and another of colonial Spaniards, as well as by regionalism and lack of internal communication — made Mexican society for a long time a pre-national one. Perceptions of security were strongly affected by this. The defense of national interest — an interest which was basically theoretical, given that the nation had not even begun to construct itself — concentrated on the most elemental aspects, such as creating a minimum internal unity and defending territorial integrity against threats from within and without: regional secession, European imperialism, and North American expansionism, among others.[3]

The consolidation of a central government in Mexico and the consolidation of the United States as a great geopolitical entity after its Civil War, the achievement of North American interoceanic communication as a result of the construction of a canal in Panama and not in Tehuantepec, and the decreased political and military European presence in Latin America, favoring U.S. hegemony, were some of the other factors that diminished, to a large degree, the external threat to Mexican territorial integrity. After the 1910-1920 Revolution, Mexican efforts in national security stopped concentrating on territorial defense and until very recently concentrated on two areas with little or no military content: 1) expanding its capacity for political self-determination vis-à-vis the United States, and 2) promoting economic development based on protection of the internal market and direct state intervention in the production process. In reality, those two areas became the main elements of revolutionary nationalism, which was the backbone of postrevolutionary Mexican politics until the crisis of the economic-political model in 1982 (Meyer 1990, 259-271).

Today, as this volume demonstrates, Mexico is living through a radical redefinition of the concrete, operational meanings of national interest, independence, and sovereignty. Currently, the rapid diminution of the state as economic actor and the opening and integration of the Mexican economy into the international market are distinctive elements of government policy — the main objective of which is the modernization of the production apparatus. This will require an operational definition of national security different from the one that could be applied until 1982.

The analytical efforts of this volume's contributors focus on this new stage of the Mexican historical process. In the international arena, this new phase is marked by the end of the East-West confrontation. In the domestic arena, it is marked by a shift in economic growth strategies from one based on tariff protection to one whose dynamic derives from the opening and integration of the Mexican economy with that of the United States. This volume is an effort to clarify, in relation to those new factors, Mexico's strong points and its "windows of vulnerability" and how best to close them.

If during the Cold War the concept of national security in Latin America was determined by the political, military, economic, and ideological struggle between the United States and the Soviet Union, at the end of this confrontation, the concept of national security defined in anticommunist terms has (even for conservative groups and governments) little or no reason for being. In the new circumstances — where the socialist bloc no longer exists — the idea of national security in Latin America finally has the possibility of freeing itself from its conservative, anticommunist, and largely illegitimate past, concentrating on constructive themes of greater interest and relevance for the bulk of political actors of the region, including Mexico.

As previously noted, those at any given time with the responsibility for and control of the state apparatus are basically (but not exclusively) the ones who give concrete definition and operationalization to national security. It is thus not a definition that remains fixed once and for all, but one that must change as the nature of government's endeavors changes. Just as the consensus of political actors around a concrete government project can be greater or lesser but never total, so will there always be space for alternative definitions of national security; that is, the proposals of the counter elite. In a pluralist and open political system, it should be society itself, through the use of discussion, partisan political activity, and electoral and parliamentary competition, that chooses the definition of national security most appropriate to a national project. In theory, it should be this way in Mexico, but in practice, the persistence in our country of a state party and of a presidency with broad metaconstitutional powers limits the possibilities for social bases which could produce representatives who influence the operational substance of national interest and national security.

In spite of all this, the real definition of Mexican national security is not something entirely arbitrated by those formally responsible for the conduct of the state or by its critics. As different sections of this volume make clear, there are objective conditions that determine much of the definition. On the other hand, it is to be conceded that within the government, the opposition, and, to a lesser extent, academia, there is no agreement on what should be included on the Mexican security agenda, nor its order of importance, since that depends in good measure on how narrow or wide is the definition employed. For example, for some, drug trafficking is a threat to national security, whereas for others, it is a matter of state security. The same can be said with respect to the deterioration of the traditional economic system. But whether the definition of national security is wide or limited, there are some basic points of agreement among most interested observers and participants. The first is that for present-day Mexico, given the asymmetry of the relationship with its neighbors to the north and south, it is not very useful to emphasize the traditional (military) sense of national security. The practical definition of Mexico's security as a national society depends and will continue to depend largely on the

United States' vision of its own national security and the place Mexico holds on its agenda.

In effect, the Mexican vision of security of the nation will depend heavily on how those north of the Río Bravo manage themselves and the weight they give to problems like the relationship between industrialized powers, drug trafficking, the migration of undocumented laborers, the Third World's external debt, the Mexican transition to democracy, the Central American political process, pollution and ecological deterioration on the northern Mexican border, and the importance of natural resources and the Mexican market. One of the characteristics of security in peripheral national societies is its dependence on the political processes of the core societies, processes that always echo throughout the spheres of influence of the core powers but which are difficult indeed to influence from the periphery.

No matter what the elements are that make up the operational definition of national security and its agenda, one thing should be clear. This concept has not been, and cannot be, free of concrete political and moral values. These values can change according to the times and the definitions that each author or actor gives the concept, but the term will never be neutral or innocent. Thus, the first and inevitable question we must ask ourselves before adopting national security as part of our analytical tools is whether its definition and use truly contribute to a better description and explanation of the Mexican reality. If the answer is yes, as it is for the majority of the authors in this work, then it must be managed in a way that truly contributes to a positive development of Mexican life.

From the sad story of national security in other countries, it is clear that the fundamental obligation of those who, in the name of national security, offer analysis, formulate proposals, and make and implement decisions, is not to confuse national security with the security of a state, government, or special interest group. From this confused thinking to the idea of an "internal enemy," of political adversaries as traitors who must be destroyed rather than tolerated, is a small step, easily taken when the political order weakens and enters into crisis, but whose consequences have always been tragic, lengthy, and damaging to a sane and democratic political evolution (Buzan 1983, 32).

Notes

1. For an analysis of the theoretical nature and the terrible practical consequences of the national security concept in the hands of military regimes in Argentina, Brazil, and Chile, see Tapia, 1980.

2. For discussion on interdependence in the Mexican case, see Torres, 1990.

3. For an analysis of the role of conflict with the United States in the Mexican historical process and its defense of national interest, see Meyer, 1990, 251-271.

References

Buzan, Barry. 1983. *People, States, and Fear.* Brighton, Sussex: Wheatsheaf Books Ltd.

Gori, Umberto. 1988. In *Diccionario de política,* eds. Norberto Bobbio and Nicola Mateucci I. Mexico: Siglo XXI.

Meyer, Lorenzo. 1990. "The United States and Mexico: the Historical Structure of their Conflict." *Journal of International Affairs* 43 (2) (Winter).

Tapia, Jorge A. 1980. *El terrorism de Estado. La doctrina de la seguridad nacional en el Cono Sur.* Mexico: Nueva Imagen.

Torres, Blanca, ed. 1990. *Interdependencia, un enfoque útil para el análisis de la relación México-Estados Unidos?* Mexico: Colegio de México.

Introduction:
In Search of Security

Bruce Michael Bagley, Sergio Aguayo Quezada,
and Jeffrey Stark

Introduction
Why this Volume?

Since the rise of the United States to global "superpower" status at the close of the Second World War, both the theory and practice of national security in the West have been largely the domain of North Americans. As a result, academic and policy discussions of this concept over the last forty-five years have consistently reflected the assumptions, perceptions, and interests of U.S. policymakers and analysts who have typically been steeped in the traditional "power realist" approach to international politics and who have been predominantly concerned with East-West tensions and U.S.-U.S.S.R. rivalries. To the limited extent the term has been used in the Third World at all, it has usually been invoked by anti-democratic elements of local ruling elites (both right and left) to rationalize and justify their authoritarian suppression of internal oppositions — as in the dictatorial military regimes of Latin America's Southern Cone countries during the 1960s and 1970s,[1] which relied on variants of the infamous National Security Doctrine, or in Castro's Cuba, which relied on revolutionary communism and anti-imperialism.

Rhetoric aside, neither version — whether the hegemonic or the *criollo* (home-grown) — paid much attention to the vital concerns and essential needs of the impoverished majorities of the developing world: for example, the amelioration of hunger and misery; the equitable distribution of the benefits of economic growth; the improvement of health, education and welfare; the defense of human rights; the institutionalization of democracy; the control of environmental

1

degradation; and the observance of the principles of self-determination, non-intervention, and national sovereignty. In practice these issues were routinely eclipsed by the "Cold War" East-West focus on national security questions prevalent in the United States and/or subordinated by repressive domestic governments to the narrow interests of specific elite groups. Not surprisingly, such results tainted the field of national security studies among many Third World scholars and led most to avoid use of the term altogether, especially in Mexico.[2]

At the outset of this book, therefore, it is essential to address the question of whether or not the notion of national security can be properly and meaningfully applied to Mexico or any other Third World nation-state. Given that most Mexican intellectuals are keenly sensitive about past aggressions carried out by the United States against Mexico (or by successive Mexican governments against internal oppositions) in the name of national security and are justifiably leery of a concept historically laden with ideological baggage, a second, related question is whether there is any analytic value or conceptual utility to be derived from an examination of contemporary Mexico from a national security perspective. And even if such a book is deemed at least potentially worthwhile, should it include contributions from North American scholars or be restricted to Mexican participants only?

In all honesty, we must admit that we are not absolutely sure of the "right" answers to these questions. Our intention in this introduction is to share with our readers both our lingering doubts and the logic that, nevertheless, persuaded us to proceed with the publication of this volume on the "national security" problems confronting Mexico in the final decade of the twentieth century. While we certainly hope that our arguments prove as convincing to skeptics as they were to us, we in any event submit that the analyses presented here will help to clarify the central issues and basic controversies involved in any attempt to apply the concepts and logic of national security analysis to Mexico or other Third World nation-states.

Is the Concept of National Security Worth Saving?
Realism and the Traditional Concept of National Security

Current definitions and interpretations of national security evolved out of the school of international politics known as "realism." This analytic framework or conceptual approach has a long and venerable history in Western political thought, extending from Thucydides through Machiavelli to present-day international relations theorists.[3] For many contemporary analysts and policymakers, the temporary waning of realist perspectives during the years between the World Wars, which witnessed the idealistic experiment of the League of Nations and British Prime Minister Neville Chamberlain's "appeasement" of Hitler at Munich, has served as an object lesson vindicating realism's enduring salience to the understanding of international politics and the problems of war and peace.[4] In adopting a realist approach to the international system after World War II, therefore, U.S. policymakers were explicitly building upon what they perceived to be lessons of history.

These "lessons" are grounded in a few core propositions, the most important of which is that the international system is inherently anarchical or conflictual. Unlike individual nation-states, which seek to construct internal order through the establishment of accepted patterns of authority, the international system lacks clear lines of command or any ultimate repository of decision-making power. The implications of this harsh reality for national security are far-reaching and sobering: In an anarchic world each nation-state is responsible for its own survival and can, in the final analysis, rely only on self-help to protect itself from the depredations of others; but in a hierarchical international system composed of formally sovereign nation-states separated by vast differences in wealth and power, and whose interests persistently come into conflict, "self-help" is often simply another name for war or domination.

Through the writings of such theorists as Hans Morgenthau and Kenneth Waltz, among others, the corollary propositions of realist thinking received further refinement.[5] Consisting essentially of logical extensions of the fundamental security dilemma faced by all nation-states as set forth above, these include the assertions that: 1) nation-states are the preeminent actors in world politics; 2) nation-states are best understood as rational, self-interested entities; and 3) the exercise of power is ultimately the means by which nation-states protect and promote their interests.[6] From the realist perspective, therefore, the defense of national security is generally understood in terms of (mainly military) power and inevitably ranks at the top of the hierarchy of issues for every nation-state. Thus, in the wake of the destructive and costly war against Nazi Germany and Japan, and with the Soviet Union and Eastern Europe under Stalinist control, U.S. leaders were understandably predisposed to conceptualize Western national security in realist terms, and they possessed the military capacity and economic clout to implement such a strategy on a global scale.

In practice, the escalating competition for world dominance between the United States and the Soviet Union in the immediate aftermath of World War II propelled U.S. policymakers to design a strategy to restrain and check the expansion of Soviet influence around the globe: containment. The principal components of the U.S. containment doctrine were strong conventional military and nuclear deterrents and the incorporation of regional allies into the global struggle against communism.[7] In Latin America this strategy took concrete form via the creation of the 1947 Rio Pact (Interamerican Treaty of Reciprocal Assistance).[8] As a world superpower and regional hegemon, the United States was, in effect, able to take Latin American acquiescence as a given. Within this framework, Mexico was viewed as an important linchpin and compliant ally in the anticommunist struggle.[9]

Over the ensuing four decades, the United States steadfastly pursued its containment strategy in Latin America. Examples of forceful, "self-help" actions taken against perceived threats to U.S. national security interests include Washington's involvement in the overthrow of the Jacobo Arbenz government in Guatemala in 1954, failed efforts to topple the Fidel Castro regime in Cuba in the 1960s, direct intervention in the Dominican Republic in 1965, CIA involvement in the military coup against the democratically elected, socialist government of Salvador Allende in Chile in 1973, the military invasion of Grenada in 1982, and covert and overt efforts to destabilize the Sandinista regime in Nicaragua in the 1980s.[10] While undeniably successful in preventing or "rolling back" communist regimes during the last forty-five years (with the notable exception of Castro's Cuba), it is also evident that the U.S. containment strategy in the region, by and large, tended to subsume or ride roughshod over the basic needs, developmental aspirations, and nationalist sentiments of large sectors in many Latin American countries. In the wake of the 1959 Cuban Revolution, President John F. Kennedy's sponsorship of the Alliance for Progress did reflect heightened U.S. concern for Latin American development and socioeconomic reforms, but even during this relatively progressive phase, U.S. policy was vitiated by a concomitant, contradictory emphasis on internal security, which effectively limited or thwarted political reform in many nations in the hemisphere (LaFeber 1986).

Herein lies evidence of an important point of inflection in the U.S. operationalization of the concept of national security. Whereas pre-World War II European notions of national security essentially focused on external threats, the postwar U.S. containment doctrine encompassed *ideological* as well as military concerns and thus brought with it the easily abused idea of "the enemy within." While hardly innocuous within the United States itself — it spawned, for example, the era of McCarthyism in the 1950s — the expansion of potential security threats to include elements of the body politic wreaked havoc on democracy in many Latin American nations lacking the counterbalancing presence of strong civil societies, effective democratic institutions, and independent media. Furthermore, because U.S. security concerns were primarily global in scope, while those of Latin American countries were mainly oriented toward internal issues, U.S. policymakers often proved willing to work with abusive and dictatorial governing cliques, as long as they remained firmly anticommunist and loyally pro-American in their foreign relations.

Rapid modernization in Latin America during the 1950s and 1960s generated a dramatic upsurge of new social forces demanding socioeconomic and political reforms. U.S. adherence to anticommunist doctrines and containment strategies, however, inclined Washington toward maintenance of the status quo, making it wary of all but gradual, incremental change and justifying its use of unilateral power to preempt potential threats or preclude unwanted outcomes. The gap between U.S. and Latin American perceptions of national security became increasingly palpable and provoked rising levels of tensions in U.S.-Latin American relations in the 1970s and 1980s.

The evolution of Mexican foreign policy in the postwar era provides an excellent case in point. As early as the U.S.-backed intervention in Cuba in 1961, the Mexican government formally dissented from the security policies pursued by the United States on the grounds that they violated the principles of national independence, sovereignty, and self-determination. Successive Mexican leaders raised similar objections to U.S. actions in Latin America from the Dominican Republic through Chile to Grenada and Nicaragua (Vázquez and Meyer 1985, chapters 9 and 10). In the early 1970s, under President Luis Echeverría Alvarez, Mexico became increasingly preoccupied with its own economic development and more outspokenly critical of U.S. policies and actions in Latin America. Under President José López

Portillo in the late 1970s and early 1980s, in the context of the country's deepening debt crisis, Reagan's interventionist policies in Central America, and the intensification of the arms race between the superpowers, Mexico emerged as a leading Latin American critic of the strategies of global, regional, and national security advocated by Washington.

Shortcomings of the Traditional Concept

In light of the fact that the dominant interpretation of national security employed by realist scholars and policymakers implicitly or explicitly influenced by them has been consistently U.S.-centric, narrowly focused on issues of military defense, and highly ideological (i.e., anticommunist) — and, thus, often open to a variety of political abuses — some participants in this project argued that the concept should be abandoned altogether and replaced by a more rigorous and neutral category (or set of categories) appropriate to the particular historical circumstances, cultural traditions, and social and political priorities of Mexico and other Third World nation-states. While recognizing the ethnocentric distortions and ideological bias embedded in the traditional usage of the term, however, most members of our study group were not persuaded that abandonment of the intellectual terrain of national security studies and withdrawal from present and future debates over the meaning of the concept would in practice help prevent its continued misuse and abuse by either scholars or policymakers in the United States or elsewhere. Indeed, many participants noted that the term has become so central to political and academic debates on contemporary national and international affairs that it is unlikely that a substitute terminology can be found, much less widely accepted, in the foreseeable future. From this perspective, the most viable intellectual alternative was posited to be not a quixotic search for a replacement terminology of our own invention, but rather, a reformulation of the traditional concept to take into account the security needs and perspectives of the many "subordinate" states and societies that heretofore have not been fully incorporated in the calculus of hegemonic analysts and practitioners or their Third World counterparts.

Among the majority of our colleagues who concluded that the term "national security" could not (or should not) be jettisoned completely, most concurred that attempts to expand the parameters of the concept beyond its customary military and national defense focus were, at least in principle, worthwhile. Several, however, demurred on

the grounds that such a strategy runs the risk of dilut_
beyond recognition, thereby reducing it to a residual cat_
of analytic specificity or clarity. They proposed, instead, to
of the concept exclusively to questions of national defense   _.ving
threats of external aggression or subversion emanating from abroad,
and to employ terms like national interests, objectives, priorities, and
goals to refer to issues such as economic growth, social progress,
democratic stability, and environmental protection.

The principal justification advanced in support of this strict
construction of the concept was that it would facilitate greater analytic
precision in the field of national security studies. A secondary line of
reasoning was that a restricted approach would impede Third World
military elites from adopting open-ended definitions of national
security to justify usurpation of political power from civilian authorities
and indiscriminate internal repression. In short, our dissenting colleagues warned that efforts to broaden the term might inadvertently
become a dangerous invitation to further abuse of an already much-
abused concept. Although both arguments unquestionably highlighted potentially serious obstacles to the reformulation of the notion
of national security, in the end neither was sufficient to dissuade our
study group from its attempts to reconceptualize and expand the
meaning of the concept.

The claim that narrow scholarly definitions would, in practice,
deter military or other anti-democratic leaders from invoking national
security arguments to legitimate their de facto interventions was
dismissed on the grounds that intellectual rationales for military coups
and authoritarian rule in the name of national security already exist, have
been repeatedly adduced in the past to justify force and repression, and
would likely be so used in the future, whether intellectuals like it or not.
Indeed, various participants argued that it was precisely because the
traditional concept — however loose and imprecise — has usually been
construed to refer to the military dimensions of security, while excluding
considerations of economic growth and diversification, social welfare,
human rights, and democracy, that it has been so useful to authoritarian
leaders of all stripes. In this context, a suitably broadened concept of
national security — one that sought to specify the relations between
economic, social, political, and military variables and national security
— was seen to offer potential deterrents to, rather than justifications for,
future dictatorships.

The possibility that expansion of the concept of national security beyond its traditional boundaries to include a range of non-military issues could reduce it to an amorphous, residual category was, in contrast, recognized by all as a very real danger. In supporting the quest for a broadened conceptual approach, in spite of the pitfalls, various colleagues emphasized that the extensive interdependence characteristic of the contemporary international system has so greatly increased the sensitivity and vulnerability of states and societies around the globe to non-military challenges to, and constraints upon, their national autonomy, that the issues of national security have inevitably become more complex and inclusive, extending well beyond traditional military defense problems to questions of "development," social "progress," and global environmental protection.

Six fundamental transformations within the international system were seen to have contributed to the steady erosion of the utility of realist approaches to the conceptualization and resolution of national security issues in the postwar era. The first was the demise of colonialism and the attendant rise and spread of nationalism among Third World states and peoples. The newly independent states of Africa and Asia, along with those of Latin America seeking economic development, faced enormous obstacles in meeting the basic needs of their populations — needs that were far removed from the power games of *Realpolitik*.[11] In places like Algeria, Zaire, Mozambique, and, most spectacularly, Vietnam and Afghanistan, defiant nationalist elites backed by popular resistance movements proved able to thwart the designs and dictates of more powerful industrialized countries. In the Americas, the Cuban Revolution jolted the United States into awareness of the potential power of disenchanted and oppressed social groups once mobilized by radical leaders.

This change was closely tied to a second more important transformation — the diminishing effectiveness of military force (Keohane and Nye [1977] 1989, 27-29). As military interventions in the Third World became more protracted and costly, citizens of powerful countries increasingly balked at open-ended conventional wars. This trend was paralleled by the growing realization among the major world powers that nuclear weapons were, in fact, unusable. While realism had provided the conceptual rationale for a massive conventional and nuclear weapons buildup, in practice realist strategies and tactics based on self-help became progressively less applicable to the world scene they had helped to create.

A third major transformation further undermined the relevance of traditional realist formulas for ensuring national security. In the aftermath of World War II, U.S. security concerns had made it imperative that Western Europe be rebuilt as quickly as possible in order to serve as a bulwark against Soviet-communist expansionism. This, the Marshall Plan was able to accomplish. By the late 1960s, however, increased economic competition from a revitalized Western Europe, in conjunction with the surging economy of Japan, began to place strains upon the U.S. economy. By the 1980s, with U.S. workers increasingly displaced from non-competitive industries and the economy plagued by inflation, high interest rates, and unsustainable fiscal and trade deficits, world economic issues moved higher on the political and security agenda of even the powerful United States.[12]

Underpinning such problems was a fourth transformation of truly global scope: the increasing integration or interdependence of the world economy. While state-to-state relations remained central to world politics, the proliferation of transnational corporations and banks, the dramatic increase in subnational and international organizations concerned with citizens' basic needs and human rights, and the development of technologies capable of transferring information, capital, and commodities around the world in lightning fashion, converged to create an ever more complex web of relationships that tended both to diffuse sources of power and produce cross-cutting interests that were difficult to decipher for even the wiliest of statesmen (Keohane and Nye 1974; Jacobson, Reisinger, and Mathers 1986; Spero 1988; Gill and Law 1989; Garten 1989; Islam 1990). In effect, the use of superior power capabilities became more problematic as nationalist resistance intensified, as domestic and international constraints grew stronger, and as the secondary consequences deriving from increased interdependence became more important.

Only in the last decade or so have significant numbers of scholars and policymakers come to recognize fully the potential consequences of the fifth transformation — the rapidly accelerating degradation of the world environment (Matthews 1989). This "new" issue has presented nation-states — whether weak or strong — with problems that are simply beyond their capacity to solve unilaterally and that cannot be resolved through the use of force. Even the most intransigent realists have been forced to accept the fact that environmental threats such as acid rain and global warming can neither be stopped at the water's edge nor subdued by military force: They clearly require concerted and sustained international cooperation.

Finally, the sixth transformation is the massive increase in citizen-to-citizen contacts and forms of organization, originating in the increased "analytic skills" of individuals, the strengthening of civil societies in many countries, and new technologies of information, communication, and transportation (Rosenau 1990). A wide array of independent groups have developed their own international agenda with respect to issues such as human rights and disarmament, and their actions have proved to be obstacles to the implementation of the preferred foreign policies of various governments.

Taken together, these six transformations have dealt the realist approach to world politics heavy blows and caused analysts and policymakers alike to reassess the validity and appropriateness of traditional realist assumptions about the international system and the national security doctrines and policy prescriptions that have resulted from them. This process of reassessment has not produced an alternative paradigm or a wholesale repudiation of realistic precepts. It has, however, introduced new variables and more complex formulations of the linkages among variables in an effort to account more fully for the transformations that have occurred and are occurring in the evolving international system. Taken as a whole, this alternative perspective or approach has become generally known as "interdependence" theory.[13]

As in realism, the international system is seen in this school of thought as anarchical and conflictual, but interdependent perspectives emphasize that the existence of myriad, interdependent relationships and the decreasing utility of military force place a premium on the construction and maintenance of mechanisms of cooperation. Furthermore, unlike traditional realists, interdependence theorists recognize that the accelerating complexity of global interactions means that there is no fixed hierarchy of issues, but rather sets of shifting concerns that include many non-military priorities as well. In such a world, the notion of national security unavoidably becomes a broader category extending well beyond traditional military defense problems.

Broadening the Frame of Reference: Reconceptualizing National Security in the Era of Interdependence

Mere recognition that increasingly complex forms of regional and global interdependence have given rise to a variety of new, nonmilitary issues relating to national security does not, however, resolve the problem of conceptual boundaries or cut-off points raised earlier. Operationally, which non-military issues should, or should not, be considered questions of national security under conditions of interdependence? Even more to the point, what are the criteria for inclusion (or exclusion) that analytically delimit the expanded version of the concept, regardless of the manner in which it is ultimately recast to take into account the consequences of accelerating interdependence and the concerns of non-hegemonic nations and states?

Our study group's discussions produced no infallible recipes or stock formulas for making such determinations. To the contrary, it was generally accepted that the term "national security" could not meaningfully be defined in the abstract, but rather, had to be constructed via examination of the socio-historical contexts and cultural values, as well as needs, perceptions, and expectations of the specific peoples and states under study. The logic behind this position was that the notion of national security is not an absolute, that is, objective or universal category, but rather a relative, that is, subjective, socially conditioned perception; its meaning and content vary according to perceived interests, vulnerabilities, and sensibilities. In the jargon of the social sciences, the problem of defining this concept is ontological, not epistemological, theoretical, or methodological in nature: Individual human beings and the collectivities they identify with regularly perceive and interpret the external world and its threats differently, according to their own life-chances, historical experiences, values, and priorities.

A second area of general agreement was that traditional definitions — cast as the absence of danger from direct military attack, political pressures, or economic coercion — constituted a necessary but insufficient conceptualization of the category. As Javier Elguea notes in his contribution to this volume, in addition to the negative side of the national security equation (i.e., the preservation of national sovereignty and independence), there is also a positive side (i.e., realization of autonomously defined national goals or self-determination). Incorporation of this second, positive dimension means that issues such as economic development, health and welfare, and political legitimacy are not secondary or derivative interests but are central considerations in the analysis of national security problems and priorities for all countries, whether weak or strong, rich or poor, capitalist, socialist, or hybrid. Recognition that specific national security priorities (or core values) vary in different historical and cultural settings implies that the precise positive security agenda particular to individual nation-states cannot be identified deductively via assumptions or stereotypical generalizations. They must, instead, be discovered through the empirical study of concrete national experiences, cultures, values, beliefs, and attitudes.

A third major point of consensus within our study group was that the notion of national security could not be fruitfully conceptualized as a simplistic, Manichaean dichotomy: Either a nation is sufficiently rich and powerful to defend its national security, or it is not. Instead, it was posited that national security objectives or priorities should be located on a continuum and their pursuit (and achievement) viewed as a matter of degree rather than a question of all-or-nothing. Adopting such an approach, it was suggested, would not only prevent reducing the notion of national security to the capacity to resist external aggression, but could also help to clarify the costs or trade-offs involved in pursuit of specific national security goals vis-à-vis others. In the same vein, it was posited that such an approach could facilitate analysis of the trade-offs involved in adoption of one or another national security strategy over time; that is to say, short-term costs versus medium- to long-term gains, and vice versa.

A fourth area of agreement concerned the need to distinguish between principals (society) and agents (state authorities) in order to avoid the reductionist fallacy of equating state security with that of the nation or society as a whole. As Richard Moss and Richard Rockwell highlight in their essay in this volume, policies that purport to secure state (regime or government) security need not, and often do not in practice, promote the security of either society as a whole or its individual members.

A final point of consensus that emerged during our discussions involved the need to move analysis beyond static lists or inventories of vital national security interests (whether negative or positive) in order to examine the complex interconnections or linkages among the agenda items and the strategies adopted to attain them, both nationally and internationally.

Mexico in Search of Security
in a Changing World System

The conviction that the modern world system is experiencing major realignments in the locus and distribution of economic and political power was a decisive consideration in our decision to seek to recast, rather than to accept a narrow definition of national security or abandon the term altogether. Among the basic trends highlighted within our discussions were the decline in the relative hegemony of the United States, the amelioration of East-West tensions, and the consolidation of Japan, Germany, and Western Europe as major actors in the world political economy. These trends were seen to imply major shifts in the ways that Mexico, the United States, and others around the globe perceive their national security. Such alterations in the political economy of the international system, combined with structural and attitudinal changes within Mexican society itself, it was argued, presented new opportunities and new dangers for the security of the Mexican nation-state and its citizenry. The majority of participants in our project agreed that these fluid circumstances offered greater possibilities than at any time in this century for Third World intellectuals generally, and Mexicans in particular, to rethink their own views, and to reshape U.S. perceptions of national security.

The dramatic changes that took place in the Soviet Union and Eastern Europe in recent years unquestionably opened a new stage in the debate over national security in the United States. Most of the group concurred that if Mexican intellectuals opted not to engage in the process of redefinition, the U.S. debate would not end; Mexican concerns and interests would simply be glossed over or ignored as they have so often been in the past.

The burgeoning interconnections between Mexico and the United States were seen to involve not only deepening economic interpenetration, socio-cultural ties, and political contacts, but also an expanding social and intellectual dialogue that provides the basis for a mutual exploration of national well-being, national interests, and collective security. In this potentially fruitful context, it seemed to most of us neither realistic nor politically advisable for scholars from either side of the border to retreat from the intensifying discussions over the meaning and implications of alternative formulations of national security concepts.

In practice, social scientists have historically played significant roles in the development of prevailing perspectives on national security. Reflecting upon the development of U.S. foreign policy in the transitional period after World War II, Stanley Hoffmann noted that "what the scholars offered, the policymakers wanted. Indeed there is a remarkable chronological convergence between their needs and the scholars' performances" (Hoffmann [1977] 1987, 10). This observation reflects a more general point fundamental to this volume's raison d'être: In periods of rapid change, policymakers will, as a matter both of logic and necessity, turn increasingly to the academic and intellectual community for guidance. In recognition of this dialectic, many of our colleagues felt that despite the often antagonistic relationship between policymakers and academics or intellectuals, it was important to recognize the inevitable linkages between theory and practice and to join the debate, rather than to shy away from it.

In our view, the new realities of the evolving international system imply that scholars and practitioners from both sides of the Mexican-U.S. border have the opportunity and the responsibility to reexamine to what extent the continuing search for national security in each nation will affect, positively or negatively, the other. Both countries are marked by high degrees of nationalism, although the specific content of that nationalism is clearly the result of the different historical background and the economic, political, and socio-cultural contexts characteristic of each. Any putative unilateral resolution of national security challenges on either side of the border unavoidably risks exacerbating mutual incomprehension and national resentments, as well as limiting the chances for mutual cooperation and joint action to confront common problems and threats.

In practice, neither the much rehearsed security debates in the United States nor the more embryonic security discussions in Mexico have ever systematically analyzed the roles of their immediate neighbor in the definition and defense of their own national security. Although unquestionably short-sighted, this is not especially surprising on the part of the United States, which, as the hegemonic power in the hemisphere, historically has taken Mexico and the rest of Latin America for granted. It is, however, far more surprising on the part of Mexico, which has been obliged to live in the shadow of the "Colossus of the North" for much of the last two centuries. In light of the rapidly changing contours of the international system, neither country can afford to continue such a myopic approach toward the conceptualization of its own, or its neighbor's, national security problems. This is particularly true because the references to national security in both countries are so replete with jingoistic rhetoric, ideological premises, untested assertions, and questionable conclusions.

Mexican scholars and policymakers have never articulated clearly or completely their own views of national security. The force of current changes in the international system is now driving them to do so. How Mexicans conceive of their own security has implications for the national security of the United States and vice versa. Thus, we conclude that an effort to bring together both Mexicans and North Americans to discuss these differing perspectives at this juncture in our collective history — to identify both commonalities and divergences and to consider how best to deal with them — is a justifiable enterprise, however complex and difficult it ultimately proves to be.

Equity and mutual understanding obviously require that the implications of changing U.S. perceptions of national security also be discussed by both North Americans and Mexicans, for the outcome of the U.S. debate will ineluctably affect Mexico's own national security and policy options. We thus hope to continue the dialogue begun with the meetings that produced this volume by undertaking a second series of seminars involving scholars from both nations to explore the implications of changing definitions and perceptions of U.S. national security for Mexico, Mexican interests, and Mexican security. It is our hope that the present volume and its planned companion will jointly provide the groundwork for a subsequent reexamination of the sore questions of concern to us here: Do the U.S. and Mexico have common or divergent security interests? What are they? How can they best be reconciled or managed?

For Mexico, the last decade of the twentieth century presents in stark fashion both the opportunities and dangers mentioned above. If a relatively less hegemonic United States does opt to put into practice antiquated and outmoded notions of national security, it is most likely to do so with its nearest neighbors, especially those who present particularly troubling problems of rapid social and political change. This could prove disastrous for Mexico, as well as for U.S. society. Hence, we contend that Mexican analysts have a vested interest in, first, striving to understand the ongoing shifts in interpretations of national security in the United States and elsewhere, and, second, engaging fully in the reconstruction of the concept in ways beneficial to Mexico's economic development, political autonomy, and social well-being.

Mexico is currently being catapulted toward fuller integration into the international system. This integration cannot take place solely at the level of the export and import of commodities; it requires the creation of a safer and more secure international environment within which national projects can reach fruition. In our judgment, it would be a serious error to think that only governmental elites can or should participate in and contribute to these debates. These are questions that engage destinies of entire societies, and in which civil society must take an active part; they are simply too momentous to be to left to policy elites alone.

The problem is not one only for Mexicans. The U.S. public, intellectuals, and political leaders must also strive to understand and accept rapid social and political changes. This need is especially urgent regarding U.S. security thinking vis-à-vis Mexico. The profound processes of economic, social, and political transformation that Mexico is currently experiencing require that U.S. analysts abandon traditional and static notions of U.S. national security in order better to comprehend and adapt to the accelerating changes through which its southern neighbor is passing.

The tasks are monumental. Neither country is in a position to redefine its own national security unilaterally. The possibilities for fruitful interchange in this critical moment of our shared history appear great; failure to reach impartial understanding implies unacceptable costs to both countries. To refuse even to try, seems to us, at least, an inconceivable position.

The Logic of the Volume

The chapters compiled in this volume are the revised product of a conference held at the Universidad Nacional Autónoma de México in Mexico City 22-24 February 1989. Prior to this meeting the editors had asked the contributors to prepare a draft version of their essays for presentation at the conference. Each essay was discussed and debated in turn, and the authors were then given the opportunity to incorporate the new ideas and critiques developed during the conference's sessions. Thus, these essays encompass a time frame extending through the first year or so of both the Salinas and Bush administrations.

The participants in this conference were invited on the basis of their individual expertise and with an eye toward including a broad range of disciplinary and analytical perspectives. Not all of them were specialists in the field of national security studies. Our concern was rather to bring together individuals knowledgeable about Mexico, the United States, and Mexican-U.S. relations in the hope that these individuals, interacting with specialists in security studies, would be able to inform our discussion of the new security agenda confronting both nations. An effort was also made to incorporate varying ideological perspectives.

After lengthy discussions among the project organizers, we decided not to invite military personnel from either Mexico or the United States. Our rationale was that defense policies form only one part of national security studies and are among the themes that, in relative terms, have been more fully treated in the national security literature in both countries. Instead of rehashing highly technical and purely military questions, we consciously sought to broaden the debate to include non-traditional themes. We agreed, however, that in future discussions between our two countries on security issues, the inclusion of military analysts specializing in national defense and security problems would be beneficial. To avoid getting bogged down in unproductive debates over specific aspects of current official policies in either country, we also decided not to involve government representatives.

Beyond military issues, several other key aspects of Mexican national security are not dealt with in detail in this volume. Among the most important of these, in our view, are questions of food self-sufficiency, the impact of demographic trends, the problems along Mexico's southern border, ethnic and racial conflicts, and Mexican external relations (e.g., with Europe, the former U.S.S.R., the rest of Latin America, as well as with international organizations such as the United Nations or the Organization of American States). Also missing is any attempt to compare Mexican security needs with those of other countries. To compensate, at least partly, for these and other omissions and deficiencies in this volume, the final essay, prepared by Mexican social scientists Luis Herrera-Lasso and Guadalupe González, puts forward an agenda for future research on Mexican national security issues.

The book is organized into five parts. The first, entitled "Thinking About the Concept of Security," contains four essays that review and critique the breadth of national security. The opening chapter by Richard Rockwell and Richard Moss explores the theoretical and methodological challenges inherent in efforts to reconceptualize national security. Their analysis concentrates on three key questions which must, they argue, be addressed by any adequate reformulation: Whose security? Which threat? By what means?

The first of these questions introduces the problem of the possible disjuncture between the state and the nation. Rockwell and Moss pose this in theoretical terms as a potential de-linking between "principal" and "agent"; while the nation is the principal on whose behalf security must be assured, the state serves (whether well or badly) as the agent to effect this. The authors also highlight the considerable theoretical difficulties which may arise when security is considered at the multiple levels of the state, the nation, the society, and/or the individual: If national security is a socio-cultural goal decided by individual nations, what are the prospects for development of a general theory of national security?

In the second essay, Javier Elguea contends that to understand Mexican national security priorities, it is necessary to distinguish between the country's "positive security" agenda (expectations of economic and social progress) and its "negative security" agenda (defense of national territory from external threats). However, this amplified spectrum of security considerations poses a further serious conceptual problem; namely, which socio-economic problems, at what moments, put national security in jeopardy? When applied to the Mexican case, these questions lead Elguea to assert that the crisis of political stability in Mexico is one related to development, not security.

The broadening of the notion of security posited by Elguea contrasts with the position taken by Gene Sharp, who is concerned with the dangers inherent in a broader definition. Sharp feels that an expansive reconceptualization of national security could provide a pliable vocabulary by which political elites might manipulate public discourse to their own advantage and to the detriment of the broader interests of civil society.

Echoing Sharp, Cathryn Thorup also voices serious doubts about the appropriateness of efforts to broaden the concept of national security to include issues such as development, debt, poverty, and the environment. She focuses her critique on the need for specificity in the use of the concept and precision in the development of its operational meaning. If the concept of national security is to be expanded beyond the traditional reference to military defense issues, she believes intellectual clarity and coherence are essential.

In the second part of the book, "The Theory and Practice of National Security in Mexico," the changes and contradictions in Mexican views on national security are explored. Sergio Aguayo opens discussion on these matters by analyzing the evolution of Mexican national security concerns. He finds that in both Mexico and the United States studies about Mexican national security dramatically increased in the late 1970s. This sudden shift, however, resulting from changes both within Mexico and in its geopolitical setting, lead to widely varying interpretations of Mexican national security. Aguayo systematically reviews these often contradictory perspectives in order to move toward greater understanding of the historical parameters of Mexican national security studies. A continuing effort to reconceptualize Mexican national security more adequately, he believes, requires both intellectual and political advances that will allow the social participation necessary to a real determination of the meaning of Mexico's national security.

In his analysis, Roger Bartra uncovers the contradictory and conflictive relations between the nation and the state in contemporary Mexico. According to his assessment, it is a notable historical irony that Mexican nationalism led to a form of capitalist industrialization and transnationalism that eventually undermined the *caciquismo* (labor paternalism) and corruption that served as functional mechanisms of the revolutionary national project. Looking at the present moment in Mexican history, Bartra asks whether President Salinas can manage a political project that is both transnational and parochial — that is to say, one which seeks economic liberalization and export-led growth, while still maintaining the old political machinery.

"Economy, Environment, and National Security" are dealt with in part three. In order to provide the necessary historical context for the well-known recent shifts in Mexican economic policy, Matthew Edel and Candace Kim Edel examine in their essay the trajectory of the Mexican economy over the past fifty years. After contrasting three stages — an accumulation model based on expansion of the internal market, the exhaustion of that strategy, and the search for a new mode of integration within a rapidly changing world economy — they view Mexico's present neoliberal economic policies as in some measure a reaction to the failures of the earlier economic model, rather than a fully coherent reading of Mexico's present economic situation. They ask, "Is there not some middle ground better suited to the nation's needs?"

Discussions about the economy can no longer avoid the planning challenges presented by the fact that Mexico is now experiencing serious conditions of environmental degradation. Diana Liverman points out that, insofar as a sound environment is the prerequisite for basic life-support systems, Mexico's increasing environmental problems may well be considered a matter of national security. She emphasizes the nature and scope of Mexico's proliferating environmental difficulties by examining such wide-ranging concerns as soil erosion, biodiversity, air and noise pollution, toxic wastes and pesticides, water resources, and the effects of urbanization — as well as the concomitant health problems resulting from many of these problems.

Liverman observes that addressing these environmental difficulties is all the more challenging, given the constraints imposed by Mexico's current economic crisis. She feels that an acritical emulation of the developmental path followed by other industrialized countries could be especially damaging. One crucial first step toward advancing Mexico's environmental self-awareness, says Liverman, would be a much-needed effort to study the potentially devastating impact of global warming trends.

Richard Nuccio, Angelina Ornelas, and Iván Restrepo approach the same environmental problems with an analytical framework that relates them to Mexico's prior import-substitution model. They point out, for example, that Mexican economic development came to revolve around the urban poles of Guadalajara, Monterrey, Puebla, and Mexico City, creating concentrations of population that have outstripped capacities for housing, water, and sewage. Similarly, Nuccio et al. see difficulties with the modern neoliberal economic model in that export promotion and liberalization reduce the government's ability to monitor and control deleterious environmental effects. They believe that such an approach often relies unrealistically on the initiative of private industry in relation to environmental matters. Therefore, they are led to ask whether a serious assault on Mexico's ecological degradation may not require a fundamental rethinking of Mexico's economic strategy.

The environment is just one of several matters of great importance to Mexico and the United States, as is made apparent in part four's examination of "Bilateral Issues and National Security."

In turning to issues of labor migration, Jorge Bustamante's essay employs the systematic approach characteristic of many traditional security studies. First, he summarizes the main elements of Mexican migration to the United States by analyzing the various factors contributing to the Mexican and U.S. joint supply and demand for labor. On that basis, Bustamante looks to the future by building several scenarios around two sets of variables: economic growth or recession in the United States and political stability or instability in Mexico. Utilizing those variables, Bustamante then details each scenario in order to examine the resulting impact on Mexico's national security.

In the accompanying essay on bilateral issues, María Celia Toro considers the relationship of Mexican and U.S. attempts to counter drug trafficking and governmental statements concerning national security. Despite the considerable commitment of resources devoted to anti-drug efforts by the Mexican government, she questions whether the nature of the problem is best defined as a matter of national security.

The volume concludes with a summary essay under part five's theme of "Rethinking Mexican National Security." Luis Herrera-Lasso and Guadalupe González's concluding essay seeks to take account of the preceding chapters in an effort to develop the guidelines for an expanded definition of national security that incorporates Mexico's traditional values. They believe that the need for a redefinition of Mexican national security derives from a host of new issues demanding attention. These include the discovery of oil, the debate over Central America, the intensification of anti-drug efforts, the internal disequilibrium flowing from economic and political difficulties, and the desire of the military to clarify its own role.

Herrera-Lasso and González clearly pose the dilemmas attached to any effort to operationalize the concept of Mexican national security. Their analysis shows that the underlying conundrum is that while the government acts as the effective agent of civil society and the nation, only the citizenry can substantively determine the actual content of national security concerns. Herrera-Lasso and González find it disquieting to note that a nation recently in crisis, such as Mexico, is highly susceptible to abuses resulting from a blurring of the categories of state, government, and nation — allowing individuals within each level to seek what they perceive to be in the interest of their own security.

As is clear from the foregoing review of this volume's rationale, content, and intellectual and historical antecedents, the collection of essays that follows is better seen as an initial effort to analyze systematically the problems of Mexico's national security in both conceptual and practical terms, than as an attempt to assert facile solutions. It is hoped that discussions of Mexican national security will be thereby stimulated and advanced. But whether that proves to be the case or not, the path to a secure Mexico in the coming century will have to pass through some of the thickets inspected here.

Notes

1.   For example, during Brazil's authoritarian experience of those years, the powers of control and repression were centralized under its National Security Council, which "was the holy of holies in a regime that by definition put questions of national security in first place" (Rouquié 1987, 293). Similarly, it has been noted that "according to the Argentine military, from the point of view of its strategic national security doctrine, the very real crisis generated by Peronism's collapse, and the general perception of a swelling wave of insidious subversion, the 'dirty war' against its citizens was fully justified" (Smith 1989, 231).

2.   For example, according to one prominent observer, the East-West focus of U.S. security policy in the Americas was driven by "a logic that is perverse for almost everyone" (O'Donnell 1986, 354-357).

3.   Robert Gilpin has gone so far as to say, "In honesty, one must inquire whether or not twentieth-century students of international relations know anything that Thucydides and his fifth-century compatriots did not know about the behavior of states" (Gilpin 1981, 227).

4.   This was, for example, a considerable part of the message of Carr ([1939] 1951).

5.   The key texts are Waltz 1959 and 1979, and Morgenthau [1948] 1986. An excellent review of the main propositions of realism may be found in Gilpin 1986.

6.   For a critical analysis of the "binary divisions" — order and anarchy, war and peace, "realism" and "idealism" — that result from the persistent privileging of the nation-state in international relations theory, see Walker (1990).

7.   Two key documents in the development of this strategy were "The Sources of Soviet Conduct" by "X" (George F. Kennan) and NSC-68 (National Security Council paper 68). For the first, see Kennan [1947] 1987, and for an analysis of the origins of the second, see LaFeber (1989, 479-482).

8.   On the signing and subsequent development of the Rio Pact, see Gil (1971, 196-98); Molineu (1986, 26-27); and Schoultz (1987, 179-81).

9.   Nevertheless, as Lorenzo Meyer has pointed out (Vázquez and Meyer 1985, 165), "The political support Mexico gave the United States had certain limits." See Vázquez and Meyer 1985, chapter 9.

10.   On Guatemala see S. Schlesinger and Kinzer (1982) and Immerman (1983); for Cuba, see Johnson (1964) and A. Schlesinger (1965); for the Dominican Republic, see Lowenthal (1972); Gleijeses, (1978) and Kryzanek

(1988); for Chile, see Sigmund (1977) and Davis (1985); for Grenada, see Schoultz (238-248); and for the Central American policy of the Reagan Administration, the best single-volume treatment is to be found in Blachman, LeoGrande, and Sharpe (1986).

11. Many volumes have addressed this topic, from a variety of perspectives. For example, Loup (1983) tackles it from the standpoint of development planning; the anthology edited by Seligson (1984) provides an analysis grounded in political economy; Worsley (1984) has authored an account derived from the insights of social anthropology; and Tucker (1977) forcefully argues against the idea that issues of economic development can somehow be disentangled from realist power politics.

12. The mounting concern and conflict over world economic issues is reflected in Brittan (1983) and Garten (1985). By 1987, from a North American perspective, Robert Hormats (1987, 478) was saying that international economic issues presented "major challenges" of such significance that "The prosperity and, ultimately, the security of the United States hang in the balance."

13. The classic analysis of interdependence in the international system is Keohane and Nye ([1977] 1989), especially chapters 1 and 2. The dimensions of sensitivity and vulnerability in an interdependent world are defined and discussed in the same volume, 12-19.

References

Blachman, Morris J., Douglas C. Bennett, William M. LeoGrande, et al. 1986. "The Failure of the Hegemonic Strategic Vision." In *Confronting Revolution: Security Through Diplomacy in Central America*, eds. Morris J. Blachman, William M. LeoGrande, and Kenneth Sharpe. New York: Pantheon.

Blachman, Morris J., William M. LeoGrande, and Kenneth Sharpe, eds. 1986. *Confronting Revolution: Security Through Diplomacy in Central America*. New York: Pantheon.

Britton, Samuel. 1983. "A Very Painful World Adjustment." *Foreign Affairs* 61(3): 541-568.

Carr, E.H. [1939] 1951. *The Twenty Years' Crisis, 1919-1939: An Introduction to the Study of International Relations*. London: Macmillan.

Davis, Nathaniel. 1985. *The Last Two Years of Salvador Allende*. Ithaca, N.Y.: Cornell University Press.

Gaddis, John Lewis. 1990. "Coping With Victory." *The Atlantic* 63(5)(May): 49-60.

Garten, Jeffrey E. 1985. "Gunboat Economics." *Foreign Affairs* 63(3): 538-59.

Garten, Jeffrey E. 1989. "Trading Blocs and the Evolving World Economy." *Current History* 88(534)(January): 15, 16, 54-6.

Gil, Fredrico G. 1971. *Latin American-United States Relations*. New York: Harcourt Brace Jovanovich.

Gill, Stephen R., and David Law. 1989. "Global Hegemony and the Structural Power of Capital." *International Studies Quarterly* 33(4)(December): 475-99.

Gilpin, Robert. 1981. *War and Change in World Politics*. New York: Cambridge University Press.

Gilpin, Robert. 1986. "The Richness of the Tradition of Political Realism." In *Neorealism and Its Critics*, ed. Robert O. Keohane. New York: Columbia University Press.

Gleijeses, Piero. 1978. *The Dominican Crisis: The 1965 Constitution-alist Revolt and the American Intervention.* Baltimore: Johns Hopkins University Press.

Hoffmann, Stanley. [1977] 1987. "An American Social Science: International Relations." In *Janus and Minerva: Essays in the Theory and Practice of International Politics.* Boulder, Colo.: Westview Press.

Hormats, Robert. 1986. "The World Economy Under Stress." *Foreign Affairs* 64(3): 455-78.

Hunter, Robert E. [1987] 1989. "The Reagan Administration and the Middle East." *Current History* 88(534)(January): 41, 57-8.

Huntington, Samuel P. 1988. "The United States-Decline or Renewal?" *Foreign Affairs* 67(2): 76-96.

Hyland, William G. 1990. "America's New Course." *Foreign Affairs* 69(2): 1-12.

Immerman, Richard H. 1982. *The CIA in Guatemala: The Foreign Policy of Intervention.* Austin: University of Texas Press.

Islam, Shafiqul. 1990. "Capitalism in Conflict." *Foreign Affairs* 69(1): 172-82.

Jacobson, Harold, William Reisinger, and Todd Mathers. 1986."National Entanglements in International Governmental Organizations." *American Politic Science Review* 80(1)(March).

Johnson, Haynes. 1964. *The Bay of Pigs.* New York: W.W. Norton.

Kennan, George F. [1947] 1987. "The Sources of Soviet Conduct." *Foreign Affairs* 65(4): 852-68.

Keohane, Robert O. [1977] 1989. *Power and Interdependence,* 2nd ed. Boston: Scott, Foresman and Co.

Keohane, Robert O. 1984. *After Hegemony.* Princeton: Princeton University Press.

Keohane, Robert O., and Joseph S. Nye, Jr. 1974. "Transgovernmental Relations and International Organizations." *World Politics* 27(1)(October): 39-62.

Kryzanek, Michael J. 1988. "The Dominican Intervention Revisited: An Attitudinal and Operational Analysis." In *United States Policy in*

Latin America, ed. John D. Martz. Lincoln, Neb: University of Nebraska Press.

Kubálková, V., and A.A. Cruickshank. 1989. *Thinking New About Soviet "New Thinking."* Berkeley, Calif.: Institute of International Studies.

LaFeber, Walter. 1986. "The Alliances in Retrospect." In *Bordering on Trouble: Resources and Politics in Latin America*, eds. Andrew Maguire and Janet Welsh Brown, 337-88. Bethesda, Md.: Adler & Adler.

LaFeber, Walter. 1989. *The American Age: United States Foreign Policy at Home and Abroad Since 1750*. New York: W.W. Norton.

Loup, Jacques. 1972. *Can the Third World Survive?* Baltimore: Johns Hopkins University Press.

Lowenthal, Abraham. 1972. *The Dominican Intervention*. Cambridge: Harvard University Press.

Matthews, Jessica Tuchman. 1989. "Redefining Security." *Foreign Affairs* 68(2): 162-77.

Maynes, Charles William. 1990. "America Without the Cold War." *Foreign Policy* 78(Spring): 3-25.

Mead, Walter Russell. 1987. *Mortal Splendor: The American Empire in Transition*. Boston: Houghton Mifflin.

Molineu, Harold. 1986. *U.S. Policy Toward Latin America: From Regionalism to Globalism*. Boulder, Colo.: Westview Press.

Morgenthau, Hans J. [1948] 1986. *Politics Among Nations*. 6th ed. New York: Alfred A. Knopf.

Nye, Jr., Joseph S. 1988. "Understating U.S. Strength." *Foreign Policy* 72(Fall): 105-29.

O'Donnell, Guillermo. 1986. "The U.S., Latin America, Democracy: Variations on a Very Old Theme." In *The U.S. and Latin America in the 1980s: Contending Perspectives on a Decade of Crisis*, eds. Kevin Middlebrook and Carlos Rico, 353-75. Pittsburgh: University of Pittsburgh Press.

Rosenau, James N. 1990. *Turbulence in World Politics: A Theory of Change and Continuity*. Princeton: Princeton University Press.

Rouquié, Alain. 1987. *The Military and the State in Latin America*. Berkeley and Los Angeles: University of California Press.

Schlesinger, Stephen, and Stephen Kinzer. 1982. *Bitter Fruit: The Untold Story of the American Coup in Guatemala.* New York: Doubleday.

Schoultz, Lars. 1987. *National Security and United States Policy Toward Latin America.* Princeton: Princeton University Press.Seligson, Mitchell A., ed. 1984. *The Gap Between Rich and Poor: Contending Perspectives on the Political Economy of Development.* Boulder, Colo.: Westview Press.

Sigmund, Paul E. 1989. *The Overthrow of Allende and the Politics of Chile, 1964-1976.* Pittsburgh: University of Pittsburgh Press.

Smith, William C. 1977. *Authoritarianism and the Crisis of the Argentine Political Economy.* Stanford: Stanford University Press.

Spero, Joan. 1988. "Guiding Global Finance." *Foreign Policy* 73- (Winter): 114-134.

Tucker, Robert W. 1977. *The Inequality of Nations.* New York: Basic Books.

Vázquez, Josefina Zoraida, and Lorenzo Meyer. 1985. *The United States and Mexico.* Chicago: University of Chicago Press.

Waltz, Kenneth N. 1959. *Man, the State and War: A Theoretical Analysis.* New York: Columbia University Press.

Waltz, Kenneth N. 1979. *Theory of International Politics.* New York: Random House.

Worsely, Peter. 1984. *The Three Worlds: Culture and World Development.* Chicago: University of Chicago Press.

Part One

Thinking About the Concept of Security

Reconceptualizing Security:
A Note About Research

Richard C. Rockwell and Richard H. Moss

For a small child, as Charles M. Schulz once noted, "Security is a thumb and a blanket." Unfortunately, as we grow older, this particular method of making ourselves feel secure becomes less effective. We adopt more expensive and rather more dangerous means, and then we disagree about what we have achieved.

In the United States, the term "security" has become a potent political symbol. Disagreements about its prerequisites and the means that should be adopted to attain it are intense and politically heated. The term can imply quite different things, but current political discourse rarely restricts the meaning to the ability of a nation-state to defend its borders against foreign invasion. Today policy makers and politicians argue that national security is threatened by many non-military conditions and events, such as the wave of illegal drugs flooding the United States, setbacks in the international race to design and market high-definition television receivers, and the poor performance of the U.S. educational system relative to those of its major economic competitors. The struggle among persons of all ideologies for control of the definition of national security has become part of the struggle for control of national power — an attempt by such persons to redefine national priorities by claiming that their view of the nation's

We express our appreciation to Cary F. Fraser and Robert H. Sprinkle for their helpful comments and to Nancy Lustgarten for research assistance. We bear full responsibility for any remaining errors or omissions.

most pressing national problems is encompassed in the politically potent concept of security.

The struggle for control of the definition has spilled over into academic discussion. Consensus among researchers regarding the meaning of the term is breaking down, invoking political and professional as well as scientific disputes. The scholarly literature increasingly challenges former meanings and old assumptions but has not yet begun to converge on a new consensus. However, enough research which challenges and redefines traditional meanings has now accumulated that it is possible to make some preliminary observations about what we have learned about security through attempts to reconceptualize it.

The following discussion assumes that the study of security can be part of the endeavor of social science. This means that the same methodological canons that have worked in other research areas can be consulted here. It means that cross-fertilization can and should occur between the study of security and the study of other subject matters, as indeed it has in the past. It means that the study of security ought to contribute to the general goals of social science: understanding how humans live together in societies, develop as individuals, produce and consume, engage in and resolve conflicts, and pass on to other generations their understanding of what it means to be human. Some might argue that research on security cannot be carried out as a social scientific enterprise, that there is no possibility of a scientifically acceptable theory of security. We do not share this view but instead seek to develop criteria for such a theory.

Traditional Concepts and Theories of Security

The term "security" popularly connotes freedom from danger, or more broadly, freedom from anxiety, care, or fear, according to Webster. Its meaning in public debate and in social science research depends upon the modifier appended to it. Thus we speak of "personal security," freedom from fear of assault; "food security," freedom from fear of starvation or malnutrition; and "economic security," freedom from concern for an individual's or group's financial well-being.

The traditional concept of national security owes much to the post-World War II writings of political realists such as Hans Morgenthau, and to earlier definitions advanced by such writers as Walter Lippmann.[1] Informed by these treatments and by more recent writing on national security affairs, we offer the following statement of the traditional concept of national security as a starting point for discussion: A nation has security when its national government possesses sufficient power and military capability to deter attack on its legitimate interests by other states and, if attacked, to defend its legitimate interests by waging war.

Whatever criticisms one might make of the traditional concept, at least it does embody a coherent if limited theory of national security: national security is sought by the application or potential application of military, economic, or political power. According to this conceptualization, national security is the security of the state and is protected by the ability of states to resist foreign invasions. It involves maintaining a military capability sufficient to repulse or deter invasion, buttressed by military alliances that increase the costs and dangers that any would-be invader would face. One can make an error in believing that a particular security action will deter an invader, just as a physician can make an error in assuming that a particular antibiotic will restore health. Nevertheless, a theory is being employed in both cases, and errors can lead to refinements in both theory and practice. Assessing the capacity to deter enemy missile attacks is an example of a tractable analytic problem within this framework, a matter of physics and military intelligence.

There are three important components embedded in the traditional concept of security that need further elaboration. Consideration of these components will also provide a basis for discussing some of the questions that have been raised about the concept. First, the traditional conceptualization assigns to a state (the national government) the role of agent in providing security for a collectivity, the nation or the society. Second, this conceptualization assumes that the particular purpose of state action is the protection of "legitimate" national interests. And third, the threats to national interests are viewed as emanating from the actions and policies of other states, also acting to protect what they view as their own legitimate interests.

The State as Agent

One of the most fundamental and, at first glance, seemingly non-controversial elements of the traditional concept of security is its assignment to the state of the role as provider of security for a society. Nation-states emerged in Europe as an efficient and potent means of organizing certain types of social activity and aggregating economic and military power. In the modern era they continue to dominate all forms of social organization. Traditional analysis assumes that states *must* provide security for nations because there is no entity better placed to do so. Individuals or societies are assumed to be unable to act to provide for their security in the absence of a state, and so, by default, the state becomes the provider of security.[2]

This line of reasoning has led many scholars of international relations and national security to go one step further and to equate state security with national security. In many traditional analyses, the motivation of state action becomes ensuring the survival of the state; pursuit of the survival and security of the state is also assumed to promote simultaneously the security of the society or the nation.[3] By "society" we mean the largest possible collection of people inhabiting a common physical environment who share a cultural identity and interact in patterned ways.[4] In traditional security analysis, the state is assumed to be coterminous with the society: The society is defined and bounded by its government.

This is a leap that threatens analytical confusion and ignores political outcomes such as repression, one of the measures states may use to ensure their continued dominance over societies. While a state's efforts to secure its survival may result in ensuring the survival and security of the society, in fact, it also may not. As a number of analysts have pointed out, state and societal security need not be the same. Policies designed to enhance state security need not necessarily promote simultaneously the security of either the society or individuals for two reasons: first, the state may seek to enhance its security at the expense of broader national interests; second, even assuming that the state acts in the interests of the dominant national group, the interests of marginal groups within a society may not necessarily be advanced by pursuit of the interests of the dominant group.

In some cases, what economists and rational choice theorists have termed "principal-agent problems" lead the state to pursue its own interests above those of the nation. Principal-agent problems have two basic characteristics: 1) The "agent" (in our analysis of national security policy, the state) has information that the "principal" (the society) does not have, and 2) there is a conflict between the interests of the agent and the principal, which leads the agent to try to exploit its informational advantage to advance its own interests at the expense of those of the principal.[5] Traditional national security analysts have pointed to one form of such problems: Military services can become committed to a particular means of securing a goal as well as to the goal itself. Hence they advocate strategies, weapons systems, and missions which promote their own service-specific interests at the expense of a more unified, rational approach to achieving national security.[6]

Research has addressed some potential principal-agent problems in the provision of security. Particularly in the context of developing countries, analysts have noted the ways that states may attempt to manipulate security policies and external conflicts in order to advance domestic political agendas.[7] Other researchers have observed that in the United States, the "military-industrial complex" may advocate policies and the procurement of weapons not because they enhance national security, but because they benefit the economic interests of a select group of industrialists and policy makers.[8] Principal-agent analysis of the ways in which states may or may not actually provide security for their societies is an area ripe for further research.

Other researchers have pointed out that when the goal of state security becomes paramount, it is possible for state actions to alter the nature of social and political life within a nation and to reduce the security of the individuals living within it. Harold Lasswell called attention to the possible impact on U.S. domestic life of massive militaries that stand at a high state of readiness. Lasswell suggested that because of the complexity of nuclear weapons systems and the need for secrecy, there was a danger that citizens would be cut out of the decision-making process, and a "garrison state" dominated by military specialists would evolve.[9]

In other cases, deep political, social, or religious divisions among a nation's peoples can mean that the security of the state may not be coterminous with the security of all the society. The concept of the nation-state implies that the state is the definer and guarantor of identity for the nation, organizing a society's people and setting them apart from those outside. But states do not always succeed in their attempts to become synonymous with nations, and the legitimacy of established claims is sometimes threatened by separatist movements. Ethnic and racial groups often straddle state boundaries, and in many societies there are "marginal groups" (such as indigenous native American or Indian populations within the United States and Mexico) whose identity is threatened, not guaranteed, by the state.

Edward Azar and Chung-in Moon have examined the potential consequences of the pursuit of security policies in Third World countries with deep domestic political divisions. They contend that "fragile political legitimacy, fragmented societies, incomplete nation-building, and rigid policy capacity" can have extremely serious consequences for security policy. Azar and Moon focus on the implications of these problems for the ability of the state to protect its own security, rather than on these problems as reasons why an evolving society may have to challenge the security of the state. Their concern for the ways in which pursuit of state security may be incompatible with security for opposing or marginal national groups is secondary (Azar and Moon 1988).

The repression of minority populations within states continues to be one of the major problems in the world today. Recent data on one hundred sixty-six countries show only one-third to be ethnically homogeneous. A number of separatist parties and movements which seek to establish separate states or autonomous regions within states are challenging the authority of primary national governments. In at least sixteen countries (about 10 percent of the total), the "national" government was engaged in overt violent conflict against separatist guerrilla movements.[10] States have frequently used force to protect themselves against portions of their own populations (Stohl and López 1984). Joseph Stalin, Adolf Hitler, Idi Amin, Hafez al-Assad, and the Afrikaners only head the list of those who have used force against their populations to ensure the survival of their regimes. In Kenneth Waltz's terms, "If such cases constitute aberrations, they are uncomfortably common ones. We easily lose sight of the fact that struggles to achieve and maintain power, to establish order, and to contrive a kind of justice within states, may be bloodier than wars among them" (Waltz 1979, 103). For these reasons, we argue that additional research is needed into the ways in which state security and the security of social groups within the state may not be identical.

In the vast scope of human history, the nation-state is a historically recent phenomenon that arose in a particular economic, political, geographic, technological, and security context. Its present efficacy in dealing with international problems and its future roles in international and domestic affairs are by no means clear, as analysts are increasingly pointing out. The extent to which societies will continue to see the nation-state as key to their security is an open question; while nation-states continue to be extremely powerful political and economic actors, their continued primacy seems increasingly less certain.

Protection of "Legitimate" National Interests

A second fundamental aspect of the traditional concept of national security is the specific purpose attached to the actions of the state: the protection of "legitimate national interests."[11] Every state must, according to the argument, be the final judge of its own legitimate interests, which creates the potential for both conflicting judgments of interests and for misunderstandings about a state's definitions of its interests. Every state must provide the means to attain and protect its interests in the absence of any other agent to perform this task.

The centrality of this particular aspect of the traditional concept of national security grows out of one of the major dilemmas of national security, namely, the lack of an international sovereign or magistrate with impartiality and authority to adjudicate disputes in cases of conflicting legitimate interests. "Anarchy" is held to distinguish relations among sovereign states from relations among individuals and groups within states. According to Waltz, "An effective government...has a monopoly on the *legitimate* use of force [emphasis in the original text], and legitimate here means that public agents are organized to prevent and to counter the private use of force. Citizens need not prepare to defend themselves. Public agencies do that. A national system is not one of self-help. The international system is" (Waltz 1979, 103-104).

Of course, deciding what is and is not a legitimate use of force even *within* nations is not a simple matter. As discussed above, what one group or clique within a state may view as the legitimate use of force to protect the state may appear to another group as brutal repression and a violation of the security that the state is theoretically obligated to defend. Thus, basing the distinction between national and international politics on the criterion of possession of a monopoly in the legitimate use of force is not without problems.

In the international arena, conflicts over what constitutes "legitimate" national interests are common. However, there is some agreement in the international system, even among ideologically hostile states, of what constitutes legitimate national interests. Most governments and analysts agree, for example, that territorial integrity and sovereignty are legitimate national interests. Respect for this principle is embodied in international common law and the charters of such international organizations as the United Nations and the Organization of African Unity. We do not mean to argue that the consensus on this principle eliminates the possibility of wars over national territory. Such conflicts continue, such as that recently between Iran and Iraq. We do assert, however, that in the context of traditional national security analysis, there is at least some agreement among states as to what constitutes a legitimate interest and hence a legitimate use of force.

In the United States during the 1950s, there were several attempts to develop an objective standard of national interests. The most notable of these, advanced by Hans Morgenthau, was based on the concept of national power. For Morgenthau, the universal drive of states for power dictated that policy makers define their state's interests in terms of power. The power at a state's command, relative to that possessed by other states, was argued to be objectively measurable and hence the only sound and rational basis of judgment for setting the foreign policy of a state.

Taken out of the broader setting of Morgenthau's writings, this formulation appears more ill-advised and simplistic than it actually was. In part, Morgenthau was arguing against U.S. national crusades "to make the world safe for democracy," and in this context, defining the national interest in terms of national power provided a relatively less dangerous and messianic criterion for setting national goals and priorities. Nonetheless, it is widely accepted that Morgenthau's attempt to define interests objectively in terms of power did not succeed. Morgenthau was unable to develop a clear method for determining exactly what a state's relative power is. While some of the elements of national power described by Morgenthau — such as population, resources, and military capabilities — may be quantifiable, other elements such as national "will" and "reputation" are less easily measured. More fundamentally, Morgenthau's conceptualization of interests defined in terms of power fails to address a fundamental question in the determination of national interests: power to do what? Power is ultimately desired by states not simply as an end in itself; it is desired primarily as a means of attaining other ends. Morgenthau's formulation provides no objective standard for determining what those ends should be.[12]

The fact that a standard such as national interests is subjective and hence likely to produce conflicts is not an argument for eliminating this aspect of national security from the traditional concept. It is simply a recognition of one of the difficulties in determining rights and interests faced not only by states, but also by individuals and groups. The political act of calculating what is in the national interest might be seen as a narrow, amoral basis for determining security policies. We disagree with this contention. The standard of carefully weighed national interest as the basis of state action in pursuit of the goal of national security can be high and exacting, particularly if the political process through which nations define their interests in representative and just and if a long-range view is taken.

Even though it may not be possible to develop an objective standard of national interests, it is possible to give the concept greater specificity. Donald E. Nuechterlein, harking back to Morgenthau, seeks to develop a hierarchy of national interests and to provide a framework for analyzing those interests of states "that are so important to the national well-being that governments may choose to use economic and military force if necessary for their protection" (Nuechterlein 1979). Drawing a distinction between when governments act "in the public interest" (in their internal environments) and "in the national interest" (in their external environments), he identifies four basic interests of a nation-state. These are its interests in 1) defense against the threat of physical violence, 2) enhancement of its economic well-being in relations with other states, 3) the maintenance of a world order in which it can feel secure and in which its citizens and commerce can operate peacefully outside its own borders, and 4) the protection and furtherance of a set of values which its citizens share and believe to be universally good. He draws particular attention to the third and fourth national interests, which were rejected in the 1950s by realist theorists in their focus on military and economic power but which he considers essential to re-establishing the concept of national interest as a useful tool for understanding state behavior.

Nuechterlein's framework implicitly addresses some of the issues raised in our previous discussion of potential principal-agent problems. According to Nuechterlein, states are the agents of societies in pursuing their interests in peaceful commerce, the furtherance of a set of values, the enhancement of economic well-being, and the protection of citizens from physical violence. He argues that there is no necessary priority of one interest over another and that they are not mutually exclusive. He acknowledges that these interests do compete for attention and resources, stressing that states do not have a single concept of "the national interest" defined by "some Philosopher-King" but, instead, many interests that are determined by their political systems. The role of political leadership is the determination of which interest is paramount at a specific time and the marshaling of resources required to defend it.

Sources of Threats

The third essential aspect of the conventional concept of national security is the identification of the origins and types of likely threats to legitimate national interests that states are likely to confront. Traditional analysis views the actions of other self-regarding states as the most likely source of threats to national security. This is because of the existence of what is termed "the security dilemma." As a result of international anarchy, a state must be prepared to act on its own behalf to protect its interests. As a final recourse, it must reserve the right to resort to violence. Because all states reserve this right, each state's security is contingent on the behavior of other states. As Robert Art and Robert Jervis argue:

> Because security is the basis of existence and the prerequisite for the achievement of all other goals, statesmen must be acutely sensitive to the security actions of others. The security dilemma thus means that statesmen cannot risk *not* reacting to the security actions of other states, but that in so reacting, they can produce circumstances that leave them worse off than before.... Because of the effects of the security dilemma, efforts of statesmen to protect their peoples can lead to severe tension and war even when all parties sincerely desire peace (Art and Jervis 1985, 3).

The traditional concept of security does not assume that all other states are necessarily aggressive, or that wars occur as a result of human greed or some innate drive for power. Rather, the structure of the international system forces states to be self-regarding and to protect themselves from the possibility that the actions of other states, no matter how well-intended, may actually harm them. Thus, traditional national security analysis focuses on the military preparations and related actions of other states even when they pose no direct threat of aggression.

However, the fact that threats to national security can emanate from events other than the military preparations of other states has long been recognized. Famine was a concern of the Egyptian pharaohs, and water has been a focal point of interstate disputes for millennia. Both internal and external political change has always been seen as a threat to governments. Other states can subvert a state's security through such nonmilitary interventions as espionage and economic warfare.. The economic basis of national power and self-determination did not become a concern only in an age of Japanese competition or crushing external debt loads. These have also been topics for study within traditional national security analysis.

Increasingly, researchers, analysts, and policy makers in the United States have been focusing on a broader range of threats to the interests of states which do not emanate just from the military preparations of other states. If anything can be said to constitute the core of attempts to reconceptualize security, it is this effort to broaden the range of threats considered to challenge national interests. These attempts also recognize the increasing permeability of societies to extra-societal influences and the challenges posed by this permeability to the doctrine that the state is the exclusive agent of a society in the domain of security. Thus we now turn to a brief survey of some of the attempts to reconceptualize national security.

The Contemporary Movement to Reconceptualize Security

Admonitions to reconceptualize security have been commonplace for some time. As early as 1966, Robert S. McNamara, then U.S. Secretary of Defense, made the point that the concept of security had become greatly "oversimplified." He noted, "We still tend to conceive of national security almost solely as a state of armed readiness; a vast, awesome arsenal of weaponry," and that most nations had gone well beyond the point at which they could "buy" more security simply by buying more military hardware.[13]

McNamara was among the first of many in the United States to argue that contemporary debate about United States national security was too strictly focused on military issues. In the mid-1980s, a wave of articles by researchers in the United States and other countries returned to this theme and called for new definitions of national security. Some of these reconceptualizations have analyzed the implications for military power and institutions of an increasingly varied set of changes and potential changes on the national and international scene. These changes include advances in biotechnology and their potential application in warfare, the implications for military manpower of such trends as the spread of AIDS and the decline of birth rates in some European nations, and the impacts on military missions and capabilities of the predicted rise of sea level due to warming of the earth's atmosphere.

Other reconceptualizations have expanded the concept of security to encompass a far broader array of potential threats to entire civil societies, not just to their military institutions.[14] These diverse potential threats include environmental degradation, population growth, depletion of natural resources, economic mismanagement and decline, the rising power of multinational corporations, the replacement of traditional values within a culture with "foreign" culture influences, increasing social and economic stratification, public health crises, authoritarianism and repressiveness, abrogation of human rights, and even natural disasters such as earthquakes. Some have investigated and questioned the applicability of the concept to Third World settings in light of its European and North American origins.[15] Still others have argued that the focus of traditional analysis on the security of states is misplaced, that research needs explicitly to focus on other levels of analysis, such as the security of individuals or the security of the international system (Buzan 1983).

One of the most comprehensive studies of the concept was undertaken by the United Nations Department of Disarmament Affairs. That study began with a definition:

> In principle, security is a condition in which States consider that there is no danger of military attack, political pressure or economic coercion, so that they are able to pursue freely their own development and progress. International security is thus the result and the sum of the security of each and every State member of the international community; accordingly, international security cannot be reached without full international cooperation. However, security is a relative rather than an absolute term. National and international security need to be viewed as matters of degree (United Nations Department for Disarmament Affairs 1986, 2).

The 1986 report takes note of worsening military developments — the continued use of force in international relations, the arms race, the diffusion of military technologies, the lack of progress in disarmament negotiations. It further notes "serious new challenges": trade deficits, resource scarcities, external debts, overpopulation, the emergence of new centers of political and economic power, natural calamities, and environmental degradation. These new challenges are said to place the world "on the thin margin between catastrophe and survival." All of these concerns are given "unprecedented" dimensions by the shadow of nuclear war. The report notes that one state's security is often another's insecurity, acknowledging that the logic of cooperation and accommodation often counts for little against the range of perceived threats and vulnerabilities. Finally, the report suggests that an attempt to review concepts of security has never been so timely and urges national policy makers to weigh its recommendations and translate them into national policies.

The report takes the developing world as a major point of departure for its broad reconsideration of the sources and types of threats to national security. It observes that for many of the four billion inhabitants of the planet, security pertains to the most elementary level of the struggle for human survival — the struggle for access to safe drinking water and the ability to obtain food. The report's analysis of security then extends to the continuation of colonialism, racism, and South Africa's system of apartheid and its aggression against its neighbors. It takes note of the interference of states with large military arsenals in the affairs of small states, particularly in regions that are regarded as strategically or economically sensitive. It acknowledges threats of proliferating arms technologies and spiraling arms races. And it concludes with the observation that new challenges have emerged in developing nations, including overpopulation and environmental resource issues.

Theoretical Confusion and Political Motivations

It is beyond the scope of this chapter to provide a systematic review of these and other efforts, although we believe that such a comprehensive review is sorely needed. However, we offer two observations about them. First, the concept of security embodied in these works remains an inchoate slogan not yet embedded in a theory of security. Second, these reconceptualizations are motivated by an implicit (and sometimes explicit) political agenda: to encourage a reallocation of public resources away from spending on the acquisition of additional military capabilities. We develop each of these points below.

The current reconceptualizations of security fail to develop an alternative theory of security. While they argue that the range of threats which face states and societies needs to be broadened, they fail to advance a coherent set of relationships among the diverse factors that are argued to affect security. These works focus on potential acts, events, or other conditions that in a worst-case scenario would pose a danger or cause fear. Three major groups of evolving threats are emphasized: 1) economic threats, 2) threats posed by energy and raw materials shortages or changes in the global environment, and 3) threats posed to national and international security by domestic social problems such as underdevelopment, political instability, and the inability of governments to meet the welfare demands of their citizens.

Of course, the list of threats is infinitely expandable. A fundamental problem is that these reconceptualizations do not resolve contradictions that arise when security with respect to one sort of threat is bought at the expense of another. They fail to provide a basis for handling tradeoffs among different threats to security; they sometimes even fail to acknowledge that such tradeoffs exist. Finally, the reformulations do not provide methodological or conceptual guidelines that would assist researchers in building on current knowledge about security and enhancing our understanding of it.

In the traditional conceptualization of national security, the state acts as agent in protecting the security of the nation from threats emanating from the self-interested actions of other states. Under these terms, a theory of national security is at hand. But as analysts consider the decline in the abilities of states to act in their own interests and in the interests of their people and consider domestic obstacles to determining and reconciling national interests, this underlying theory begins to totter. Many of the threats to national interests that are seen to be increasingly pressing do not seem tractable to a model based on the national power of sovereign states. The "security dilemma" seems to have taken on a new shape, in that threats increasingly emanate not from the political-military actions of other states but from powerful forces beyond the ability of any single state to control or manage. This poses major analytical problems for traditional theory as well as for the making of policy.

For example, examine the potential threats posed to national interests by global environmental change. In the abstract, a powerful and rich state could assume leadership on such global environmental issues as reducing the emission of greenhouse gases — it could define the problems, find solutions, develop needed technology, disseminate knowledge and equipment, pay the costs, and monitor the results. But no such preeminent state is willing and able to take on these leadership tasks and costs exists today, if it ever did. Some other solution seems required, perhaps based on coordination and cooperation among sovereign states or on control by a supranational authority. Even this kind of solution is not without problems, because not all states have the power to implement domestically what they agree to internationally: International protocols on the reduction of biomass burning, for example, might have little effect on the practices of farmers and ranchers in remote parts of nations with weak governments.

As the list of potential threats is expanded — some might say is bloated — many of the reconceptualizations argue that it is problematic whether the traditional state-centered concept of security can encompass them. If the meaning of security includes economic development, political stability, democratic forms of governance, human rights, environmental quality, and the living conditions of a people, the traditional concept becomes inadequate as a guide for research. Moreover, starting from the traditional concept may be antithetical to attaining the goals sought. For example, the precepts of the traditional means of maintaining national sovereignty collide with the fact that for emerging issues such as economic competitiveness and environmental change, the national interest may dictate some loss of sovereignty, as indeed the member nations of the European Community (EC) have illustrated by moving toward economic integration. Foreign invaders and war are by no means least among the concerns of societies worldwide today, but security in the sense in which many are beginning to understand it has little to do with preparations to deter or repulse foreign invasion or with the maintenance of national sovereignty.

While we agree that these observations and trends have validity, the problem is that there is nothing in the reconceptualizations that proposes an alternative analytic framework. There are assumptions, explicit or implicit, that could lead to a new theory — for example, that the state is not and should not be the sole agent for determining the security agenda — but the assumptions do not add up to an analytical framework. The works are fundamentally exhortations to national governments to alter their priorities and to adopt a more internationalist outlook, one that replaces concern with national security with concern for the security of the international system or humanity.

This brings us to our second observation about current efforts to reconceptualize security: Calls for reconceptualization of security often have been driven not by the goals of greater scientific clarity or explanatory power, but by political aims and events — by values. A particular concern will be drawn under the umbrella of security if doing so furthers a political end. That motivation will not necessarily yield theoretical gains. The literature consists mostly of arguments that a particular nonmilitary threat to societies is as important as, or more important than, the possibility of military aggression. While military threats were an important source of insecurity in the past, these are argued to be becoming less central for a variety of reasons — always acknowledging the overriding threat of nuclear annihilation.

We would not contend that it is possible or even desirable to avoid the political motivations that underlie these calls for reconceptualization of security. The concept of security is inherently political. In this respect, it seems logically different from such concepts as social class and social interaction in that it represents a goal, not a form of social organization or a social process. It inextricably entails the deepest values about humanity and societies. Constructing a theory of security is made more difficult by this circumstance.

A "social class" is, to be sure, epistemologically different from a mammal or a planet; one cannot see a social class. But one can conceptualize its attributes, measure its characteristics, tell its history, place it within a society, and observe how its existence plays a role in social and economic life without, for example, reference to the political goal of much traditional Marxist analysis — raising the class conscious-ness of the proletariat. Similarly, "social interaction" in its various forms can be observed, measured, and analyzed separately from the question of the types of social interaction that a particular analyst may find desirable. Both represent large classes of phenomena that can be studied through the clarifying and simplifying lens of a concept without the intrusion of personal value judgments. This is not to say that such value judgments are immaterial or inappropriate, but simply that analysts need not share these value judgments in order to contribute jointly to research on social class or on social interaction.

Behind the concept of social class lies an articulated theory, perhaps Marxist, social-functional, or social-psychological. That theory informs the core concept, structures links to other concepts, provides descriptive, explanatory, and sometimes predictive power, and tells us what is relevant and what is irrelevant. Each theoretical stance shapes the usage of the concept, and each points the investigator in a slightly different direction. Theorists of different schools can profitably discuss their findings as well as their points of agreement and disagreement. As these theories are challenged and evolve, so do the concepts: Their usefulness turns both upon their designating a phenomenon that is worthwhile to study and upon their openness to new meaning.

But security is a political concept as well as an analytic one. It embodies the values of the politicians or researchers who define it — their choices of those goals to seek and those goals not to seek, those means to employ and those to abhor. Moreover, it is not a phenomenon that can itself be directly studied. It is instead the absence of phenomena like threats of destruction, foreign invasion, insurrection, economic domination, or circumscription of political choices. More abstractly, it is the *capacity* to avert, avoid, or mitigate such threats if and when they arise, as in the capacity to destroy enemy missile sites before launch. Even more abstractly, it is *freedom from the fear* of such threats. There is an endless string of threats from which people might like to be free, and given the fact that public resources are limited, it is necessary to establish priorities, which is fundamentally a political process.

Given that analysis of security is inherently political, it is important to be specific about the particular historical and political circumstances in which the analysis takes place. A fundamental difference among these reconceptualizations is whether they start from the context of the developing world or that of the industrial nations. In much of the developing world, the very existence and viability of the state may be in question, as well as the ability of the society to provide for basic human needs. In the industrial world other challenges are raised, including those to the exclusive domain of the state as the agent of a society in providing security and to the military as the means to security. The divergence of critiques and reformulations is partly attributable to these differing contexts.

This observation is particularly important in the context of this volume because what may be an appropriate strategy for addressing the political aim of reestablishing priorities in one country may be inappropriate for others. In the United States, for example, the calls for reconceptualization of security take place within a political context that seems to require definition of a public problem or issue in terms of some threat it poses to national security for it to receive attention and resources.

Historically, the United States has become involved in international affairs only to the extent that its failure to do so constituted a threat to national interests and security. During the 1950s, this entailed responding to the perceived threat to U.S. interests posed by Soviet expansionism. This particular historical condition, coupled with the fact that during this seminal period the U.S. economy was strong and its society cohesive, accounts for the definition of threats to U.S. national security as originating in the actions of other states. Now, however, the continued well-being of the U.S. economic and social system seems less certain, and as a result, many individuals are arguing for a reordering of priorities. Because of U.S. political culture, this usually entails arguing that a particular problem is a security problem, because that continues to be the dominant political strategy for securing access to public resources. Such arguments can distort national responses to public problems: Today's clamor for improved elementary and secondary education comes not from the intrinsic desirability of learning, but from an urge to improve economic competitiveness and thus to increase U.S. national security.

Within other states, perhaps particularly within such developing countries as Mexico, the recourse to the language of national security has not been as important historically. Other arguments were used to mobilize public action to address pressing national needs. Hence, from a political point of view, we must question whether attempts to reconceptualize security to encompass a broad array of threats — not just those posed to Mexico from the self-interested activities of other states such as the United States — are necessary or even desirable. It is at least conceivable that such a strategy will have a paradoxically negative outcome, that of strengthening the role of the military in national decision making and hence shifting priorities away from other problems and toward military threats and solutions. More generally, we counsel caution in attempting to use the language and analysis of national security to argue for greater governmental attention to nonmilitary threats and problems.

We have noted that reconceptualizations of security are grounded not in theoretical understandings, but in political goals. This has important ramifications for their utility in adding to our knowledge of security and in developing more broadly based theories of security. Ideally, what would a more theoretically adequate reconceptualization accomplish for research? We turn now to a brief discussion of the role of concepts in social science research.

Concepts and Research

The complexity of the world of social, economic, political, and cultural life forces on the social scientist the necessity to form abstract concepts. It is through concepts that we study abstract phenomena such as social class, reference groups, marginal utility, and kinship networks — each a collection of diverse phenomena sharing some theoretical trait. These concepts simplify the social world, necessarily shedding much of its richness but enabling the formulation of systematic theories and the conduct of research.

While politicians look to experience, history, and public opinion for their concepts, often preferring to keep them fuzzy to maximize political support or minimize opposition, the social scientist seeks clarity and analytical power. That search, even without political overtones, would lead to disputes. Dispute over concepts is not new to social science; it is, in fact, a basic aspect of scientific advance.

Philosopher of science Abraham Kaplan describes the purposes and uses of concepts and implies some abstract standards by which their usefulness can be judged (Kaplan 1964, 46-54). Most broadly, according to Kaplan, if a concept is to do anything at all useful, it clarifies the complexity of the social world by introducing into discussions a hope of theoretical order. It does so by being embedded in a theory about the linkages between actions and their results. For example, concepts like "social class" help us to identify relationships among other key concepts such as family background, income, occupation, education, political opinions, personality, and culture. Mill saw this criterion in causal terms: A scientifically valid concept should identify properties which are causes of many other properties (Kaplan 1964, 51). This criterion is usually relaxed in the social sciences to a requirement for statistical relationships.

Drawing freely from Kaplan's analysis, we identify three specific functions of concepts that seem relevant to research on security. First, a useful concept should identify relationships among key phenomena and levels of analysis. This involves understanding the relationships of variables that measure threats to security and variables that measure actions that can be taken to obtain security. These variables must be studied in at least four distinct levels of analysis: the individual, the society, the state, and the international system. Second, a useful concept should enable researchers to classify something as a threat to security, as an action that will promote security, or as something that is irrelevant to the security calculus. Third, the concept should provide a guide as to which measurements are relevant and appropriate and enable researchers to compare potential threats and the probable increments to security yielded by alternative policies.

If national security is conceived in terms of military threats emanating from the actions of other states, the traditional concept, in fact, could fulfill all three of these functions. It is embedded in a theory that identifies critical relationships between national military power and national security, structures analytical classifications, and leads states to take certain actions based on their expectations of favorable results. It provides guidance to the researcher concerning relevant and irrelevant phenomena, measurement operations, and analytical strategies. It permits researchers to assess the effectiveness of different military policies to counter potential military threats.

However, as the range of security threats is expanded, the traditional concept comes up short because of its focus on the potential state application of military power to counter external threats of aggression. It does not enable us to conduct research that compares potential military threats with nonmilitary threats or to measure the increments to security potentially yielded by alternative policies. It does not provide guidelines for determining whether particular actions enhance or diminish security against nonmilitary threats. It also fails to point the way to research that may enable us to better understand the connections among such problems as underdevelopment, environmental degradation, and political instability.

Failure to specify "causal" relationships in the reconceptualizations renders them unable to assess trade-offs — across different kinds of threats and among different levels of analysis — that arise when states attempt to ensure their security. Policies intended to increase the security of the state sometimes have the effect of decreasing security at the individual, societal, or international levels of analysis. And even within the state level of analysis, the traditional concept fails to give adequate attention to contradictions that result when attempts to increase security by enhancing military preparedness result in economic, political, or social costs that endanger other core national interests or values.

This failure to specify causal relationships also leads researchers to analyze security as a thing in itself rather than as a part of the cultural, political, economic, and social life of a society. It has not been an important concept in broader social science theory or research, although traces of the idea can be found, for example, in systems analysis in its recognition of the systemic role of organizations that guard national borders (Miller 1978, 770-71). Despite the centrality of the national security apparatus in the life of most societies, it rarely is considered in basic textbooks or studied as part of the national social system. Although researchers such as Morton Kaplan have attempted to view national security as an aspect of social behavior, most research on security is entirely dissociated from the rich body of theoretical and empirical work on social phenomena. The needed intellectual bridge is not there between traditional national security analysis and other concerns of the social sciences.

Clearly, the traditional theory of security cannot readily support research on a vastly broadened new concept of security. It would have to be extended or supplanted. What would be needed in the emerging reconceptualizations is a new security theory that encompasses a far wider range of relationships among social, economic, cultural, political, and environmental phenomena, that lays out the actions that can be taken to attain security on all these fronts, and that guides analysts to the construction of useful classifications and models. The state might or might not play a central role in this new theory. Interests might be defined at the level of societies or at some broader level, perhaps at the level of the entire human race. In any event, a new solution would have to be found for principal-agent problems. However, there is as yet no consensus on elementary issues among those who seek to reconceptualize security: What kinds of analytical classifications will structure research, which variables are relevant or irrelevant, or which measurement operations are appropriate or inappropriate. There could hardly then be consensus on relationships among security threats and actions to counter them, which actions are likely to produce the desired results, or how the increments to security of possible actions can be assessed. We see no indications of the rise of a nascent theory of security in the writings of those who seek to reconceptualize it.

For such a theory to be developed, analysts will have to make choices leading to a coherent concept embedded in a model of relationships among threats, capabilities, and actions. Is economic growth to be taken as part of the calculus of national security or not, and if so, which forms of economic organization can achieve this goal?

Is ensuring a high quality of life for its citizens part of the security concerns of a nation? How about freedom from repression? What is the continuing theoretical role of the necessity for a nation to be able to defend itself against foreign aggression? How do we factor into the security calculus the potential for rise of sea levels and the possible devastation that this will wreak in numerous nations on their economic and social structures, and even on their territorial integrity?

This last question leads us to pose the issue of whether any new theory could encompass the means that a state can employ to ensure security when the threats come not from the self-regarding actions of other states, but instead from an agglomeration of world economic and environmental changes. Which means to ensure international security can be used when, according to the only cogent theory of security that now exists, the steps taken to maximize one nation's security can undermine the security of others? Is it possible to develop a theory that admits both the preservation of national sovereignty through the military defense of borders and the forfeiture of national sovereignty in the interests of improvement of the global environment? What is gained by considering most national and international concerns under the rubric of security, other than laying a claim for a politically potent concept? Do the reconceptualizations lead to greater clarity and analytical power, or do they further obfuscate what was already a complex and problem-ridden idea? It is premature to judge these questions, but surely the time has come to raise them.

In spite of this negative assessment, it is unrealistic to expect that the development of new concepts would be more advanced. Kaplan writes of "the paradox of conceptualization": "The proper concepts are needed to formulate a good theory, but we need a good theory to arrive at the proper concepts" (Kaplan 1964, 53). The bind is, of course, handled by approximations: Weak concepts lead to weak theories that, nevertheless, give rise to research, research refines theories and concepts, and successively both concepts and theories are made more useful. We are, at best, at the first level of approximation in reconceptualizing security.

Research and the Reconceptualization of Security

The groundwork for a coherent, theoretically powerful reconceptualization of security is yet to be laid. Simple steps toward theoretical development, not polemical argument, seem needed.

What we suggest as a beginning is that researchers might profitably address three fundamental questions in their attempts to think about alternative concepts of security: "Whose security?" "What threats?" "Which means?"[16]

Whose Security? Are we discussing the security of individuals, of the collectivity called the society, of the state regime, or of a regional or international system? Research should focus more explicitly on the tradeoffs that are believed to exist among these levels of analysis in order to develop better theories as to the relationships among individual, social, national, and international security. Such research could make a valuable contribution in linking the current study of national security to other traditions of social research. It could also enrich these other traditions by pointing to some of the ways in which factors at the level of the international system can influence other types of social interaction.

What Threats? Is the focus of future research to be on the threat of an enemy to use its military power, on nonmilitary threats that might undermine the capacity of a state to maintain military power, or on nonmilitary threats to "legitimate interests?" Is the latter focus on short-term threats such as famine and flood, or on longer-term threats such as loss of economic competitiveness and depletion of the ozone layer? Research that begins to explore the impacts of diverse developments in the international system and to compare the likely probability-weighted costs of those developments for states and societies would assist in beginning to develop a better categorization of potential threats.

We again turn to the analysis put forward by Nuechterlein, who rates potential challenges to national interests at four levels of intensity. In doing so, he presents a hierarchy of issues that makes explicit the necessity for a long-time horizon in consideration of national interests and the means of pursuing them. Nuechterlein's analysis distinguishes between "survival issues," short-run threats to the very existence of a society that invoke the defense interest, and "vital issues," long-run threats that can invoke all four interests. He further considers "major issues," events and trends in the international environment which can become vital issues unless corrective action is taken, and "peripheral issues" that do not affect the well-being of the society but do affect the foreign activities of private citizens and corporations. Attempting to flesh out this scheme may assist in the process of developing a more encompassing and still cogent theory of security.

Which Means? Do the means to security lie in strengthening military power, in changing society so that it can better support military power, or in measures that might achieve security even without military power? The consideration of this question must go hand-in-hand with the previous questions that we have posed. Means cannot be considered in the absence of the consideration of goals and of potential obstacles to the attainment of those goals. Research should carefully integrate assessments of potential means for attaining security into the consideration of whose security is being promoted and in response to what threats. Consideration of the appropriate means for attaining security will also enable researchers to understand better some of the important relationships among different policies designed to enhance security and to discover some of the ways policies are designed to protect against others.

We propose more explicit consideration of this third question not only as a question of means but also as a question of agency: Who in a given society is responsible for protecting the security of the society — the state, the people themselves, or some international actor? Again, the level at which one is seeking to enhance security and the type of development which is seen to threaten security are integral to the analysis. As not all means are available to all agents, issues of strategy and tactics are intertwined with issues of agency.

Conclusion

How the researcher addresses each of these questions necessarily involves choices on political or moral values; it accomplishes nothing to ignore that fact. *Whose security*: Is it right for the international community to suppress rogue states in the interest of international security? *What threats*: Is there a universal human entitlement to adequate nutrition and clean water? Is autocratic rule antagonistic to the human spirit? *Which means*: Is it ethical to kill when the alternative is that one's fellow citizens will be killed? The necessity for such value choices cannot be denied. Nevertheless, we argue that researchers who would make different political choices all ought to be able to contribute to common research.

Many analysts hold that values inevitably affect the outcomes of research, initially in the selection of problems and then in the choice of theories, concepts, and methods. We concur and believe that researchers should make their values known so that these factors can be taken into account. Some go so far as to assert that there is no possibility of scientific communication across gaps in values. This dismal view renounces the possibility of cumulative research spanning ideological boundaries. At the root of cumulative research — indeed, to us, at the root of the claim of social science to be "scientific" — is the concept of replicability: Can one researcher's finding stand up to the scrutiny of another? A convincing test of the replicability of a finding, whether on cold fusion or the origins of World War I, requires that the researcher not slavishly imitate the predecessor, mistakes and all, but instead test the resilience of the finding under differing conditions, perhaps including differing beliefs. Other analysts, fearing that their values will bias their observations, eschew theories in the hope that "immaculate perception" will render their data objective. This is a naive stance and truly dangerous to "objectivity." Thus, while not assuming the worn facade of "value-free" social science, we assert the necessity for the independence of values and research findings and see as key to this that values are announced rather than hidden.[17]

Our review of the failings of both the traditional concept of security and attempts to reconceptualize it has not produced a satisfactory resolution for those who seek a concept that will prove a sound guide for research. We reserve judgment on whether the most profitable direction will be further attempts to reconceptualize security, attempts to subsume traditional military security concerns under a different concept, or the separation of the concept of military security from the new agenda of national and international concerns. Given the political nature of this task, it may not be possible to reach a universally generalizable answer to this question; what may be appropriate in one national context may not be appropriate in another. While this volume does not provide a definitive answer to this question, we believe that it constitutes an important attempt to explore whether scholars can grapple with important problems under the rubric of security to produce valid insights into the diverse issues and problems confronting Mexico. It also shows, we think, the necessity for reflection as to next steps toward methods, concepts, and theories.

Notes

1. Lippmann, for example, defined national security as follows: "A nation has security when it does not have to sacrifice its legitimate interests to avoid war, and is able, if challenged, to maintain them by war." See Walter Lippmann, *U.S. Foreign Policy: Shield of the Republic* (Boston: Little Brown & Co., 1943), 5. See also Morton Berkowitz and P.G. Bock, "National Security," vol. 11 of *International Encyclopedia of the Social Sciences*, ed. David L. Sills, 40-45, (New York: MacMillan, 1968) for a discussion of the development of the concept.

2. In *The Politics of Nonviolent Action* (Boston: Porter Sargent Publishers, 1973, three vols.), Gene Sharp explores the potential of a variety of civilian-based defense schemes that limit the role of the state in providing for defense and national security.

3. See, for example, Kenneth Waltz, *Theory of International Politics* (Reading, Mass.: Addison-Wesley, 1979), chap. 5, "Political Structures," especially 91-93. The state assumes exclusive importance in Waltz's analysis; the goal of ensuring the survival and security of the society drops from sight. Waltz writes, "I assume that states seek to ensure their survival.... Survival is a prerequisite to achieving any goals that states may have, other than the goal of promoting their own disappearance as political entities."

4. The society of industrial societies has tended to treat societies and nation-states as coterminous, but contemporary thinking recognizes that the boundaries of modern societies are often permeable. This increasing permeability poses one of the major challenges to the nation-state as it does to sociology. States conceivably can contain several societies; the Soviet Union was arguably an example. Societies can also include parts of several states; not only has this understanding been behind wars of conquest to reabsorb ethnic minorities in adjacent states, but some analysts are speculating about the possible emergence of a European society. One analyst has noted that "analytical conceptions must not be inflexibly tied to the concept of the national boundary." Leon H. Mayhew, "Society," vol. 14, of *International Encyclopedia*, ed. David Sills, 577-586.

5. See Jonathan Bendor, 1988. "Review Article: Formal Models of Bureaucracy," *British Journal of Political Science* 18: 353-95, for an extended discussion of principal-agent models.

6. See, for example, Samuel Huntington, *The Common Defense* (New York: Columbia University Press, 1961) for an early example of this sort of analysis.

7. David J. Finlay, Ole R. Holsti, and Richard R. Fagen, *Enemies in Politics* (Chicago: Rand McNally, 1967), discuss some aspects of the functions

which the image of the antagonist serves in politics. See especially Chapter 4. See also Richard H. Moss, *The Limits of Policy: An Investigation of the Spiral Model, the Deterrence Model, and Miscalculations in U.S.-Third World Relations* (unpublished Ph.D. dissertation, Princeton University, 1987) for an extended discussion of the domestic political costs and benefits of external conflicts for leaders in the United States, Cuba, Egypt, and Indonesia.

8. While early statements of this argument attribute this possibility to the profiteering of industrialists and atavistic aggressiveness of certain social classes, more recent work sees it as rooted in modern industrial and scientific systems. For discussions of the role of such considerations in military procurement in the United States, see James R. Kurth, "Why we buy the weapons we do," *Foreign Policy* 11(Summer 1973): 33-56. See also Richard J. Barnet, *The Roots of War* (Baltimore: Penguin, 1972) for a discussion of the obstacles which such military-industrial interests may present in attempts to achieve disarmament.

9. Harold D. Lasswell, "The Garrison-State Hypothesis Today," in *Changing Patterns in Military Politics.* ed. Samuel P. Huntington, (New York: Free Press, 1962), 52-70. This is an updated version of "The Garrison State," *American Journal of Sociology,* 46 (1941): 455-68.

10. See John Clements, *Clements Encyclopedia of World Governments,* vol. 7 (Dallas: Political Research, Inc. 1986), and Arthur S. Banks, *Political Handbook of the World: 1986* (Binghamton, N.Y.: CSA Publication, 1986), cited in Bruce Russett and Harvey Starr, *World Politics* (New York: W.H. Freeman and Co., 1989).

11. The concept of "national interest" is itself both an analytic tool and an instrument of political action. As will be discussed more fully below, it is essentially rooted in personal values and judgments about "what is best" for a nation. For a discussion of the concept, see James Rosenau, "The National Interest," vol. 11, of *International Encyclopedia,* ed. David Sills, 34-40.

12. See Hans J. Morgenthau, *Politics Among Nations: The Struggle for Power and Peace,* 6th edition (New York: Knopf, 1985), 4-17. See also James N. Rosenau (referenced in note 11 above) for a longer discussion of the application of the concept of the national interest and Robert H. Sprinkle, *The Conscience of Power: States, Corporations, and the Life Sciences* (draft Ph.D. Dissertation, Princeton University), chap. 3, "States, Corporations, and the Ethics of Political Realism," for an in-depth critique of realist ethics.

13. McNamara refers to this address and further develops his point regarding the limits to attaining security through additional military expenditures in "Population and International Security," *International Security,* 2,2(Fall 1977): 25-55.

14. See, for example, Richard H. Ullman, "Redefining Security," *International Security,* vol. 8, no. 1(Summer 1983). Additional works will be cited

throughout this chapter. Ullman's analysis and a study by Neville Brown, *The Future Global Challenge: A Predictive Study of World Security, 1977-1990* (London: RUSI, 1977), both argue for the necessity of conceptualizing security much more broadly than is the case in traditional studies of national military strategy. Their empirical arguments point to developments in the international environment that are changing the nature and substance of international security problems.

15. See Davis B. Bobrow and Steve Chan, "Simple Labels and Complex Realities: National Security in the Third World" and Barry Buzan, "People, States, and Fear: The National Security Problem in the Third World" in *National Security in the Third World: the Management of Internal and External Threats*, eds. Edward Azar and Chung-in Moon (College Park, Md., Center for International Development and Conflict Management, 1988).

16. Or, as Carl von Clausewitz might have expressed similar questions, "Which goals? What obstacles? Which means?"

17. Some analysts argue that values themselves cannot only be systematically studied but also objectively grounded. See Abraham Kaplan, *The Conduct of Inquiry: Methodology for Behavioral Science* (San Francisco: Chandler Publishing Company, 1964), 370-97.

References

Art, Robert J., and Robert Jervis. 1985. "The Meaning of Anarchy." In *International Politics: Anarchy, Force, Political Economy and Decision-Making*, eds. Robert J. Art and Robert Jervis. Boston: Little Brown & Co.

Azar, Edward, and Chung-in Moon. 1988. "Legitimacy, Integration and Policy Capacity: The 'Software' Side of Third World National Security." In *National Security in the Third World: The Management of Internal and External Threats*, eds. Edward Azar and Chung-in Moon. College Park, Md.: Center for International Development and Conflict Management.

Banks, Arthur S. 1986. *Political Handbook of the Third World.* Binghamton, N.Y.: CSA Publication. Cited in Bruce Russett and Harvey Starr. 1989. *World Politics.* New York: W.H. Freeman and Co.

Barnett, Richard J. 1972. *The Roots of War.* Baltimore: Penguin.

Bendor, Jonathan. 1988. "Review Article: Formal Models of Bureaucracy." *British Journal of Political Science* 18:353-95.

Berkowitz, Morton, and P.G. Bock. 1968. "National Security." In *International Encyclopedia of the Social Sciences*, ed. David L. Sills, 11:40-45. New York: Macmillan.

Bobrow, Davis B., and Steve Chan. 1988. "Simple Labels and Complex Realities: National Security in the Third World." In *National Security in the Third World: The Management of Internal and External Threats*, eds. Edward Azar and Chung-in Moon. College Park, Md.: Center for International Development and Conflict Management.

Buzan, Barry. 1983. *People, States and Fear: The National Security Problem in International Relations.* Chapel Hill: University of North Carolina Press.

Clements, John. 1986. *Clements Encyclopedia of World Governments* 7. Dallas: Political Research, Inc. Cited in Bruce Russett and Harvey Starr, *World Politics.* New York: W.H. Freeman and Co.

Finlay, David J., Ole R. Holsti, and Richard R. Fagen. 1967. *Enemies in Politics.* Chicago: Rand McNally.

Grier Miller, James. 1978. *Living Systems.* New York: McGraw-Hill.

Huntington, Samuel. 1961. *The Common Defense.* New York: Columbia University Press.

Kaplan, Abraham. 1964. *The Conduct of Inquiry: Methodology for Behavioral Science.* San Francisco: Chandler Publishing Company.

Kurth, James R. 1973. "Why We Buy the Weapons We Do." *Foreign Policy* 11:33-56 (Summer).

Lasswell, Harold D. [1941] 1962. "The Garrison-state Hypothesis Today." In *Changing Patterns in Military Politics*, ed. Samuel P. Huntington, 51-70. New York: Free Press. (New version of his article of 1941).

Lippmann, Walter. 1943. *U.S. Foreign Policy: Shield of the Republic*, Boston: Little Brown & Co.

Mayhew, Leon H. "Society." In *International Encyclopedia of the Social Sciences*, ed. David Sills, 14:577-86. New York: Macmillan.

McNamara, Robert. 1977. "Population and International Security." *International Security* 2, no.2, 25-55 (Autumn).

Morgenthau, Hans J. 1985. *Politics among Nations: The Struggle for Power and Peace.* 6th. ed. New York: Knopf.

Moss, Richard H. 1987. "The Limits of Policy: An Investigation of the Spiral Model, the Deterrence Model, and Miscalculations in U.S. Third World Relations." Ph.D. thesis. Princeton University.

Nuechterlein, Donald E. 1979. "The Concept of 'National Interest': A Time for New Approaches." *Orbis* (Spring): 73-93.

Rosenau, James N. 1973. "The National Interest." In *International Encyclopedia of the Social Sciences*, ed. David L. Sills, 11:34-40. New York: Macmillan.

Sharp, Gene. 1973. *The Politics of Nonviolent Action.* Boston: Porter Sargent Publishers.

Sprinkle, Robert H. *The Conscience of Power: States, Corporations and the Life Sciences.* Chap. 3. Princeton University.

Stohl, Michael, and George A. López. 1984. *The State as Terrorist: The Dynamics of Governmental Violence and Repression.* Westport, Conn.: Greenwood Press.

Ullman, Richard H. 1983. "Redefining Security." *International Security* 8, no. 1 (Summer).

Ullman, Richard, and Neville Brown. 1977. *The Future Global Challenge: A Predictive Study of World Security, 1988-1990.* London: RUSI.

United Nations Department of Disarmament Affairs. 1986. *Report of the General Secretary: Concepts of Security*, 2. New York: United Nations.

Waltz, Kenneth. 1979. *Theory of International Politics.* Reading, Pa.: Addison-Wesley.

International Security and National Development

Javier A. Elguea

Introduction

The crisis of security through which the countries of Latin America are passing is a recent addition to the intellectual agenda of international security experts and specialists. The acute economic crisis and the ineffectiveness of many national economic programs, the region's enormous international debt, the difficult and vulnerable political transitions taking place, and, above all, the persistence of endemic internal violence and the escalation of regional conflicts have made the 1980s one of the most uncertain and collectively insecure decades in modern Latin America's history.

This uncertainty, and its accompanying violence, have so exceeded national as well as regional geographic boundaries that the matter has been transformed into a problem of international security. The fact that security experts and specialists have only recently incorporated Latin American problems in their analyses has, at times, obscured the true nature and origin of the issues involved. Contemporary Latin American security problems date back at least several decades and have been affected by disputes over territory and sovereignty, but above all they have been exacerbated by internal political, social, and economic factors.

In this sense, the essential components of the conventional notion of security — the defense of territory and national sovereignty — are insufficient to explain the current security crisis of practically all the countries in the region. The problems these countries face in the development process, facing rapid growth and social change as well as frequent reversals of these same processes and the explosions of

63

violence they generate, oblige the countries of the region to conceive of and deal with the national security question in different ways than do the countries of the developed world. The following pages represent an effort to reflect analytically on the characteristics the concept of security has assumed for Latin American countries in recent decades, the ways this concept is used by them, and the distinctions between this concept and the current definition of security for the developed countries and major powers.

Security: Its Definition and Its Problems

In general terms, the notion of "security" has been associated with protection and avoidance of danger or risk. The majority of specialists in the discipline refer to "national security" as the capacity of a nation-state to defend itself from outside attack and the ability to defend its "national interests," understood fundamentally as territorial integrity and political sovereignty.

The great emphasis the specialized literature has placed on the military aspects of national security and on the nuclear arms race and confrontation between powers is, without a doubt, partially responsible for the success achieved up to now in the maintenance of a stable and enduring peace between the powers. However, for some time this emphasis has shown great limitations, both in the developed and underdeveloped world.

Academics and experts have recently entered into an intense discussion on the necessity for and dangers of expanding the semantic limits of the definition of security. Those in favor of a broad version emphasize the myopia of the conventional definition and its incapacity to account for new nonmilitary national and international security problems. For their part, proponents of a restricted version point to the dangers of relaxing definitional limits that could lead to the inclusion of problems that really do not belong as security issues.

For some time, adherents of a broader version have advocated the incorporation of a long list of phenomena excluded until now from the security problematic, which include not only issues of political survival but also of general well-being, such as ecological concerns, the exhaustion of nonrenewable resources, illegal international migration, and drug trafficking. In the case of the Third World, where the discipline has shown a serious inability to deal with security problems arising from multiple regional conflicts, there has been insistence on the need to fit the significance of the notion of security to the reality of the problems of developing countries, where poverty and inequality as well as the absence of political consensus and the recourse to internal violence are serious threats to peace and national and international security.

Defenders of the conventional definition, for their part, claim that the majority of the attempts made to expand the definition have been inapt and dangerous. Some of the recent efforts, according to them, have done no more than increase conceptual confusion, erase key conceptual limits, and convert the term "security" into a cliché applied hither and yon without any rigor.

The restriction or expansion of a conceptual definition is, in itself, neither a vice nor a virtue; definitions are good or bad, useful or useless, independent of their expansion or restriction. In the case of the contemporary debate over the definition of the term "security," the justifications for its expansion or restriction reflect nothing more than the two extremes of a semantical continuum, along which one seeks to define the meaningful limits of the term and its object of study. In this sense, the definition of these limits (expanded or restricted) will allow students of security to establish a minimal consensus about the object of their analyses and a minimal agreement on adequate methodologies for its study.

Seen from this perspective, the discipline seems to have entered a period of "scientific crisis" in which the previous paradigms or research projects are competing with novel revisions and new ideas. It is an intellectual struggle in which the best projects and theories should triumph, as occurs in any intellectual debate that aspires to contribute to scientific progress. The question the specialist must ask, then, is: What are the criteria for deciding which theories are better than others? A discussion of the extensive literature on the progress of scientific knowledge and theoretical evaluation is beyond the scope of this article. Suffice it for now to suggest that a definition of this type should at least satisfy two requirements: explanatory power and practical utility.

On the one hand, the heuristic or explanatory power of a definition determines its generalizability as well as its capacity to encompass a large number of cases in a logically consistent manner. On the other hand, the practical utility of a definition can be evaluated in light of its capacity to resolve real problems. The first requirement permits us to adequately describe *what security is;* the second orients us toward *how to avoid insecurity.* In this sense, expanded or reduced definitions are nothing more than the two opposite extremes of the continuous dialectic within which we should be able to locate the definition of security to guide future research and practice.

At one end of this continuum, the restricted conventional definition has begun to show signs of exhaustion. For one thing, it has been unable to explain adequately the emergence, development, and proliferation of internal wars in the Third World. Any war is — by definition — a problem of national security for the country in which it is fought and can become a problem of international security. For another thing, it has ignored the causes of insecurity that issue from phenomena unrelated to territorial defense or sovereignty.

The other extreme, that of expanded definitions, has fallen into excesses of various kinds, such as treating problems better defined as economic or political as if they were security problems, and the elaboration of long lists of synonyms that describe analogies and metaphors but are consistently said to define the term "security."

Both versions fail to meet the criteria of explanatory power and practical utility. Neither is capable, at present, of adequately defining the limits of the object of study or orienting its practice. New theoretical efforts, then, are still needed.

In the following pages, I will explore the term "security," taking especially into account Third World security problems that have arisen in the decades since World War II.

Security and Underdevelopment

> No, Mascarita, the country had to develop. Didn't Marx say that progress would arrive streaming blood? As sad as it was, we had to accept it. There was no alternative. (Mario Vargas Llosa 1987)

Since the end of World War II, Third World regional conflicts have increased exponentially. War, apparently becoming obsolete as a form of conflict resolution between developed nations, has proliferated in the same period in the underdeveloped world, threatening not only the stability and security of entire regions, both domestically and internationally, but also the maintenance of the balance of forces between powers.

Since 1945, there have been approximately three hundred wars, the great majority of them occurring in the Third World (Kidron and Smith 1983). These wars have been fought for traditional reasons: rivalry between states for control of regional power and domestic power struggles. These wars have been fought in a context of international restructuring that came as a consequence of the rise and fall of powers after the Second World War, an era during which all regional conflicts have taken on global significance. Independence and anticolonial movements, revolutions and civil wars have been the keynote of armed conflicts during the so-called "decades of development." An important element of armed conflicts in these decades has been their internationalization, not only because superpower intervention has been a characteristic common to all, but also because on repeated occasions there have been systematic efforts to export conflicts to neighboring countries or to intervene in existing ones.

On the American continent, from the end of the Second World War through the 1980s, all the armed conflicts took place in Central and South America and the Caribbean. There have been thirty-eight domestic armed conflicts and eleven international ones (Kidron and Smith 1983). Of those, fourteen occurred in Central America, thirteen in the Caribbean, and twenty-two in South America.

The death count from these conflicts in Latin America alone in the 1970s and 1980s exceeded three hundred thousand (taking into consideration the conflicts in El Salvador, Guatemala, Nicaragua, Colombia, Peru, Chile, and Argentina). The refugee and exile count for the same period in Latin America come to more than four million people (Stevens 1988; Fagen 1987).

The collateral damage done by the militarization of the region can be seen in its negative correlation with illiteracy, education, public health spending, and life expectancy and its positive correlation with infant mortality. The statistics in other regions of the underdeveloped world are even worse: more than sixty armed conflicts in Africa between 1945 and 1982, forty in the Middle East, and almost eighty in Asia and Southeast Asia for the same period (Kidron and Smith 1983).

The majority of cases of organized violence in the Third World are of an internal nature. A great number of the conflicts are civil wars, making "defense from external attack" irrelevant or nonexistent in terms of territorial protection and sovereignty. Nevertheless, despite certain resistance in the specialized literature, these are real wars in every sense of the word. They involve at least two contentious groups with incompatible objectives that resort to organized force and violence with high death rates directly caused by the massive violence, and they sometimes cross borders to become international conflicts. For these reasons, attempting to explain these conflicts using the conventional notion of security is, for the most part, a useless activity. The origin of the violence is internal in nature and must be examined on a case-by-case basis, using a different conception of security, one capable of explaining the origin and characteristics of this modality of armed conflict.

The literature on the origins and causes of the violence, revolutions, and fall of regimes in the Third World is no longer useful in predicting the occurrence of these phenomena, nor in the explanation of the relative weight of factors that cause violence and instability in specific situations. However, the investigation and elucidation of the causes is now and will continue to be a central problem in the adequate definition of security problems in the Third World. In this sense, and despite their theoretical deficiencies, some recent efforts have properly tried to provide both historical and conceptual reasons for the expansion of the definition of security in the Third World.

From a historical perspective, the experience the great powers have gone through provides a very powerful reason for the expansion of the concept of security. Since 1945, there has been growing pressure to raise the consciousness of developed countries about the role dependent and underdeveloped territories play in their own security and in the international system in general. At the same time this awareness has been growing, the great powers have repeatedly shown an inability to understand the origin and nature of regional problems in the Third World. The great powers have paid dearly for their indifference and incapacity to understand the problems of the developing countries, the most notable example being that of the United States in Vietnam, where sophisticated arms technology failed as a substitute for political acumen and perceptiveness. Something similar has occurred in Latin America where the military containment of communism has overtaken the promotion of regional development as a priority on the North American security agenda, when in the judgment of the Latin American countries, the priorities should be reversed.

It is clear, given the experience of recent decades, that international insecurity in the underdeveloped world can turn into considerable insecurity for the nations of the developed world through the effects of regional instability and interventionism.

There are some important considerations to take heed of with respect to the expansion of the meaning of national security. For one thing, there is the defense of "national interest" as an essential component of the notion of security. Stephenson (1981) has criticized the inclusion of "national interest" in security definitions because of its lack of clarity and semantic precision. "National interest," he believes, is an amorphous term used much more by politicians than by careful researchers (1981, 2). Patterson (1981) holds that the specific "national interests" of countries tend to change over time and are more variable than fixed. In this sense, a country still concerned with reaching minimum standards of health and education for its population, with international debts that oblige it to delay its growth, with a weak and vulnerable political system, will tend to define its "national interests" in a fundamentally distinct fashion from an industrialized nation with a stable political system and a high commercial and financial surplus. "National interest" is, then, a relative term. As P. O'Neill asserts:

> Nation-building, cohesion, quality of government, capacity to hold elections, sense of national identity, cultural autonomy, and the creation of disciplined public servants under government control, especially the military — all these, realities that Western democracies take for granted — have to be actively promoted if we want to construct secure nations in the Third World (O'Neill 1988).

This, of course, does not mean that every one of a country's "national interests" necessarily involves problems of security, nor are all the security problems of an underdeveloped country domestic rather than international in nature. Much contemporary literature has inaccurately stretched the term to include as security issues such items as economic, food, population, pollution, and migration problems, when in reality they are no more than development issues that do not seriously compromise peace or national stability. Without any doubt, there are diverse examples where the coming together of problems of this type has provoked instability and the eruption of armed violence in the region. But there are also many examples where this has not occurred; security specialists should be interested in only those development problems that have placed peace and stability in question. In sum, only those national interest priorities that represent a threat to the survival of the nation and cause recourse to armed force and violence constitute true national security interests.

The common denominator of almost all the armed conflicts in the Third World is the frustrated expectation of economic and social progress. Whether the sudden and unexpected reversal of growth processes; the differences of opinion on the criteria for distribution of the benefits of growth; the conflicts of interest that social, political, and economic change necessarily bring; or differences of opinion about the nature of the development model to be followed — a concern with progress, or the lack of it, has been almost always present in Third World armed conflicts over the last few decades.

All this seems to indicate that a broadening of the meaning of the concept of security for Latin American countries should include as another important component, in addition to defense of national territory and sovereignty, the maintenance of the capacity for economic growth and social progress. This entails all the reasons explaining why the people or governments of many developing countries in Latin America would be willing to eschew peace and resort to force. In the next section, we will further analyze this characteristic of the notion of security in the underdeveloped world, most specifically with respect to Latin America.

National Security and Development: Latin America

From the time of the Greeks until the present, the idea of progress has driven Western civilization. The notion of human history as a slow, gradual, uniform ascent toward some better future goal has been the dominant historical idea in the West. Similarly, the attainment of other important Western values, such as justice, freedom, equality, and knowledge, has been conditioned by a belief in progress.

One of the crucial characteristics of nineteenth and twentieth century conceptions of progress is the close relationship between social evolution or growth and economic development. Classical economists, from Adam Smith to David Ricardo, took the desirability of material progress and economic growth for granted. For Karl Marx, the panorama was more or less the same. They all agreed that the objective of social progress was the well-being of the people and that material progress, in one form or another, was essential toward that end.

At the beginning of the twentieth century, interest in growth and national development became even more accentuated. Besides the Marxists, Joseph Schumpeter was the first to tackle systematically the problem of economic growth. During the Second World War, the social sciences, along with the other branches of the sciences, centered their activities on confronting the dangers and problems brought on by the war. At war's end they directed their attention toward more peaceful objectives. The most important of these was, undoubtedly, analyzing the problem shared both by war-torn and Third World countries — the question of national development.

To understand the massive mobilization of resources designated for national development in the decades following the war and the enormous impact these efforts had on nations of the underdeveloped world, several factors must be kept in mind. First, there was outside the United States a predominant interest in growth and full employment, resulting from the desire to prevent a repetition of the worldwide depression that followed the First World War. Second, there was the Cold War and the competition between powers for regional control in the Third World. Third, there was the massive enthusiasm of underdeveloped nations embarking on national modernization and development projects in hopes of becoming part of the industrialized world.

The decades of the 1950s and 1960s witnessed the proliferation of economic development and modernization projects in a large part of the underdeveloped world, but nowhere so intensely as in Latin America, undoubtedly due to the fact that Latin America has been part of the Western tradition of progress almost since the time of its conquest. Frequently, this process of cultural transformation, changes in modes of existence, the rise of nations, political projects, and enormous economic investments was characterized as a "revolution of rising expectations" in the Third World.

Despite the fact that the decades of the seventies and eighties taught us that the road to progress and development is rocky, and that it is easier to generate aspirations than to satisfy them, the ideal of progress and economic development has not been abandoned by Latin American countries.

In this sense, the idea of development represents more than a collection of technical knowledge; rather, it involves aspirations and visions of the collective future. The idea of development has penetrated and transformed the cultures of the region, convinced populations of its goals and objectives, translated the ideas into successful and unsuccessful projects, and modified individual and institutional behavior. In short, it has generated distinct modern national projects that Latin Americans are unwilling to abandon and — more important for our purposes — for which some are willing to resort to the use of force and organized violence. Progress and development are now such an essential part of Latin American cultures that they conceive of themselves as a group of societies in the process of change and improvement, within an all-encompassing vision that is reflected not only in literature, art, social problems, politics, and economics, but also in internal conflicts and international disputes.

The ideal of development has been introduced so profoundly into Latin American societies that most of the functions attributed to the structures that constitute them are evaluated by their capacity to promote effective development. Such is the case with the state, the different forms of government, different economic actors, education, foreign aid, and even the definition of national security policy. The capacity to generate growth and development is today a powerful social legitimator in these countries, used as often to justify the need for order, stability, and peace as it is to justify war and the use of force.

Organized Violence and Development

It is a known fact that, in practice, growth and development create both internal and external conflicts that polarize regions and nations and may foster militarism and the use of force in the process of social change in underdeveloped countries. Similarly, rapid social, political, and economic change tends to bring about conflict between local and national interests, national and regional interests, and national and international interests. The conflicts and disputes over the methods and goals of development, the speed with which it can be reached, the justice of the distribution of goods produced, the political models that should accompany it, and the ideologies that make it up have multiplied almost without end in the Third World, sometimes accompanied by enormous violence. In other words, development and its concomitant ideologies have also become powerful tools for the legitimation of the use of armed force and organized violence.

In a context of tension and poverty, militarization and the eruption of organized violence — from the regional arms races to revolutions and civil wars overseen by guerrillas and their repressive counterparts — constitute the most alarming trend in the underdeveloped countries. In some regions, this tendency has placed the objectives of social progress and economic development at risk; in others, it has brought the process of growth to a complete standstill or even reversed it. It has created a flourishing international market in arms specially designed for the war needs of the Third World. The public expenditure in arms and militarization has become a tremendous burden for many fragile economies. Worse still, as mentioned in the previous section, this tendency has endangered not only internal security, but also international peace and security.

However, despite the fact that organized violence and the use of force are a daily reality in a large part of the Third World, the study of peace and security and its relation to development has been one of the most ignored topics in both security and development literature.

In the case of Latin America, at least three phenomena frequently associated with security and development should be considered in future analyses on the subject. These are revolutionary movements and civil wars, the instability of political regimes, and interventionism.

These three phenomena, which normally bring about resort to force and armed organized violence, have been legitimized in their various manifestations by virtue of conceptions of progress and development wielded by revolutionary groups, aspiring governments, and countries interested in influencing the internal conflicts of another country. These phenomena go beyond the bounds of this article. Suffice it to say that given the dimensions of these phenomena, their proliferation in the last few decades, and their influence on international peace and stability, they have become events of great importance for regional and international security that merit the systematic and profound attention of researchers and specialists. Researchers must dedicate themselves to the study of the relationship between development and national and international security if we wish to understand the violence some development processes have generated and if we wish to promote a peaceful climate of security and development in the Third World. It is no exaggeration to say that in vast areas of the underdeveloped world, security and peace studies have become as important as, or more important than, development studies.

Security: The Search for a Concept

For several decades, specialists have searched for a clear, yet limited, definition of security that can explain the great variety of existing security problems in the contemporary world and provide a lucid and precise orientation for practical decision making.

The conventional conception of security has already been discussed, with its emphasis on the militaristic aspects of external attacks on territory and sovereignty. It has limited utility in the analysis of contemporary Third World security problems with internal conflicts caused by processes of change characteristic of a country in the midst of development. What, then, is the appropriate path to a concept of security for Third World countries? What are the challenges and dangers we should understand and communicate to the leaders in underdeveloped nations?

A different way of conceiving the dichotomy of the broad-to-restricted continuum of the definition of security is by making a distinction between negative and positive security.

Negative security implies the capacity to cut off or stop a negative relationship where threats exist to the population, the borders, or stability. Militaristic definitions are most useful within this type of security. Positive security, on the other hand, implies the ability to continue or maintain a positive relationship. It requires the certainty of the continuation of the satisfaction of the population's basic needs in terms of food, health, education, or in terms of natural resources, systems of communication, energy, and so on. The loss of this certainty can easily become a threat to national and regional peace and stability. When that occurs (and it occurs frequently in the Third World), it is possible to speak of a problem of national security. Another alternative is found in the distinction between external and internal security, where external security refers to the capacity of the nation-state to prevent external attacks and internal security refers to the capacity to prevent generalized outbreaks of internal violence.

Given these definitional specifications, negative or external security would be at one end of the semantic continuum, and positive or internal security on the other.

In the case of developing countries, as is the case with Mexico and all of Latin America, the concept of security is closely related to *peaceful management of social, political, and economic change* in national as well as international spheres. Developing countries are, by definition, countries undergoing transformations and processes of rapid change that frequently generate conflicts of interest that can result in violence. In this sense, the outer limit of our definition of security is constituted by the need to explain, manage, and prevent not just any social change, but the unique issue of *violent change*. That is to say, *our definition of security must be concerned with the analysis of the use of force and organized violence in social, political, and economic change.*

To summarize, in line with the aforementioned requirements of explanatory power and practical utility, at one extreme — or lower limit — the new concept of security should be capable of the following:

1. Explaining past violence and preventing its occurrence in the future. (In other words, it should be capable of describing external and internal threats to peace and stability in developing countries.)
2. Establishing, clearly and precisely, the hierarchy of priorities issuing from these threats to peace and stability.
3. Defining the legitimate means, including force, to prevent and confront these threats.

I have earlier insisted that, in countries like those of Latin America, the capacity for growth and development should be included within the essential components of the concept of security, especially since these same notions of growth and development are used to justify force.

The other extreme — or upper limit — of the definitional continuum is more problematic because, as we have said, at this level it is easier to commit the error of including phenomena that can be more properly described as problems of development. It is undoubtedly true that development problems (for example, economic crises, loss of governmental legitimacy, violent opposition movements, frustrated expectations) can become problems of security, but it is important to keep in mind that only those problems of development that compromise peace and stability can be considered security problems.

A fruitful step toward an enhanced definition would be empirical research on the conditions under which internal peace and stability have been disturbed in the past, and an accounting of the reasons put forth as justifications for the use of force. In particular, we must analyze those cases in which the problems of the upper limit or extreme (positive security) threaten to become problems approaching the lower limit or extreme (negative security). Put simply, we need to understand under what conditions a development problem may become a security issue.

The common denominator of the upper and lower limits of this concept of security is, on the one hand, the avoidance of violence and the use of force in the process of change and development, and on the other, the restriction of the use of force when necessary. Understood in this way, it becomes easy to approach the term "security" conceptually by describing insecurity. The notion of security, with idealistic and even utopian casts to it, has proved to be slippery or even unattainable. Conversely, insecurity can be described in clearer, more concrete terms as related to the rise in organized violence and force. In other words, it is easier to describe what security *is not* than to describe what it is.

That being the case, it is more informative and helpful to define national security by beginning with a definition of what insecurity is and how to avoid it. In this way, we avoid the idealistic and utopian coloring of the definition as well as fitting it to the realities of the Third World whose nations are, for the most part, far from the ideal status of "secure nations."

The definition of national security is also, in a way, the definition of the criteria of justice in the use of force. In the definition of national security, limits are established beyond which a nation is determined to resort to force in the elimination of obstacles and threats and in reaching its national objectives. But it is also in the definition of national security that strategies are established that will permit the avoidance of the greatest danger to security: war, whether external or internal. The best and most useful definition of security will be one that effectively avoids recourse to force and violence, anticipates its need when inevitable after using peaceful political conciliation strategies, and limits the use of force when it has to be used. The utility of this way of conceiving security is that it offers guidelines concerning the problem of insecurity.

It has been repeated over and over again that the state is, by definition, the monopoly of force. Perhaps it is important to add to this that, in the contemporary world, a legitimate government is one that does not need the systematic, massive use of force to maintain its power, nor does it need to sacrifice peace on the altar of stability. Moreover, its legitimacy is reflected in its national security policy. If there is something important for the leaders of the First, Second, and Third Worlds to understand, it is that development, peace, and stability are concepts and realities intimately connected with security, and that organized violence and the use of force are, in themselves, causes of insecurity even when used in the name of national security.

Conclusion

As mentioned earlier, the idea of progress has had great importance for Western civilization, to which Latin America belongs. In this region, the idea of development, heir to the notion of progress, has proved to be a powerful motivation, one that can forge nations, creating "economic miracles," or destroy them violently. It can unite and solidify entire populations, or divide them, causing bloody confrontations. It can foment cooperation and international exchange or provoke the rise of hostilities and wars.

In Latin America, and in a good part of the underdeveloped world, growth and progress are imperatives as fundamental as territorial defense and national sovereignty. The viability and political, economic, and social survival of these countries depend on all these factors. As history has demonstrated, they constitute sufficient reasons to resort to the use of force and organized violence, making them necessary components of any pertinent definition of security for the Third World.

Progress and development are challenges facing two-thirds of the world's population. To bring peace to the Third World and find development alternatives for these countries is the challenge the entire world must accept if there is to be any hope of leaving behind much of the uncertainty, threats, and insecurity that characterize the end of the twentieth century.

References

Elguea, J. N.d. *The Bloody Road to Utopia: Development Wars in Latin America.* Forthcoming.

Fagen, R. 1987. *Forging Peace: The Challenge of Central America.* Santa Cruz, Calif.: PACCA Books, Blackwell Publishers.

Kidron, M., and D. Smith. 1983. *The War Atlas.* Concord, Mass.: Pluto Press (Paul and Co. Pubs. Consortium, Inc.).

O'Neill, P. 1988. "A Historical Perspective on International Security Analysis." *ITEMS* 42/1,2 (June).

Patterson, H. 1981. "A Historical View of American Security." *Peace and Change*, VLI, 4 (Autumn).

Stevens, R. 1988. "Special Report," *On Beyond War* 38 (April).

Stephenson, C. 1981. "Alternative International Security Systems." *Peace and Change.* 7:4, 1-6.

Vargas Llosa, Mario. 1987. *El Hablador.* Mexico: Joaquín Mòrtiz.

Commentary:
On the Definition
of National Security

Gene Sharp

I agree with the view, expressed by others, that it is desirable to view "national security" in a wider context than is often done. I agree that the welfare of society as a whole also needs to be considered in addition to military threats and military responses. In view of this, the definition we use for "national security" is fundamental. It is, however, a very tricky term. Whoever introduced or popularized it in past years was at the least very clever, for how many sincere people can be in favor of "national *insecurity?*" This fact helps to explain the tragic history of the "national security state" and the use of claims of "national security" to justify dictatorship and all kinds of repression, including torture, disappearances, and jailing. Clearly, those institutions and actions have been contrary to any genuine consideration of what should be included under the term "national security."

These experiences illustrate the problems in having a very broad definition of national security. If one includes "national interests" within national security, does that not open the way for justifying repression of internal groups that supposedly endanger those interests and for military intervention in foreign countries with which one has an economic, political, or other significant difference? If one expands the idea of national security so that underdeveloped countries may

A commentary on the papers by Sergio Aguayo ("The Uses, Abuses, and Challenges of Mexican National Security: 1946-1990") and by Javier Elguea ("International Security and National Development").

include economic resources, then the argument becomes weak against including economic resources (such as oil) in the scope of national security for the industrialized superpowers and provides "justification" for their military intervention to secure those resources as part of their "vital interests." If one includes, as does Richard Ullman (1983, 133), anything that "threatens drastically... to degrade the quality of life...[or] to narrow the range of policy choices available to the government of a state or to private nongovernmental entities," does that not elevate private economic interests to national priorities and open the way to various types of military intervention in other countries in the name of national security?

Abstract terms are inherently dangerous. If defined broadly and loosely, or if hardly defined at all, they open the way to fundamental errors in thinking, judgment, and action. It was Alexis de Tocqueville who reminded us that "an abstract term is like a box with a false bottom: You may put in it what ideas you please, and take them out again without being observed" (1889, 63).

The problem is that not only can "good guys" attempt to put good ideas of democracy, justice, and development into the box of national security but, as events have demonstrated, "bad guys" are equally capable of effectively putting bad ideas into that box, and they are likely to attempt to do so again. Their ability to do this will be facilitated by our acceptance of "national security" as a broad and inclusive term. If national security becomes, in effect, what is "good for the society," then *whose views* of that "good" are to be decisive, and are groups with opposing views not endangering the national security and therefore meriting suppression?

These problems are not solved by refining the term national security to distinguish between "positive security" and "negative security." Those terms still open the way for similar confusions and misuses.

A better solution would be to use the term "national security" very narrowly and to give those other highly important principles and objectives, such as social justice, democracy, progress, and humane development, some other inclusive term such as "national priorities," "national objectives," or "national principles." National security, narrowly defined, would become one of these. This would, in practice, not reduce the importance of these principles but rather elevate them and help prevent them from being relegated to a lower rung of the national security "ladder." Instead, it would be necessary to address those principles and objectives squarely on their own merits.

National security would then cease to be the all-encompassing goal of society and become one of several goals, all of which require the formulation of carefully prepared agendas to secure and defend them. These agendas would consider not only threats and obstacles confronting each goal but also the setting of positive policies and forms of action to secure them.

National security would then refer to condition in which a nation or country is relatively safe from attack, whether internal (as from an executive usurpation, coup d'état, or other violent means) or external (as from military invasion or acts of massive destruction). This safety could conceivably occur because such dangers did not exist, but that situation is rare. The secure condition would more likely be the result of dissuading potential attackers by means which cause them not to launch hostile activities, or by some deterrent which causes them — though still hostile — nevertheless, to avoid the consequences of a contemplated attack. When national security is violated by an actual attack, effective means to defend against it and to protect the population are required. The defense objective then is to end the assault and restore the society's independence of action and condition of safety. How this is done is then highly important, but the means should not automatically be military.

As viewed here, national security is not identified with the ability to secure from other parts of the world all desired economic resources on one's own terms, nor with the capacity to control the economies, politics, and military actions of other countries or to intervene militarily throughout the world. Indeed, such actions would, in time, contribute to national insecurity. Similarly, under a democratic constitutional system, national security does not condone internal repression and violation of civil liberties, abrogation of democratic procedures, and the like (Sharp 1985, 50-51).

This concept of national security does, however, assume that genuine internal and international threats are likely to continue to exist and that preparations to repel and counteract them are going to be required. In other words, it is not sufficient simply to advocate the pursuit of peace, the practice of negotiations, or the acceptance of demilitarization of individual countries or regions as an alternative to submission or to civil or international war without providing another means of defense. It is not even adequate to call for a shift from "national security" to "international security." International security is itself the subject of major controversies, with some states wishing to maintain or even expand their positions of dominance, while other countries wish to change the international order in very fundamental ways.

The search for peace, or for alternative ways to achieve national security, must recognize the existence and continuation of acute conflicts in which neither side will see itself as able to compromise, in which each side believes (rightly or wrongly) that it must fight for its principles and goals, and in which at least one side will not "play by the rules" when those are seen to mean submission to injustice, oppression, or unjustified violent attacks. In such conflicts, in any part of Latin America or elsewhere, the questions will be how to conduct and resolve major internal conflicts and how to act to defeat external aggression or foreign-assisted coups d'état.

Yet, we should never ignore the importance of the growth of democracy, or the achievement of greater justice or humane types of development. Indeed, attention to conflict resolution will facilitate the achievement of those goals, because it will represent an alternative to both submission and war.

In pursuing "national priorities," careful attention must be given to their content. For example, too often the actual development processes considered have resulted in extreme political and economic centralization of power and the destruction of traditional societies and cultures. This situation leads not only to economic impoverishment and political powerlessness but also to a cultural "lostness" as well.

In addition, careful attention is required to the relationships between economic development, political systems, and violence and war. The relationships may be more complex than the view that change in a political system or internal political violence can usually be traced back to economic changes and conflicts over development. We may also need to reconsider the assumption that increasing economic internationalization is clearly a good thing. The loss of local, regional, and even national control over the economic welfare of a people in their society may be an excessive price to pay for certain types of internationalization of economies.

Similarly, the commonly accepted means of achieving national security through large military systems and expensive high-technology weapons systems may have disastrous economic consequences for a society, as well as contribute to the possibility of both military coups d'état and guerrilla wars.

Despite the many problems which Mexico has experienced and now suffers, the situation might have been far worse if military expenditures and the power of military organizations had not, over the years, been kept low. In times of recent conflicts, the country has been fortunate that the opposition parties have rejected the path of political violence and that one major opposition party has, in the face of claimed election fraud, specifically urged *nonviolent* resistance.

As others have pointed out, there are genuine security dangers for Mexico which arise from developments or potential events which have been, or would be, initiated either by the United States or in Central America. Both the U.S. military bases near the Mexican northern border and civil wars in Central America provide strong motives for Mexico to adopt foreign and defense policies which are likely to reduce the possibility of war and contribute to peaceful resolutions of conflicts. In terms of Central America, a neglected option is for Mexico to help conflicting parties to understand that the violence of guerrilla wars and repression to prevent change are not the only options. Even in face of violence by the other side, nonviolent struggle is an option, as has been shown in past decades by significant cases in Central American and Latin American history.

It is significant that the Mexican government has stated that the internal strength of a society is important in meeting external threats. Carried further, it points to the potential of using that internal strength as the predominant means to repel internal usurpations or foreign aggression, operating primarily through the capacity to maintain self-direction despite the actions of usurpers and invaders and to apply massive nonviolent noncooperation and defiance to make the country ungovernable by attackers. This would constitute a powerful reserve capacity to help preserve constitutional government internally and to discourage any foreign military aggression.

One can observe the negative influences of militarization and violence in developing countries and the frequent justification of this violence for reasons of progress and social development. Unfortunately, efforts to achieve constructive social development are commonly made in the context of civil wars, political instability, and foreign intervention.

Both violence of internal origins and the violence of United States or other intervention (direct or by proxy) are based on the assumption that violence and war are the most powerful means available in acute conflicts. It is that confidence which has led to the tragedies of civil wars in Central America, to coups d'état, and to military regimes in Argentina, Guatemala, Brazil, and Chile, to name a few. Unfortunately, in Latin American countries, continued reliance by groups, with whatever objectives, on civil war and military repression will not only bring increased economic impoverishment and impediments to positive development, but in time will produce more military regimes in Latin America.

In 1984, then-President of Colombia Belisario Betancur said, "Without peace, it is not possible to have development, and without development it is not possible to have peace. We must break this vicious circle." There is a possible way to do this and to provide powerful means to achieve national security which are fully compatible with the achievement and defense of other "national priorities." This is not achievable through the continuation of civil wars and the expansion of military systems but through looking to other historical experiences in various Latin American countries, including Guatemala and El Salvador in 1944, which saw the use of "people power" to fight dictators and oppression. The mobilization of the popular masses in nonviolent protests, economic boycotts, labor strikes, political noncooperation, civil disobedience, and various types of nonviolent intervention can give to political societies, governments, and mass populations alternative tools compatible with progressive economic and social development, democracy, and national security. The conflicts in Third World and underdeveloped countries, and the means of providing national security for them, only take violent and military forms if the other options remain ignored and undeveloped.

Specific limited steps can be taken soon in exploring these options. They include 1) the development of plans for massive noncooperation to defeat future coups d'état in Latin America; 2) the development of basic strategies of nonviolent struggle to democratize or disintegrate existing dictatorships in Latin America and to ensure transitions to democratic political systems; 3) the examination of the possibilities of massive nonviolent noncooperation against foreign military aggression (which would, for example, be more likely to be successful and produce far fewer casualties than guerrilla warfare); and

4) the development and practice of nonviolent forms of struggle in face of violence to achieve substantive social change toward greater justice and vital democratic systems in Latin America (Sharp 1973, 1990).

These steps would open new options in breaking the cycles of violence, war, dictatorships, and economic deprivation. They would make struggles for social justice and democracy compatible with a move against political violence by the state and non-state groups. There would be major economic, social, and political benefits.

In this way, many nations could be freed from the dilemmas which have sometimes forced new imitations of past disasters. Past cycles of violence and oppression could potentially be abandoned, if citizens decide to pioneer the development of policies able to provide new hopes, policies which make peoples and governments the masters in their own countries, dedicated to building societies of justice and democracy.

References

De Tocqueville, Alexis. 1889. *Democracy in America*. Vol. 2. London: Longmans Green & Co.

Sharp, Gene. 1973. *The Politics of Nonviolent Actions*. Boston: Porter Sergeant.

Sharp, Gene. 1985. *National Security Through Civilian-Based Defense*. Omaha: Association for Transarmament Studies.

Sharp, Gene. 1990. *Civilian-Based Defense: A Post-Military Weapons System*. Princeton: Princeton University Press.

Ullman, Richard. 1983. "Redefining Security." *International Security* 8(1)(Summer).

Refashioning a National Security Agenda for the 1990s: the Dilemmas of Redefinition

Cathryn L. Thorup

The Changing Nature of National Security

The meaning of the term "national security" was very much influenced by the specific geopolitical setting in which the concept originated and by the reigning world view it reflected. For this reason, current efforts to reformulate the meaning of the concept — to make it more inclusive or to alter its content entirely — must be approached with some degree of caution.

The term "national security" first appeared in the United States in the aftermath of World War II and was, from the outset, heavily influenced by Cold War and military-strategic thinking. The term fell out of vogue in the aftermath of the Vietnam War and received only marginal usage during the period of détente. Some U.S. analysts in the 1970s, reflecting growing scholarly interest and public policy attention to U.S. economic interdependence, sought to rework the concept by expanding its definition to include economic and social criteria, but, by and large, the negative connotations associated with the term overrode those efforts.

With the arrival of the Reagan administration and the resurgence of the Cold War ideology that guided its forays into Central America, the term "national security" was rehabilitated. The ideology of the new administration was succinctly captured by Robert Tucker, who wrote of "the restoration of a more normal political world, a world in which those states possessing the elements of a great power once again play the role their power entitles them to play" (Tucker 1980/81, 273).

This return to a traditional definition of national security provoked considerable debate in academic and policy circles in the United States. To a large extent, though, it was as much a political battle as it was a theoretical struggle. Those who were concerned by the resurgence of East-West tensions and were opposed to U.S. policies toward Central America stressed the need to incorporate economic and social criteria into the definition of security. Supporters of the Reagan administration's tough, high-profile U.S. foreign policy, designed to "make America proud again," emphasized traditional military and geostrategic thinking, imbuing the concept of U.S. national security with a content reflective of the resuscitated Cold War ideology.

During the course of the 1980s, the hard-line approach to security issues gained many adherents. Even the principal philanthropic organizations in the United States altered their funding priorities to place a heavy emphasis on security studies. Toward the end of the decade, though — with the advent of *glasnost* and the weakening of the concept of an external enemy — there was a growing sense in both academic and policy circles in the United States that the militarization of the concept of security had gone too far and that it was time to redress the imbalance.

Once again, momentum was generated for a broadening of the concept of security. This was further promoted by a growing consensus in the United States on a variety of other issues that seemed more threatening to U.S. national security, when defined as not only the ability of a state to protect its territorial integrity but also its capacity to provide for the well-being of its people. Among these new issues were debt, both in terms of the U.S. deficit and the debt owed by a variety of countries to a wide array of international creditors; drugs; terrorism; Japanese economic competition; and the environment (Tuchman 1989).

Support for a demilitarization and a broadening of the definition of national security has not been limited to analysts in the United States. In other nations as well, there is an attempt to reclaim the concept from the "cold warriors" through a process of redefinition. There are a variety of reasons behind this effort. First, the concept of national security traditionally referred primarily to external threats to the stability of the state and was defined in terms of nuclear deterrence, superior weaponry, military intelligence, alliances, containment of aggressor nations, and stability in the U.S.-Soviet relationship. One problem with this definition is that there is a point at which more arms do not necessarily mean greater security and may actually mean less. Moreover, in the post-Cold War era, a strictly military definition of national security seems markedly anachronistic.

Second, it is argued that the "real" security threats facing the developing world — and, by extension, U.S. national security — have their roots in economic deprivation. Thus, the threat derives not from an external enemy but from internal causes originating in profound problems of development. In this case, a country's social and economic conditions must be taken into account in any discussion of national security.

Third, some analysts stress that it is impossible to control the evolution of an idea — that, like it or not, it may be that security encompasses a broader array of concerns today than when the term was first coined. They point out that a concept should not be avoided simply because it has a bad reputation, since it may be possible to rectify the distortions through redefinition.

These arguments have produced a variety of efforts to "rescue" the notion of national security from the hands of military planners and broaden its meaning. The results, however, may be dangerously disappointing.

The Perils of Redefinition

There are six basic risks — some with particular relevance to U.S.-Mexican relations — associated with a broadening of the national security agenda:

1. *The increased risk of military responses to nonmilitary problems.* Definitions contain inherent policy implications. Since it is every nation's right and obligation to protect its national security, there is an increased likelihood of direct government involvement and the possibility of a military response when an issue is defined as "a question of national security." As the number of issues "worth fighting for" expands, higher risks are incurred. Thus, there is a danger that, by couching issues in national security terms, a strategic response will result.

The elevation of the "war on drugs" to the status of a national security concern, for example, produced discussions in the United States of the advisability of involving the military or the reserves in drug interdiction efforts and led to speculation regarding the effectiveness of digging a ditch along the U.S. border with Mexico to stem the flow of drugs. Moreover, when the drug issue is cloaked in the mantle of national security, the U.S. government feels justified in taking a more direct interest in Mexico's war on drugs — as evidenced by the annual certification process to which Mexico is subjected by the U.S. Congress.

For years it has been argued that Mexico should be at the top of the U.S. foreign policy agenda and that no other country is more important to the United States. It is not at all clear, however, that an elevation of Mexico's position among U.S. foreign policy concerns is desirable. When an issue is a strategic priority, there is a tendency among policymakers to think that something must be "done" about it. In this scenario, U.S. security concerns could increase Mexican insecurity.

2. *The definition of national security is country-specific.* It is unrealistic to assume, for example, that the United States and Mexico share a common definition of what constitutes national security or that Mexico's security will promote that of the United States. The *content* of security for each country reflects *different* national interests. Efforts to meld the two may produce conflict.

Nor is it useful to incorporate all of the issues on the U.S.-Mexico bilateral agenda onto the national security agenda of either nation. Advocacy groups determined to win a higher profile for their particular issue have argued that immigration, narcotics, debt, and/or the environment constitute national security issues. If all of these suggestions were pursued, it would be impossible to differentiate the national security interests of the United States and of Mexico from the bilateral agenda of the two nations, thus confusing the issues and forcing the bilateral relationship into a rigid security framework. It would not capture the richness and complexity of U.S.-Mexican relations, and it might, in fact, result in unwelcome policy consequences.

Finally, it should be remembered that definitions are socially grounded in the biases associated with the needs and concerns of particular societal groups. It is important to pay attention to the fact that there are many different views of "the" national interest in each country.

3. *The problem of overloading.* There is a danger that if the notion of national security is overloaded, it will become entirely unwieldy. Means and objectives may become confused. For example, are drugs and debt national security issues in and of themselves, or are they the tools used to influence "real" national security issues, such as securing

Mexican compliance in the mid-1980s on U.S. policy toward Central America?

For reasons of conceptual clarity and administrative manageability, some issues must be considered of greater security concern than others. If everything is critical, then nothing is "truly" critical. In this situation, it becomes more difficult to ascertain what is not an issue of national security than to know what is. How is a government to allocate scarce resources if everything is of vital importance?

Many topics *could* be included on the security agenda, but which *should* be included — global warming, debt, democratization, development? If all development problems, for example, are viewed as security problems, both concepts lose meaning. It would be more productive to explore the nature of the link between security and development. When does a development problem become a security problem (Sewell 1989)? To what extent is the social and economic security of the Third World a cornerstone of U.S. national security?

4. *The need for specificity.* It is not enough to say that debt is a national security issue for Mexico without explaining how, when, and in what circumstances. Is it any debt, a lot of debt, or a lot of debt owed to one country? There needs to be more content and specificity to the discussion of the meaning of national security.

5. *Who defines the terms?* It matters what groups, sectors, or classes determine the national security agenda. Assume, for example, that Group A has as its hidden agenda to secure debt relief for Mexico. In pursuit of this objective, Group A convinces U.S. policymakers to place Mexican political stability on the U.S. security agenda. Group A reasons it will then be able to use the argument that the debt burden is threatening Mexican political stability — and, therefore, U.S. national security — to obtain debt relief for Mexico.

Group B, however, has a different hidden agenda, having decided that democratization — and the social mobilization and sweeping political changes that would imply — constitutes the principal threat to Mexican political stability. Group B uses the national security argument regarding Mexican political stability — placed on the U.S. agenda by Group A — to convince U.S. policymakers that political liberalization in Mexico is not in the U.S. interest.

Clearly, definitions are not bias-free, and there are no guarantees that an issue placed on the national security agenda for a "good" reason will not be used to a "bad" end. Broadening the agenda of national security to include a variety of new issues may, therefore, produce unanticipated results.

6. *The security of the state — or of a particular regime — is not synonymous with the security of the nation*. When leaders talk about national security, they may mean the security of the ruling political elite. It is important, therefore, to differentiate between state security (preservation of the government apparatus) and the security of civil society. When President Carlos Salinas de Gortari states that drugs are an issue of Mexican national security, he is referring not to their societal impact — drug addiction among Mexican youth, for example — but rather to the ability of traffickers to control portions of the state apparatus and, therefore, his administration's ability to govern effectively.

Future Directions for Research

In light of these constraints, the refurbishing of the concept of national security should be pursued with great care, leading not to an automatic and indiscriminate broadening of the concept, but rather to a painstaking and detailed process of analysis and review.

A more academically rigorous and conceptually tidier alternative to a catch-all notion of security would be to utilize the term "national interests" for nonmilitary issues, leaving the concept of national security for more traditional usage. It is in this context also that it would make sense to talk about those issues — such as the greenhouse effect, drug trafficking, terrorism, or the unraveling of the international financial system — that transcend national boundaries to become of joint concern to the United States and Mexico or of global concern.

It seems intellectually suspect to attempt to secure attention for issues by retooling them to fit the current academic fashion. Democracy, economic development, and a sane environmental policy are laudable goals, but that is not reason enough to include these items in the definition of national security, and it may result in military approaches to nonmilitary problems.

The term "national security" was developed in a specific historical setting to refer to a very concrete set of issues. Expanding that definition in order to imbue an old concept with a new meaning is a complex enterprise that must be approached with a clear awareness of the inherent risks. We should be clear about the potential pitfalls.

References

Sewell, John W. 1989. "Security and Development: What Is the Relationship?" Paper presented at the Heads of Institutes Meeting. Wilton Park, United Kingdom: The International Institute for Strategic Studies (15-17 November).

Tuchman, Jessica Mathews. 1989. "Redefining Security." *Foreign Affairs* 68(2)(Spring).

Tucker, Robert W. 1980-81. "The Purposes of American Power." *Foreign Affairs* 59(2)(Winter).

Part Two

The Theory and Practice of National Security in Mexico

The Uses, Misuses, and Challenges of Mexican National Security: 1946-1990

Sergio Aguayo Quezada

There are few references to Mexican national security from 1946 to the end of the 1970s. That changed in the 1980s, when transformations inside Mexico and in its geopolitical milieu stimulated references and research about Mexican national security and its effects on U.S. security.

A key question behind this volume is the scholarly and political viability and appropriateness of using the concept of security when referring to Mexico. The introduction gives a number of reasons why we consider its use unavoidable, although on the condition that the concept be reformulated. This chapter will support the same proposi-

Research for this essay was carried out by the author as a member of the Program for International Peace and Security of the Social Science Research Council and the MacArthur Foundation (1987-1989). In Washington, I had the assistance of Claudia Franco and Eugenia Mazzucato and in Mexico, of Pilar Morales. Subsequent drafts were prepared while I was a visiting researcher at the Johns Hopkins School of Advanced International Studies, the Instituto Latinoamericano de Estudios Transnacionales (ILET), and Georgetown University. Different versions were discussed at the Colegio de México, the Centro Latinoamericano de Estudios Estratégicos, and El Colegio de Defensa Nacional. The comments of Luis Herrera-Lasso, David Ronfeldt, and General Gerardo R.C. Vega were especially important. I thank them and many more for their support and advice.

tion, starting with the following premise: In spite of ambiguities and deficiencies, the concept of security is a mirror reflecting the aspirations and fears of a society. It follows that before proposing any definition or agenda, we have to understand the ways in which the concept of security has been used and misused both in Mexico and in the United States.

Thus, the thrust of this essay is to gather scattered information in an attempt to prove that Mexican national security (and, in a way, U.S. security as well) faces two important and deeply interrelated challenges. One is intellectual: to advance in the solution of the theoretical problems raised by the concept of security and, simultaneously, to gather the information necessary to formulate an agenda based on and oriented toward democracy, social justice, and sovereignty. The other is eminently political: to highlight that Mexico needs to create or strengthen those practices and institutions which will make possible an agenda synchronized with the above-mentioned principles.

The Literature in the United States

Those U.S. scholars or policymakers writing about Mexico and its security share a basic agreement: A stable, prosperous, and friendly Mexico is fundamental to U.S. interests, security, and global strategy.[1] To understand Mexico's key role, it should be kept in mind that until very recently, U.S. security doctrine has been driven by the containment of communism. That goal has been instrumentalized through global deployment of a military apparatus that has been made possible because in Mexico and the Caribbean Basin, the United States has applied an "economy of force," that is, the use of a minimum of military resources (Cunningham 1984; Jordan and Taylor 1984; Ronfeldt 1983). From this perspective, a "hostile" regime in Mexico would lead to a modification of that strategy and to more direct and immediate consequences.

This explains, in part, the American obsession with Mexican stability and allows one to divide the literature into two main periods: from the end of World War II to the second half of the 1970s and from the second half of the 1970s to the present day. The fundamental characteristic of the first stage is indifference: In spite of its importance, Mexico is ignored in detailed policy making.[2] I will refer to just two examples. The 1949 Continental Defense Plan of the United States (CONUS) is a single-spaced, fifty-page document which dedicates only seven lines to Mexico.[3] On the other hand, American magazines specializing in military issues published only some twenty-five articles on Mexico, basically on historical matters or praise for Guadalajara as the paradise for retired military (Aguayo 1990).

There were, however, some isolated references which should be mentioned as a precedent to the discussions of the 1980s. For example, the Central Intelligence Agency (CIA) and other sectors considered oil production or the construction of highways in Mexico as the way in which the nation was contributing to U.S. security (CIA 1951; Carmical 1948 and 1949; Krock 1948; Wohl 1950). Besides those topics, the CIA considered that the "only foreseeable threat to U.S. security in the Mexican economy is that from labor or saboteurs." Some U.S. officials also mentioned the risk presented by communists infiltrating the United States disguised as *braceros*.[4] The 1968 Student Movement and the "dirty war" which followed also provoked some references to security and, although short-lived, are harbingers of a future scenario. In all, the general consensus was that Mexican national security was not threatened and did not represent a threat to U.S. security (J.I.S.-248M 1946; DOS 1951; CIA 1951; WH 1953).

Such a broad consensus was based on several factors, such as a flourishing Mexican economy, a stable political system, and generally cordial relations with the United States. Mexico's economic protectionism and independent diplomacy were occasional irritants, which did not hinder a conclusion reached by the CIA in 1977: The established order in Mexico had only brought "benefits to the United States" (CIA 1977). Finally, this perception about Mexico was also founded on the premise that "in the event of war... Mexico will ally with the United States" (DA 1949, 1, 6; CIA 1951; White 1955).

The consensus started to change in the mid-1970s, when some sectors viewed Mexico through a security prism. The first *Presidential Review Memorandum* (PRM-41) dealing with Mexico-U.S. relations was completed in 1978. In 1979 and 1981, two papers appeared explicitly linking Mexico with U.S. security (Fagen 1979; Deagle 1981). These documents were motivated by the economic and political turmoil surrounding the 1976 presidential election and the discovery of large oil fields which supposedly counterbalanced the "erosion of (U.S.) security" provoked by the oil embargo of 1973 (Fagen 1979, 43).

To ensure oil supply, the United States resurrected the old premise that in case of problems, they could "surely count on Mexico"

(Fagen 1979, 46; CIA 1977, 8, 19). There was an initial reluctance on Mexico's part, but this was soon overcome when the United States confirmed that Mexico did not have all the oil it was originally thought,[5] and when the economic problems and the asymmetries of power finally forced the Mexican government to sell the United States all the oil it wanted. This also put an end to the possibility of Mexico's becoming a middle power, which, in turn, had been considered a potential modifier to U.S. security schemes (Deagle 1981).

At the same time, different sectors started to argue that the production of and trafficking in drugs, immigration, the environment, the effects of Central America on Mexico, and Mexican stability should be included in the security agenda.[6] Given the lack of space and the inclusion in this volume of chapters dealing with the first three topics,[7] this chapter will only elaborate upon two issues which were interrelated for several years: domestic stability and Central America.

The 1980s were a turbulent decade for the region and the world as a whole, and, as discussed in the introduction, this led to discussions in the United States about problems that the Caribbean Basin and Central America could cause for its security. This, in turn, led to a broader debate on the meaning of "security." In this context, it was natural that if stability had been the cause of U.S. indifference toward its southern neighbor, any transition in the Mexican established order would lead to a reassessment of the "strategic importance" of what a military analyst had called the "ultimate prize in the U.S. backyard" (Leighton 1988, 13).

As a matter of record, Mexican stability and its effects on U.S. security started being discussed by the end of the 1970s. In 1977, the CIA recognized, in passing, that Mexico had "entered a period of internal transition" (CIA 1977, 8). Two years later, and this time from an academic point of view, Richard Fagen concluded that, according to the establishment, the "primary Mexican security threat...is a Mexico torn by civil and political strife" (Fagen 1979, 48). At the same time, James Dalessandro produced the first of a series of apocalyptic predictions issuing from the far right; however, the far right has always been marginal in the debate (Dalessandro 1977/78, 52-53).

Over the years, the number of references to security has increased. They can be divided into those which refer to the effects of Mexico on U.S. security and those which specifically discuss Mexican national security. The first ones — which will be treated in more detail

— show differences and agreements. The main point of agreement is that instability in Mexico affects the United States.[8] Mexican instability opens up the possibility of external and/or hostile interests taking power, and that could endanger U.S. investments, access to oil, and maritime routes in the Gulf of Mexico and the Caribbean, and it could result in the arrival of millions of refugees. Another concern has been that the United States could be forced to militarize its southern border at great economic cost, to restructure its "Grand Strategy," and to incur a further loss of power in the world (Hannon 1984, 1986 and 1987; Linn 1984; Sanders 1987; Wilson 1989).

Among the factors that have been mentioned as producing instability (economic crisis, unequal income distribution, drug trafficking, foreign debt, corruption, the international communist conspiracy, and so on), the effects of Central American turmoil were paramount in the first half of the 1980s (Erb and Thorup 1984; Anderson and Atta 1987; Leighton 1988). Beginning in 1980, Central America became an obsession for the Republicans — so much so that in 1983, Ronald Reagan stated before Congress that "the national security of *all* the Americas is at stake in Central America." From this perspective, during the first five years of the decade, officials like Constantine Menges took advantage of the idea that Mexico's destiny was being decided in the Central American morass (Menges 1988, 27, 48). Indeed, this sort of opinion had some influence. Thus, a study commissioned by the U.S. Army states that "a dominant U.S. security concern for Mexico during mid-1984 centered on the belief that the Central American conflict, if not checked, would spread into Mexico" (Green Walker 1984, 332).

Any theory — even those ideologically influenced by the Central American "domino" — must be proved, and some U.S. sectors tried to use the events on Mexico's southern border (especially Chiapas) for that purpose. For example, in 1985 a U.S. military officer wrote that the region is, "and will continue to be, very important to our national security" (Russo 1985, 35). The statement was based on the following ideas: Chiapas is of great economic importance to Mexico; it is a poor and stratified state, where independent social and political movements have proliferated; and, since 1981, it began to receive a massive exodus of refugees from Guatemala and Central America. It followed that the South was seen as a "receptive host for the contagion of the revolutionary epidemic advancing from Central America," and even a place where Mexican guerrillas could be nurtured.[9]

These writings had a minor impact on mainstream U.S. security thinking. This was either because those who wrote about Chiapas lacked information or analytical rigor (in other words, they did not know the region), or because other analysts were concluding that Mexican institutions were still solid (Thorup and Ayres 1982; Cunningham 1984; Linn 1984; Williams 1984), or, finally, because many analysts perceived those arguments as biased in favor of the Republican policy in Central America.[10] At some moments, the discussion took unexpected turns. For example, Democrats backed the Mexican position, not only because they considered it to be the correct one but also as a means of opposing the Republican definition of security in Central America. Thus, they counterargued that if the thesis of the Mexican government was that U.S. policies "threatened regional security," then the Republican policies were threatening "Mexican stability," considered so important by all parties concerned (Levy 1986, 240; Thorup and Ayres 1982; Erb and Thorup 1984). Note that underlying this discussion was a more fundamental debate on the concept of security and its significance in a troubled region.[11]

Attempts to "persuade" Mexico to change its position in Central America came about as a logical consequence of the Republican analysis (Menges 1988; Aguayo 1985). However, they did not succeed, not even at top federal levels. This frustration can be found in the memoirs of Constantine Menges, an officer of the CIA and the National Security Council during the first years of the Reagan administration. The determining factor in this failure was a structural obstacle: Exerting pressure on Mexico risked the unleashing of social and political forces, which could affect its stability and, eventually, have repercussions on the United States.

Imbedded in the discussion of Central America was the major issue: Mexican stability. Peter Smith captured the U.S. core perception with a statement and a question: "Mexico stands on the brink of far-reaching transition.... Where is Mexico going?" (Smith 1986, 101). There have been several answers. The most zealous conservatives have insisted on their apocalyptic premonitions. For example, Colonel Rex Applegate stated in 1985 that Mexico "possesses most of the elements and conditions needed for a communist-inspired takeover" (Applegate 1985, 87). Even more sophisticated analysts, like Brian Latell of the CIA, foresaw in 1986 that "Mexico's stability will be threatened by a deepening crisis that is inextricably economic and political" (Latell

1986, 3). However, this school of thought was superseded by a cautious optimism.

In 1984, the CIA reached the conclusion that "most Mexicans still accept the legitimacy of the PRI-dominated system" (Harper's 1987, 21). A National Intelligence Evaluation concluded, "We judge that in the end the Mexican political system is likely to remain intact" (Anderson and Atta 1987, 42, also 1987). Finally, a group of experts on Mexican affairs who prepared a series of papers for the State Department reached similar conclusions in 1985 (Camp 1986).

The observers certainly agreed on the need for reforms in Mexico, but most of them believed in the possibility of an ideal scenario for the United States: gradual reforms, headed by Mexicans belonging to either the PRI or the PAN, who would lead the country on the way to the liberal reforms that had been recommended repeatedly and unanimously. A natural corollary was to consider that, as time went by, Mexico would overcome its anti-American nationalism and end up in economic fusion with the United States (Douglas 1985; Baer 1988). This relatively optimistic approach explains the permanence of the long-standing recommendation of not intervening in Mexico's internal affairs.

During the 1980s, researchers in the United States also focused on the study of the evolution of the concept and practice of security in Mexico. They reported that the term was most frequently used as a consequence of Central American events, that it has a broader meaning which gives priority to socioeconomic aspects over military ones, that it is more oriented toward domestic affairs, and that the role of the military is changing (Cunningham 1984; Ronfeldt 1984; Williams 1984 and 1986; Baer 1987; Sereseres 1984). Although, in a sense, this analysis recorded what was happening in Mexico, we can now see that it displays some potentially dangerous limitations.

Whenever the changing role of the army within the political system — or the modernization of its equipment and training — is discussed, one of the main concerns is whether "the modern Mexican military [will] continue to fulfill its security and development roles responsibly and in subordination to civilian authority."[12] The discussion even goes so far as to confuse this process with that of national security. The mistake is to equate Mexican national security with internal (or governmental) security, and there is an implicit militarization of the concept. This may be the result of a somewhat peculiar situation: Those who are thinking about or discussing the meaning of

U.S. security do not include Mexico,[13] and, with a couple of exceptions, those who write on Mexico and security rarely conceptualize it.[14]

Another distortion is that, with one exception, none of the essays considers the possibility that the United States can pose a threat to Mexican national security.[15] This stems from a hidden but fundamental assumption: It is thought that, in the final analysis, Mexico and the United States share the same security interests. Notwithstanding the importance of the notion, it has never been proved.[16]

This weakness in U.S. analysis became relevant as change in Mexico accelerated in 1988. Two years earlier, in 1986, Georges Fauriol wrote, "few events in the world could have a deeper impact on the United States [than] a conclusive Mexican shift to the left" (Fauriol 1986, 397). However, at the time, he discarded this possibility. The surprise in 1988 was not the diminishing support for the PRI, but the appearance of a nationalistic left which, once considered a piece out of the Mexican museum of rhetoric, was becoming a real contender for power. Since this has rapidly brought about change and uncertainty regarding the future, it is necessary to question where the U.S. discussion on Mexico and security is heading and what its potential effects on Mexico and the United States may be.

Because of the way in which security has been understood, it is possible that a growing pluralism in Mexico could nurture an alarmist approach that would promote intervention in Mexican politics on behalf of the established order, without even considering that such a move could become a threat to Mexican security. On the other hand, as the forces in favor of change are very powerful, the conceptual inertia could bring the U.S. government to an all-out support of the Mexican school of security, which also confuses national with internal security. U.S. literature has not captured the essence of the Mexican debate. In order to appreciate the potential scenarios, one must analyze the uses and misuses of the concept of security in Mexico.

Mexican Literature and Practice

For Mexico, it is possible to make a chronological division similar to that used for U.S. literature. Between 1946 and the end of the 1970s, economic growth, social peace, and secure and stable borders made it unnecessary to think systematically in terms of security. Even without theoretical consideration, the government used the concept as synonymous with control of dissidence by force (an interpretation still in vogue). This was clearly shown during the 1968 student movement which, in spite of its moderate demands, was repressed with a massacre on the night of October 2.

In his memoirs, General Luis Gutiérrez Oropeza, head of the military during the term of President Gustavo Díaz Ordaz, explained the decision to put a violent end to the student protest: "Gustavo Díaz Ordaz had no alternative but to resort to force as the way to contain the violence which was about to engulf us. Whenever *order and national security* are involved, the government cannot, must not, run the risk of failure, error or a lack of guts because it is the life of a nation which is at stake" (Gutiérrez-Oropeza 1988, 49).

This interpretation fed the growth of armed movements which emerged in several parts of the country. The administration of Luis Echeverría (1970-1976) fought them with policies that included programs for economic development, co-optation of opposition leaders and intellectuals, some political openings, and the use of force. It is precisely at the peak of the virtually unknown Mexican "dirty war" that the concept of national security appears for the first time in an official document.

In 1973, the Internal Regulations of the Ministry of the Interior assigned the Federal Directorate for Security (Dirección Federal de Seguridad or DFS) several functions, including "analyzing and notifying about any acts related to the security of the nation" (DO 1973). In 1947, the DFS was created by presidential order, as Mexico's political police.[17] Officially attached to the Ministry of the Interior, it really obeyed presidential orders and acted autonomously from Congress or the judicial system. Although lacking any respect for human rights, the DFS was relatively efficient in controlling the opposition movements which emerged periodically in different parts of the country.

The year 1980 is a key moment in the evolution of this concept in that, while the concept's repressive connotation is confirmed, there are also hints of some of the changes that would appear over the course of the decade. During that year, the last group of armed opposition (the "Liga Comunista 23 de septiembre") was formally dismembered with the death of one of its leaders, Miguel Angel Barraza; in February, the Internal Regulations of the Ministry of the Interior confirmed that the DFS was the only bureaucracy expressly in charge of issues related to "national security" (DO 1980). But in April, the 1980-82 Global Development Plan prepared by the Ministry of Planning used the concept to discuss the role of the armed forces, thus mistaking national security for national defense[18]; and in September, the Minister of Defense, General Félix Galván López, added an important nuance, when he defined national security as the "maintenance of the social, economic, and political equilibrium, guaranteed by the armed forces" (Vizcaíno 1980).

These differences of opinion were motivated by the main assumptions supporting two official interpretations of security: One of these is broad and establishes linkages with development, democracy, and social justice; the other is narrow and equates national security with internal control. Throughout the decade, the two definitions have remained in a tense coexistence that has not been resolved and that is a symptom of Mexico's unfinished transition. Just as in the United States, one of the factors influencing the use of the concept was oil. As Olga Pellicer de Brody and other analysts point out, a security approach started to be used during the López Portillo administration (1976-82) because, it was argued, there was a need to defend oil facilities from the greed or aggression of neighbors. Another rationale was to prepare the country against the potential effects of the Central American conflicts (Pellicer de Brody 1981; Granados 1982). The use of security was also influenced by the short-lived governing elite's illusion that the time had come to project national power abroad, especially in Central America.

After 1980, then, changes in Mexico and the region brought about more frequent references to the concept of security. First, I will discuss the ways in which the government has used the concept and then mention the formulations which have emerged from some political parties and the academic community. More time is spent dealing with the government's use of the term because of the enormous weight it has in Mexico's life and because it is necessary to evaluate the way in which it has fulfilled the prerogative assigned to the state by the traditional definition (the state as being in charge of defining and implementing security policies).

The first dimension to consider is conceptual. At this level, the trend has been to broaden the concept. The 1983 National Development Plan (PND-83) was the blueprint for the government of Miguel de la Madrid. In this document, there is the first attempt to give an explicit meaning to national security, which is defined as the "integral development of the nation" and "the instrument used to maintain liberty, peace, and social justice within the constitutional framework" (PND 1983, 61). Furthermore, it clarifies the fact that the function of the armed forces is to "collaborate," "support," or "contribute" to national security.

Another novelty is the attempt to give the concept an operational meaning. Thus, it is mentioned that one objective is to formulate an "integral security policy" which, based on tradition (for example, Mexican nationalism), is able to harmonize foreign and internal policies (PND 1983, 59). However, the PND-83 only refers to educational and cultural activities that strengthen national identity, communications policy, administrative practices, the defense of institutions, the search for social justice, and economic strength. It concentrates, therefore, on internal aspects and does not define the "integral security policy" which was supposed to include foreign issues (the PND-83 only makes a reference to the traditional principles of foreign policy, which had a defensive and legalistic connotation).[19] In conclusion, we then come up against a broad, yet cautious and somewhat inexplicit, explanation of the meaning of security.

As time went by, "national security" was increasingly used by officials.[20] Even the ruling party (PRI) felt obliged to include, in its Declaration of Principles, a chapter on "National Security and the Armed Forces," characterized by rhetorical devices and without conceptual innovation (PRI 1988). There are, of course, some exceptions which ought to be mentioned. In 1983, the Minister of Foreign Affairs, Bernardo Sepúlveda, gave the topic an important turn when he mentioned that the "true objective" of security is, "above all,...internal political harmonization" (Sepúlveda 1983). The Minister of the Interior, Manuel Bartlett, rounded off the idea when he stated that security is a "function of consensus and national unity" (Sandoval, Guerrero, and del Valle 1985, 120). Nevertheless, these are still incomplete definitions because they do not specify, for example, the threats and their origin, which make imperative the maintenance of internal unity.

The May 1989 National Development Plan of Carlos Salinas de Gortari (PND-89) includes a fundamental conceptual modification that may have great future consequences. This change is not in the definition because the administration reverted to that of 1983, nor in the role of the armed forces, whose function is still to "contribute" and "support" security; nor is it in the actions which should be taken to achieve the "condition" of security. The change is, first, that the term is used more frequently and freely (although not very accurately);

second, there is a change in the way Mexico's security vis-à-vis the rest of the world is viewed; and third, there appears explicitly an agenda of threats to national security.

The relation of Mexico vis-à-vis the rest of the world is a peculiar mixture of the old and the new. First, there is an assertion of traditional foreign policy principles (mainly defensive in character), and then there is a 180-degree turn when it is stated that one of the objectives of Mexican security is to "*act firmly and in anticipation, in order to avoid any external action* which can become a threat to national security" (PND 1989, viii). Taken literally, the last idea reminds us of the arguments given by the superpowers to justify their worldwide presence. However, other parts explain that the drafters of the PND-89 were only thinking of economic issues, although even in this dimension, it is never specified which external actions could become foreign threats or where they could originate.

This wider view reflects the new Mexican reality: The external dimension clearly conditions the Mexican economy, and there is a new model of economic development, based on an opening of the economy to foreign goods and investment, giving private exports the key role in the recovery. Undoubtedly, national security is more than ever dependent on external events, and it is a pity that the document was not used to substantiate the conceptual revolution.

Another novelty of the PND-89 is the inclusion of drug trafficking as the main threat to security, which leads one to the subject of how the government has developed a security agenda. An agenda should include the problems or phenomena which the state considers to be a real or potential threat to security and which, therefore, require a mobilization of national power. During the 1980s, some government officials mentioned (usually as a personal opinion) different problems that should be part of the agenda. Representative examples include the expansionist conception of security held by the United States, the Simpson-Rodino Act, and the fall of international oil prices (Gómez Ortega 1985 and 1988; Heller 1986; Lasse 1988). These are, nevertheless, not discussed in this essay, because in Mexico only the president has the power to set the security agenda.

The first issue publicly related to security by a president was Central America. In 1984, Miguel de la Madrid wrote that if Mexico ignored the conflict, it would mean that it was "giving up the defense of our own national interest and security" (de la Madrid 1984).

Although the president never explained why Central America should be considered an item on the security agenda, other government officials did. The main rationale was linked to the potentially deleterious effects of the Central American conflicts on Mexico; mentioned were problems, such as the arrival of hundreds of thousands of Central Americans escaping from violence; tensions with Guatemala and the United States; and an increase in military spending, which could lead to an increasing involvement of the armed forces in certain decision making processes. As the southern border is a strategic and rather conflictive area, fear existed that a regionalization of the Central American conflict would magnify those effects (Santos Caamal 1985; Cabrera 1987; Solana 1989). For such reasons, Mexico decided to resist Washington's policies and to interpret them as one of the causes of the region's violence.

The southern border, however, was an issue of heated internal debate within the bureaucracy. Some sectors pushed in favor of the coercive version of security, as they shared the U.S. thesis about the dangers of contamination. Just as happened in the United States, this interpretation did not succeed in Mexico. Most accepted that the origins of the tensions were rather complex. Thus, an essentially economic, political, and diplomatic response was devised, which only marginally involved the military or the police. This approach was made clear by the fact that the first two regional development plans of the Miguel de la Madrid administration were those of the southeast and Chiapas. Thus, to deactivate internal and international tensions, the federal government allocated enormous sums to development, and, in a more discrete way, increased its military presence.

It can, therefore, be stated that the "integral security policy" mentioned in the PND was rehearsed on the southern border. The policy was successful in attaining a relative normalization of the problems created by the Guatemalan refugees and in reducing tensions with Guatemala. Nonetheless, it failed in its objective of raising Chiapas to the level of development of the rest of the country and in diminishing political tensions. Three factors prevented that: the inefficiency and/or corruption of some government institutions, the resistance to change of the local elites, and, as a consequence, the impossibility of giving local independent organizations a share of power commensurate to their political strength.[21] Altogether, the southern border became a part of the security agenda, although not explicitly so. In this way, the reluctance to use the concept and define an agenda were made apparent.

The next problem defined as a threat to national security was drug production and trafficking. Since 1987, de la Madrid and Salinas de Gortari have been labeling it as the most important threat to security (de la Madrid 1988; Salinas 1987, 1988 and 1989). In spite of this, both presidents have been very reluctant to explain why it is considered so. The former made a blunt statement that drug trafficking is a risk to "national security"; the latter added that it was also a threat to the "health of Mexicans." On another occasion, he also added that it was a "problem of international solidarity" (de la Madrid 1988, 17; Salinas 1988, v and 1989, 20). A high official from the Attorney General's office was more precise. In his opinion, drugs threaten security because they erode "political stability," endanger the "strength of government institutions," contaminate "economic, financial, and agricultural" structures, and damage "Mexico's prestige abroad" (Reyes Estrada 1989).

The argument seems convincing enough, but it is still incomplete. One of the weak points is that it never clarifies where the most important enemy is. Depending on how one looks at the problem, the enemy could be the drug traffickers, the corruption of Mexican officials, the demand for drugs in the United States, or any combination of the three. It is important to note that the diagnosis of the threat is what determines the strategy to fight it.

Finally, in 1989, the concept of security was used on two different occasions. On one hand, the PND mentioned external economic threats, although without specifying them; on the other, the dismantling (and arrest) of PEMEX's union leadership by the army was justified on the basis that it was a "national security problem" (Moffett 1989).

The official agenda has another threat, which is hardly ever made explicit in public but which determines the operative use of the concept: Just as in the past, national security is equated with internal security, opening the space for the possible use of force to control the opposition. The thesis may be substantiated by mentioning, first, the authority held by different sectors of the bureaucracy. In the PND-83 the only ministry linked to security is the armed forces (their role is to "contribute" to and "support" security). Nevertheless, the 1986 "Organic Law of the Mexican Army and Air Force" does not include in its functions "supporting" national security. Significantly enough, the Law only includes references to internal security (SDN 1986). In 1985,

President de la Madrid issued the Internal Regulations of the Ministry of the Interior, and, although it was not mentioned in the PND, he assigns to this office — for the first time ever — the power to "coordinate all actions related to national security" (DO 1985, 3).

This situation was further complicated during the first weeks of the Salinas de Gortari administration. On 7 December, 1988, also by presidential decree, the "Coordination of the President's Office" was created. This document also announced the creation, for the first time ever, of a national security cabinet, which includes the Ministry of the Interior and which is accountable "for its functions and operation" to this coordinating office (DO 1988, 4). One would suppose that the "coordinating" functions in security matters which were under the Ministry of the Interior would pass to this coordinating office, but it did not happen that way. On 13 February, 1989, the president issued a new set of internal regulations for the Ministry of the Interior where its functions of "coordinating actions related to national security" are ratified (DO 1989, 26). In May 1989, another PND was issued, which vaguely mentions the armed forces and never defines which of the different bureaucracies is responsible for the coordination of security activities.

It is evident that the functions of the bureaucracy are not clear, and it is plain that the difference between national security and internal security is not defined either. This can also be demonstrated from another perspective. The DFS was a political police force with the objective of analyzing and providing information about the security of the nation. However, more than an intelligence organization, it was an operational structure with considerable autonomy from the Ministry of Defense and, in some moments, from the Ministry of the Interior with which it was formally associated. The impunity enjoyed by the DFS fostered corruption, as it protected gangs involved in the production and trafficking of drugs.

This complicity was not new. For example, in 1951 the CIA stated that "some of the unscrupulous chiefs of this group [the DFS] have abused the considerable power vested in them by condoning and actually conducting illegal activities such as narcotics smuggling" (CIA 1951, 58). What did change was the increase in the magnitude of the problem. Moreover, with the murder of the Drug Enforcement Administration (DEA) agent Enrique Camarena, the complicity of some members of the DFS in drug trafficking activities became public. Partly due to U.S. pressure, the Mexican president ordered the disbanding of the DFS in 1985. A presidential decree created a substitute: the General Directorate of Investigation and National Security. This organization tried to fuse the operational functions of the DFS with those of intelligence carried out by the General Directorate of Political and Social Investigations, also created by presidential decree in 1947. Through this same system of decrees, in February 1989, President Salinas de Gortari transformed this Directorate into the Center for Investigation and National Security, which has among its functions that of "establishing and operating an investigation and information system for the security of the country" (DO 1989, 40).

This sketch outlining the dimensions of the official use of the security concept shows a number of ambiguities and contradictions. In the conceptual dimension, it is never clear why the term is broadened, nor does the agenda of threats ever explain the criteria used to formulate it. It is possible to argue that the use of the army indicates that one is dealing with a security threat. Furthermore, the fight against drug trafficking or the detention of oil leaders could be used to support this hypothesis. Nevertheless, the armed forces had a secondary role on Mexico's southern border, and it is not clear how they can be used to "avoid any external action which could become a threat to national security," as mentioned in the PND-89. In this sense, the government's reluctance to define who the enemy is and reluctance to omit the possibility that the United States could threaten Mexico's security is a significant weakness. The lack of specific criteria is important because it makes it difficult to assess the validity of the government's agenda or to propose the inclusion of other problems. For example, the PND-89 mentions international economic problems as an abstract phenomenon which poses a potential threat. This would open the way to include such problems as foreign debt and food dependency.

Another criticism comes from a review of the contradictions among dimensions. Two examples are quite significant. At the conceptual level, national security is defined as the "integral development of the nation." This contradicts the operational aspects, because the National Security Cabinet, created in 1989, only includes the ministries of the Interior, Foreign Affairs, Defense, and the Navy, as well as the Attorney General's Office. With the exception of Foreign Affairs, the function of the others is to maintain internal order, whereas if the broad definition had some operational validity, this cabinet ought to include some of the ministries dealing with the social area.

A second example comes from an idea included in the PND-89: The security of the nation is "sought by the people and the government" (PND 1989, xi). By using these words, the government seems to recognize the importance of consultative mechanisms (which would fit into the concepts of Bernardo Sepúlveda and Manuel Bartlett about "concertation," "consensus," and "unity" as the essence of security). Nevertheless, the 1988 decree creating the Coordination Office and the National Security Cabinet mentions that the "President of the Republic may determine that the heads of other offices or agencies be present at the meetings of the Cabinets, as well as other government officials whose presence, according to the topics under discussion, might be required" (DO 1988, 4). In other words, matters of national security are decided by a cabinet controlled by the president and the participants invited by him.

These and other ambiguities and contradictions make it impossible to understand what the federal government really means by national security. It is even possible to conclude that the broad definition is a rhetorical exercise concealing the coercive nature of security. On the other hand, if one looks at the process from another perspective, the concept has been undergoing a transformation and could evolve either into a broad concept or into a tight and repressive one. Before trying to give some ideas for the future, I would like to enumerate some of the factors creating confusion. Among others are the lack of a tradition in security studies, the absence of institutions linking government and society, and the deficiencies of a centralized but uncoordinated bureaucracy. Nevertheless, the chief cause lies in an authoritarian system where the president has the power to decide what is and what is not national security, to decide what the threats are, which threats should receive priority, what resources might be allocated, which institutions will participate, and what methods will be used. In other words, the uses and misuses of the concept of security have reflected the nature of the political system, and it follows that the concept will evolve according to the changes in the political system.

That is, a democratic Mexico is incompatible with the current conceptualization and practice of security. But authoritarianism is considered outmoded in Mexico, and the uses and misuses of security have become dysfunctional, even for the government. For example, although it is not easy to pinpoint exactly what influence the Federal Security Directorate (DFS) had in the rise of drug trafficking, what we know is sufficient to conclude that it was this official agency, in charge of safeguarding national security, which contributed to the creation of what is now considered to be the main threat to security. Corruption of agencies fighting drug traffickers is common, but it was perhaps facilitated by the impunity enjoyed by the DFS ever since its inception. There is an obvious conclusion: Some sort of accountability is indispensable to ensure a socially secure use of security.

The lack of interest by society in official management has made such abuses easier. The opposition parties, for example, only consider the coercive dimension of security. Thus, Héctor Ramírez Cuéllar, from the Partido Popular Socialista, thinks that "intelligence functions are meant to safeguard national security" (Fuentes 1986). Ricardo Valero, from the Partido de la Revolución Democrática, thinks the same, as he considers the Minister of the Interior to be "responsible for national security" (Caballero 1990). Other sectors make a similar mistake when they confuse national and public security (Cabrera Parra 1983).

In these cases, they point to only one dimension of security. Scholars have shown a more consistent interest in defining national security or in making a follow-up of the way it has been used by the government. In 1981, Olga Pellicer de Brody published the first essay discussing national security (Pellicer de Brody 1981). Her purpose was twofold: to explain why the concept has started being used in Mexico and to promote a broader interpretation equating national security with the general objectives of the 1917 Constitution.

Her essay revealed some of the main traits characteristic of Mexican academia. First, there is an explicit rejection of the repressive definitions of security that originated in South America, although there is hardly any mention of the Mexican government's operative use of the concept, which follows the same pattern. Second, there is a conscious effort to adapt the theoretical discussions of security to Mexico's history (especially to nationalism) and to the changing conditions of the country. The basic platform is the national project embedded in the 1917 Constitution. This conceptual effort has led to the discussion— among other issues— of judicial guidelines, the need to distinguish between national interests and security, and the relation of this concept to the national project (Aguilar 1986; Castillo 1990; Herrera-Lasso 1988; Meyer 1989; Lassé 1989; Sarmiento 1986; Sepúlveda 1986; and Zárate 1986).

The academic community has also actively discussed some of the threats and issues included by the government in the security agenda. The most outstanding case where this may be seen was the debate about Central America and its effects on Mexico. When the bureaucracies were still undecided how to interpret the situation, scholars produced solid arguments to demonstrate that the Central American conflicts were fundamentally internal and that aggressive U.S. policies nurtured them, increasing the negative effects for Mexico. On the other hand, based on the old premise that the main threats to Mexico's sovereignty come from the north, it was stated that the presence of the United States in the south could mean that Mexico shared a double border with that country. A logical conclusion was that the best defense for national security lay in the consolidation of independent regimes in Central America (this interpretation coincided with official theses) (Pellicer de Brody 1982; Aguilar 1986; Aguayo 1987; and Benítez and Bermúdez 1990).

In the discussion about the refugees along the southern border, or about the possibility that the latter would be susceptible to ideological contamination, the academic community produced studies demonstrating the fundamentally humanitarian character of Guatemalan immigration and the domestic origin of the problems in Chiapas. It should be noted that the influence of the academic sector (always difficult to determine) was made easier because the southern border and the country itself continued to be relatively stable. Perhaps the results would have been different had this massive immigration coincided with the political movements of 1988. (The speculation is significant because of the possibility that, in the future, the worsening of the Guatemalan civil war and political readjustments in Mexico could occur simultaneously.)

In drug trafficking, the academic contribution has been less significant. Most research focuses on the effects of the drug issue on Mexico-U.S. relations, but the social, political, cultural, and economic effects are not known. The reluctance to delve into the matter is a consequence of lack of resources and awareness of risks. A reminder is the murder of the well-known journalist Manuel Buendía in 1984, during his investigation of narcotics issues. This act was apparently ordered by the ex-director of the DFS. Nevertheless, it continues to be essential to do more research in order to assess the real threat posed by drug trafficking to Mexico's security.

The intellectual community has also proposed some topics for the agenda. Although ignored by the government, they should in any event be mentioned. Adolfo Aguilar Zinser, among others, points out that "Mexicans have always been wary of their northern border, which is where the most obvious aggressions and threats against our security come from" (Aguilar 1983; González 1986; and Herrera-Lasso 1989). Sofía Méndez Villareal argues that the economic policies of the current administration affect the country's economic security for several reasons: They perpetuate social and economic inequalities; they postpone "indefinitely, the need to produce domestically most of Mexico's capital goods"; and finally, they increase the extent that the "present crisis may bring about greater integration to the U.S. economy" (Méndez Villareal 1990, 22-23).

Luis Herrera-Lasso concludes that the "state has lost spaces and has multiplied the windows of vulnerability to outside players," both in the economic and the political spheres (Herrera-Lasso 1989, 11, 12). In 1984, I mentioned the need to base national security on "the respect and the broadening of the democratic process" (Aguayo 1985, 73). Finally, the research carried out by several Mexicans on the armed forces should be acknowledged. With few exceptions, Mexicans have avoided the U.S. mistake of confusing national with internal security when discussing the evolution of the army (Boils 1985).

This brief summary of what has been written in the country during the past few years shows that our research is still insufficient. There have been some advances, but most research is still in process or shelved in unpublished documents or has been given limited circulation and is therefore difficult to obtain.[22] As with any other subject, theoretical thinking will improve as more Mexican and foreign research is carried out, and the opinions of other sectors, which are at present absent from the discussion, are included.

On the other hand, it is essential to conduct many more case studies that analyze, support, or reject the issues or threats which should be included in the security agenda (which is one of the objectives of this book). Of course, to do this, one needs resources and, above all, information. This situation has created a vicious circle for which the academic community can be held only partly responsible. That is, some of the security topics are politically sensitive (in part, because they have been defined as part of security), and that erects obstacles to the acquisition of information (generally withheld by government officials). It would seem logical to establish and/or maintain a dialogue between academics and the state, but this is not an easy task in a country like Mexico where, besides authoritarianism, we lack the institutional mechanisms that allow social participation in the formulation or discussion of security.

There are, of course, some exceptions. For example, in 1981 the Ministry of Defense and the Ministry of the Navy created the College of Defense and the Center for Higher Studies in Leadership and National Security, respectively. The college has fostered one of the most systematic and serious analyses on security. Probably, this process was influenced by the constant presence of Mexican lecturers of different political leanings. The Latin American Center for Strategic Studies (CLEE) could be considered the civilian equivalent. The center was founded by a group of scholars and officials interested in security issues and has gradually become a forum for analysis. These are, however, limited exercises which do not substitute for the need for other mechanisms to allow the Mexican people to discuss what is and what is not a threat to the security of the nation. On the basis of this review of the literature, I can now offer some concrete propositions.

Some Elements for a Definition of Mexican Security and Criteria to Formulate an Agenda

This review of what has been said and done about security gives a foundation for returning to the initial question: Is it feasible to apply the concept of security to the Mexican case? The evidence is not very encouraging. In the United States, some statements are based on premises of rather dubious validity but, nevertheless, bear definite political weight. In Mexico, the official use of the concept is characterized by contradictions in the different dimensions, although they all have as a common denominator the authoritarian decree. For its part, the intellectual community in Mexico has not yet overcome theoretical obstacles or gathered the information needed to tackle extremely complicated issues.

In consequence, it does not seem advisable to use such a risky concept. However, that does not mean that all those sectors that have used it will accept some sort of moratorium on the use of the concept until an agreement is reached as to its advisability or limitations. This would be an unrealistic expectation, because the popularity of the term is not the result of an intellectual fad; it is a direct consequence of a

generalized perception of real or potential threats to which governments, scholars, and society react. This has been shown in the review
of the literature: From 1946 to the end of the 1970s, "security" was used
on rare occasions, because realities made it unnecessary. When reality
changed, so did indifference, and we had an unsatisfactory proliferation of the concept.

It follows, then, that the permanence of structural problems
(among others, readjustments in the global balance of power; debate
in the United States about the meaning of such changes and of security;
violence and economic crisis in Central America; and drug trafficking,
economic problems, and political tensions in Mexico) will continue to
affect Mexico and the United States. In consequence, different groups
or individuals will continue to justify their actions with a politically
powerful concept: security. Governments will certainly do so, because
there are bureaucracies — the National Security Council in the United
States and the National Security Cabinet in Mexico, just to mention two
— whose *raison d'être* is "security." They will do so independently of
whether society takes part in the discussions or is just informed of what
is being done in its name. Perhaps, it would be better not to use the
concept. However, there is a certain inevitability in its use. One cannot
ignore it; indifference means leaving the field to those sectors which
have already used it to postpone or obstruct the changes required by
democracy, social justice, and sovereignty. This, in turn, leads to
another question: Is it possible to have a definition and an agenda
grounded on such principles?

This is slippery ground, because I share the concern of some
colleagues about the risks of a broad definition of security which can
lead to an unlimited and dangerous expansion of the agenda. I,
therefore, propose the following ideas, keeping in mind existing
literature, historical trends, and the arguments given in the introduction
to this book. What seems most appropriate is to start with a broad
definition, complemented by an agenda narrowed by two factors: the
evidence of research and the legitimacy given by national consensus.

Mexico already has the conceptual elements required by a
definition. In his book, General Gerardo C. R. Vega defines national
security as the "permanent condition of liberty, peace, and social
justice provided by the three branches of the state within an institutional and legal framework." This is to be achieved internally, through
"political, social, economic, and military actions that will be oriented

to the provision of a dynamic balance among the aspirations and interests of the different sectors of the population and the country. In its international context, the goal is to safeguard territorial integrity and exercise sovereignty and independence" (Vega 1988, 46).

Although this definition does not explicitly refer to Mexico, I consider it appropriate for a number of reasons. First, because it is broad enough to include the many challenges faced by Mexico, both domestic and international. Second, because it contains the essence of the best Mexican definitions (from inside and outside the government), which are based on the Constitution of 1917. Third, because the "condition" of security is provided by the "three branches of the state," which could reduce the concentration of power in the executive (the latter being one of the reasons for abuses of the concept). By redressing this problem, we would be moving toward the creation of the institutional mechanisms that would give legitimacy to a security agenda.

To my way of thinking, a very important shortcoming of this definition is that it is oriented toward a "positive" agenda; that is, it speaks of "actions" which will "be oriented to the provision" of an already existing "condition." This is, therefore, the broad definition of a secure country. As Mexico is not at present a secure country, the agenda would have to be complemented with certain criteria which would allow for the integration of a "negative" agenda of challenges, problems, and threats, since it is in their name that the abuses already mentioned have been committed. This negative agenda should be integrated very carefully, in view of the fact that the concept of security is so flexible; and given that the literature on security lacks criteria to differentiate between real and potential threats, there is always the possibility that an individual, group, or government will try to transform a challenge or a problem into a threat to security.

In other words, more precise criteria should be established to disentangle threats, problems, and issues of security. In this sense, and considering what has been done in Mexico, I think that a realistic and sensible formula would be for any proposed threat to fulfill the following requirements: First, it should be permanent and should affect the nation, not just the government or a small group — and certainly not an individual. This must be demonstrated through case studies which will, in turn, polish the conceptual framework. Another challenge is mainly political in nature. As I mentioned earlier, in Mexico there has never been sufficient presidential accountability — for example, of the 62

Congressional committees, there is not one that deals with national security issues. This can only be modified through reforms of the state and the political system, and that means democratization.

Does a Nuclear Neighbor Pose a Threat to Mexican National Security?

Security is an ambiguous term surrounded by relative truths. Thus, it needs the filters of theory, information, and common sense. For example, it is not enough for someone to say that a certain issue is a threat to security; it has to be proved. And it is precisely here that the literature on Mexican national security shows gaps and weaknesses. There are plenty of unfounded premises as well as threats created by invisible enemies, but we do not have demonstrations based on information and logic.

U.S. analysts, for example, never consider the possibility that some of their country's actions could become a threat to Mexican security, which is an oversight running counter to the most elementary logic. Therefore, when choosing a case study, I decided to review this assumption by considering the implications of being a neighbor to a nuclear power. I chose this topic because nuclear issues are a recurrent issue in the security literature of the industrialized nations, because it has never been included in the discussion about Mexican security, and because it will illustrate the difficulties that exist when it comes to differentiating between issues of concern and threats to security.

The case can be approached from different dimensions. From January 1951 to July 1962, some one hundred atmospheric explosions were carried out in the Nevada Test Site (Cochran and Arkin et al. 1987). Twenty-three of them produced thirty-nine clouds with radio-active debris that fell on Mexico (Miller 1986, Appendix C). In the summer of 1963, the United States and the USSR signed an agreement banning atmospheric testing. That did not eliminate the risks for Mexico. In a secret memorandum (25 March, 1964), McGeorge Bundy, special assistant to the president for national security affairs, informed President Lyndon B. Johnson of an accident that had occurred on 13 March during an underground test. Through a crack in the earth, "measurable quantities of debris did, in fact, cross into Mexico." The Mexican government was never informed (NSC 1964). According to Philip L. Fradkin, there were at least another "dozen" similar accidents which may have sent nuclear debris over Mexico (Fradkin 1989, 137).

Although the effects of this fallout were never studied, research carried out on the U.S. population affected by the fallout suggests that the health of many Mexicans could have suffered similarly.

Along the border with Mexico, the United States has over one hundred major military bases (DOD 1982 and 1988). Some of them have aircraft carrying nuclear weapons, which could have accidents and pose a potential threat to Mexico. There are precedents: The best known is Palomares, Spain, where in January 1966 four atomic bombs fell. The damage they caused to the health of the civilian population is still a matter of dispute. I was able to document similar accidents in Mexico (although it has been impossible to determine whether or not the bombs had nuclear warheads). In 1958, for example, the Mexican ambassador to the United States complained about "missiles" falling near "highways and populated towns" in Sonora (DOS 1958, 2). In September 1967, the United States Embassy in Mexico informed the Department of State about the fall of a "Pershing" missile in the neighborhood of El Cuervo, Chihuahua. This document also makes reference to another incident in which a Target Drone Jet of the American navy fell over Sonora (DOS 1967). It is possible that there are more accidents still hidden behind the "classified" seal.

The possibility of leaks of radioactive material used by government institutions or private companies near the Mexican border also represents a potential threat to Mexico's security. Using as a criterion the distance between the Nevada Test Site and the Mexican border (this is the area from which the nuclear clouds emanated, as was previously mentioned), there are twenty installations handling radioactive material (six nuclear plants, several laboratories, factories, and the Pantex Company, where all the nuclear warheads of the U.S. arsenal are assembled) (Cochran and Arkin et al. 1987; and FEMA 1989). Finally, we ought to mention nuclear waste deposits or the irresponsible handling or transportation of radioactive waste near the border (take, for example, construction rods which affected the population of Ciudad Juárez, Chihuahua).

The greatest risk is, of course, the possibility of a nuclear war. It would seem unnecessary to include this possibility when the confrontation between the United States and the USSR has withered away. However, the United States and other industrialized countries continue to explore threatening scenarios which could affect their security. It would, therefore, be justifiable for Mexico to undertake a similar exercise, as we have so many nuclear targets close to the border. Some are civilian; others, industrial; and many are military. The information obtained was considerable, and due to the lack of space, I will summarize it graphically.

Chart 1 shows the "potential targets" (that is, those that would be attacked by nuclear weapons) according to U.S. government classifications. Based on official information, Chart 2 attempts to show the effects of direct impact and the resulting radioactive fallout in the United States. Something that has to be highlighted is that the consequences for Mexico are not taken into account in U.S. studies, even though, as Octavio Miramontes has mentioned, the electromagnetic pulse and radioactive fallout could be devastating for our country (Miramontes 1989 and 1989a).

On the other hand, these charts assume that the missiles will be very accurate, because they ignore the possibility of a "probable circle of error." Alejandro Nadal reviews this assumption and concludes that "there is enough information to believe that the calculations concerning the accuracy of the intercontinental ballistic missiles (ICBMs) are too optimistic and that, in the event of a nuclear conflict, there is a high probability of 'accidental' direct impact in countries neighboring the superpowers" (Nadal Egea 1989, 112).

A nuclear war would have further consequences: Millions of U.S. refugees would seek refuge in Mexico. This irony demonstrates the limitation of the U.S. literature, insofar as it assumes that only Mexican events constitute a threat to Mexican security. It is common to read or hear in the United States that an unstable Mexico would produce millions of Mexican refugees and that such an event would create a threat to U.S. security. When discussing this scenario, or Mexican undocumented immigration, U.S. analysts have an acute awareness of the border dividing the two countries and are not reluctant to conceive of it as a salutary barrier. But the concept of a border disappears when some sectors speculate about escape routes for U.S. citizens in the event of a holocaust. In one of those popular survival manuals, Mexico is explicitly mentioned as a haven ("south of Monterrey"), without taking into consideration the opinion of the Mexican people (Clayton 1989, Chapter 3).

This outline of the main elements constituting this case study has to be complemented with the reactions of Mexican officials. When interviewed, an official of the Ministry of Foreign Affairs, Zadalinda

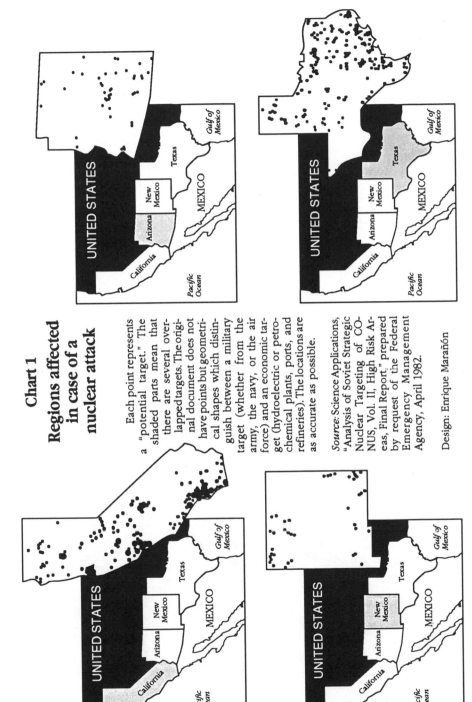

Chart 1
Regions affected in case of a nuclear attack

Each point represents a "potential target." The shaded parts mean that there are several overlapped targets. The original document does not have points but geometrical shapes which distinguish between a military target (whether from the army, the navy, or the air force) and an economic target (hydroelectric or petrochemical plants, ports, and refineries). The locations are as accurate as possible.

Source: Science Applications, "Analysis of Soviet Strategic Nuclear Targeting of CONUS, Vol. II, High Risk Areas, Final Report," prepared by request of the Federal Emergency Management Agency, April 1982.

Design: Enrique Marañón

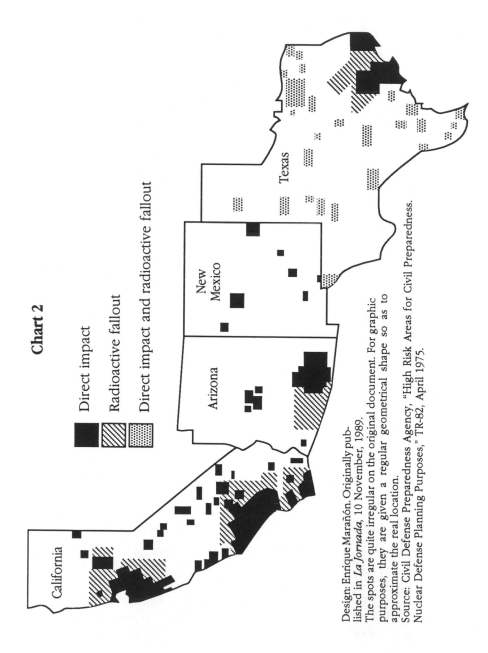

Chart 2

Direct impact

Radioactive fallout

Direct impact and radioactive fallout

Design: Enrique Marañón. Originally published in *La Jornada*, 10 November, 1989. The spots are quite irregular on the original document. For graphic purposes, they are given a regular geometrical shape so as to approximate the real location.
Source: Civil Defense Preparedness Agency, "High Risk Areas for Civil Preparedness. Nuclear Defense Planning Purposes," TR-82, April 1975.

González, stated that "because of lack of resources, Mexico has not carried out studies or evaluations, nor has it established contingency plans in case of an accident or a nuclear war." Put succinctly, the issue "is not included in the Mexican-U.S. agenda."

What does the nuclear factor mean for Mexican security? Can it be considered an issue, a problem, or a threat to national security? Or is it a public health issue or problem? Should Mexico continue accepting silently the nuclear risk and validating the idea that it is the cost to be paid for the protection of the U.S. umbrella? There are perhaps many answers, but if one were guided by the criteria of U.S. analysts, one would conclude that we are facing a threat to Mexican national security, because large cities could be destroyed, workers and markets for our products could disappear, the most important sources of inputs for our industry could close down, and we might as well receive millions of refugees. All of this would happen despite Mexico's rejection of the presence of nuclear weapons within its territory.

However, this conclusion has to be qualified with an assessment of the risk. Thus, to have a nuclear neighbor is, at present, a matter related to security rather than a threat to security. This has not always been the case. For example, in moments of great tension between the superpowers, such as the 1962 Cuban Missile Crisis, the threat was so evident that it should have been the first item on the security agenda. Likewise, as a return of nuclear tensions is always possible, a confrontation between the superpowers should not be discarded from a future agenda of Mexico's security.

On the other hand, the nuclear aspects have been a public health problem, especially between 1951 and 1964, when the fallout of radioactive waste was so constant that it could have affected a large percentage of the Mexican population. We do not have details on this, because there was no information then available. This was partly the result of a lack of awareness but also a lack of political will to assign the necessary resources to evaluate it. Nevertheless, there is no doubt that even in this obvious case, the nuclear factor is not seen in the United States as a threat to Mexican security. The lack of security-oriented research means that other aspects of the relationship should be analyzed before concluding that Mexico and the United States share the same interests. Perhaps, this is valid in some aspects but certainly not in all, and this case study substantiates the conclusion.

Of course, there are more immediate concerns for Mexico's security.

Democratization and Security in Mexico

Two opposing concepts of security coexist in present-day Mexico: a broad one, within the constitutional framework, which is based on democracy, social justice, and sovereignty; and a coercive concept, which confuses national with internal security (and in some cases, even with government security). The latter is potentially very dangerous because it is used by the president, in an authoritarian manner, and without any social control. Since both concepts reflect contemporary Mexico in transition, the conflict between them can be solved in a relatively short period of time. In order to discuss the possible outcomes, it is necessary to address some aspects of Mexico at the turn of the century.

Mexico is changing. There is an economic crisis which is aggravating income inequalities; a new development model is being tried in order to resume growth; drug trafficking has become a very serious problem; traditional political institutions are losing effectiveness; groups within society are organizing; opposition is growing in all sectors; and, in 1990, some guerrilla groups reappeared. The geopolitical environment and the world are also changing. To the south, the apparent solutions to the wars in Nicaragua and El Salvador leave pending unresolved conflicts in Guatemala. To the north, the traditional border is undergoing modification because of a double and contradictory set of forces: There is an economic opening, leading to a free trade agreement, which takes place in the midst of problems of drug trafficking and immigration. Since some of these problems will continue for some time, it is quite possible that references to security will also.

During the past few years, a new group took power and started to implement an economic revolution. Although some measures were inevitable and necessary, the new plan has not yet shown that growth can again be resumed or that it can resolve social inequalities. Social justice requires adjustments in the distribution of wealth, which means a readjustment in the distribution of power. This, in turn, depends on the ability of different social groups to organize themselves and obtain answers to their demands.

At the political level, a recent characteristic has been society's accelerated organizational drive, something that was noticeable during the 1988 elections. Even though left- and right-wing opposition, as well as the official party, have had considerable internal problems, social organization has continued (and even increased in some regions). This poses a dilemma to Mexico's (and the United States') established order. It can accept the new realities and democratize the system, or it can use repression against independent or opposing organizations. If a variant of the second option is chosen, it is possible that the coercive definition of security will be used in an authoritarian way (that is, through the decrees). Although it is, indeed, possible to use it, generalized repression would face several obstacles in Mexico.

First, it would require that the coercive apparatus be consistent, something which has been gradually disappearing as a result of several factors. For geopolitical reasons, government institutions in charge of internal security have been relatively small for such a large country. Among the military and federal police, there are no more than 160,000 effective members. For several decades, these were sufficient, because the other control mechanisms (co-optation and corruption) were functioning well — resources were available — and because the coercive structures were built on the assumption of an isolated, divided, and regionalized opposition.

The sudden emergence or consolidation of several opposition groups all over the country means that the authoritarian regime must monitor more people, with fewer allies and resources. For example, the popularity of the nationalist left (*Cardenismo*) in the rural areas, combined with the expansion of drug trafficking, has attracted the support of broad sectors of the peasantry. This has reduced the effectiveness of the "Rural Guards" (a peasant-based paramilitary organization that acts as informant in the internal security scheme). Events at the southern border and the fight against drug trafficking (to which, according to some sources, a third of the armed forces and some fifteen hundred police officers are committed) have resulted in the dispersal across the country of much of this personnel.

On the other hand, the armed forces maintain their loyalty to the government, although they seem to be reluctant to use force to repress discontent. It is not likely that there will be a repetition of the highly uncritical role they played in the 1968 student movement. Some of the reasons behind this reluctance are their sympathy for *Cardenismo* (a large percentage of them voted for this party in 1988), the popular class origins of the military, the general uneasiness caused by the crisis, and a re-evaluation of the origin of national problems and the military's role in them (Aguayo 1988).

In spite of their hermetic public posture, the Mexican military has shown some indicators of a greater sensibility toward change. In 1982, the Secretary of Defense declared that the "Mexican army would respect any political regime that ruled the country by popular support" (Hinojosa 1982). October 1988 was an especially tense month because, although Carlos Salinas de Gortari had been declared president by his party, the opposition was strong, and people were dissatisfied; some analysts thought this could escalate to a violent confrontation. In that context, the Secretary of the Navy stated, in front of Salinas de Gortari, that the navy would not accept foreign theories which give priority to the "eradication of internal dissidence and the denationalization of the armies so as to transform them into instruments of dominant groups, using them against their own people and thus imposing schemes of domination" (Gómez Ortega 1988). In 1990, amidst a tense atmosphere due to frauds committed by the official party in the local elections of Guerrero and Michoacán, the Secretary of Defense, General Antonio Riviello Bazán, said in front of the president that "reason and dialogue" are the "means to solve conflict" (Ramírez 1990).

Another set of obstacles to the use of force is international. Two notable examples are the wave of democracy which is sweeping the world and the premium given to stability by the new development model, dependent as it is on foreign investment, social peace, and predictability. A regime which continues to show lack of respect for the vote or popular will, and which decides to use force to repress opposition and violate human and political rights, will be exposed to international criticism and, because it fosters instability, will put the economy at risk.

A changing Mexico also forces the United States to face the traditional dilemmas of its foreign policy: respect for democracy and the defense of its own interests. In the first two years of the Salinas administration, Washington has backed the established order in Mexico, and it will probably support the coercive variant of security (in the literature previously discussed, one can find the theoretical foundation). However, there are also some reasons why the United States can support a transition toward a pluralist regime in Mexico. The most important limitation is that any interventionist miscalculations on the part of the United States toward Mexico would almost immediately have negative repercussions back in the United States. Another reason is the current lack of internal consensus regarding processes of change in countries in its immediate sphere of influence. In this sense, the debate over Central America can be considered a rehearsal for any discussions about change in Mexico; thus, some U.S. groups would support the democratization option. And in such an open society, minorities can, indeed, become an effective opposition.

The last factor limiting the use of force is intellectual. In his *Encyclopedia*, Hegel wrote, "In our reflecting and reasoning age, a man is not worth much who cannot give a good reason for everything, no matter how bad or how crazy. Everything in the world that has been done wrong has been done wrong for the very best of reasons." The South American militaries attempted to create a sort of intellectual legitimacy for their National Security Doctrine. But the misuses of the concept of national security in Mexico and the United States have been the result of unfolding bureaucratic practices, and they have no coherent foundation in reason. None of the reviewed documents mentions a single definition which *explicitly* justifies a South American-style interpretation, and, in spite of the limitations of the Mexican or U.S. literature, there has been no academic willing to make an intellectual argument legitimizing repression.

Because of these and other reasons (which include the decision of the opposition to act within the law), I would argue that, in spite of the reluctance of the group in power, a gradual democratization of the system is possible. It is clear that this will not be an easy transition and that the possibility exists for an increase in authoritarianism. The transition will be facilitated by the consolidation of the broad definition of security. However, the success of a broad definition of security depends on the ability of the nation to carry out the political and economic reforms needed to support a condition of security based on democracy, social justice, and independence.

Notes

1.   Among others, see War Department 1942; J.I.S. 248/M 1946; CIA 1951; DOS 1951. The importance of the assumption is confirmed by its continuous presence in more recent material: Deagle 1981; Linn 1984; Moorer and Fauriol 1984; Douglas 1985; Fauriol 1986; Sanders 1987. In Neuchterlein 1985, one can find the most systematic revision of Mexico's importance for U.S. national security.

2.   Among other documents, see NSC-56 1949; DOS 1952; and NSC-144/1 1953; Deagle 1981.

3.   In eight other lines, Mexico and Canada are mentioned together (DA 1949).

4.   For the U.S. officials, see Special 1951 and 1954; Gruson 1953.

5.   One of the most relevant papers on this subject was Ronfeldt et al. 1980.

6.   Fagen 1979, 47-48; Douglas 1985; Anderson and Atta 1987. For other perspectives, see Thorup and Ayres 1982; Erb and Thorup 1984; Baer 1987 and 1988; Dziedzic 1988.

7.   See Toro, Bustamante, Liverman, and Nuccio, et al. in this volume.

8.   During the past two centuries, "stability" has been the main security objective of the United States in Latin America. See Schoultz 1987 for a critical and sophisticated discussion and Jordan and Taylor 1984 for a conventional one.

9.   Williams 1984, 187; Linn 1984. On the Mexican guerrillas, see Hannon 1984. For a criticism of this argument, see Aguayo 1987.

10.   Salaverry 1988; and for a broader analysis, Aguayo 1985.

11.   As an example of the different positions in this debate about security, see Domínguez 1982; Ronfeldt 1983; Moorer and Fauriol 1984; Blachman et al. 1986; Fauriol 1988. For a contextualization of Mexican foreign policy, see Bagley 1981 and 1983.

12.   Ronfeldt 1984, 28. See Walker 1984; Colson 1989; Williams 1984; Wager 1989; Hannon 1984; Fauriol 1986. Ronfeldt illustrates the evolution of the term "national security"; in a 1975 essay on the Mexican military, he does not refer to national security; in 1984, he relates the military to the concept.

13.   About the few references to Mexico, see the general works of Brown 1983; Jordan and Taylor 1984; Schoultz 1987.

14.   The authors who provide a theoretical framework are Ganster and Sweedler 1987 and Dziedzic 1988.

15. Cunningham 1984; Ronfeldt 1984; Moorer and Fauriol 1984; Baer 1987. The only exception is Dziedzic 1988.

16. For some examples of this idea, see DAF 1955; DOS 1956; DOS 1959; Fauriol 1986; Ganster and Sweedler 1987; Wilson 1989.

17. The antecedents of the DFS were the "Confidential Department" created in 1929, which in 1938 became the Office of Political Information, and in 1942, the Department of Political and Social Investigation; DO 1929; DO 1938.

18. PGD 1980. President López Portillo made the same mistake. See González 1982.

19. The PND mentions that "this concept includes any actions taken in favor of peace, respect to self-determination, and the rejection of a policy of blocs or hegemonies." PND 1983, 58.

20. Among others, Santos Caamal 1985; Gómez Ortega 1985 and 1988; Cabrera 1987; Hernández Haddad 1988. I have not included some other references made in passing in the press.

21. For a more detailed analysis, see Aguayo 1987.

22. This is the case, for example, of Vega 1988; Castillo 1990; and the transcription of the internal seminars of Latin American Center for Strategic Studies (CLEE). An exception is the book by Saxe-Fernández 1984.

References

Aguayo, Sergio. 1985. "La seguridad nacional y la soberanía mexicana entre Estados Unidos y América Central." In *Las relaciones de México con los países de América Central*, comp. Mario Ojeda. Mexico: El Colegio de México.

Aguayo, Sergio. 1987. *Chiapas y la seguridad nacional mexicana.* Mexico: Centro Latinoamericano de Estudios Estratégicos.

Aguayo, Sergio. 1988. "Los militares y las elecciones." *La Jornada*, 1 September.

Aguayo, Sergio. 1990. "México en la literatura militar estadounidense, 1949-1988." In *El espejo roto: percepciones mutuas México-Estados Unidos, 1968-1988,* comp. Guadalupe González. Mexico: Siglo XXI.

Aguilar Zinser, Adolfo. 1983. "México y la crisis guatemalteca." In *Centroamérica. Futuro y opciones,* eds. Olga Pellicer de Brody and Richard Fagen. Mexico: Fondo de Cultura Económica.

Aguilar, Zinser, Adolfo. 1986. "En torno a la seguridad nacional." *El desafío mexicano.* Mexico: Océano.

Anderson, Jack, and Dale Von Atta. 1987. "The Mexican Time Bomb." *Penthouse*, May.

Anderson, Jack, and Dale Von Atta. 1987a. "CIA: Disorder Could Overwhelm Mexico." *The Washington Post*, 5 June.

Applegate, Rex. 1985. "The Evil Empire Eyes the Big Enchilada." *Soldier of Fortune*, August.

Baer, Delal. 1987. "Mexico: Ambivalent Ally." *The Washington Quarterly* (Summer).

Baer, Delal. 1988. "Between Evolution and Revolution: Mexican Democracy." *The Washington Quarterly* (Summer).

Bagley, Bruce. 1981. "Mexico in the 1980s: A New Regional Power." *Current History,* November.

Benítez, Raúl, and Lilia Bermúdez. 1990. "La militarización centroamericana, reto a la seguridad nacional de México." In *La seguridad nacional mexicana,* eds. Sergio Aguayo and Carlos Payán. Mexico City: Claves Latinoamericanas.

Blachman, Morris J., William Leo Grande, and Kenneth E. Sharpe. 1986. *Confronting Revolution: Security Through Diplomacy in Central America.* New York: Pantheon Books.

Boils, Guillermo. 1985. "Los militares en México (1965-1985). *"Revista Mexicana de Sociología,* 47:(January-March).

Brown, Harold. 1983. *Thinking About National Security: Defense and Foreign Policy in a Dangerous World.* Boulder, Colo.: Westview Press.

Caballero, Alejandro. 1990. "Denuncia formal del PRD por los asesinatos de sus militantes." *La Jornada,* 26 January.

Cabrera Muñoz Ledo, Jesús. 1987. "La seguridad nacional de México y la pacificación de Centroamérica." *Revista Mexicana de Política Exterior,* 16:(July-September).

Cabrera Parra, José. 1983. "Terror y policía. Asunto de seguridad nacional." *Ultimas Noticias,* 17 January.

Camp, Roderic (comp.). 1986. *Mexico's Political Stability: The Next Five Years.* Boulder, Colo.: Westview Press.

Carmical, J.H. 1948. "Ready Oil Reserve for Navy Is Cited." *The New York Times,* 13 June, 1.

Carmical, J.H. 1949. "Prospect Revived for Oil in Mexico." *The New York Times,* 2 January, 1.

Castillo Costa, Miguel. 1990. "Los intereses nacionales de México frente a los de Estados Unidos: Teoría y práctica de las relaciones internacionales." Ph.D. Thesis, UNAM.

Central Intelligence Agency (CIA). 1951. Mexico, SR-18, 24 January.

Central Intelligence Agency (CIA). 1977. "The Forces for Change in Mexican Foreign Policy," June.

Clayton, Bruce D. 1980. *Life After Doomsday: A Survivalist Guide to Nuclear War and Other Major Disasters.* New York: The Dial Press.

Cochran, Thomas B., William M. Arkon, and Milton M. Hoenig. 1987. *Nuclear Weapons Data Book,* Vol. II, U.S. Nuclear Warhead Production. Cambridge, Mass.: Bollinger Publishing.

Colson, Harold. 1989. "National Security Affairs and Civil-Military Relations in Contemporary Mexico: A Bibliography." *Vance Bibliographies*. Monticello, Ill.

Cunningham, Alden M. 1984. "Mexico's National Security in the 1980s-1990s." In *The Modern Mexican Military: A Reassessment*, ed. David Ronfeldt. La Jolla: Center for U.S.-Mexican Studies.

Dalessandro, James. 1977-1978. "Where Are the Next Revolutions." *Military Electronics/Counter-measures*. December 1977-January 1978.

Deagle, Edwin A., Jr. 1981. "México y la política de seguridad nacional de los Estados Unidos." In *Las relaciones México-Estados Unidos*, eds. Carlos Tello and Clark Reynolds. Mexico: Fondo de Cultura Económica.

de la Madrid, Miguel. 1984. "México, nuevos desafíos." Translation of an article published in *Foreign Affairs* 63 (1) and in *La Jornada*, 28 September.

Department of the Air Force (DAF). 1955. "Outline Plan of Operations for Mexico." Memorandum. Washington, D.C., 9 September.

Department of the Army (DA). Plans and Operations Division General Staff. 1949. "Defense Plan for the Continental United States (DA-DPI-49)." Washington, D.C., 4 April.

Department of Defense (DOD). 1982. *Map of Major Military Installations*. Washington, D.C.: Directorate for Information, Operations and Reports, June.

Department of Defense (DOD). 1988. *Atlas/Data Abstract for the U.S. and Selected Areas*. Fiscal Year 1988. Washington, D.C.: Directorate for Information, Operations and Reports.

Department of State (DOS). 1951. "Policy Statement, Mexico." Washington, D.C., 1 October.

Department of State (DOS). 1952. "Latin America and U.S. Policy." Washington, D.C., 11 December.

Department of State (DOS). 1956. "Outline Plan of Operations for Mexico." Washington, D.C., 13 January.

Department of State (DOS). 1958. "Miscellaneous Items of Irritation in United States-Mexican Relations." Memorandum of conversation. Washington, D.C., 17 June.

Department of State (DOS). 1959. "Memorandum for the President. Visit to Acapulco, Mexico, February 19-20, 1959." Washington, D.C., 14 February.

Department of State (DOS). 1967. "Pershing Missile Overshot." Telegram from American Embassy Mexico to Secretary of State, Mexico, D.F., September.

Diario Oficial (DO). 1929. "Reglamento Interior de la Secretaría de Gobernación." 28 November.

Diario Oficial (DO). 1938. "Reglamento Interior de la Secretaría de Gobernación." 25 August.

Diario Oficial (DO). 1973. "Reglamento Interior de la Secretaría de Gobernación." 27 July.

Diario Oficial (DO). 1980. "Reglamento Interior y Reglamento de Escalafón de la Secretaría de Gobernación." 21 February.

Diario Oficial (DO). 1984. "Reglamento Interior de la Secretaría de Gobernación." 14 June.

Diario Oficial(DO). 1984 or 1985. "Reglamento Interior de la Secretaría de Gobernación." 14 June, 1984 and 21 August, 1985.

Diario Oficial (DO). 1988. "Acuerdo por el que se crea la Oficina de Coordinación de la Presidencia de la República." 7 December.

Diario Oficial (DO). 1989. "Reglamento Interior de la Secretaría de Gobernación." 13 February.

Domínguez, Jorge I. 1982. *U.S. Interests and Policies in the Caribbean and Central America*. Washington, D.C.: American Enterprise Institute.

Douglas, H. Eugene. 1985. "The United States and Mexico: Conflict and Comity." *Strategic Review* (Spring).

Dziedzic, Michael J. 1988. "The Mexican Challenge. Managing Change and Preserving a Strategic Relationship." Draft.

Erb, Guy F., and Cathryn Thorup. 1984. "U.S.-Mexican Relations: The Issues Ahead." *Development Paper 35*. Washington, D.C.: Overseas Development Council, November.

Fagen, Richard. 1979. "Mexican Petroleum and U.S. National Security." *International Security* 4(Summer).

Fauriol, Georges. 1986. "Mexico: In a Superpower's Shadow." In *Emerging Powers. Defense and Security in the Third World,* eds. Rodney W. Jones and Steven A. Hildreth. New York: Praeger.

Fauriol, Georges. 1988. *The Third Century: U.S. Latin America Policy Choices for the 1990s.* Washington, D.C.: The Center for Strategic and International Studies.

Federal Emergency Management Agency (FEMA). 1989. "Commercial Nuclear Power Plants." Washington, D.C., April.

Fradkin, Phillip L. 1989. *Fallout. An American Nuclear Tragedy.* Tucson, Ariz.: The University of Arizona Press.

Fuentes, Gloria. 1986. "El concepto de seguridad nacional." *El Sol de México,* 31 December.

Ganster, Paul, and Alan Sweedler. 1987. "U.S.-Mexican Border Region: Implications for U.S. Security." San Diego, Calif.: UCSD, April.

Gómez Ortega, Miguel Angel, Admiral. 1985. *La Secretaría de Marina y su influencia en el desarrollo del país y en la seguridad nacional.* Mexico: Secretaría de Marina.

Gómez Ortega, Miguel Angel, Admiral. 1988. Speech given during the breakfast offered on 7 October by the Secretaría de Marina Armada of Mexico in honor of Carlos Salinas de Gortari, president-elect of Mexico. Typed.

González, Guadalupe. 1986. "Estados Unidos y la seguridad nacional de México." Transcription of the internal seminar of the CLEE, 17 July.

González, Roberto. 1982. "Modernizar el ejército, garantía de seguridad: JLP." *Excélsior,* 5 January.

Granados Roldán, Otto. 1982. "¿Regreso a las armas?" *Nexos* 50 (February).

Green Walker, Phyllis. 1984. "National Security." In *Mexico. A Country Study,* ed. James D. Rudolph. Foreign Area Studies. Washington, D.C.: American University.

Gruson, Sidney. 1953. "Mexicans Vitiate `Wetback' Drive." *The New York Times,* 27 January, 32.

Gutiérrez Oropeza, Luis, General. 1988. *Díaz Ordaz. El hombre. El gobernante.* Mexico: Gustavo de Anda.

Hannon, Esther Wilson. 1984. "Mexico's Growing Problems Challenge U.S. Policy." *The Backgrounder,* 16 August. Washington, D.C., Heritage Foundation.

Hannon, Esther Wilson. 1986. "What the U.S. Should Do As Mexico Heads for Crisis." *The Backgrounder,* 17 July. Washington, D.C., Heritage Foundation.

Hannon, Esther Wilson. 1987. "Keys to Understanding Mexico: Challenges for the Ruling PRI." *The Backgrounder,* 7 April. Washington, D.C.: Heritage Foundation.

Harper's. 1987. "The CIA Sizes Up the Mexican Domino," May.

Heller, Claude. 1986. "La concepción de seguridad de Estados Unidos, traba a la determinación de AL." *La Jornada,* 26 February.

Hernández Haddad, Humberto. 1988. "Seguridad nacional en la frontera sur." *FENASE,* 4(13).

Herrera-Lasso, Luis. 1988. "Democracia y seguridad nacional." In *El reclamo democrático,* ed. Rolando Cordera, 7. Mexico: Siglo XXI.

Herrera-Lasso, Luis. 1989. "La condicionalidad geopolítica en la seguridad nacional de México." In *La seguridad nacional de México,* eds. Sergio Aguayo and Carlos Payán. Mexico: Claves Latinoamericanas.

Hinojosa, Oscar. 1982. "Cualquier régimen de gobierno, con apoyo popular, será respetado por el ejército." *Proceso,* 29 March.

Joint Intelligence Services (J.I.S.), 248/M. 1946. "Report by the Joint Intelligence Committee, Joint Basic War Plan-Mexico." Washington, D.C., 29 April.

Jordan, Amos, and William J. Taylor, Jr. 1984. *American National Security: Policy and Process.* Baltimore: The Johns Hopkins University Press.

Krock, Arthur. 1948. "The Vital Question of Mexican Oil." *The New York Times,* 30 December, 18.

Lassé, Oscar de. 1988. "Seguridad de la nación; doctrinas y estrategias." *El Financiero,* 27 October.

Lassé, Oscar de. 1989. "Seguridad nacional y seguridad interna en México." Transcription of the internal seminar of the CLEE, 7 December.

Latell, Brian. 1986. *Mexico at the Crossroads: The Many Crises of the Political System.* Palo Alto, Calif.: Hoover Institution.

Leighton, Marian. 1988. "Moscow's Courtship of Mexico." *The Backgrounder,* 5 July. Washington, D.C.: The Heritage Foundation.

Levy, Daniel C. 1986. "The Implications of Central American Conflicts for Mexican Politics." In *Mexico's Political Stability: The Next Five Years,* comp. Roderic Camp. Boulder, Colo.: Westview.

Linn, Tom, Major, U.S. Marine Corps. 1984. "Mexico and the United States: Recognition at Last." *Defense and Foreign Affairs,* December.

Méndez Villareal, Sofía. 1990. "La seguridad económica nacional de México." In *La seguridad nacional mexicana,* eds. Sergio Aguayo and Carlos Payán. Mexico City: Claves Latinoamericanas.

Menges, Constantine C. 1988. *Inside the National Security Council.* New York: Simon and Schuster.

Meyer, Lorenzo. 1989. "Seguridad nacional, seguridad del Estado y seguridad del gobierno: perspectiva política." Transcription of the internal seminar of the CLEE, 26 October.

Miller, Richard L. 1986. *Under the Cloud. The Decades of Nuclear Testing.* New York: The Free Press.

Miramontes, Octavio. 1989. "Consecuencias para México de una guerra nuclear: el pulso electromagnético." DI-9. Mexico: El Colegio de México, Programa sobre Ciencia, Tecnología y Desarrollo, March.

Miramontes, Octavio. 1989a. "Consecuencias para México de una guerra nuclear: la precipitación radiactiva." DI-10. Mexico: El Colegio de México, Programa sobre ciencia, Tecnología y Desarrollo, May.

Moffett, Matt. 1989. "Mexico Arrests Powerful Chief of Oil Union." *Wall Street Journal,* 11 January.

Moorer, Thomas H., and Georges A. Fauriol. 1984. *Caribbean Basin Security.* New York: Praeger.

Nadal Egea, Alejandro. 1989. "Trayectorias de misiles balísticos intercontinentales. Implicaciones para los vecinos de las superpotencias." *Foro Internacional* XXX 1:(July-September).

National Security Council, NSC-56. 1949. A Report to the National Security Council: "U.S. Policy Concerning Military Collaboration under the Inter-American Treaty of Reciprocal Assistance." Washington, D.C., 31 August.

National Security Council, NSC-144/1. 1953. A Report to the National Security Council. "United States Objectives and Courses of Action with Respect to Latin America." Washington, D.C., 18 March.

National Security Council. 1964. "Memorandum for the President." McGeorge Bundy to President Lyndon B. Johnson. Washington, D.C., 25 March.

Neuchterlein, Donald E. 1985. *America Overcommitted: U.S. National Interests in the 1980s.* Knoxville: Kentucky University Press.

Partido Revolucionario Institucional (PRI). 1988. *Documentos básicos.* Mexico: PRI.

Pellicer de Brody, Olga. 1981. "La seguridad nacional de México: Preocupaciones nuevas y nociones tradicionales." In *Las relaciones México-Estados Unidos*, eds. Carlos Tello and Clark Reynolds. Mexico: Fondo de Cultura Económica.

Pellicer de Brody, Olga. 1982. "Política hacia Centroamérica e interés nacional en México." In *Centroamérica, crisis y política internacional.* Mexico: Siglo XXI.

Plan Global de Desarrollo, 1980-1982(PGD). 1980. Mexico: Secretaría de Programación y Presupuesto.

Plan Nacional de Desarrollo, 1983-1988(PND). 1983. Mexico: Secretaría de Programación y Presupuesto.

Plan Nacional de Desarrollo, 1989-1994 (PND). 1989. *La Jornada,* 1 June.

Ramírez, Aníbal. 1990. "Razón y diálogo, vía para solucionar conflictos: Riviello." *La Jornada,* 10 February.

Reyes Estrada, Jorge. 1989. "Narcotráfico, grave peligro para la seguridad nacional: SDN y PGR." *Unomásuno,* 27 June.

Ronfeldt, David. 1983. *Geopolitics, Security, and U.S. Strategy in the Caribbean Basin.* Santa Monica, Calif.: The Rand Corporation.

Ronfeldt, David. 1984. "The Modern Mexican Military: An Overview." In *The Modern Mexican Military*, ed. David Ronfeldt. Santa Monica, Calif.: The Rand Corporation.

Ronfeldt, David, Richard Nehring, and Arturo Gándara. 1980. *Mexico's Petroleum and U.S. Policy: Implications for the 1980s.* Santa Monica, Calif.: The Rand Corporation.

Russo, Daniel L., Jr., Lieutenant Colonel, U.S. Air Force. 1985. *Conflict on Mexico's Other Border. A Challenge for United States Political and Military Relations.* Miami, Fla.: University of Miami, Graduate School of International Studies.

Salaverry, Jorge. 1988. "Evolution of Mexican Foreign Policy." *The Backgrounder*, 11 March. Washington, D.C.: The Heritage Foundation.

Salinas de Gortari, Carlos. 1987. "El narcotráfico: el reto más grande a la seguridad nacional." *La Jornada*, 13 November.

Salinas de Gortari, Carlos. 1988. "Discurso de toma de posesión." *La Jornada*, 2 December.

Salinas de Gortari, Carlos. 1989. *Primer Informe de Gobierno.* Mexico: Presidencia de la República, 1 November.

Sanders, Sol. 1987. "Crisis Looms Down Mexico Way." *Pacific Defense Reporter*, April.

Sandoval, Juan M., Francisco J. Guerrero, and M. Eugenia del Valle. 1985. "La política de seguridad nacional y las fronteras de México." *Nueva Antropología* VII(16).

Santos Caamal, Mario, Rear Admiral C.G. 1985. "México frente a Centroamérica. Un concepto estratégico nacional en acción." *Revista del Centro de Estudios Superiores Navales*, VII(51): (August).

Sarmiento, José E. 1986. "La seguridad nacional en el marco jurídico mexicano." Transcription of the internal seminar of the CLEE, 18 September.

Saxe-Fernández, John. 1984. *De la seguridad nacional.* Mexico: Grijalbo.

Secretaría de la Defensa Nacional (SDN). 1986. Ley Orgánica del Ejército y Fuerza Aérea Mexicanos. Mexico: SDN, Col. Legislación Militar V, 12th ed., May.

Sepúlveda, Bernardo. 1983. Speech given during the celebration of Benito Juárez's birthday. Guelatao de Juárez, Oaxaca, 21 March. Typed.

Sepúlveda, Isidro. 1986. "Lineamientos para el estudio de la seguridad nacional en México." Transcription of the internal seminar of the CLEE, 11 September.

Sereseres, Caesar. 1984. "The Mexican Military Looks South." In *The Modern Mexican Military*, ed. David Ronfeldt. Santa Monica, Calif.: The Rand Corporation.

Schoultz, Lars. 1987. *National Security and United States Policy toward Latin America.* New Jersey: Princeton University Press.

Smith, Peter. 1986. "Leadership and Change, Intellectuals and Technocrats in Mexico." In *Mexico's Political Stability: The Next Five Years*, comp. Roderic Camp. Boulder, Colo.: Westview Press.

Solana, Fernando. 1989. "Puede afectar a la seguridad de México la guerra salvadoreña." *La Jornada*, 21 December.

Special to *The New York Times.* 1951. "Accord is reached on Migrant Labor." *The New York Times*, 21 June, 17.

Special to *The New York Times.* 1954. "Bill Authorizing the Admission of Migrant Labor Goes to White House." *The New York Times*, 4 March, 18.

Thorup, Cathryn, and Robert L. Ayres. 1982. "Central America: The Challenge to United States and Mexican Foreign Policy." U.S.-Mexico Project Series, 8. Washington, D.C.: Overseas Development Council, July.

Vega, Gerardo C.R., General. 1988. *Seguridad nacional. Concepto, organización, método.* Unpublished.

Vizcaíno, Roberto. 1980. "*La seguridad del país, fin primordial del Estado.*" *Proceso*, 22 September.

Wager, Stephen, J. 1989. "A Repoliticized Military?" *Hemisphere*(Winter).

War Department General Staff. 1942. "War Department's Objectives Respect to Mexico." Memorandum. Washington, D.C., 5 February.

White, Francis, Ambassador. 1955. "Letter to the President." Mexico, D.F., 9 August.

White House (WH) Memo. 1953. "Background Information for Meeting with President of Mexico." Washington, D.C., 19 October.

Williams, Edward J. 1984. "The Mexican Military and Foreign Policy: The Evolution of Influence." In *The Modern, Mexican Military*, ed. David Ronfeldt. Santa Monica, Calif.: The Rand Corporation.

Williams, Edward J. 1986. "The Evolution of the Mexican Military and Its Implications for Civil-Military Relations." In *Mexico's Political Stability: The Next Five Years*, ed. Roderic Camp. Boulder, Colo.: Westview Press.

Wilson, Michael G. 1989. "The Security Component of U.S.-Mexico Relations." *The Backgrounder*, 26 January. Washington, D.C.: The Heritage Foundation.

Wohl, Paul. 1950. "New Railroad Opens Mexican Wonders." *The New York Times*, 11 June, 35.

Zárate, Alfonso. 1986. "Proyecto nacional del régimen actual en materia política." Internal Seminar, CLEE.

Revolutionary Nationalism and National Security in Mexico

Roger Bartra

Colonel Alden M. Cunningham — a Latin American specialist from the U.S. Army War College — believes that up until the end of the 1970s, Mexico had no need for a fully integrated national security policy (Ronfeldt 1984). For about a quarter of a century, problems of national security did not seem to be important to anybody, not even to the CIA operative stationed in Mexico, judging from Philip Agee's description. Until 1967, CIA operations in Mexico had a modest budget of $5.5 million to be spent on a station that, according to Agee, had the reputation of having many bones and little muscle, and where the bored and gray operations of the agents were limited to maintaining contacts with Mexican officials and indifferently watching over the Soviets, the Cubans, and the Communists. According to Agee, the insipid character of the intelligence operations resulted from the fact that "Mexican security services are so effective in eradicating the extreme left that we don't have to worry about it. If the government was less effective, we would, of course, have to promote their repression" (Agee 1975).

After resolution of an imbroglio concerning an alcoholic agent who was involved in both pornographic activities with a female employee of the U.S. embassy and a dubious relationship with a Polish spy, the most passionate CIA operation in Mexico took place in 1966,

This essay is based on a study conducted at La Jolla, California, between September 1987 and February 1988, while I was a visiting researcher at the Center for U.S.-Mexican Studies, University of California, San Diego. I would like to thank Sergio Aguayo for his stimulating commentary and analysis, without which my reflections on national security would not have been possible; I would also like to thank Paul Haber for his acute observations.

143

when a coded telegram was sent to Washington with the information that the government secretary, Luis Echeverría, had been selected as the *tapado* and therefore, as the future president of Mexico (Agee 1975). During this time, Karl Schmitt, an obscure former analyst for the U.S. Department of State, published a book about communism in Mexico, whose subtitle was rather revealing: "A Study in Political Frustration" (Schmitt 1965). U.S. national security — and by extension Mexico's — did not appear to be threatened by Mexican communism. Even from this aggressive and reactionary perspective of national security, nothing clouded the political horizon. It was insistently repeated that Mexican national security was protected by a hard nationalist crust that immunized the country against communist contamination. Even though the official revolutionary nationalism occasionally adopted anti-imperialist hues, intelligence operative specialists agreed that a political system with many security guarantees for the United States was more significant.

Today, the situation has obviously changed. Three principal factors have disturbed the tranquility of national security: the war in Central America, the economic crisis, and the growing opposition to the political system. Either directly or indirectly, these three factors have changed the relationship between nationalism and the political system, as Mexico has a more active role in international politics and the Partido Revolucionario Institucional (PRI) government has less legitimacy.

Many observers now ask themselves whether the possibility of a breakdown in Mexican nationalism presents a threat to national security. In the same manner that nationalism has been a keystone to the institution building that shelters the governments of the Mexican revolution, it is thought that its erosion and weakening can occasion serious difficulties not only for national sovereignty but also for continental security. The purpose of this essay is to show that a crisis in nationalism should not be looked upon as a threat to national security, unless attempts at pluralist democracy and representation — with its peculiarities of alternating governments — are considered to be against the interests of the geopolitical bloc headed by the United States. The tendency to view nationalism as a stabilizing instrument for the state, constructed with the goal of resolving social conflicts and as a means of domination, can be linked to its association with national security.

The obvious fact that nationalism acts on innumerable occasions as a legitimizing mechanism of modern political systems adds an aura of conviction to this idea. Nevertheless, it is necessary to introduce doubt: Why is it that a functional relationship has to produce an instrumental explanation? The doubt is pertinent if we wish to understand the profound nature of the mechanisms of domination and legitimacy that uphold the modern state. Mexican nationalism highlights the structures of power that gradually consolidated after the 1910 revolution, and it presents a good example for the illustration of a common myth. A great many of the "specialists" on the theme have arrived at the conclusion that Mexican nationalism is "a means to resolve conflict between groups," "a useful device in social control,"[1] or a project of the revolutionary state to integrate the interests of all classes under capitalist development (Monsivais 1978). It would appear that we are facing a problem of political technique in which the basic formulas for national security are found in order to create the so-called "civic culture." In other words, one develops a form of participation in which a congruence between culture and political structure is achieved (Almond and Verba 1965). But really, Mexican nationalism, as consolidated after the revolution, fulfills a highly important regulatory function in relation to the consensus upon which the state is based. It is impossible to understand the stable succession of post-revolutionary governments without the study of revolutionary nationalism.

In this manner, nationalism takes on an important ideological function insofar as it consolidates itself as a political tendency that establishes a structural relationship between the nature of the culture and the peculiarities of the political system. Nevertheless, the mere analysis of this ideological function can easily lead us to see the relationship between culture and politics as unilateral and, in the last analysis, instrumental. Nationalism (like other compound ideas) would only be a mediating bridge between society and politics, between culture and institutions of coercion. From this narrow perspective, a crisis in nationalism could be looked upon as a threat to national security insofar as the government depends on it for stability.

The problem is very complex, as the nationalist myth inserts itself in Mexican society in a paradoxical manner. Nationalism has undoubtedly contributed to the legitimation of the political system, but it established itself in a mythic form hardly coherent with the development of Western capitalism typical of the twentieth century. In other words, the nationalist myth is efficient in its legitimation of the PRI's power but inefficient in legitimizing the rationality of modern industrial development. Or, it can be said that the myth corresponded to the peculiarities of a capitalism that was behind the times, corrupt, and dependent. Today, the nationalist revolutionary myth is becoming a dysfunctional element, but it is also necessary to point out that this "dysfunctionality" comes in large part from its "popular" and "anti-capitalist" origins. The myth of nationalism shelters a large measure of bitterness, protest, revolt, and resistance. We now face a confused situation in which there coexist functional relations, expressions of class interest, and elements out of sync that reveal a dysfunctional conjuncture.

It is proper to point out that I understand nationalism as a body of political theory that expresses the hegemonic vocation of the dominant class under the form of a multi-class alliance founded in the supposed originality, subjectively reconstructed, of national peculiarities and their identification with the character of the state. It is, therefore, clear that nationalism is not a permanent phenomenon of society; it appears in many forms, but under specific historical conditions. In Mexico, the specificity of nationalist politics, with its variegated sociocultural base, has resulted in a democracy tinged with stinginess so as not to choke on the original underdevelopment, a unionism of "horsemen" protected by the shadow of the state, a destruction of indigenous cultures justified as a sacrifice that encourages the official state culture, and an intellectual life which, in order to be "cultured," sees itself obliged to beg the favor of the strong (Bartra 1977).

In order to analyze the relationship between nationalism and national security, it is necessary to remove the idea that the nation cannot exist without nationalism. Although tightly linked, these are realities that operate on different planes: One is the territorialization of political power based in the nation-state, and the other is the form in which one legitimizes the constitution of a national space. It is true that nationalism virtually accompanies the creation of a modern state; the subsequent modernization, as the expansion of urban industrial capitalism is usually called, is a process that includes the expansion of nationalist currents. One can mistakenly fall into the temptation of associating nationalism with conditions of backwardness and under-development. Studious Americans who, for obvious geopolitical reasons, have enormously interested themselves in Mexican national-ism, frequently leave the impression that Mexico is a country domi-nated by strong national passions, in contrast to the United States, which is conditioned by a cold materialist culture that revolves around a world based on interests. These observations have contributed to the strengthening of the false idea that nationalism is an inherent passion of the Mexican people; furthermore, they have contributed to hiding a fact that must not escape analysis: The United States is today (and has been for decades) one of the most fertile territories for the growth of nationalism; in reality, this country harbors a nationalism that is deeper and more aggressive than that of Mexico. It is impossible to explain Mexican nationalism without understanding its U.S. counterpart, in which the exaltation of national values is clearly and intimately associated with so-called national security and modernization (Kohn 1957; Van Alstyne 1970; Pullen 1971).

Technocracy vs. Nationalism

During the 1980s, Mexico witnessed the ascendance of the political technocracy.[2] This fact has been pointed out by many observers of Mexican politics, but its consequences in the area of political culture have been little examined, notwithstanding the fact that the antagonism between the traditional nationalist discourse and the technocratic style of government would appear quite evident. The problem requires closer scrutiny.

Revolutionary nationalism is minimally defined by four large series of attitudes and postulates.

1. A mistrust of the superpowers (particularly the United States), accompanied by varying amounts of xenophobia and anti-imperialism.

2. An affirmation of nationalization as a way to limit the ownership of land, control natural resources, and avoid the concentration of capital — as evidenced in the *ejido* "communal lands" system, the state control of petroleum, and the legal limitations placed on foreign investment.

3. A strongly interventionist state, whose exceptional strength is legitimized by its revolutionary origin and by its broad popular base (the "institutionalized revolution"). The security of the state is subsumed in national sovereignty that resides — according to the constitution — in the people.

4. A premium on Mexican identity as an inexhaustible source of political energy.

Of course, the political technocracy in its discourse has not renounced the postulates of revolutionary nationalism.[3] But if the curtains of demagogy are opened and one peeks in on what the technocracy is doing, it is easy to see that revolutionary nationalism is no longer its source of inspiration. The technocracy not only does not distrust the United States but even became an active collaborator with so-called "Reaganomics"; really, the official Mexican economic policy — in its whims, as well as in its technocratism — cannot be understood without knowing the most recent trends in the University of Chicago or Harvard. In the Mexican technocracy, there remain only vestiges of the former xenophobia: Nothing causes one of the freshly minted Mexican officials more horror than an anti-imperialist attitude, which is now considered an antiquated weapon that should be locked up in a showcase at the museum of the revolution. The contradictions that periodically bring the government of the United States into conflict with Mexico are increasingly managed within a logic of interests that revolves around the U.S. economy and that reveals itself as a pragmatic movement toward a North American common market.

It is also evident that the technocracy, with hopes of exiting the crisis, is bent on "rationalizing" the limits the system imposes on property ownership, control of natural resources, and the concentration and circulation of capital. Because of this, the technocracy has endeavored (with uneven success) to displace the traditional nationalist policy of three key sectors of the economy: agriculture, petroleum, and foreign investment. This process has attempted to bring down the three great bastions of revolutionary nationalism — agrarianism, union-based populism, and protectionism — so as to impose a "modern" perspective on economic policy.

This confrontation has seriously eroded the popular base of the PRI regime and has produced serious fractures and dislocations in the unity of the "revolutionary family," the most serious of which gave birth to the movement headed by Cuauhtémoc Cárdenas that seeks to recover the nationalist values that the PRI is abandoning. Nevertheless, the "modern policy" has not managed to extract Mexico from its acute economic crisis. Attacks against agrarianism, union populism, and protectionism are rather more than ideological aggression; they form part of a general tendency that has eroded mass support for the state and has been eroding the Mexican mechanisms of agrarian political bosses, union strongmen, and protectionist corruption. Even though it is evident that agrarianism cannot be reduced to a political boss, unions to *charro* leadership, nor protectionism to bribery or favoritism, there is no doubt that without these odious "national" peculiarities, the Mexican political system would not be able to work. The tragic paradox of the system lies in the dual and ambiguous character of the mechanisms that produce it: At the same time that they guarantee popular support, they are the source of repression, violence, corruption, and fraud. It seems difficult, if not impossible, to correct these "deficiencies" without affecting the communication channels between the government and the popular organizations that support it. At the same time, disquieting tendencies are surfacing that subordinate the notion of national sovereignty to the supposedly superior calculations of security. Mexican technocracy has not yet developed a precise political position regarding the relationship between the state and national security.[4]

Modernization and Democratization

Faced with the economic crisis that exploded in 1982 and the symptoms of a latent political crisis, the leaders of the system — especially the technocrats — proposed a "new policy" that can be summed up in a single word: modernization. It is suggested that certain changes need to take place within the political system in order to put it in tune with the new winds of change that are blowing around the world. This has to do with an implicit recognition that power structures are lagging behind the requirements of modern society; consequently, it is said that it is necessary to modernize these structures in order for the state apparatus to return to its traditional levels of efficiency and effectiveness. The technocratic origins of modernization policy are obvious, even if only because of the implicit message: The system is no longer efficient, given the relative dysfunctionality of its relationship with civil society. In reality, modernization is a proposal for "refunctionalization."

On the other hand, the new winds of change that are stirring Mexican civil society can be summarized in one word: democratization. Social forces with an appetite for democratic processes are growing every day. The important thing is that this democratization of the civic culture is occurring in diverse, and even antagonistic, sectors of society: Today we see that the democratic ideal spans the entire political spectrum, from the extreme right to the extreme left. Even the official party is feeling the reverberating tensions and has suffered an important schism: Its "democratizing" current split in order to support the independent candidacy of Cuauhtémoc Cárdenas in the 1988 presidential elections, in which he obtained a high percentage of the votes (officially 32 percent, but surely much higher).

Political conflicts are now emerging due to the confluence of two problems. The first is the growing difficulty within the political elite in trying to maintain cohesion in the government apparatus during periods of electoral transition. The second problem is the growing difficulty of the governing group not so much to stop the economic crisis but rather to administer it with a minimal efficiency. The 1982 political crisis that provoked the spectacular nationalization of banks bluntly revealed the advanced loss of cohesion (or "harmony," to use the technocrats' word of choice) within the governing elite. The most visible aspect of the crisis is the generalized demand for a representative democracy: The tragic fact that the extension of "social democracy" (the elimination of private bankers) occurred in such a despotic manner is one more symptom that proves the government's incapacity to harmonize social democracy with political democracy. The 1982 crisis opened a period characterized by the rapid extension of a new phenomenon: the need for a democratic exit, surfacing in all the strata of political society and in ever-broader sections of civil society. The precariousness of democratic mechanisms had become an obstacle for various currents and tendencies that operate within the government; the PRI manner of authoritarian government is no longer operative nor efficient for the reproduction of the mediating and legitimating functions of the state.

Nevertheless, the conflicts are also seen and lived from a technocratic perspective that intends to check the sclerosis of the mediating channels that link the state with society. If the traditional PRI methods are inefficient, then it is right to "modernize them," that is to say, to find a new technique of government that allows the unblocking of the processes of control and removes from the political scene the leftovers of a useless past. Modern technique lends more importance to administration, efficiency, and economic measures than to political pacts between factions, the manipulation of leaders, and the distribution of areas of influence.[5]

The critical tensions that today characterize the Mexican state are expressed at the level of political culture in the apparent contradiction between "modernization" and "democratization." This situation has been able to develop due to important changes that the political elite has undergone in the last ten years. The governing group that developed in the post-Cárdenas years was essentially formed by a peculiar confluence of interests between the dominant economic classes and the bureaucracy which holds power in the name of the masses of peasants, laborers, and workers. More precisely, the political elite was composed of three groups: the technocracy, the "new" business class, and the bankers. Three political and economic groups exercised, in a certain way, the representation of a diverse and complex ensemble of allied interests under the "government of the revolution." The technocrats formed the group that headed and represented other parts of the bureaucracy (unions, agrarianism, "popular" organizations). The new nationalist businessmen (especially the bourgeoisie of central Mexico that emerged thanks to protectionism) assigned themselves the role of directors of the entire business class (thanks to their solid channels of influence in the governments of Mexico City and the state of Mexico, the Secretariat of Commerce and Industrial Development, and so on). Finally, there were the bankers who had positioned themselves in a powerful and dangerous balancing act between the right-wing business groups to the North (the "Monterrey Group" and others) and the political bureaucracy (Saldívar 1980).

Nevertheless, in 1982 it became obvious that along with the economic crisis, new factors had appeared. In the first place, there was a deepening of the division between the technocrats and the rest of the political bureaucracy (the management of revenues from petroleum had much to do with this, as well as the poor government response to the economic crisis). At the same time, political differences between the "nationalist" sectors and the "right-wing" business sector had diminished (as a result of the abandonment of a populist position of the no longer "new" business sector). Nevertheless, the elimination of private bankers as a group in 1982 generated an overall distrust of the political bureaucracy on the part of the business sector. At the heart of the state apparatus, there was a weakening of both the PRI's agricultural sector and its network of traditional *caciques* in the provinces, accompanied by a strengthening of the bourgeoisie and the regional middle classes. Furthermore, there was a relative strengthening of the union bureaucracy, accompanied by an increase in the splits that separated different groups and currents bidding for power. It is also important to underscore the enormous importance of the new popular urban movements that developed as a result of the accelerated decomposition of the traditional urban lifestyle, creating a critical fabric of new democracy in the cities; this was dramatically and spectacularly proven in Mexico City after the devastating earthquake of 1985.

Due to these factors (and many others not mentioned here), recent years have seen an extraordinary political strengthening of the technocrats; but at the same time, a type of vacuum has arisen with regard to the new power nucleus, since the old agreements that allied the diverse political factions have become worn or are no longer respected. The hegemonic technocratic nucleus has had to propose a restoration of the ensemble of agreements, but pressure groups want a reformulation of political alliances, as opposed to a mere restoration of agreements. Thus, many in the business sector distrust any restoration of previous alliances with the government; they want to see substantial changes, and some are even wagering on an alternative that is totally different from the current system. Paradoxically, the union bureaucracy is, perhaps, the faction that houses the most conservative elements. This is expressed in their wish to renegotiate on the basis of traditional arrangements and in their distrust of all democratizing changes within the structure of the system; they poorly tolerate the technocratic politics of austerity that has caused the workers' quality of life to deteriorate.

In order to complete the panorama of crisis, it is necessary to emphasize that two great powers — one material, one spiritual — have initiated a decisive turn in relations with the Mexican state: the U.S. government and the Catholic Church. The Reagan administration manifested a certain distrust of the stability of the Mexican state (which, in turn, contributed to its destabilization), and the ecclesiastical hierarchy began to tire of the old rules of the game that have been in place since 1940 and have marginalized it from politics. In sum, we have a bourgeoisie that is less "Bonapartist," a more unsociable middle class, a broken workers' movement, a less complacent U.S. government, and a less "Caesarist" church. All of this is reflected in electoral tendencies, in which the strengthening of the opposition is observed (mostly from the right).

This is, in broad terms, the context within which the Mexican technocracy proposed a modernization project to the country, a project of pacts and alliances to rectify the imperfections suffered by the political apparatus, in order to avoid foreseeable failure and to confront the tormenting winds that would not cease. It is a modernization project directed at avoiding, or at least manipulating, the spirit of democratization that looms as a threat to the enormous privileges accumulated by the hegemonic political bureaucracy.

On various fronts, the complexity of tensions stirs a summoning of nationalism, symbol of a variegated collection of pacts that have maintained the government of the Mexican revolution for almost half a century. From this viewpoint, it is worthwhile to pose this question: Is the nationalist political culture able today to perform the legitimizing function that the system appears to demand? A part of the political bureaucracy is aware of the complexity and the enormous difficulties that arise in the attempt to renew Mexican nationalism under the critical conditions through which the country is passing. It realizes that Mexican nationalism contains ingredients that are no longer acceptable to large and significant sectors of society, and it sees in nationalism the stamp of a period of time that must be superseded.

Revolutionary nationalism clashes as much with the so-called modernization process as it does with representative democracy; its fundamental presuppositions do not adapt well to the indispensable competition that would be introduced by a clean and impartial electoral system or to the criterion of efficiency in political decision making and the management of public finances. Nationalism is so intimately associated with the corrupt authoritarian system of the dominant official party that it is difficult to hide the contradictions between the paths to exit the crisis and the old hegemonic political culture. Setting aside these contradictions and incongruities, the challenge facing the dominant bureaucracy is the modernization of nationalism. A similar challenge also confronts the neo-Cardenist opposition group, to be sure. It is obvious that if its revolutionary nationalist ingredients are not diluted in the search for an alternative democracy, the movement that has crystallized in the Democratic Revolutionary Party (PRD) will be seen as enmeshed in the same difficulties as the PRI party belonging to Salinas de Gortari.

National Security and Regional Powers

Revolutionary nationalism also faces other dangers. One of these is found in the growing strength of regional systems of power. In this we can observe another of the effects of so-called modernization, which has not only increased the yearning for efficiency on the part of the political bureaucracy but has also propelled the economic and political development of various regional centers of power. The geopolitical map of the Republic is rapidly changing in such a way that transformations in the regional power structure considerably affect the problems of defining national security. International borders have become more complex, and corporate powers have managed to obtain firm regional footholds.

Since nationalism goes hand in hand with centralism, it is obvious that any change in the correlation of forces that increases the strength of the provinces affects the very principles that undergird nationalism. The new situation also directly threatens electoral fraud, whose existence guarantees the high percentages that are assigned to the official party during voting time. This "fringe of fraud" is formed by extensive rural areas that are controlled by small and medium-sized regional power centers; it is a question of places where the opposition finds itself totally excluded and where nobody exercises the least vigilance over electoral procedures.

In this way, the changes in the relations between the center and the provinces not only affect the traditional forms of political culture but also contribute to the periodic crises that PRI government structures suffer in diverse places. Even though they are not the only ones, political conflicts in Chihuahua, Baja California, and Michoacán are among the most spectacular and best prove that a new period is fast approaching in which the operation of a centralized authoritarian system is fraught with difficulties (Aziz 1987).

Three factors should be pointed out as having contributed to this new situation. In the first place, the last twenty years have seen a slow but inexorable process of weakening of the traditional forms of rural power, which manifested itself first after the Calles administration and most notably after Cárdenas. These mediation structures — in which *caciquismo* (or the informal leadership of a local boss) plays a key role — established themselves as a strong political structure knitted into a web comprised of institutions for agrarian reform, peasant organizations, and agricultural communities. I have written extensively on the subject (Bartra 1974 and 1982), in order to show the manner in which the processes of political mediation in the country have been changing to the point that the structure of official power is enormously weakened in certain rural zones, while in many others the systems of power are found in the hands of a new political class of functionaries and technocrats that has replaced the old guard of *caciques*.

This phenomenon leads to the second factor that is changing the political panorama in the provinces: the creation of new regional powers, or the expansion of some of those already in existence, under the rubric of economic-technical-administrative conglomerates linked to petroleum, the more prosperous regions of irrigation, the *maquiladora* industry, the large centers of electrical energy, other large businesses (such as steel mills and petrochemicals), and the tourist centers.

These processes have generated an expansion of dense bureaucracies and regional technocracies that have invaded the pores of quiet rural life. Perhaps the most dramatic case is that of petroleum production, whose boom has permanently changed living conditions in several of the coastal areas of the Gulf. Along with petroleum came highways, oil pipelines, engineers, labor union corruption, pollution, and waves of businessmen. In a less spectacular manner, similar processes have occurred in other areas of the provinces.

All of this has taken place within the framework of the third factor I wish to mention: the extraordinary strengthening — especially during the latter part of the 1960s and the beginning of the 1970s — of the provincial bourgeoisie, not only that of Monterrey, but principally that of a multitude of small and medium-sized cities linked to the economic-technical-administrative conglomerates to which I have referred. The economic bonanza prior to the crisis that erupted in 1982 contributed to the rapid reproduction of the business class of the entire country, as well as the middle classes that usually gravitate around it.

These three factors — along with some others not mentioned — have contributed to the strengthening of regional power systems, resulting in very interesting paradoxical effects. One of these is what Luis González calls *matriotismo*, whose meaning and resonances I now propose to discuss (González 1987). It is understandable that the strengthening of regional power systems causes emerging social groups in the provinces to look around their environment in order to seek a means by which to confront the authoritarianism of the central powers. What do they find in their search? They find the hundreds of *matrias*. According to Luis González, "half of the Mexicans insert themselves in mini-societies in villages, municipalities, parishes, *patrias chicas* [small fatherlands] or *matrias*" (González 1987). One is speaking here of two thousand municipalities of rustic and semi-rustic dimensions where people base their livelihoods on agriculture, livestock, and handicrafts, where there frequently exists a *cacique* and a certain Catholic conservatism that, without quarreling with the desire for change, seeks to conserve the customs of the place. Luis González movingly exalts the values of *matriotismo*, which directly confronts the nationalism or patriotism of the leaders of the Mexican state. And it is the Mexican state that "frequently exercises aggressive actions against *matriotismo* or the sensibilities of *the patria chica*, love for an ancestral birthplace, and the desires of two thousand municipal minorities" (González 1987).

The conflict between urban authoritarian patriotism and conservative rural *matriotismo* is better captured as a part of cultural imaginings than as a contradiction of the political system. Of course, the opposition between rural life and the large cities expresses itself in thousands of ways and possesses powerful influence over political styles. But this does not hide the fundamental fact: One of the principal supports of the Mexican political system is precisely the existence of the two thousand municipalities on the matriarchal margins. Luis González himself describes it this way: "The *cacique* is a powerful and autocratic person in the *matria* or local community...and counts on the support of the nation's authorities, who are fearful of democracy. Besides the *cacique*, the republic's towns have a municipal government. The majority of the *matrias* rely on a group of councilmen. According to law, they are freely elected by the citizens of the municipality; in reality, they are assigned by the supreme government in connivance with the *cacique* of each *matria*. In return, the *caciques* team together with local forces: the shopkeepers and other wealthy people, the municipal president, the kibitzer, the doctor, the lawyer, and the fixer (González 1987).

This moving caricature, which reminds us of the rural world described by Balzac, corresponds with reality: Despite all the oppositions or different levels, there exists a relation between municipal *matriotismo* and centralized patriotism. In no way does it have anything to do with a violent and proud imposition of authoritarian patriotism over clumsy, ingenuous, rustic, and folkloric inhabitants of the *matria* living hunched over in their rural niches. Mexican authoritarianism, shrouded in patriotism and nationalism, has deep historical roots. Authoritarian centralism can exist, in great part, because of the presence of the *matrias*; furthermore, these two thousand municipalities are, broadly speaking, the same type that compose what can be called the "fringe of fraud," that enormous area that supports the statistical alchemy needed to invent a crushing electoral majority. The so-called "patriotic fraud" finds its natural base in the "matriotic" fringe.

It must be noted that this situation has begun to change, which helps to explain why diverse conservative sectors are seeking to find antidotes to the patriotism of the central government within the "matriotic" fringe. What Luis González expresses with his exaltation of *matriotismo* are the profound changes that have occurred in the Mexican provinces, whose most evident symptom is the growth and multiplication of new power centers. These centers have begun to dispute the central government's hegemony over the rural fringes, in which traditional ties between the *cacique*, his community, and state powers have begun to weaken.

These tendencies demonstrate something more than the difficulties of authoritarian centralism in trying to maintain itself. We also find a serious threat to nationalist hegemony, a threat that takes the form of the renovation of a never totally extinguished regionalism that Luis González tenderly baptizes as *matriotismo*. This is not a resurgence of antiquated centrifugal and *caudillista* tendencies but rather the fruit of the modernization of broad rural areas — with its corresponding frustrations — produced in part by the hundreds of thousands of Mexicans who have traveled and worked in the United States. *Matriotismo* is a new conservatism that looks for its *raison d'être* more in life's moral and religious values and the world of small cities and towns than in "great national problems." It is a post-modern conservatism that has lost faith in progress and seeks tranquility; it is a conservatism similar to that found in small cities and the suburban areas of the Midwest and Southwest of the United States, which is not based on the antiquated conservative impetus of military men like Almazán or the synarchic movements. The PAN, especially in Northern Mexico, captures a great part of this regionalist conservative spirit.

Nevertheless, *matriotismo* is still, to a considerable degree, a silent bastion of the official party and one of the main supports of the currents within the government that oppose the technocrats in the name of traditional revolutionary politics.

The Insecurity of Fraud

It is usually thought that the vast masses of Mexicans who abstain from voting comprise a type of silent support system for the PRI government. From this, one would presume that electoral fraud merely fills the ballot boxes for all of those who abstained, and who, had they voted, would invariably have supported the PRI. This rationale seeks to give a vestige of legitimacy to electoral fraud, with the assumption that abstentionism merely conceals PRI forces.

A survey taken in 1959 by Almond and Verba (1965) — whose interpretation greatly influenced many in academia — demonstrated that in spite of great political indifference, there existed in Mexico a widespread legitimacy of the system. Political indifference was at a very high level: 44 percent of the sample declared that they had no interest in politics; the percentage of those who were indifferent must have been, in truth, much higher, since the sample excluded communities consisting of fewer than 10,000 inhabitants. Another survey taken twenty years later, in 1982 (Hernández Medina 1987), showed that in rural areas, 55 percent of those asked had no interest in politics. This study also revealed that, of those questioned in the entire country, 70 percent had little or no interest in politics.

The authors of the 1959 survey found that in Mexico there was a greater level of national political pride than in either Germany or Italy (although it was lower than in the United States or Great Britain). Despite the distrust and rejection of concrete forms of politics, Mexicans considered the 1910 revolution as a symbol of national identity. In the 1959 survey, there is strong support for the PRI (even though the data are a bit confused and doubtful and exclude rural communities); there is also little evidence of support for the PAN. A little over half of those questioned expressed their preference for the official party and only 7 percent expressed a preference for the PAN.[6]

According to the later survey (Hernández Medina 1987), the situation in 1982 revealed very little sympathy for the PRI. Indeed, only 19 percent of those questioned expressed their support for the governing party (6 percent supported the PAN, and 1.6 percent supported the PSUM), while the great majority showed no sympathy for any political party (71.5 percent). Even though the survey does not mention how those questioned intended to vote, there is no doubt that the survey indirectly reflected such attitudes. If we compare these percentages with electoral results, we can guess at the huge dimensions of electoral fraud; for example, assuming that those who do not sympathize with any political party abstain from voting, the PRI still obtained 66 percent of the votes in the sample taken; the PAN received 21 percent; and the various parties on the left received 10 percent (the PSUM received only 5.6 percent). But let us attempt to observe more closely what occurs on the potentially abstentionist and non-party margins whose silence appears to legitimize the system.

The 1982 survey gives an idea of the political inclinations of the silent "fringe of fraud." Paradoxically, in spite of constituting the concrete power of the PRI, the greater part of the surveyed population had right-wing preferences. Fifty-six percent of those surveyed indicated that they leaned toward the right; 33 percent were in the center; and 11 percent leaned to left of center. It can be observed that this political spectrum is not reflected in preferences for political parties (nor does it appear in the electoral results). It can be assumed that two phenomena occur which are not mutually exclusive: 1) the majority of those who lean to the right or to the left tend not to vote, and 2) a significant portion of those who define themselves as right-wing or left-wing vote for the PRI. There are definite reasons to assume that the first case is the one that is clearly predominant.

Nevertheless, the Mexican political elite does not wish to admit publicly to the existence of a deep-rooted electoral problem; what is important for the elite is that Mexican society thinks that the elections are clean, even if, in reality, they are not so. They want to convince society that it is possible to overcome the legitimacy crisis through an improvement of efficiency that resolves the economic crisis. For many technocrats, the crisis has an essentially economic character not a political one. This attitude has led them to abandon the classic ideas of political representation. In the United States, similar political tendencies have signaled a retreat from the typical norms of the modern state, which are sustained in the representative mechanisms connecting the mass of the citizens with the government apparatus. In the United States, there is increasingly an expansion of multilateral negotiations with monopolies, diverse pressure groups, and ethnic minorities with the end of establishing forms of representation that are no longer based in the mass of free and equal individuals — which the classics describe as a civil society. Political parties are weakened, and they thrust into the forefront the battle between personalities within a context of mass communications combined with the financial means on which every politician relies.

Is it possible that in Mexico this political tendency might be successful, little by little supplanting classical democratic forms with a plurality of technostructures that go beyond civic (and national) mechanisms of political control? Is it possible that before arriving at democracy, Mexico must suffer a post-democratic regime?

This might be the intention of the political current headed by Salinas de Gortari. There is strong reason to suspect that the combination of the so-called "modern politics," along with the imposition of fraudulent elections, could create a paradoxical effect — that is to say, doing away with the obsession for innovation and revolution in order to make way for what is usually rejected by modernization: those things considered parochial, traditional, or ornamental. This non-democratic political culture would tolerate a sort of soft authoritarianism, provided that channels of communication and negotiation were not closed and that Mexico integrated itself much more into the areas of consumption and investment dominated by the United States.

The question that must be posed is the following: Are the PRI and the political system positioned to pick up the tacit support of the enormous conservative fringe that has expanded in Mexican society, in order to head up an alternative that is, at the same time, transnational and parochial? It appears to be a difficult task, and should it happen, it will be an alternative that is both unstable and short-lived. It is true that the conservative fringe coincides with the fringe of fraud at many points, that is to say, those rural or semi-urban areas in which the opposition can't even stick their noses, except through the church, the Lion's Club, or the semi-clandestine radical leftist groups. But it appears that fringe — which, to a certain degree, also coincides with the two thousand rural municipalities of *matriotismo* mentioned by Luis González — is beginning to mobilize in a manner not entirely parallel with the official party.

The July 1988 elections proved that the PRI was unable to channel the conservative vote. One of the more notable results of the elections was the relative failure of the turn to the right of the hegemonic PRI group, which coincided with the PAN's movement toward the center, did not produce a significant electoral advance for the official party on the right, and further provoked a profound schism within the dominant PRI party apparatus. As a consequence, there was an abrupt drop in votes for the PRI, and the PAN's advance was stopped. (The parties obtained 50 percent and 17 percent, respectively, according to available data.)

The split within the PRI's hegemonic apparatus took away the support of so-called parastatal leftist and center organizations and created a front that took away close to 5 million votes from the PRI candidate. Added to this was the volume of votes that were on the left and those who supported PAN candidates, not so much as a definition of their political character but as a protest against the establishment. The result was that neo-Cardenism became the strongest political current in modern Mexico (and obtained 32 percent of the officially recognized vote).

Maybe the most spectacular failure of PRI politics is the comical contradiction of its supposed vocation for "modern politics" and the fact that the official party has as its primary electoral base the least modern areas of the country. In almost all of the poles of modernization — in the center and north of Mexico — the opposition headed by Cárdenas and the PAN has the majority of the vote. The PRI is increasingly identified with rural backwardness and marginal votes; the party of an unmodern Mexico and, as a result, of a pre-democratic Mexico. This situation can even be proved with official results that demonstrate a notorious negative correlation (of -0.5 percent) between a modernization index and state voting for the PRI.[7]

Official data states that these elections were plagued by high levels of abstentionism, close to 50 percent. At the same time, it is clear that these were the best-attended elections in Mexico's recent history. This is the unequivocal sign that in previous elections, votes were fraudulently inflated. There is no indication that the 1988 elections were not fraudulent; on the contrary, a preliminary examination of the results allows one to suspect that fraud continued to play an important role. Without it, it is highly unlikely that the PRI's candidate would have achieved the voting levels required to win the elections. The new situation is a result of the diminution of the fraudulent groups as a result of a greater vigilance by the opposition parties in the counting of electoral results.

The opposition (Barberán, Cárdenas, López, and Zavala 1988) pointed out numerous incongruencies in the official electoral count. These results, as has been repeatedly shown, reveal the existence of two different countries: a democratic country where the official party is often placed in the minority and a country where voting for the PRI is virtually unanimous and where abstentionism is suspiciously low. This curious duality can be observed in a graph that shows the voting for a specific candidate in each electoral precinct, ordered from lowest to highest. In the graphs portraying the results of the PRI, the curve begins with 30 percent but, at a certain point, rises sharply up to those precincts giving the PRI 100 percent of the vote. This peculiar type of statistical configuration I call the "dinosaur tail" effect, and not only because of the zoomorphic form adopted by the graph's profile. This "dinosaur tail" contrasts notably with the so-called normal distribution or bell-shaped curve (Gauss curve) which PAN and PRD graphs tend to resemble.

Besides the peculiar "dinosaur tail," the statistical behavior of the data is completely aberrant, in that it not only is an assault against democracy but also goes against the rules for the calculation of probabilities. Those in charge of inventing votes for the PRI at uniparty polling stations chose — with little imagination — an abnormally high level of figures ending in zero. This was as improbable, according to the authors of *Radiografía del fraude* (Barberán et al. 1988), as tossing a coin one hundred times in the air and having it always land on the same side.

The reigning confusion after election day confirmed that the governing group is undergoing a grave political crisis. There are clear differences that separate the technocrats of the Salinas team from the aging hardliners of the traditional political system. Everyone is asking: Can modern "technocracy" divest itself of the corporative interests of the Old Guard PRI leaders? Doubtless, a new pact would have to be negotiated; however, the relationships between factions are so weakened that it is doubtful that any alliances would be particularly durable. Mexico has entered a critical and confusing period. The dominant party's tragic paradox lies in the fact that it has lost legitimacy in almost every modern area of the country (especially the northern and central regions of the country) and, in a notorious and spectacular way, in the capital city. The PRI's pretension to lead Mexico's modernization process reveals itself as erroneous: The civil society that lent its support to the opposition taught a lesson in modernization to a system that is both archaic and barbaric. Cuauhtémoc Cárdenas, contrary to predictions and in spite of his populist origins, headed the impetus of a modern Mexico opposed to a barbaric Mexico. The PRI's technocrats, against the predictions of many and in spite of their cult of efficiency, carry the burden of a Mexico of corruption and authoritarianism. This change of roles reveals the profound upheavals that are occurring within the system.

The political crisis Mexico is undergoing is not the result of traditional opposition, especially from the left, but rather provides evidence of the profound division that took place within the hegemonic group, after which even the mechanism for fraud began to rot. The Cardenists took away from the PRI at least 5 million votes, which were added to the electoral totals of the left. Faced with this surprising situation, the official vote-falsifying machine, expecting a less arduous task, jumped in and produced bizarre and perverse results. The almost incredible electoral folklore confirmed that the Mexican government is fraught with unstable fissures that can split apart at any time.

The elections created new conflicts: Who was responsible for the slip-ups? For some, it was the technocrats who lacked the sagacity of the old wolves of the PRI. For others, the blame fell on the leaders of the mass organizations incorporated into the government system, whose boundless corruption alienated support from society. Others said that the causes stemmed from the economic crisis and from pressures exalted by the Reagan administration, inducing the PRI to move toward the political right into places already occupied by the opposition.

At any rate, it is evident that the crisis had, if not as its origins, at least as its detonator the break from the official party which created the Cardenist movement. What type of movement is this? What does Cuauhtémoc Cárdenas represent? Is it a massive complaint against economic austerity led by nostalgic leaders who wish to return to a populist and patrimonial past? Those who respond affirmatively usually believe that at the head of the PRI is a group of dynamic, modern politicians who wish to bring about democratic reforms. This assertion does not stand up to cold, hard facts; the group of technocrats that is trying to consolidate its hegemony over the PRI and the government has not been freed itself from the peculiarities that characterize the system: authoritarianism, inefficiency, and corruption.

The Mexican political system has reached a new stage in which electoral fraud produces extraordinary insecurity and disorder. The situation has inverted itself: For decades the cynically named "patriotic fraud" took place, assuring an undisputed PRI legitimacy, supposedly defending national interests. Now fraud, combined with the residual effects of an inefficiently and incapably run public administration during a time of economic crisis, has provoked waves of insecurity in civil society.

Towards a Culture of Security?

M exico is undergoing a period of transition; it is passing through important transformations in its political coalitions and in the correlation between pressure groups and class alliances. Do these changes create, perhaps, a national security problem? Or does the problem lie within the definition of national security? It appears to be the latter; national security is neither a patrimony nor a nonrenewable limited resource, defined once and for all and subject to threats from changes in the correlations of social and political forces. Traditionally, the Mexican government has refused officially or publicly to recognize the need to define national security in either military or political terms. David Ronfeldt (1984) states that the political leaders and Mexican intellectuals "would prefer that a concept of Mexican national security never develop but, if it were necessary to do so, they would like to define it in terms of defending the social and economic objectives of Mexican nationalism."[8] In this sense, one might think that a crisis involving "nationalist objectives" would make it necessary to define national security; in the absence of economic and social security, a need would arise to resort to the forces of order in hopes of guaranteeing the equilibrium of the political system. I believe, on the contrary, that it is revolutionary nationalism that is converting itself into an element of imbalance and disorder, in that it stops the expansion of a democratic alternative to the present authoritarian political system. It seems pertinent to examine this problem from the perspective of political culture, which, in the long run, is the fabric from which definitions of security and national unity filter and develop.

The post-revolutionary state achieved national unity in the realm of political structure but not completely in the area of political culture, despite efforts to confuse nationalism with national culture. We can recognize two tendencies that have halted cultural unification. First, there is the already mentioned transnationalism and expansion of mass culture. Second, but equally important, there is the multiplicity and heterogeneity of a political culture whose roots were not only formed by the long processes of syncretism and formation of the mestizo but also by the ancient coexistence of political traditions of diverse orientations. Cultural transnationalization has not changed this latter phenomenon: on the contrary, it has expanded the already rich spectrum of cultural alternatives by adding elements issuing from the Anglo-Saxon "global village."

Capitalist industrialization was promoted in the name of nationalism. It was the post-revolutionary government that promoted urbanization, and, paradoxically, national unity was the vehicle for transnationalization. The national state established the means for political secularization and the expansion of radio and television broadcasts. In the name of revolutionary nationalism, labor organizations and peasant movements were squashed in order to expand free enterprise and authoritarian statism. Nationalism brought modernity and with it, the new winds that have modified the frontiers of national culture. This change in the limits of national culture — along with the fissures it has opened — is what has occasioned the crisis of revolutionary nationalism. Nationalism is no longer merely ceasing to be an effective means of domination but has reached such a level of inherent incongruence that it has made difficult its reproduction as the culture of the hegemonic class. Nationalism has lost efficacy as a legitimating element of PRI hegemony and as a unifier of the dominating class. In other words, the official nationalism has lost credibility before the masses and is losing coherence as the ideology and culture of the governing group.

Modernity — it was inevitable — came from the hand of a transnational mass culture shot through with a strong Anglo-Saxon flavor. Hollywood movies, rock and roll, television series, and thousands of articles on consumption modeled after "international" tastes invaded Mexican territory and populated consciousness with a new type of fantasy and frustration. As a result, spaces that were specifically national were displaced from their original places; the popular, traditional interlocutor of nationalist politics changed location. From the perspective of the masses, the official discourse increasingly appeared as a mute nationalist gesticulation whose symbols were ever less understood and converted into objects of contempt. Mexican political culture has had increasingly less tolerance for the idolatry of the state machine that characterizes Mexican nationalism.

To a certain degree, the nationalist political culture banished (or buried) problems relative to national security. The people's nationalism and the peculiar political system were sufficient forces for guaranteeing the security of the national state. Nevertheless, in the last decade, things began changing. A critical situation developed for nationalism because not only did it not achieve full-scale unification of the political culture, but, having been constituted into a symbol of authoritarianism, it was confronted by a growing democratization of civil society. Democratizing ideas were channeled by means of the two just-mentioned tendencies, the transnational mass culture and the evolution of Mexico's cultural multiplicity. Do these new tendencies provide room for a reconsideration of national security themes? Let us briefly examine some of the problems with reference to mass culture, which has traditionally been accused by nationalists of being not only a threat to security and national unity but also a carrier of anti-democratic, imperialist tendencies. It has also irritated the cultural elites, who consider it a sort of degeneration and a low and vulgar expression of high spiritual values. As opposed to transnationalization, national unity was supposedly based on "authentic" cultural traditions. The tragedy of Mexican nationalism lies in the fact that the national state has converted itself into the principal vehicle of mass culture in order to form the best institutional channel for capitalist modernization. Furthermore, the "authenticity" of the culture explicitly defended by nationalism is as doubtful or as valid as the expressions of the new society of the urban, migrant, and intensely proletarianized masses.

Jean Franco has correctly pointed out that mass culture — as much in the "center" as in the "periphery" — cannot be seen unilaterally as a process of uniformity and adaptation of the individual consciousness to the needs of an industrial capitalist society. She asserts that in Latin America "the trans-nationalization" of culture can be considered from various points of view and not only as an absolute disaster. This is, above all, true for those areas and groups that were in a disadvantageous position when culture was articulated around nationality and national identity. Women and ethnicities, marginalized and under the thumb of nationalism, can now establish a network of alliances above national frontiers" (Franco 1987). It must be added that in Mexico it is not only indigenous peoples and women who are treated in a paternalistic manner by the national authoritarian state; in fact, large sectors of the population are trapped in the peculiar corporate paternalism of the system.

The messages from transnational culture can be read in many ways. Even though a large proportion of the readings suggested by its producers seeks to expand the typically ethnocentric, colonialist, and imperialist influences, cultural interaction has produced a great variety of results, among them new forms of radicalism and democratic movements against established power and oppression.[9] The fact that many of these new cultural forms have oscillated to the right of the political spectrum is due to the fact that the left has practiced a cheap anti-imperialism that has isolated it from important crossroads in contemporary culture. What is interesting about this is that transnational cultural interests on the right have initiated a democratization and liberalization of conservative ideas. The archaic, sanctimonious Catholic Hispanization that characterized a large sector of the right has had to recede before the influence of profoundly sexualized life-styles, stuffed with ultra-modern imagery and marked by a tolerant pragmatism.

A curious phenomena is produced: that which in the eyes of revolutionary nationalism is a hateful denationalizing process generates a liberating effect in conservative culture. To put it another way: The syncretism of "the American way of life" and the traditions of Guadalupe produce an implosion of the meanings that are mined by the traditional right. The result is not only the birth of a new right but the expansion of a more critical and less manipulable civil society. This paradoxical situation has fostered the crisis of nationalism and the broadening of democratic expectations within Mexican society. However, there have appeared disquieting fissures.

It is evident that the political mechanisms of democratic representation, among many requisites, require a precise delimitation of a territory whose inhabitants are endowed with civil rights — most especially the right to effective suffrage. The definition of these limits is fundamental at all levels: local, regional, and national. And it is so important that its manipulation (with the end of dividing masses of votes with the same political loyalty) has been one of the most-used instruments in many countries to block the access to power of opposition parties.

It is clear, therefore, that all processes of de-territorialization can threaten the functioning of representative government (and consequently, of national security). The most obvious example is the migrants: Millions of people around the world are unable to exercise fully their democratic rights either in their countries of origin or in their countries of residence. Another obvious case results from the situations created by large transnational corporations; any political decision regarding them has difficulties in finding a democratic grounding, as the object upon which they must decide lacks a precise territorial base.

In this sense, the existence of territories that delimit and guide the processes of representation is an essential aspect of democracy. It could be thought that the crisis of nationalism weakens self-determination and sovereignty insofar as it could erase national frontiers that separate Mexico from the United States. This argument is based on the false presumption that it is nationalism that draws Mexico's borders, but it has been precisely that identification between nationalism and nation that has been one of the factors that has blocked the expansion of any democratic system in Mexico. We can ask ourselves: Up to what point can a national differentiation maintain itself if based on the absence of democracy? Nationalism has become the symbol of an authoritarian political regime that has not yet been able to establish either a solid economy or avoid its transnationalization. Today, in spite of revolutionary nationalism, millions of Mexicans live in the United States not only on the margins of democracy but outside the law. Many millions more in Mexico find themselves in a similar position: Their vote is manipulated by an authoritarian system. And they live in a crisis economy against which the ballot box can do little; inflationary processes, or those linked to external debt, have been increasingly located in the territory of national political decisions.

Traditional revolutionary nationalism cannot offer a solution to the crisis. The revolutionary discourse is very worn, and today it can be seen that the ideological-cultural mechanism that identifies the PRI with the nation does not lie in its "revolutionary" character. On the contrary, it presents itself as the only party that can contain the revolution, disorder, and chaos. The revolution is its property, and the PRI has it locked up in a Pandora's box and appears to tell the nation (and the government of the United States): "If you support me, I will keep the box closed." That which legitimizes the PRI is fear of revolution. The PRI offers security not revolution. The PRI is the revolution domesticated, in other words, institutionalized.

Due to this, one of the few things that can still be demonstrated, with dubious pride, is the disquieting fact that social tranquility has been maintained since the onset of the terrible economic crisis of 1982. But every day, more Mexicans begin to suspect that the tranquility is due more to the broad presence of tolerant and democratic tendencies in civil society than to the hegemony of revolutionary nationalism. There is a widespread suspicion that the forces of a "Bronco Mexico" are found in the state rather than in society. These authoritarian forces with repressive tendencies — and with which the technocrats have evidently made a pact, with the objective of maintaining a certain stability — are the ones that put forth the idea of defining national security. The authoritarian government feels the need to watch its social environs in order to check preventively any tendencies that threaten the security of the state.[10] The enormous increase of crime and violence in urban and industrialized areas stimulates tendencies for the expansion of what we could baptize as a culture of security: security against anti-patriotic elements, against foreign influences, against drug trafficking, against the underworld, against corruption — in sum, security of the authoritarian political system against the tendencies that supposedly destabilize it. The danger that traditional nationalism will be substituted by a culture of security is very real. This could lead to a dangerous escalation, since it is well known that the cult of security winds up sponsoring the expansion of insecurity.

Notes

1. Turner 1971. For another perspective, see Freeman Smith 1972.

2. A political interpretation of the 1980s can be found in Bartra 1986.

3. A discussion with the technocrats can be found in Bartra 1983.

4. Fifteen years ago, in a symptomatically rude and common form, Miguel Nazar expressed this idea when he was the torturer for a political prisoner: "With what regards the national security of the Constitution and the law, it isn't worth a fuck." (Declaration made August 1973. *La Jornada* 1988).

5. For the origins of the political crisis, see Bartra 1982 and 1986.

6. For an interesting critique, see Craig and Cornelius 1980.

7. Using the data from Zavala 1988.

8. Nevertheless, we must remember that in a well-known declaration in 1980, General Félix Galván, defense secretary, introduced new and disquieting elements by making public a definition of national security that included the maintenance of "political equilibrium" (as well as social and economic) as an assignment for the armed forces (*Proceso* 1980).

9. See Gómez-Peña 1987 as a good example.

10. See the interesting book by Donner 1981.

References

Agee, Philip. 1975. *Inside the Company: CIA Diary*. Penguin.

Almond, G.A., and S. Verba. 1965. *The Civic Culture*. Boston: Little, Brown and Co.

Aziz, Alberto. 1987. "Chihuahua y los límites de la democracia electoral." *Revista Mexicana de Sociología* XLIX 4: (October - December).

Barberán, J., C. Cárdenas, A. López Monjardin, and J. Zavala. 1988. *Radiografía del fraude: Análisis de los datos oficiales del 6 de julio*. Mexico: Nuestro Tiempo.

Bartra, Roger. 1974. *Estructura agraria y clases sociales en Mexico*. Mexico: Era.

Bartra, Roger. 1977. *La jaula de la melancolía: Identidad y metamorfosis del mexicano*. Mexico: Grijalbo.

Bartra, Roger. 1982. *Campesinado y poder político en México*. Mexico: Era.

Bartra, Roger. 1983. "Presagio eficiente y no represión?" In *México '83: a mitad del tunel*. Mexico: Nexos/Océano.

Bartra, Roger. 1986. *La democracia ausente*. Mexico: Grijalbo.

Craig, Ann L., and Wayne Cornelius. 1980. "Political Culture in Mexico: Continuities and Revisionist Interpretations." *The Civic Culture Revisited*. Boston: Little, Brown and Co.

Donner, Frank J. 1981. *The Age of Surveillance*. New York: Vintage Books.

Franco, Jean. 1987. "Recibir a los bárbaros." *Nexos* 108.

Freeman Smith, Robert. 1972. *The United States and Revolutionary Nationalism, 1916-1932*. Chicago: University of Chicago Press.

Gómez-Peña, Guillerma. 1987. "Wacha esa border, son." *La Jornada Semanal*, October 25.

González, Luis. 1987. "Suave Matria." *Nexos* 108.

Hernández Medina, Alberto, and Luis Narro Rodríguez. 1987. *Como somos los mexicanos*. Mexico: CREA.

Kohn, Hans. 1957. *American Nationalism.* New York: MacMillan.

La Jornada. December 23, 1988.

Monsivais, Carlos. 1978. "1968-1978: Notas sobre cultura y sociedad en México." *Cuadernos Políticos* 17.

Proceso. December 22, 1980.

Pullen, J.J. 1971. *Patriotism in America.* New York: American Heritage Press.

Ronfeldt, David, ed. 1984. *The Modern Mexican Military: A Reassessment.* San Diego: Center for U.S.-Mexican Studies.

Saldívar, A. 1980. *Ideología y política del Estado Mexicano (1970-1976).* Mexico: Siglo XXI.

Schmitt, Karl M. 1965. *Communism in Mexico: A Study in Political Frustration.* Austin, Tex.: University of Texas Press.

"The Modern Mexican Military: An Overview." 1984. *The Modern Mexican Military: A Reassessment.* Center for U.S.-Mexican Studies, La Jolla, Calif.

Turner, F.C. 1971. *La dinámica del nacionalimo mexicano.* Mexico: Grijalbo.

Van Alstyne, R.W. 1970. *Genesis of American Nationalism.* Waltham, Mass.: Blaisdell.

Zavala, Iván. 1988. "El nuevo régimen." *Cuadernos de Nexos* 1 (August).

Part Three

Economy, Environment, and National Security

Mexico's Accumulation Crisis in Historical Perspective

Matthew Edel and Candace Kim Edel

Introduction: Accumulation and Security

Examining the Mexican economy and its implications for U.S. security has been a frequent exercise for investigators from the North. Debates within the Central Intelligence Agency over whether Mexico is a "time bomb" (Woodward 1987) are merely the most recent example. Thirty years ago, a study for the Council on Foreign Relations concluded that Mexican development had created opportunities for improved relations with the United States, but that "the dependency relationship between the two countries" might cause tension (Lewis 1960, 344). Despite different diagnoses of current conditions, all U.S. political factions would give at least lip service to the view that an economically stable and secure Mexico is in the United States' interest.

But too often forgotten in the North is the obvious point that Mexico's economic stability, independence, progress, and its ability to

Research in Mexico for this chapter during the 1987-1988 academic year was supported in part by a grant from the William and Flora Hewlett Foundation to the Bildner Center and by grants from the Fulbright Americas Research Program and the P.S.C./B.H.E. faculty research awards program at City University of New York (CUNY). The opinions presented are not necessarily those of the sponsoring organizations.

Editors' Note: It is with deep regret that we note the death of Matthew Edel prior to the publication of this volume.

satisfy popular needs and aspirations are, first and foremost, issues for *Mexico's* security (Pellicer de Brody 1983). The relation of economic and political developments within Mexico forms an important part of that nation's defense of its own security and sovereignty.

This is particularly true in the present economic crisis. Memories of the revolution's violence and of postrevolutionary turmoil, as in 1968, as well as the historical awareness of past U.S. interventions, are strong enough to make Mexicans cautious about their security. Thus, the Mexican "man in the street" is likely to mention a fear of U.S. intervention in a discussion of what may happen in Mexican politics. Government planners, while not fearing military seizure of customs houses for unpaid debt, can still see payment as a defense of sovereignty. In the design of austerity programs, as well as future development plans, the question of what the Mexican populace can bear is, or ought to be, a serious consideration. Thus, it is fitting that consideration of issues in Mexico's security should include the economic crisis.

But the economic crisis, like the binational relationship itself, is a complex object of study. The economy of a nation must be seen both as an object in itself of study and policy manipulation and as part of an increasingly internationalized system. The world economy is becoming increasingly interdependent, limiting the maneuvering room of individual states (Sanderson 1985).

Nor can the approach be strictly economic. The literatures of economic development and of economic crisis have both concluded that one must go beyond purely economic variables to the relationship of the economy to society as a whole. Thus, James O'Connor argues for examining whether, or in what sense, there is a crisis that requires attention to economic, social, political, and even personality issues. His diagnosis of a crisis of the U.S. pattern of accumulation turns on whether an ideology and a personality structure of "ultra-individual-ism" have proved barriers to appropriate response to economic change (O'Connor 1984, 1987). In Mexico, decades of industrialization have answered old questions of whether traditional attitudes and peasant or entrepreneurial conservatism were insuperable barriers to change. But economic crisis has led to arguments over whether entrepreneurs or public officials are sufficiently "outward looking" and over the role of nationalism and national character in the crisis (Bartra 1987).

A broad approach is needed to Mexico's accumulation crisis, one that looks at the overall economic pattern in each major period of growth or crisis and relates it to the overall social and political structure. Mexico's noteworthy growth between the 1930s and the 1970s involved economic and social elements. The eventual undermining of that pattern came about not only because the economy came up against limits or obstacles; development also undermined social factors that originally had favored growth. In the subsequent periods of inflation and austerity, social response has affected even economic policy, narrowly defined. Proposals for a new model of accumulation must take into account economic, political, social, and psychological aspects, both nationally and internationally.

The analysis is also made difficult because much of the discussion about Mexico's future direction takes place with a weak base of information. In part, due to the economic crisis, micro-level information on the condition and productivity of different industries and agricultural sectors, and on the population's living conditions, is nonexistent or scattered. Time and funds for research are limited; what studies are done often focus at extremely local levels; and communication among researchers in different regions, universities, and faculties is difficult. Government data sources are also severely curtailed; data flows between agencies have atrophied; and lack of time and resources impede data collection, integration, dispersal, and analysis. Macro-level policy debates, thus, tend to go on without a sufficient link to what is happening at the micro-level base, and even macro data may be compromised by deficient micro data collection.

There is clearly a need for information as a component of policy making. Some of this information is of an historical-analytic nature: What accounts for the successes and problems of the postrevolutionary growth model must be seen in balanced, rather than myth-making, terms. Some is focused on current situations: to determine what margins for experimentation and what surpluses for investment there are in Mexico requires more knowledge of living and working conditions, production processes, and coping mechanisms than is readily available to the policy maker or scholar who seeks to deal with Mexico as a unit.

A further need is for the specification of possible development models, for Mexico and for its current or potential trading partners, in ways that go beyond a simple dichotomy between nationalist and neoliberal alternatives. At present, the production and exchange of ideas and information are made difficult by a cautiousness of imagination and a lack of realization of how much change has already occurred. And, perhaps more so, exchange is hindered by the difficulties of scholarly production and distribution in a crisis economy, in which time and money are scarce and effort is compartmentalized.

A short paper cannot provide a complete analysis. Nor would greater length alone be sufficient, given our position as outside observers of the society involved. Yet we can point to possible approaches and raise questions for further thought and study. We begin, in the following section, with a discussion of the cycle of rapid accumulation, through which Mexico passed between the 1930s and 1970s and whose supposed exhaustion set the stage for the current crisis. Then, we turn to the analysis of policy, performance, and response during the different crisis stages. Finally, we raise some questions about possible new accumulation models. The separation of short- and long-term issues is not merely one of exposition; rather, we fear, the difficulty in turning from short-term coping to a long-term solution is a principal challenge to Mexico's security.

Postrevolutionary Growth and Its "Exhaustion"

M any analysts of the Mexican economy argue that the present crisis reflects the exhaustion of a previous development model (Boltvinik and Hernández Laos 1981; Solís 1981; Silva-Herzog 1987). They differ over the characterization of that model and why it ceased to generate growth. For some, the degeneration of a pattern of growth into crisis is a normal phenomenon, which will occur to any growth pattern after several decades. This is the message of both Marxist and non-Marxist discussions of the long or "Kondratiev" cycle in Western capitalism, which suggests that capitalism has an innate tendency toward alternations of long periods of growth and those of stagnation or crisis. For others, crisis is a one-time historic event, not reducible to any such pattern (FitzGerald 1983; Edel 1985).

Whatever one's metatheory of crisis, one must specify what pattern of institutions and innovations led to growth. For growth to be sustained, social and economic factors must reinforce each other, as must technology and investment incentives, as well as patterns of production and demand. One must also examine what factors undermined the pattern that promoted accumulation in order to characterize the subsequent crisis.

History may be of use in suggesting possible strategies to inaugurate a new round of accumulation, since past events created present opportunities and constraints. However, one cannot argue simplistically that a development model should be used because it worked the last time or that it should be avoided because it was tried before and became "exhausted." A polarization of the two positions has appeared in Mexican policy discourse (including the 1988 election campaign). We would argue that neither position in its extreme form is correct. Analysis of the complexity of the past cycle is necessary to avoid policy that is blinded by myths. Only if it is not taken in an either-or sense may analysis of past experience be useful for analysis of present possibilities.

Mexico's gross national product grew at a rapid and nearly constant rate for almost half a century, from about 1933 to 1981. Within this period, one can identify a number of constant elements, both economic and institutional, that may have contributed to growth, although analysts will differ on their meaning and importance. One can also identify a number of changes in economic policy that occurred within this cycle and may have been crucial to its long duration.

Economic growth throughout this period can be characterized as capitalist accumulation, in that values obtained by the sale of commodities produced by wage labor were the prime source of reinvestment. But the state, as investor and as regulator, as supporter or as antagonist of private capitalists, had an unusually high profile for a capitalist economy. Accumulation occurred in an economy that was, at least partially, autocentric (Amin 1976) or delimited from the wider North American or world economy. Much of the production expansion was geared to domestic markets; much of the capital accumulated was generated within Mexico; and many of the opportunities for accumulation were reserved for Mexicans, including peasants and state agencies as well as capitalist groups. This partial closing of the economy went through various stages, including different phases of import substitution, and it responded to various growth strategies and the interplay of various internal interests. But it also reflected a concern for nation building and a nationalist ideology, whose importance for postrevolutionary accumulation should not be underestimated.

In the 1930s, much of the attention of the Lázaro Cárdenas government was directed to matters of social reform and nation building. The centralizing of effective power in the national government and the official party, the incorporation of indigenous peoples, the distribution of land and education to the peasantry, and the nationalization of petroleum are all well-known aspects of this period. But the government also helped to stimulate and consolidate a national bourgeoisie.[1] This bourgeoisie would become more openly the principal support and beneficiary of the state after 1940, although its formal organs (unlike those of the peasantry, organized labor, state workers, and certain petit bourgeois sectors) remained outside the official party. It was no mean accomplishment that nationalist feeling and nation building institutions could pull together a widely varying set of interests and create a national market and the institutions for development over four decades (see also Reynolds 1970; Trejo Reyes 1987, 1988).

Economic growth in Mexico actually recovered earlier in the 1930s depression than did growth in the United States (Edel 1985). Enrique Cárdenas (1982) dates the beginning of import-substituting industrialization from this time, although René Villarreal (1976) suggests it should be dated after the war. Stephen H. Haber (1985) argues that growth in the 1930s involved a restoration to full capacity of industries that dated from the Porfiriato (1876-1910) and that new industries developed only after 1940, first in internal market consumer goods and then in intermediate goods. The expansion of a domestic market through national integration and through the effects of agrarian reform on demand were important in both the initial recovery of production and later expansion (Flores 1961). Government economic stimulation and investment were also important: Import-substitution policy did not just mean a high level of tariff protection.

This inward-focused development process faced several challenges. The first was the reestablishment of international participation, within the Western bloc, after the rounds of radical nationalization of the 1930s. This reinsertion was accomplished by Cárdenas's choice of a successor and the rapprochement that occurred during World War II.[2] Clearly, a turn to the "right" was involved, but one which allowed Mexico to remain an exception within the West in terms of its degrees of government control, protection, and foreign policy independence. Nor did more open support for big capitalists by the Miguel Alemán government after the war imply an indiscriminate opening of Mexico to foreign capital. The overall course of the 1930s to 1970s growth cycle shows a move from a more closed or autocentric economic pattern to a much more open or dependent one, but the reorientation was gradual, not a sudden reversal of course.[3]

Postwar inflation was another challenge. The consumer price index increased 42 percent between 1948 and 1953 and 50 percent between 1953 and 1958. Two attempts to bring inflation under control were made. From 1952-1954, and again in 1957-1958, the money supply increase was limited to the real increase in Gross National Product (GNP). In the first case, the peso was devalued, and price increases resumed. In the latter case, although monetary growth resumed and overall economic growth was not delayed enough to make a major dent in annual figures, prices did not jump upward with the relaxation of monetary restraint. The new period of growth, referred to by President Adólfo López Mateos as *desarrollo estabilizador* (stable development), was one of low price increases: only 11 percent from 1958 to 1963. There was no devaluation in this second stabilization; indeed, the exchange rate remained stable until the mid-1970s (Edel 1969).

Several factors seem to have favored this stabilization, which was unusually successful by Latin American standards. International reserves had increased greatly after the 1954 devaluation; this and the devaluation itself are often given credit for the change. But another factor was also important — food supply. The 1952-1954 attempt at monetary stabilization had been affected by poor harvests in 1951 and 1952; the first had driven food prices up sharply, the second was met by an increase in food imports which drew down the country's reserves, setting the stage for devaluation. But thereafter, food production increased sharply, reducing the need for imports and diminishing inflationary pressure. Thus, increased liquidity in 1959 and after could be absorbed with little inflationary impact. The increase in food supply itself may be related to the return to two distinct types of government-sponsored agricultural investment: 1) investments made, either in direct labor or with government credits, by recipients of *ejido* lands in the land reforms of the 1930s; and 2) investments in irrigated commercial agriculture begun and subsidized by Alemán's postwar administration. The former investments may have taken a little longer to have their impact, but both contributed to the positive output "shock" of the 1950s (Edel 1969).

Around the time that inflation was brought under control, fears began to be heard of a new barrier — the limits to import- substitution imposed by the size of the domestic market, or at least its middle class sectors. Raymond Vernon's warnings (1963) were, perhaps, the most ringing, but domestic concern with the distribution of income among individuals and regions was also voiced at the time (Martínez de Navarrette 1960; González Casanova 1965).

These warnings proved to be premature. Despite increasing economic centralization, the economy did continue to grow in the 1960s, and the second through fourth deciles from the top of the income distribution increased their shares of income (Trejo Reyes 1988). Continuing growth and this increasing middle class provided a market both for durable consumer goods and for some capital and intermediate goods, allowing continuation of import- substitution. Some of the growth trickled down to lower economic strata, despite their declining relative share. The handling of macroeconomic and income distribution policy to accomplish this was itself a major feat.

Distribution problems were eventually forced into the center of the economic and security policy agenda when the 1968 troubles brought home the importance of regional and personal inequality. The responses of agrarian populism, regional decentralization policy, and government spending and borrowing to maintain markets, as occurred during the Luís Echeverría and José López Portillo administrations, are now sometimes seen as the origin of Mexico's problems (e.g., Silva-Herzog 1987). These policies may have been too improvisational, too little and too late, and they left a dangerous legacy of international debt (Trejo Reyes 1987). However, it would be a mistake to see them simply as political demagogy; they were an attempt to respond to some of the barriers to further growth that had been created by the growth cycle — and they staved off problems for a time.

It is no mean accomplishment that all of these transformations, from Cárdenas's revolutionary policies to postwar developmentalism to *desarrollo estabilizador* and redistributive development, were accomplished without major changes either in Mexico's overall growth rate or in the political order. The high degree of legitimacy that Mexico's political system brought into the present era of crisis, despite severe cynicism about its failings, stems both from the length of the growth cycle and from the Partido Revolucionario Institucional's (PRI) demonstrated ability to change course without major political upheaval and, through these changes, to absorb creative young people from all political sides.

It is easy in retrospect to point to the changes that did not take place during the boom years. Had protectionism in nondurable consumer goods industries been reduced as import- substitution extended into larger durables and capital goods, foreign competition might have spurred productivity, and job displacement would have occurred when growth was creating opportunities in other sectors, rather than in the later period of crisis. Had support of peasant agriculture not been neglected after 1960, food dependency and over-urbanization might not be as great today. Had downward redistribution and regional decentralization received more attention prior to 1968, perhaps economic imbalances and social problems would have been averted even longer. This is not to say we believe crisis is permanently avoidable in capitalism (or perhaps, in any system), but rather that Mexico's accomplishments in the postrevolutionary wave of accumulation should be seen as considerable but not perfect. That the growth cycle ended does not prove it was a mistake; that mistakes were made does not mean all of its details can be resurrected.

As to the oil boom of the late 1970s and early 1980s, what the long-cycle view suggests is that this occurred at a time when the postwar economic growth cycle was already in trouble. There is surprising agreement, indeed, between Marxist and conservative economists on some of the immediate causes. Low industrial productivity and its concomitant, declining rates of profit on domestic manufacturing investment were clearly important. (See the estimates by Valle 1985, Alberro and Nieto-Iruarte 1986, and Ortiz Cruz et al. 1986.) Rising consumer and state debt (even before the oil boom) and inflationary monetary expansion were clearly involved, and there is even some consensus that these were being used to avoid longer-run reforms (although which longer-run reforms would have been preferred will vary among analysts). The 1976 devaluation and the austerity program under the International Monetary Fund (IMF) agreement were signs that the trouble had surfaced. It was only after this agreement that the massive expansion of oil investment occurred in the southeast coast, financed by part of the proceeds of an even more massive round of international borrowing. In addition to the internal desire to resume growth through exports, external forces (including the West's "needs" to recycle petrodollars and to find politically safer sources of petroleum than the Middle East) played their role.

Once again, hindsight is easy. Part of Mexico's borrowing went for imports; these imports did not serve as a jolt to productivity because protection of established industries remained in effect. Indeed, food imports postponed serious concern about domestic food production. Given internal credit conditions, overvaluation, and the existing income distribution, a significant proportion of foreign exchange found its way into foreign accounts. There was substantial and important infrastructure investment, but even much of that investment may be faulted for accentuating geographic overcentralization. And while investment in petroleum did eventually yield increased export volumes, the increase in oil revenues did not outweigh imports of equipment for the industry. Had petroleum prices remained high, net returns would eventually have been favorable. But given the drastic decline of prices, the main beneficiaries were oil-importing nations, particularly the United States, whose dependency on Middle Eastern sources was reduced by the Mexican alternative. The "recycling of petrodollars" into what eventually became the Latin American debt also postponed problems for the Western economies as a bloc, creating markets for developed country exports, as Latin America's role as an importer increased.

The oil boom postponed Mexico's problems, but it could not eliminate the existing sources of crisis. When the boom ended, as so many Third World primary product booms had before, additional calamities were piled upon the prior problems of distribution, low industrial productivity, regional overcentralization, and lagging food production. The search for new directions for growth had to take place submerged by the day-to-day necessities of coping with austerity and in a crisis atmosphere where simplistic long-term formulas could replace earlier policy sophistication.

Austerity and Security: The Short-Term View

In the summer of 1982, Mexico found itself without the cash on hand to meet foreign debt payments. Since then, attention has been directed toward day-to-day crisis management. For the government, the problems have involved the negotiation of terms and conditions of debt rollover, the design of austerity programs, and the attempt to prevent further capital flight. Concerns for Mexicans' living conditions have been voiced, but their influence on policy is debatable. The design and implementation of economic development strategy has frequently been on the back burner, although a general long-term policy outlook, focused on opening the economy, has certainly been present.

For Mexican people at most income levels, crisis management has also been the order of the day: the attempt to survive or to maintain at least some semblance of life-styles achieved before the crash.

Much has been written about government debt policy and crisis management, although the integration of foreign and domestic policies, and of short- and long-term concerns, clearly needs further study. A good deal has also been written about the coping done by individuals, families, and communities. But this work consists of many isolated and scattered microstudies, whose integration into a national overview remains a major research task. Indeed, one of the impacts of the crisis has been on research, as scholars have less time to keep in touch with their peers in other institutions, and publication of results is cut back.

National economic policy on the crisis took one sharp turn, with the inauguration of Miguel de la Madrid at the end of 1982, and several minor turns thereafter, in terms of alternations of tightening and loosening of austerity policies. But throughout the period, the government has been concerned with at least nominal debt repayment and with the attempt to deter capital flight and attract foreign exchange. This may be interpreted as a plausible nationalist response and an attempt to regain some possibility of national independence in policy making. But in the short run, it has left policy making extremely vulnerable to the short-term jitters and longer-term pressures of the internationally mobile sectors of both Mexican and foreign capital.

Some of the measures adopted in response to this pressure are short run in nature, as in the austerity measures of the *Pacto de Solidaridad Económica*. Some other steps aimed at the opening of the economy are related to a long-term strategy of participation in a world or North American economy, but the specifics of their implementation have been dominated by short-run concerns to reassure investors. This has meant that the longer-term strategy involved has never been fully explained to the public, nor has it reassured all investors, as witness continued support from some regional and domestic market-oriented groups for the political opposition, particularly the Partido Acción Nacional (PAN). If the government's economic strategy has a potential hypothetical coherence, the articulation of policies to that goal may also have been compromised.

The details of all these policies cannot be spelled out here. But it needs to be remembered that both the nationalization of domestic banks in the last months of the López Portillo administration and the later attempts by the de la Madrid government to heal the resulting breach with private capital were driven — at least, in part — by the fear of capital flight. This fear was presented as one of the major reasons for bank nationalization, which was seen as a way to control Mexicans' use of accounts to send money out of the country (Tello 1984). It was also cited as a reason for later pro-business policies (Silva-Herzog 1987). In 1988, wage austerity, monetary policy, and other measures of the *Pacto* were also justified to the public in terms of (and probably, impelled by) the need to control capital outflow (Corro 1988; Edel and Edel 1989).

The external debt burden, loss of oil revenues, capital flight, and austerity programs have left the economy in a severe recession for the past six years. While the economy's managers have been able to stave off a full-scale economic collapse, as well as a full-scale default, total gross national product, after several rounds of fluctuation, is only about what it was in 1980. Population has, of course, continued to grow, so that per capita income is down about 15 percent. At best, therefore, the Mexicans can claim an economic stalemate on the macroeconomic front.

In foreign exchange terms, this stalemate may be claimed as a short-run accomplishment. Debt payments have been met or rolled over, with the debt on the books, therefore, increasing from $85 billion in 1981 to over $100 billion by 1988. Part of the increase was offset by an increase in dollar reserves, which had risen from virtually nothing in 1982 to over $15 billion by June 1988. (They have declined again since then.) These reserves and further stand-by credits were designed to deter further runs on the peso and to provide a reserve for buying back debt at a discount, should the opportunity present itself. (Two such opportunities, debt-equity swaps and the Morgan plan of early 1988, have provided some small relief.) Inflation has twice broken into triple digits, and both times it has been rolled back, most recently by the 1988 *Pacto de Solidaridad Económica*. But the conditions that lead to inflation have not changed, either in terms of government peso deficits (Trejo Reyes 1987; Silva-Herzog 1987) or in terms of persistent structural problems, including conflicts over relative shares (Barkin and Esteva 1979) and dependence on imports or exports subject to price shock (Barkin and Súarez 1985).

The distribution of the costs of austerity is worth noting. If per capita income has dropped by 15 percent and another 5 to 7 percent annually has been sent abroad in net debt service flow, one might have expected a drop of over 20 percent in wages. If borrowing had raised wages in the oil boom period, perhaps another 5 percent needed to be shaved. But real wages have fallen not by 20 percent or 27 percent, but apparently by 40 percent or more. While declining average individual wages may be made up, in part, by increased labor force participation, the relative share of GNP going to wages has itself fallen sharply, from 40 percent in 1976 to 36 percent in 1982, and apparently down into the mid- to upper 20s in 1988. Wage workers have, in short, taken more than their proportionate share of the burden.[4]

Businesses, or at least the smaller businesses, have also been severely hit. Here again, the evidence needs careful evaluation. Saúl Trejo Reyes (1987) finds a decline in the profit share of national income in the first three years of the crisis, but Etelberto Ortiz Cruz (1988) finds a slight increase in the rate of profit calculated using a neo-Marxist formula. (The results are not incompatible with each other, since the methods used differ.) Both suggest a tendency toward the concentration of capital in the period, suggesting that, despite the much-publicized problems of the Monterrey group, some large businesses were the gainers, and smaller businesses were the losers. The break, however, may not be strictly in terms of size, but in type of activity, with export capital favored over investors in the internal market. If interest payments are separated out as a share of GNP, it appears that this form of factor income may have risen because of payments on the rising internal debt, while indirect taxes have also risen as a share of GNP. Thus, along with the general restriction of production, there seems to have been a transfer of what remained toward larger businesses and toward renters.

The government's own share of spending (other than internal and external debt repayment) has also decreased, although it appears that the decline of real wages paid to government employees has accounted for a larger portion of this decline than has the reduction of government payrolls. Government subsidies, both to industrial inputs and to popular consumption, have been reduced, and government investment has been scaled back sharply, accounting for a large part of the net decline in total investment.

Faced with these cuts in overall income and in their own specific incomes, different groups in Mexican society have responded with a wide set of coping mechanisms. Indeed, these elements of popular response may account for Mexico's achieving stalemate rather than complete collapse in the crisis. The evidence on these responses is scattered in the works of anthropologists and other observers of local life. Some papers have been presented in the United States (e.g., Nash 1988; Cook 1988; Eckstein 1988). Others are available only locally, if one inquires from university to university. They need to be compiled systematically. From a preliminary scan, and from some limited field observation, however, the outlines of a picture emerge.

The picture includes, of course, reductions in consumption. The *Instituto Nacional del Consumidor* (National Consumer Institute) (1988) suggests that caloric intake has been maintained by substituting grains and beans for other foods. Consumption of meat, fish, and other higher value foods is clearly down, while some of the poor appear to have been forced back to tortillas and cheap pastas, although there is regional variation. Consumption of nonfood commodities has also been restricted. So, too, have recreation and festivals. Press reports and our observations during the 1987 Christmas season suggested that everything from beach vacations by the upper middle class to participation in local neighborhood pageants has been cut back.

The implications of austerity may be fairly obvious in the case of nutrition, but even a restriction of holiday rituals may have severe consequences. First, there is an impact on family and community, which rely on such rituals to symbolize unity and the sense of group and its rights and obligations and to reaffirm or expand individual memberships and commitment. Second, there is an impact on individuals, since festivals give individuals a sense of group affiliation and an internalized reason for affiliation to the social system, as well as reducing stress and offering cognitive reward (pleasure). Third, small businesses, in particular, count on such activities for marginal existence. Individuals involved in such business were doubly hit: Their own celebrations were curtailed, and their businesses were threatened by reduction in demand.

Family incomes have been protected, in part, by two factors. The first is a proliferation of individual and familial multiple job holding. Although formal labor force participation data is hard to come by (the 1980 census is weak, in this regard, and intercensual data quite sketchy), evidence of extra jobs is apparent to the casual observer in Mexico City, the northern frontier, and the tourist centers. Women's employment has also apparently increased, although in peripheral barrios of large cities the opportunities for this work are limited (Eckstein 1988).

Second, and encompassing some of this expansion of participation and moonlighting, is a development of extended family strategies, in which principal incomes from jobs and small farms are supplemented (and "portfolios" of incomes are diversified) by artisan work, migration to cities or to the United States, and street vending or other "informal" activities. It is likely that a great many families have been driven by the crisis deliberately to strengthen ties between members located in rural and in urban areas. This is particularly noteworthy, since the urban and market-oriented form of Mexico's development is one which often tends to weaken such extended networks.

Clearly, not all individuals are included in these networks, particularly not those who were most affected by classical modernization processes. Those left out are particularly disadvantaged. No good estimates are available for homelessness and destitution, either in general or for vulnerable subgroups such as single mothers and abandoned children, although estimates of *gamines* (street children) in the Federal District vary from ten thousand to forty thousand.

At the level of policy discussion, such microphenomena are often subsumed by the debate over the so-called informal sector. Several recent works have followed the lead of Hernando DeSoto's (1986) studies of Peru, to suggest that off-the-books employment and self-employment not only are major factors in coping with crisis but that they represent a strong and growing economic sector (e.g., Zaid 1987; Alberro and Cambiaso 1986). It is sometimes suggested that the increase in these activities means that official estimates of income and national product decline are exaggerations (CEESP 1987). However, despite the undoubted increase in informal activities and their importance as coping mechanisms, it is extremely doubtful that they have been able to offset as much of the decline as is suggested, for example, by television interviews with beggars who do well in the best locations.

Our own interviews and those of Susan Eckstein (1988) indicate a general and serious, if unevenly distributed, decline in living standards. Most informal activities are low in pay (although, undoubtedly, some illegal businesses are not), and some informal activity is subcontracted from formal businesses and, hence, may already appear indirectly in national accounts (Beneria and Roldán 1987).

The proliferation of multiple job holding has combined with budget cuts per se to affect public services. Some services have been curtailed officially by budget reductions, while others face increased demands for service without increased staffing. For example, as middle-class families become unable to use private doctors and turn to the Social Security hospitals, these become overcrowded, while patients squeezed out of that system by informalization overcrowd the public hospitals of the Federal District to the point that patients must sometimes bring their own bedding to sleep in the corridors. And all services suffer as workers are affected by the fatigue brought on by moonlighting.

That Mexicans have been surviving the crisis as well as they have is an important phenomenon worthy of study and, one should say, admiration. But the extent of coping has also had negative side effects. First, Mexican quiescence is taken for granted in policy discourse, with the result that government policy can be driven only by the fear of capital flight, ignoring popular privation or the fear of rebellious activity (Edel and Edel 1989). And second, long-term policy making, or even planning, takes a back seat to coping policies. These blind spots may, in the long run, be extremely serious.

Toward the Long Run

If the Mexican economic problems of the mid-1970s and the general crisis of the 1980s mark an exhaustion of the postrevolutionary accumulation model, then the question of reinvigorating economic growth must involve a general reconsideration of the contours of Mexican society and its place in the wider world economy. The country's very definitions of security and of national identity are involved. However great the immediate problems of coping, defining a long-run course for the nation is even more problematic. Mexicans are well aware of the cost paid in moving the nation from its late nineteenth century identity and model to the pattern that came together in the 1930s. Transition itself can be a threat to security; thinking about the long run can seem dangerous. But the problems of organization for accumulation in the long run will not go away. If a new Mexican model cannot be developed, the default option may be permanent crisis, continued decline of living standards and working conditions, and insertion in an externally determined model on most unfavorable terms.

It is beyond the purposes of this paper to propose a specific model of development for Mexico: The most fitting role for the outside observer may be skeptical questioning and, in the present context, where communication itself is a scarce resource, the bringing together of different options from scattered sites. Thus, this section attempts to outline some of the proposals that have been generated and to suggest what factors may make them more or less difficult.

One convenient starting point for the debate on Mexico's future is the juxtaposition of options attempted during the oil-boom respite from crisis by Rolando Cordera and Carlos Tello (1981). Cordera and Tello saw a "dispute for the nation" between two "projects" which they termed "neoliberal" and "nationalist."[5]

The authors characterize the neoliberal project as a program whose origins stem from outside of Mexico, from transnational capital. Its Mexican proponents include some policy making intellectuals, sectors of Mexican capital, and members of the middle class concerned with access to imports. This view aspires, they argue, to

> a purging of the social and economic system forged amidst the fervor of Keynesian policy making after the war.... According to transnational thinking, among the principal factors blocking accelerated development and, therefore, principally to blame for the current crisis are 1) an excess of democracy and the consequent deterioration of the legitimacy of governments and established institutions; 2) hypertrophy of the state as well as its disproportionate and inflationary deficit; 3) the growth of unions and their interference in public policy; and 4) the rebirth of nationalism. Thus, the key proposition posed by this project is that Mexico's long-run interests, as well as those of U.S. society, will best be satisfied if both economies are integrated into a global system of mutual complementarity (Cordera and Tello 1983, 52).

Cordera and Tello counterpoise to this outlook what they term a nationalist project, based on the projections, guarantees, and spirit of the Mexican Constitution of 1917, in which

> the state, as the guiding force in the process of development, is charged with the responsibility for promoting the betterment of the conditions of life for the popular majority by acting upon relations of property...and on relations among social classes (61).

This project (which might also be termed "populist") also presupposes continuation of "the social pact on the basis of which the country has evolved." The authors suggest the state can still stimulate development:

> It can now look forward to progress in attending to the needs of the majority of the population, in tempering the extremes of wealth and poverty that currently exist, and in reaching a higher and more favorable level of social evolution.... [There is an] imperative of matching production more closely to the consumption needs of those who generate that production — namely, the workers; hence, the utility of the state intervention in the economic process, by erecting institutional barriers to the "general laws" of the economy to regulate their operation and impede the dissolution of the nation's social fabric.... In the nationalist project, which entails reviving intersectoral linkages, as well as broadening and diversifying the productive base, it will be up to the state from the outset, to provide new stimuli for commodity production and accumulation (62-63).

These two projects, as presented by Cordera and Tello, are, to some extent, caricatures designed to favor the nationalist outlook.[6] The incompleteness of both as full policies is useful in that it serves to clarify two focuses of analysis and to underline the main fear held by either side: on the one hand, that state intervention and protectionism will cripple the economy; on the other, that a simple reliance on the unregulated market will tear apart the social fabric. A recognition of these fears makes clear that each side in the dispute is acting on its own vision of national security.

But fears and general visions are not really programs and strategies. Government policy during the de la Madrid sexenio, at first glance, approximated the neoliberal caricature in terms of aspirations for an open economy and in many specific policies. But many of the policies were improvised in a short-run context dominated by international debt service pressures and the fear of capital flight. There may be a faith that, in the long run, opening the market to international investment and foreign goods will stimulate productivity and accumulation. There certainly is a sense (and not only among neoliberals) that Mexico needs to establish new exports; there is also a desire to restrict monopolies and, particularly, to reduce cumbersome government interference. But these general tendencies of policy are not always coordinated with each other, even in the short run, and their effects may run counter to the general free market philosophy.

Examples are easy to come by. The sale of government assets may sometimes strengthen local monopoly rather than perfect markets; government decentralization efforts may duplicate rather than reduce bureaucracies; the generally neoliberal austerity program of 1988 (the Pact of Economic Solidarity) invoked wage controls and at least the pretense of price controls; the same austerity program, by setting into motion populist counterforces, left the PRI government more, rather than less, dependent on corporatist leadership for its legislative majorities. All of these may, of course, be short-run contradictions. They may be temporary, crisis-induced detours from an ongoing drive for openness and reliance on the market. But even if the market project is advanced further, questions remain about it. Is Mexico doomed in such a project to compete solely on the basis of cheap labor and thus require permanent containment of living standards? Or is austerity a temporary phase, to be overcome when productivity, stimulated by competition and a lack of bureaucratic constraint, leaps forward? The proponents of openness have, in general, equivocated on this issue, which suggests the model is not really thought through beyond the version caricatured by Cordera and Tello.

Proponents of a populist or nationalist model also lend themselves to caricature. The suggestion that government could, by egalitarian programs and monetary expansion, stimulate a short-term round of growth is not unreasonable. Coupling this to an aggressive stance on the debt issue could, perhaps, facilitate the mobilization of energy for some development tasks. Brazil's *Plan Cruzado* and Peru's experience early in the Alan García administration suggest the short-term possibilities. However, these cases also signal the dangers of depletion of foreign reserves and of the business confidence that short-term growth can induce. Mention of these cases, indeed, is usually considered by neoliberals as sufficient reason to ignore populist demands.

A careful analysis of these cases might reveal more specific and avoidable errors, rather than delegitimating the entire effort. But such a task is not the obligation of the opponents of populism; rather, its proponents need to develop a detailed plan for strategy during the window of opportunity created by foreign reserves. Such a plan would be cognizant of the dangers and vulnerabilities of reserve depletion; it would require a strategy to limit spending advances and imports on the upswing, perhaps by the politically difficult act of paying for income redistribution through progressive taxation rather than through monetary expansion; and it would have to address longer-run issues of how production could be restructured to meet Cordera and Tello's criterion of fitting output to domestic needs. So far, there is little evidence that the opposition has a developed blueprint, although the Cardenista opposition may be beginning this difficult task.

Thus, neither side of the neoliberal-versus-populist dichotomy yet appears to have a proper long-term plan. Nor have worked-out programs appeared from other potential positions, such as a conservative non-free market nationalism (of a Japanese or Brazilian sort), or a left-nationalist position that would go beyond populism to an explicit socialist stand (not that Mexico lacks for socialist parties and movements, but their programs rarely go beyond the defense of labor and community rights within a populist context of state-influenced capitalism). The very lack of information that the crisis has imposed makes the elaboration of well-tempered plans difficult. However, some partial aspects of long-term programs have been proposed at the margins of the overall dispute between populism and neoliberalism, which may, perhaps, work their way into the debate over the next few years. None of them present a complete policy, but they are worth examining.

Agricultural Self-Sufficiency

A first subprogram concerns agriculture and centers on the issue of food self-sufficiency. The decline in agricultural growth rates, a de-emphasis on peasant production, an increasing specialization in export agriculture, and a reliance on grain imports have been part of the exhaustion of the postrevolutionary growth model. Whether they are a problem, per se, is subject to heated debate.

From the neoliberal viewpoint, reduction of support to "inefficient" agricultural units is good policy, while export specialization and import of foods available cheaply abroad are proper uses of competitive advantage. Neoliberals outside of the PRI often suggest that a transformation of *ejidal* land into individual property might remove barriers to efficiency, while those in the PRI remain politically committed to the *ejido*, but more as a symbol and ostensible safety net than as a production unit.

Populist programs tend to stress the historical importance of the *ejido* and point out the advantage of a viable peasant sector as a counter to overurbanization. They stress the loss of national independence involved in being dependent on basic food imports. This point is often derided as a romantic call for agricultural self-sufficiency and a return to a peasant past, but better arguments can be made and have been made for a peasant-focused program of increased food production.

In the first place, serious issues of national security are involved in food self-sufficiency. The more central an imported commodity is as a wage good and as a basic input for industry, the more vulnerable a country is to external shocks, and the weaker its political hand is in international negotiations over such matters as debt scheduling. To be independent of the need for such imports on a continuing basis allows the possibility of surviving a short- to medium-term freeze on commercial credits, in response to suspension as a negotiating tactic. The importance of trade vulnerability as a security issue has long been recognized (Hirschman 1945), and petroleum supply was certainly accepted by the United States as a national security issue in the 1970s. Despite U.S. abandonment of talk of a "food weapon" in recent years, food import dependence leaves Mexico in an unnecessarily asymmetric relation with its larger neighbor.

Furthermore, the importation of a basic wage good puts severe constraints on both macroeconomic and distributional policy, since either an attempt at macroeconomic expansion or a progressive redistribution of income will likely increase food import demand. The importance of this is well demonstrated for smaller economies (Weisskoff 1985); for Mexico, the options are somewhat greater, but, nonetheless, dependence on food imports raises the costs of possible Keynesian or populist policies. (We are not suggesting Mexican neoliberal policy has deliberately sought import dependence to make alternatives more difficult, but the effect is, nonetheless, to constrain alternatives.) Thus, any program which envisions internal market development, downward redistribution, or macrostimulation must deal first with the food question.

The agricultural expansion issue has been dealt with in the past by various methods. Hopes have been fastened, at times, on new land settlement (Ballesteros et al. 1970), on new "Green Revolution" grain varieties, and on restimulation of the peasant sector. The first two appear to have gone about as far as they can, and the ecological and distributional side effects of their past successes are sobering. But redevelopment of the peasant sector has not been adequately dealt with in policy since its de-emphasis in the 1970s. The brief round of experimentation undertaken by the Mexican Food System (SAM) in the late oil boom period was not given adequate time or resources to function (Austin and Esteva 1987).

David Barkin, in a number of studies, has suggested that the peasant sector can, with better input supply and price stimulation, be induced to produce more domestic market foodstuffs (as well as reducing pressure on urban labor markets and improving nutrition). But this would require a combined package of priority measures, including ones to make older-variety seeds and poultry stocks available — those less dependent on complementary chemical and water inputs — than can be had from present agribusiness-oriented private sources. Barkin has presented a proposed policy package as part of what he terms a "War Economy" crash program for security, but, at least at some level of state priority, agricultural measures developed along the lines he has begun to investigate might be taken as part of a more diverse program to increase national security options (Barkin 1987; Barkin and Súarez 1983, 1985).

Redevelopment of peasant agriculture would do more than just reduce imports. In the past, individuals in rural and even some urban areas produced at least part of their foodstuffs — for example, corn, chilies, beans, tomatoes, and chickens for home consumption. These small producers supplied both themselves and others in their extended families and localities with basic commodities. Now they cannot easily obtain even the seed and stock for varieties not dependent on other intensive inputs. Not only has there been a reduction in production of these commodities, but because the general crisis has followed the intensification of specialization and commodity relationships, those necessities that are produced generally have to be sold away from the neediest areas. The lack of the old partial self-sufficiency creates an individual or family dependency that parallels the national dependency on imported foods, as well as forces the accelerated urbanization that has become so costly for Mexico.

Industrial Policy

A second area where simple neoliberal versus nationalist categorization of policies is insufficient is industrial policy. In this area, present policy seems to hope that freer trade and a reduction of government intervention will lead to greater efficiency and increased exports. Entry into the General Agreement on Tariffs and Trade (GATT), removal of import licensing and quota requirements, and the extension of in-bond (*maquiladora*) privileges to regions away from the northern border exemplify this policy. Where there is controversy within this free trade view, it is over the extent of divestment of government ownership and whether energy and certain basic materials (e.g., steel) are central enough in both input-output and security senses that continued state ownership and subsidy are warranted.[7] But for most consumer goods and for industrial exportables in general, the neoliberals keep the free trade faith, and even portions of the business community that may be hurt by import competition are, at present, constrained from openly advocating continuation of a protected domestic market (although they obviously support some specific continuing protective measures quietly, and the potential for deeper splits is present).

But there is no necessary congruence between government passivity and export expansion. Indeed, the cases of Japan and Korea suggest that a degree of state intervention for technological advancement and the organization of industry for export competitiveness may be quite useful. The debate over industrial policy in the United States in the early 1980s presented two different positions on how to promote technological advancement, neither of which proposed a closed economy. "Supply siders" proposed that a less-fettered free market would stimulate investment and innovation, while advocates of an explicit national industrial policy suggested major interventions targeted toward particular sunrise industries (see Edel 1983). And Brazilian policy has — at least, at times — sought to apply a state-oriented export and technology promotion model, with at least some success (Hirschman 1986).

What is most striking about the lack of long-run thinking in the present Mexican situation is how little examination of industrial policies there has been. An exception is the work of Saúl Trejo Reyes (1987), who advocates selective government involvement in technology and industry as part of a package with some liberalization measures for other industries. Although the sunrise-sunset distinction is not clearly made in Trejo Reyes' work, the logic of selective involvement would require some such distinctions, which may make such a program politically difficult. But since distinctions between different government-owned industries are already being made over extent and terms of denationalization, it would appear that selectivity need not be an insuperable problem. Trejo Reyes' identification of possible sunrise activities is very preliminary, focusing on rather unspecified "technology" and on the particular case of electronics. Further analyses of technology are beginning to be made in specific industries, and such areas as biotechnology and pharmaceuticals might be further explored. But it would appear that those who, in general, favor a more export-oriented Mexican economy should investigate the possibilities of state stimulation more seriously.

Spatial Decentralization

An aspect of economic reconstruction which has received more attention in Mexico than in many other countries, at least in terms of policy rhetoric and initial investigation, is regional or spatial decentralization. It is fairly well agreed that the central region of the country, including Mexico City and its environs and perhaps the metropolitan areas of Toluca, Puebla, Cuernavaca, and Queretaro, have become high-cost areas both for production and for the maintenance of essential services. The problems of water, sewage, and internal transportation for Mexico City involve high social costs. Health, education, and police costs are also high.

Despite these costs, industries oriented to the domestic market may have reason to locate in the Mexico City metropolitan region to minimize transport costs to market (Trejo Reyes 1987). This concentration has been furthered, over the past century, by infrastructure availability, government subsidy policies, and the need for access to a centralized bureaucracy. Until the mid-1960s, at least, it appeared that centralization brought economies of scale and furthered industrialization (Garza 1985). But rising social and economic costs have become more important since 1970 (Oliveira and Muñoz García 1989).

Thus, it is argued that spatial decentralization must become part of the attempt to generate a new, efficient model. Trejo Reyes (1987), for example, suggests situating complexes of new higher-tech industries in metropolitan areas outside the central region. Within the more common paradigms, Carlos Bazdresch (1986) takes an orthodox market approach, suggesting that Mexico City be forced to pay higher costs (marginal costs in the neoclassical economic sense) for services as part of a modernization program. Populists oppose this as an attempt to place all of the costs of adjustment on the present urban poor and suggest that development of agriculture and industry in other regions would, at least, reduce migration to the metropolis. The government has promised much in terms of decentralization since the early 1970s, but despite many interesting pilot programs, overall centralization is still dominant.

Part of the reason for this may be political. The centralization of resources in Mexico City as part of both the Porfirian and postrevolutionary economic models was, in part, impelled by a need for nation building, which meant the centralization of control away from regional *caudillos*. Although some investment had to be directed toward the northern frontier to ensure that the area would be populated by Mexicans and be immune to a repetition of the Texas secession, creation of central national power was the highest spatial priority. Whatever economies of scale Mexico City generated were useful but secondary factors. Now, however, these security concerns have been satisfied. Security interests may now favor deconcentration, to the extent that an overly large Mexico City has been recognized since 1968 as a potential source of instability, while neglect of other regions can also cause discontent, as some recent elections reveal. However, apart from the pressure of vested interests in the center, geographic-economic decentralization may be limited by the fear that it will only be feasible if real political power is also decentralized — a movement about which the central government and the PRI are, naturally, cautious.

Despite this political caution, numerous decentralization plans have been proposed. Since the PRI's own political unpopularity in Mexico City was shown in the past election, the time may be ripe for consideration of long-term plans to direct further growth away from that area (although after 1968, the response was to direct more subsidies and construction to the capital). Any discussion of a new growth strategy for Mexico has to take spatial patterns into deliberate account.

Community and National Solidarity

D iscussion of regional, agrarian, and even industrial changes raises another, apparently less economic, issue which must be faced by any new development project for Mexico: the extent to which community and national loyalties may be relied on as part of a new model. As compared with the motivational base of the U.S. development model — with its focus on individualism, social mobility, and individualized consumerism (O'Connor 1984; Edel, Sclar, and Luria 1984) — the Mexican postrevolutionary model has been more dependent on the channeling of community loyalties (most notably, in the case of the *ejido* but also in other "corporate" institutions) and on the mobilization of nationalism for motivating participation.

To some extent, this was a conscious reversal of ideological and organizational trends in the Porfirian growth cycle; to some extent, it simply reflected the de facto importance of communities and other subgroups for resource sharing at Mexico's existing economic level. The success of mass education programs in the 1930s, of many *ejidos* through the 1950s, and of self-help housing and barrio development more recently, attests to the importance of communal activity. Nor is communal activity yet obsolete. Coping with crisis is, for the moment, forcing — or at least, urging — many Mexicans into a reliance on kinship and other communal networks, some of which must be created or recreated for the purpose. (This is difficult, to be sure, because the networks and communities on which new demands for support are placed are short of resources because of the economic crisis, and they have been weakened by the spread of market relationships.)

The political project of neoliberalism would seem to require a switch to a more individualistic motivational system, with concomitant potential individual rewards. However, without rapid growth and consequent social mobility, the ability of such a system to command loyalty may be questionable. Thus, the lack of an alternative communal motivation could be a weakness to the neoliberal project, unless wages remained so low that mere survival became the permanent motivation (a situation that hardly seems compatible with political security).

Meanwhile, there has been a proliferation of community social movements (urban, rural, indigenous) and new political forms (*coordinadoras*), which seek to unify these movements nationally. These movements have largely been outside of the PRI's older corporatist networks of patronage, and they may be seen as part of a potential populist or nationalist project. Many of them rallied to the 1988 Cárdenas campaign after previously having been nonpolitical or at least nonpartisan. But their potential place in a populist project is unclear. Would they disappear after some essential demands are met, as movements in peripheral urban neighborhoods often do? Would they become permanent patronage channels in a new corporatist model? Or would a new populist model involve a more permanent role for strong local communities, with roles in production and social consumption as well as in politics? This latter seems to us to be possible, although difficult. It may, indeed, be the only real alternative to isolated poverty. But the models are still speculative; the long-term possibilities are still uncertain, as are the political consequences of ignoring them.[8]

The role of nationalism as a force in a new model is also uncertain. In the short run, some residual faith in the old leadership may remain, based on past history and a fear that loss of unity may bring outside intervention. Trejo Reyes (1987, 1988) suggests that Mexicans have been able to put up with much in the way of inequality and delayed rewards out of a combination of nationalism and hope of national progress. But as existing leadership commits itself to greater internationalization, its ability to command nationalist loyalties and symbols is reduced. Meanwhile, opposition from the right, despite the desire of some businessmen for more protection, and despite some nationalist trappings in the Manuel Clouthier 1989 PAN campaign, is limited in its nationalist appeals by past links of the PAN to U.S. ultra-conservatives. Thus, the mantle of nationalism has been ceded to the populist side, which, however, can only wear it if it can present a credible program for growth and security. (In the absence of such a program, the left can easily remain a coalition of local and sectoral interests that fragments rather than unifies the nation.) Unless a long-term project emerges from the coalition that backed Cárdenas in 1988, putting the force of nationalist loyalties behind a new development effort will be difficult for Mexico.

This is particularly troublesome as a security issue because as the crisis continues, patience and past loyalties are wearing thin. Our interviews and observations (Edel and Edel 1989) during the election campaign suggested there was a great depth of cynicism about any national political and/or comprehensive economic solution. Such an outlook was compatible, at first, with a reliance on either individual effort or community ties for survival, as long as the odds for such solutions did not seem too adverse. But after the stock market crash and the devaluation in the fall of 1987, individual and community prospects seemed to worsen, legitimating a sense that the system was to blame. The opposition campaigns of Clouthier and Cárdenas catalyzed the expression of this discontent by making people aware that others shared it. They also channeled it into traditional, electoral channels for a time. What will happen, in terms of either organized political movement or anomic outbursts, now that the election is past, and what the response of Mexico's government — and its northern neighbor — would be to such outbursts, are troubling questions for anyone concerned with Mexico's security.

Foreign Constraints and Mexico's Response

A ny discussion of longer-term development options for Mexico, involving as it does discussion of the country's degree of openness, must consider the probable state of the outside world, and particularly of the large country to Mexico's immediate north. Controversy over deindustrialization, deficit, and economic dogma in the United States and parallel controversies elsewhere (not excluding the "communist" nations) suggest that the specific pattern of growth in the United States and world economies is itself as much at issue as is the pattern in Mexico. To some extent, one can speak of a crisis of the postwar accumulation patterns of the United States and the industrial West, as one can of the exhaustion of the postrevolutionary Mexican model. Whether the world economy (or at least, the U.S., Japanese, and EC economies) will or will not be able to maintain a coordinated macroeconomic policy is uncertain. So, too, is whether the overall system can maintain a rapid pace of technological innovation and investment sufficient to serve as an engine of growth for the world economy. It is not yet possible to determine whether the partial recoveries of the 1980s are a short-term phenomenon, spurred by U.S. deficits and falling oil prices, or whether they mark the beginning of a new major phase of accumulation, and if so, what its main features are (Edel 1983; Sanderson 1985; Sassen 1988).

In this situation, Mexico cannot even tell to what extent it has sure markets for more than a few luxury exports (as well as oil) and to what extent policies either of technological development or of cheap labor-oriented export growth will put it in severe competition with other countries or even with sectors in the developed world. The answers to these questions could greatly affect the costs and benefits, or the very viability, of different development paths for Mexico.

That Mexico is constrained by outside forces is clearly part of its (at least partial) dependence. But international policy must also be part of Mexico's economic strategy. Here again, the "neoliberal" and "nationalist" sides of the debate have general stances toward policy but not fully articulated programs. The de la Madrid and Carlos Salinas de Gortari administrations have generally favored closer integration with the world economy, and certainly such acts as joining GATT and reducing constraints on imports of goods and private investment capital are part of a program. But explicit responses to U.S.-Canadian integration and to U.S. protectionism are not yet apparent, nor is it clear (as indicated above in the discussion of industrial and agricultural policy) whether specific product lines should be exempted from a general opening trend. Similarly, the Cardenista opposition's general tone of nationalism is balanced, at times, by notes of reassurance to U.S. businesses, but how much decoupling from the United States is desired remains uncertain.

Conclusion

The main conclusion of this historical and projective exercise can be simply put. Discussion of Mexican economic policy is too often dominated by simplistic views of the previous cycle of accumulation. Neither the *leyenda negra* (black legend) that the nationalist policies of the past sixty years were a disaster nor the notion that they represent a golden age (*edad de oro*) that must be resurrected in its original form is a helpful basis for policy. The history of Mexico's past cycle of accumulation, and of the origins of the present crisis, affects present options and should be understood. But simple myths cannot be the basis for a coherent overall approach to help create a new, integrated pattern of accumulation.

Notes

1. Hamilton (1982) states that the Cárdenas government actually had to create such a bourgeoisie. Other evidence suggests, however, that this class was already well represented in the government. Hodges and Gandy (1979) argue the Alvaro Obregón-Plutarco Elías Calles forces in the revolution represented an agrarian-mercantile bourgeoisie, which successfully held a middle-ground position between the *hacendado* (landowner) and export bourgeoisies mobilized by Díaz and the peasant and worker radicals. Haber (1985) suggests that a core of industrial capitalist groups survived the revolution intact.

2. The reintegration of Mexico can be considered as, in effect, a choice, whatever the details of Lázaro Cárdenas's motives in picking his successor. The decision, which had lasting consequences, came at a time when a wide range of socioeconomic models (communism, social democracy, New Deal capitalism, laíssez faire, and fascism) all had a certain degree of legitimacy as national options. Mexico's selection of state-supervised capitalism seems as if it were designed to avoid a full-scale split between left and right, which might have threatened internal peace. But the proximity of the United States and the impending shadow of World War II, no doubt, were security considerations militating against a more extreme choice. The degree of participation Mexico was able to achieve in the post-war economic system was, for a time, not unfavorable to growth. But that degree of participation also must be reckoned as an element in the crises of the 1970s and 1980s and as a constraint on future choice.

3. A parallel reorientation occurred in the previous Porfirian growth round. Although growth in the Porfiriato has been remembered as dominated by foreign capital and an export orientation, much of the early growth and policy in that period was focused on the creation and unification of a domestic market. Even foreign investment, particularly in railroads, initially helped to unify and stimulate this domestic market. Later in the cycle, the external orientation became more dominant (Edel 1985).

4. Trejo Reyes (1988) points out that the minimum wage, which is frequently cited as a measure of wages, may overstate losses, since many industrial workers are paid wages higher than the minimum. But even he describes a decline of more than a third in these wages prior to the 1988 Pact, suggesting the 40 percent figure including the effects of the Pact. The minimum wage itself shows a loss of over 50 percent from 1982 to the end of 1988.

5. The term "project" connotes a set of "long- or middle-range plans favoring the interests of particular sectors" (Gettleman 1988).

6. There is some attempt to flesh out the nationalist project, in terms of the need to develop capital goods industries and engage in certain measures

for income redistribution, and the authors do attempt to discuss some concrete measures such as entry into the GATT as proposed by the neoliberals. The authors suggest these schemes go beyond the proposals that were extant from capital and from labor when they wrote the essay during the period of the oil boom.

7. The oddest paradox in this policy field is that many opponents of government presence in production in general seem to support the government-owned nuclear power plant at Laguna Verde.

8. See the paper by Roger Bartra in this collection.

References

Alberro S., José Luis, and David Ibarra. 1987. "Programas heterodoxos de estabilización." *Estudios Económicos* Special Number (October).

Alberro S., José Luis, and María Dolores Nieto-Iruarte. 1986. "Empirical Foundations of Marxian Categories in Mexico: 1970-1975." *Review of Radical Political Economics* 18 (4)(Winter).

Alberro S., José Luis, and Jorge E. Cambiaso. 1986. "Características del ajuste de la economía mexicana." Documento de Trabajo, Centro de Estudios Económicos, El Colegio de Mexico.

Amin, Samir. 1976. *Unequal Development*. New York: Monthly Review Press.

Austin, James E., and Gustavo Esteva, eds. 1987. *Food Policy in Mexico: The Search for Self-Sufficiency*. Ithaca, N.Y.: Cornell University Press.

Ballesteros, J., M. Edel, and M. Nelson. 1970. *La colonización del Papaloapán: Una evaluación socioeconómica*. Mexico: Centro de Investigaciones Agrarias.

Barkin, David. 1987. "The End to Food Self-Sufficiency in Mexico." *Latin American Perspectives* 14(3)(Summer).

Barkin, David, and Gustavo Esteva. 1979. *Inflación y democracia: el caso de México*. Mexico: Siglo XXI.

Barkin, David, and Blanca Suárez. 1983. *El fin del principio: las semillas y la seguridad alimentaria*. Mexico: Centro de Ecodesarrollo.

Barkin, David, and Blanca Suárez. 1985. *El fin de la autosuficiencia alimentaria*. Mexico: Centro de Ecodesarrollo.

Bartra, Roger. 1987. *La jaula de la melancolía*. Mexico: Grijalbo.

Bazdresch, Carlos. 1986. "Los subsidios y la concentración en la Ciudad de Mexico." In *Descentralización y democracia en Mexico*, ed., B. Torres. Mexico: Colegio de Mexico.

Beneria, Lourdes, and Martha Roldán. 1987. *The Crossroads of Class and Gender*. Chicago, Ill.: University of Chicago Press.

Boltvinik, Julio, and Enrique Hernández Laos. 1981. "El origen de la crisis industrial: el agotamiento del modelo de sustitución de importaciones." In *Desarrollo y crisis de la economía mexicana*, ed., R. Cordera. Mexico: Fondo de Cultura Económica.

Cárdenas, Enrique. 1982. *Mexico's Industrialization During the Great Depression: Public Policy and Private Response*. Ph.D. diss. Yale University, New Haven, Conn.

Cartas Contreras, Celso. 1987. "The Agricultural Sector's Contribution to the Import-Substituting Industrialization Process in Mexico." In *U.S.-Mexico Relations: Agriculture and Rural Development*, eds., B. F. Johnston et al. Stanford, Calif.: Stanford University Press.

CEESP (Centro de Estudios Económicos del Sector Privado). 1987. *La economía subterránea en Mexico*. Mexico: Diana.

Cook, Scott. 1988. "Inflation and Rural Livelihood in a Mexican Province: An Exploratory Analysis." *Mexican Studies/Estudios Mexicanos* 4(1)(Winter).

Cordera, Rolando, and Carlos Tello. 1981. *La disputa por la nación*. Mexico: Siglo XXI.

Cordera, Rolando, and Carlos Tello. 1983. "Prospects and Options for Mexican Society." In *U.S.-Mexico Relations: Economic and Social Aspects*, eds., C. W. Reynolds and C. Tello. Stanford, Calif.: Stanford University Press.

Corro, Salvador. 1988. "El gobierno pintó a los líderes obreros una posible catástrofe." *Proceso* (616)(August 22).

De Soto, Hernando. 1986. *El otro sendero: La revolución informal*. Lima. Colombia: Oveja Negra (1989), New York: Harper & Row (1989).

Eckstein, Susan. 1988. "Urbanization Revisited: Inner-City Slums of Hope and Squatter Settlement of Despair." Paper delivered at New England Council on Latin American Studies, annual meeting.

Edel, Candace Kim, and Matthew Edel. 1989. "Mexico: From Economic Crisis to Political Confrontation." Working paper. New York: Bildner Center for Western Hemisphere Studies, The Graduate School and University Center of the City University of New York.

Edel, Matthew. 1969. *Food Supply and Inflation in Latin America*. New York: Praeger.

Edel, Matthew. 1983. "The Reindustrialization Debate in the United States and its Implications for Latin America." Working paper.

Bildner Center for Western Hemisphere Studies, Graduate School of the City University of New York.

Edel, Matthew. 1985. "Economic Long Swings: Mexico and the United States." Working paper. Stanford University Project on United States-Mexico Relations.

Edel, M., E. Sclar, and D. Luria. 1984. *Shaky Palaces: Homeownership and Social Mobility in Boston's Suburbanization.* New York: Columbia University Press.

FitzGerald, E.V.K. 1983. "Mexico-United States Economic Relations and the World Cycle: A European View." In *U.S.-Mexico Relations: Economic and Social Aspects,* eds., C. W. Reynolds and C. Tello. Stanford, Calif.: Stanford University Press.

Flores, Edmundo. 1961. *Tratado de economía agrícola.* Mexico: Fondo de Cultura Económica.

Garza, Gustavo. 1985. *El proceso de industrialización en la ciudad de México 1821-1970.* Mexico: Colegio de Mexico.

Gettleman, Marvin. 1988. "Gringos y Latinos: Bicentennial Notes on Comparative Political Discourse." *Monthly Review* 40 (7)(December).

González Casanova, Pablo. 1965. *La democracia en México.* Mexico: Era.

Haber, Stephen H. 1985. *The Industrialization of Mexico: 1890 to 1940.* Ph.D. diss., University of California at Los Angeles.

Hamilton, Nora. 1982. *Mexico: The Limits of State Autonomy.* Princeton, N.J.: Princeton University Press.

Hirschman, Albert O. 1945. *National Power and the Structure of World Trade.* Berkeley and Los Angeles: University of California Press.

Hirschman, Albert O. 1986. "The Political Economy of Latin American Development: Seven Exercises in Retrospection." *Latin American Research Review* XXII(3).

Hodges, Donald, and Ross Gandy. 1979. *Mexico 1910-1976: Reform or Revolution?* London: Zed Press.

Instituto Nacional de Consumidor. 1988. *Seguimiento del gasto alimentario de la población de escasos recursos del área metropolitana de la Ciudad de México: Primer panel de familias.* Draft circulated, Dirección Técnica, Subdirección de Estudios Socioeconómicos, Departamento de Encuestas Sobre Consumo.

Lewis, Oscar. 1960. "Mexico since Cárdenas." In Council on Foreign Relations, *Social Change in Latin America Today.* New York: Harper and Brothers.

Martínez de Navarrette, I. 1960. *La distribución del ingreso y el desarrollo económico de México.* Mexico: UNAM.

Nash, June. 1988. "Household Economy in the World Crisis." Paper presented at the Conference on Artisan Production, Graduate School and University Center of the City University of New York.

Oliveira, Orlandina de, and Humberto Muñoz García. 1989. "Concentration or Deconcentration: Mexico City and its Region." In *Cities in Crisis: The Urban Challenge in the Americas,* eds., Matthew Edel and Ronald G. Hellman. New York: Bildner Center for Western Hemisphere Studies.

O'Connor, James. 1984. *Accumulation Crisis.* Oxford: Basil Blackwell.

O'Connor, James. 1987. *The Meaning of Crisis.* Oxford: Basil Blackwell.

Ortiz Cruz, Etelberto. 1988. "Competition, Prices of Production and Crisis in the Mexican Economy." Paper presented at Conference on International Perspectives on Profitability and Accumulation, 16-18 Sept., New York University.

Ortiz Cruz, E., M. Robles, H. Dávila, and L. Rodríguez. 1986. "Estructura de valor y crisis de la economía mexicana." *Economía: Teoría y Práctica,* no. 9, Mexico.

Pellicer de Brody, Olga. 1983. "National Security in Mexico: Traditional Notions and New Preoccupations." In *U.S.-Mexico Relations: Economic and Social Aspects,* eds., C.W. Reynolds and C. Tello. Stanford, Calif.: Stanford University Press.

Rendón, Teresa, and Carlos Salas. 1987. "Evolución del empleo en México: 1895-1950." *Estudios demográficos y urbanos* 2 (2)(May-August).

Rendón, Teresa, and Carlos Salas. 1988. "Employment and Wages in Mexico: Recent Tendencies and Perspectives." Paper delivered at Allied Social Science Associations annual meeting.

Reynolds, Clark W. 1970. *The Mexican Economy: Twentieth Century Structure and Growth.* New Haven, Conn.: Yale University Press.

Sanderson, Steven, ed. 1985. *The Americas in the New International Division of Labor.* New York: Holmes and Meier.

Sassen, Saskia. 1988. *The Mobility of Labor and Capital.* Cambridge: Cambridge University Press.

Silva-Herzog F., Jesús. 1987. *Beyond the Crisis: Mexico and the Americas in Transition.* Stanford: Stanford University Americas Program.

Solís, Leopoldo. 1981. *La realidad económica mexicana: retrovisión y perspectivas.* Rev. ed. Mexico: Siglo XXI.

Tello, Carlos. 1984. *La nacionalización de la banca en México.* Mexico: Siglo XXI.

Trejo Reyes, Saúl. 1987. *El futuro de la política industrial en Mexico.* Mexico: El Colegio de Mexico.

Trejo Reyes, Saúl. 1988. *Empleo para todos: el reto y los caminos.* Mexico: Fondo de Cultura Económica.

Valle, Alejandro. 1985. "Tasa de ganancia en México." Paper presented at workshop on cycles and crises in the Mexican economy, University of California, San Diego.

Vernon, Raymond. 1963. *The Dilemma of Mexico's Development.* Cambridge, Mass.: Harvard University Press.

Villarreal, René. 1976. *El desequilibrio externo en la industrialización de México.* Mexico: Fondo de Cultura Económica.

Weisskoff, Richard. 1985. *Factories and Food Stamps.* Baltimore: Johns Hopkins University Press.

Woodward, Bob. 1987. *Veil: The Secret Wars of the C.I.A. 1981-1987.* New York: Simon and Schuster.

Zaid, Gabriel. 1987. *La economía presidencial.* Mexico: Vuelta.

Environment and Security in Mexico

Diana M. Liverman

The Debate About Environment and Security

As environmental problems in many parts of the world have become increasingly severe, some people have suggested that we must broaden our definition of national security to incorporate notions of environmental conservation and resource management (Brown 1977; Clark 1987; Galtung 1982; Maguire and Welsh Brown 1986; Mathews 1989; Myers 1988; Westing 1986). In these broader definitions, security is associated with potential destruction of the basic life support systems of land, ocean, and atmosphere; conflicts over limited and border resources; environmental bases for sustained economic development and trade; and the relationship between ecological concerns and popular political movements.

For example, N. Myers (1988), emphasizing the need to incorporate an environmental dimension into U.S. security planning, links deforestation in the Philippines, water shortages in the Middle East, and land degradation in El Salvador to U.S. strategic and economic interests. J.T. Mathews (1989), in her plea to broaden the definition of security to include resource, environmental, and demographic issues, discusses the threats posed by deforestation, species loss, soil erosion, and atmospheric pollution. She highlights the tensions created in Central America and East Africa by millions of "environmental refugees" from resource mismanagement and suggests that environmental problems make traditional conceptions of national sovereignty obsolete. Others identify the possibility of global warming and the destruction of the ozone layer as major international security threats

(Jager 1988; Schneider 1988; Usher 1989; Tickell 1977). Other environmental problems identified as security issues include transborder air and water pollution and the export of wastes and toxic products (Brown 1987; Leonard 1987; World Commission on Environment and Development 1987; World Resources Institute 1988).

But what is meant by "security," and where does the environment rank against other security concerns? Traditionally, security is defined as military defense of the physical territory of nation-states (Barnaby 1988). In this narrow conception, environmental problems would rarely be seen as security threats, except in boundary disputes over contested resources, such as water, or where environmental collapse forces refugee movements across national boundaries. Even from this limited point of view, environmental issues do affect security. For example, A.H. Westing (1986) catalogs a fascinating list of wars over resources in which he includes the 1967 Arab-Israeli war (partly over water), the 1969 El Salvador-Honduras war (land scarcity), the clashes of Iceland (1972) and Argentina (1982) with Britain (partly over fishing rights), as well as aspects of World Wars I and II. R.J. Dupuy (1983) and R.W. Arad (1979) also discuss a number of conflicts over scarce and shared natural resources.

In fact, the traditional definition of security as defense of physical territory has often been expanded to include defense of strategic resources and markets and of a nation's political and social values. In this sense, many states have intervened to defend or secure access to resources in their former colonies and in regions where they have important economic interests (Choucri 1984).

Contemporary definitions of security are becoming much broader, extending both above and below the nation-state to incorporate conceptions of shared global security as well as the security of individuals. The definition of security has been extended beyond the military to include economic, ecological, food, and psychological security. N. Behar (1985) discusses nonmilitary aspects of European security, including the need to consider common interests in economic, energy, and environmental security. In a landmark essay, R.H. Ullman (1983) suggests that defining security in narrow military terms is misleading and dangerous, because it ignores other important threats and promotes a militarization of international relations. He proposes a redefinition of security threats to include crises which degrade the quality of life for a state's inhabitants and those factors which narrow the range of policy choices to governments and other groups. He submits that natural disasters, rapid population growth, energy crises, and environmental degradation can be grave threats to national and international security. On the other hand, authors such as L. Schoultz (1987) and J.S. Nye and S.M. Lynn-Jones (1988) view security much more narrowly and do not mention environmental issues.

Of course, as the definition of security is broadened conceptually and geographically, approaches to security can become incompatible. The security of the state (or more specifically, of a regime) can be inconsistent with the security of its citizens or its neighbors. For example, weapons used to defend military security are likely to devastate the environment and threaten food and ecological security (Galtung 1982; Westing 1986). And, as broader definitions of security become accepted, it is possible that the use of military force to defend economic or environmental security may become more frequent and legitimate.

Environmental issues are clearly moving up a broadly defined security agenda in many regions, especially when longer-term concerns are discussed. Some still assert that environmental security is a luxury, claimed only by those who are economically prosperous and at peace, or an excuse for some richer nations to hinder the development of poorer regions. This perceived contradiction between economic and environmental security has been part of a debate within nations as well as between nations, with pollution control seen to threaten employment and trade and nature conservation viewed as taking land away from agricultural production or resource extraction (Almeida, et al. 1972; CEPAL 1980; Farquarson 1988). Nevertheless, many reports, groups, and political figures are beginning to describe serious environmental threats to security and to point out that environmental protection is consistent with, not antagonistic to, economic development, strategic interests, and social justice (IUCN 1980; Repetto 1985; Salinas de Gortari 1989; Usher 1989; World Commission on Environment and Development 1987).

Environment and Security in Mexico

M any of the environmental problems identified as security threats in different parts of the world can be encountered in severe forms in the Republic of Mexico. Climatic change, soil erosion, loss of crop diversity, and pollution imperil Mexico's food security; border resource

competition, trade in toxic wastes and risky technologies, and environmental refugees elevate tensions with its neighbors; and the widespread deterioration in living conditions diminishes health security and
motivates popular movements which are questioning the legitimacy of
the governing party and the economic structure.

Other essays in this volume report on relationships between
Mexican security and factors, such as economic dependence, political
trends, and relations with the United States and Central America. These
issues, at first glance, seem much more urgent than the environment
(Castañeda 1986). Several of them, such as economic decline and the
debt, are major causes of environmental problems. This essay argues
that more traditional security concerns, as well as the sustainability of
Mexican development and the satisfaction of the Mexican people's
basic needs, are intrinsically and inevitably linked to questions of
environmental security.

Natural Environment and Security in Mexican History

The country of Mexico is richly endowed with a variety of natural
resources and ecological conditions (Bassols Batalla 1983; García
and Falcon 1972). The objective of foreign intervention and conquest
has frequently been to gain access to Mexico's rich resources of
minerals, lands, and water. In turn, foreign intervention, particularly
the Spanish conquest, dramatically transformed Mexican ecology and
culture (Crosby 1976). Mexico's resources are unequally distributed in
both space and society (Bataillon 1969). For example, water flows
freely in southern Mexico, where topography, heat, and disease have
historically limited agriculture and industrial development. In the north
and central highland regions, where other resources are abundant and
where most of the population lives, water is more limited, and rain-fed
agriculture is very vulnerable to meteorological extremes (Lee 1976;
Looney 1978). This uneven distribution of resources, combined with
a social structure in which some people control more of these
resources than others, has created patterns of unequal development
and impoverishment, which have consistently influenced Mexican
political stability and international relations.

Mexico's tropical location and geology, while providing a range
of useful resources, expose the Mexican people to the risks of
environmental extremes such as droughts, hurricanes, earthquakes,
and volcanic eruptions (Amerlinck 1986; Claxton 1986; Ortiz 1947).

Archaeological evidence suggests that a number of early civilizations in Mexico were destroyed by such events, although others were more resilient (Byers 1967; Claxton 1986; Humboldt 1966; Kandell 1988; Sanders, et al. 1979). Historians suggest that environmental extremes have interacted with political economy to create social crises and political instability. In 1629, heavy rains flooded rapidly growing Mexico City. In the five years it took the floodwater to recede, commerce and daily life were disrupted, and severe famine conditions emerged (Boyer 1975; Hoberman 1974). E. Florescano (1969, 1980) has shown how drought, in combination with market manipulation of maize prices, created destitution and famine among the Mexican poor in the sixteenth century. Authors such as E. Florescano (1980), J. Kandell (1988), and S. Sanders (1986) also tend to find environmental factors in tracing some of the causes of more recent political events in Mexico, such as the struggle for independence and the revolution. In the last ten years, the 1982 drought, 1983 El Chichón volcanic eruption, the 1985 Mexico City earthquake, and Hurricane Gilbert in 1988 have illustrated the regional and national effects of natural disasters on food security, social welfare, and political legitimacy. The Mexico City earthquake, in particular, has been identified as a critical blow to hopes for economic recovery and to support for the government (Aguilar Zinser 1986; Editorial Research Reports 1985; Musacchio 1986).

Although the examples above emphasize the role of apparently uncontrollable natural phenomena, it is nature transformed by human action, and the political and economic structures that create vulnerability to environmental variations, that must bear much of the blame for environmental threats to security in Mexican history. Human activities, organized in particular ways, have caused deforestation, soil erosion, and poor water management during (and, maybe, before) the colonial period and were responsible for agricultural crises in many regions of Mexico. Unequal access to land and lack of entitlement to food and water contributed most directly to famine under the political and economic structures imposed by the Aztecs, by the Spanish, and after independence. Poor construction, insecure land tenure, and poverty have made some people much more vulnerable to earthquakes and hurricanes than others. Most of the current environmental threats to Mexican security can be associated with human degradation of resources and the contemporary political economy of land and resource use.

Mexican security is discussed in several senses in the examples that follow. The first sense is a narrower definition of security, in which environmental risks to Mexican national security are identified with threats to territory, sovereignty, strategic resources, and markets; the second sense defines security as the satisfaction of the basic needs for food, health, water, housing, and social justice of the Mexican people; a third perspective examines the possible relationships between environmental problems and the security of the Mexican state and political system.

Border Environmental Issues

M exico shares land borders with the United States, Belize, and Guatemala and shares the Caribbean and Pacific oceans with many nations. Two major sources of conflict and insecurity along these borders are competition for scarce resources — particularly, water and fish — and transborder pollution (Armstrong 1983; Hansen 1981; House 1982; Mumme 1987; Utton 1973, 1982). A range of international agreements regulate border environmental management, particularly on the U.S.-Mexican border (Ross 1977, 1983), and despite a series of disputes, border environmental issues have not yet created major tensions between Mexico and the United States.

One potential threat to Mexican security is the quantity and quality of water resources along the border with the United States. Although Mexico is guaranteed water from the Colorado River and Rio Grande/Bravo, the share is increasingly inadequate to meet demands for irrigation, energy supplies, settlements, and industry along Mexico's rapidly developing northern border (Armstrong 1983; Day 1970; Utton 1982). Depletion and pollution of shared groundwater resources, especially in the El Paso/Juárez region, are also becoming a bilateral concern (Mumme 1988). Proposals for dams and continuing deforestation of watersheds along Mexico's southern border may also become a source of international tension.

In arid regions like the U.S.-Mexican border, competition and conflicts over water can be seen as threats to economic security and national sovereignty (Martínez 1988). J.K. Cooley (1984) traces the roots of wars in the Middle East to struggles over the water of rivers like the Jordan, Litani, and Yarmuk. Others see potential for conflict over the shared resources of the Nile and Ganges rivers (Myers 1988). Although many see boundary water management between the United

States and Mexico as a successful case in conflict resolution (Jamail and Mumme 1982; Nalven 1986), increasing demands, and possibly climatic changes, may exacerbate tension (Gleick 1988).

Contamination of rivers, from both U.S. and Mexican origins, is also a problem, especially salinity in the Colorado (Ingram 1988) and pesticides in the Rio Grande/Bravo. The United States has constructed a desalination facility near Yuma, Arizona to try to improve the quality of river water. The pollution of the Rio Nuevo/New River, flowing from Mexicali, Mexico into the United States, has also caused some conflict between the two countries. Although the contamination of this river seemingly originates in Mexico, many of the factories and waste sites causing the pollution are apparently owned or used by U.S. companies. Bilateral agreements to clean up the river, which posed dangerous health threats, were conducted at the highest levels (Mumme 1988). Sewage flows in the Tijuana-San Diego area have also been a source of contention, with untreated waste from Tijuana contaminating San Diego beaches (Herzog 1986). However, this conflict, too, has been addressed within the framework of a bilateral agreement which allows for some financial assistance from the United States to Mexico to construct treatment facilities (Nalven 1986; Mumme 1988).

Transborder air pollution has also been a cause for conflict and cooperation between the United States and Mexico (Applegate 1982; Applegate and Bath 1978; Bath 1979). Copper smelters in Cananea and Nacozari in Mexico, and El Paso and Douglas in the United States, have been viewed as health threats to citizens across the border. S. Mumme (1984) uses the Cananea case to illustrate some interesting ideas about dependence and interdependence between the United States and Mexico. A U.S. loan for expansion of the smelter was opposed, for different reasons, by a coalition of both environmental groups and the copper industry in the United States. In Mexico, concern was raised about foreign ownership and the conflict between economic needs and environmental protection.

More recently, urbanization and industrialization of border cities has led to elevated pollution levels and related health concerns across the border. In both the United States and Mexico, there is anxiety about work place health standards in the Mexican *maquiladora* factories, many of them set up or co-owned by U.S. companies, which have moved across the border to take advantage of cheaper labor, economic incentives, and perhaps lower environmental standards in Mexico

(Maquiladoras 1988; Fernández-Kelly 1983). The question of differential standards for work place health and waste management is very sensitive, especially if it results in the "export" of pollution and toxic substances across borders (Nalven 1986). Although Mexico has a number of environmental regulations which deal with work place conditions, pollution, and waste dumping, it is difficult to monitor and enforce them, especially in a time of economic crisis. There are a number of cases of illegal dumping in Mexico of toxic wastes from U.S.-based companies (Juffer 1988). In 1981, a large amount of toxic waste, (including forty-two drums of dangerous PCBs) was dumped in Zacatecas. In 1986, ten thousand gallons of toxins were illegally dumped near Tecate (Mumme 1986).

A major potential concern for Mexico is the presence of nuclear facilities and targets in the United States, adjacent to the international border. Nuclear plants in California and Arizona, nuclear waste storage and weapons testing facilities in New Mexico, and major military and strategic locations throughout the border region all pose the risks of radioactive contamination in northern Mexico (UCLA 1983). As accidents at Chernobyl and Three Mile Island demonstrated, radioactive contamination is a significant ecological and psychological threat to human health and economic activity (*The Ecologist* 1986). Mexico received dried milk from Ireland containing radioactive contamination after the Chernobyl disaster (Ortiz 1987).

Environmental Degradation and Agriculture

The degradation of the resources needed to sustain Mexican agricultural production is a serious menace to food and economic security. Widespread soil erosion, water scarcity, loss of biodiversity, pollution, and unequal distribution of productive resources diminish the sustainability of rural and urban life in Mexico, increasing poverty, hunger, and social unrest. Many authors have documented the nature and causes of environmental problems in Mexican agriculture, although the focus has generally been on the economic and social dimensions of agrarian crisis (Barkin and King 1970; Esteva 1983; Sanderson 1986; Yates 1981).

Several studies described severe soil erosion in many parts of Mexico, associated with declines in soil fertility and agricultural production (Maas 1988; Mondragon 1986; Ortiz 1987). V.M. Toledo (1985) has estimated that 15 percent of Mexican agricultural land is totally eroded, and 26 percent is severely eroded. SEDUE (1986) reports that 70 percent of the productive land is suffering from some erosion. D. Barkin and colleagues have documented the environmental and social impacts of irrigation and other rural development projects in several regions of Mexico (Barkin and King 1970; Barkin 1978), and they have analyzed related declines in food self-sufficiency (Barkin and Suárez 1982; Toledo 1985a). J.E. Austin and G. Esteva (1987), I. Restrepo (1986), S. Sanderson (1986), and A. Warman (1982) have also made general comments on the ecological problems associated with changes in agriculture, particularly the environmental impacts of new technologies such as large-scale irrigation, improved seeds, fertilizers, and mechanization. SEDUE (1986) estimates that 10 percent of the irrigated land is already too saline for crop production. Forceful case studies by C. Hewitt de Alcántara (1976), D.R. Mares (1987), and T.E. Sheridan (1988) in northwest Mexico illustrate the ecological and social transformation of communities as agriculture intensifies and becomes export oriented. Many of these authors have noted the contradictions inherent in the package of agricultural technologies termed the "Green Revolution" and in an export-oriented agriculture which increases short-term food or economic security at the national level for certain groups, yet may reduce long-term security through environmental degradation or the impoverishment of marginal groups (Pearse 1980).

The expansion of agriculture and settlement into forested and mountainous areas, due to land scarcity, population growth, and state development initiatives, is another example of how short-term attempts to increase food and economic security may decrease longer-term security. In southern Mexico, agricultural production in recently deforested areas has encountered difficulties with disease, rapidly declining soil fertility, drought, and erosion (Barkin 1978; Ewell and Poleman 1980; Restrepo 1986; Székely and Restrepo 1988). In Chiapas, the deforestation and development of the border with Guatemala has been partly designed to populate a region and increase the security of the border region (Aguayo 1987). Deforestation in Chiapas and other southern states has also been associated with refugees from political and environmental collapse in Central America (Aguayo 1985), unequal land and income distribution (Lobato 1980), and foreign capital (González 1983).

Deforestation and agricultural development also imperil Mexican and international food and health security through the destruction of biodiversity (Gómez-Pompa 1976, 1985; Halffter 1977; Toledo 1985). Mexico is one of the world's major centers of crop genetic diversity, harboring a large range of varieties of important plants like maize (Sauer 1952). These original varieties, and their ancestors like teosinte, are critical to crop breeding programs and efforts to increase yields and make them more resilient to climate and disease (National Academy of Sciences 1972). Genetic diversity is being lost through development programs and market forces which are eradicating traditional farming that uses a wide range of varieties (Altieri and Trujillo 1987; Barkin and Suárez 1983; Gliessman, García, and Amador 1981; Nahmad, González, and Rees 1988; Wilken 1987). Tropical forests are also considered to protect many plant and animal species which may have valuable medicinal properties and, thus, may to be important to local and global health (Ehrlich and Ehrlich 1981; Myers 1984). Many of the remaining areas of biodiversity in Mexico are currently at risk from development (Mexico 1988; Edwards 1986; Vovides 1981). V.M. Toledo (1985) estimates that four hundred thousand hectares of forest are being lost in Mexico each year and that 50 percent of Mexican species are in danger of extinction. Although there are a number of programs to preserve forests and biodiversity in parks, biosphere reserves, and indigenous agricultural programs, many of these projects are hampered by lack of funds, land, and public support (Mexico 1988; Iltis 1980; Romero 1987; Vargas Márquez 1984).

The health of the Mexican population is at risk from another aspect of agricultural development — the increasing use of pesticides (Simonian 1988; Sparks 1988). I. Restrepo (1988), in an important book on pesticide use in Mexico, describes the health risks to workers and consumers from the widespread use and misuse of agricultural chemicals in Mexico. His concerns are echoed in case studies by L. Albert (1980), D. Barkin (1978), E. Feder (1977), and Angus Wright (1986). The processes that led to the export of hazardous pesticides, banned in countries like the United States, to the developing world are documented in D. Bull (1982) and D. Weir and M. Shapiro (1981).

The recent degradation of the Mexican agricultural environment and associated security concerns can be connected to the selection of certain development strategies by the Mexican government (Barkin 1988; Redclift 1982). The industrialization of agriculture, associated with the use of chemical-intensive, irrigated monocultures, has increased dependency on scarce water resources and expensive, often imported, inputs (Sanderson 1986). The orientation toward export markets has focused attention away from food self-sufficiency and has made producers vulnerable to foreign markets and product standards (Barkin and Suárez 1982). The decision to accept large loans and the subsequent debt burden has put more pressure on agricultural resources and producers to produce for domestic and foreign markets, with correlated environmental degradation and health problems.

Energy Development and Industrialization

Twentieth-century development strategies in Mexico have also centered on energy developments and industrialization. The discovery of oil in Mexico augured well for Mexican energy security but created a number of social, ecological, and economic problems (Gentleman 1984). The damage to coastal ecosystems, fisheries, water resources, and agriculture from oil-related pollution on the Gulf coast of Mexico has been documented by A. Toledo and his colleagues at the Centro Ecodesarrollo (see Toledo, et al. 1983; also Pérez Zapata 1983; Reyes, et al. 1979). Contamination from the extensive oil spill at the Ixtoc I oil rig in the Gulf of Mexico has been described by M.F. Ortiz (1987) and S.A. Guzmán, et al. (1986).

Other attempts to increase Mexico's energy security include large hydroelectric schemes and a decision to build nuclear power stations. Unfortunately, the flooding of valleys in hydroelectric schemes has contributed to the loss of productive land and biodiversity, and the dams and reservoirs are vulnerable to natural hazards and terrorism.

The recent debate about the Laguna Verde nuclear power plant, located north of Veracruz, has included a number of security issues. In addition to the risks from radioactive and thermal pollution to sensitive coastal ecosystems, neighboring settlements, and agriculture, Mexican environmentalists are concerned about the costs of the plant and about dependency on foreign technology, expertise, and uranium fuel (Arias and Barquera 1988; Weinberg 1987). Others are concerned about the vulnerability of the plant to terrorist attack, hurricanes, and earthquakes and about the safety and storage of nuclear waste. And the nonproliferation question brings Mexico into debates about the links between civilian energy and nuclear weapons production and the international instability that such a link may bring.

Radioactive hazards are also associated with medical activities in Mexico. In 1982, cobalt 60 pellets from an unused piece of medical equipment were obtained by the public in Juárez. Pellets were found in homes where people became sick, and some were incorporated into some scrap metal which was then made into steel girders and restaurant equipment (Ortiz 1987).

A number of authors have pointed out that choices about energy bring a host of security concerns. Some of these concerns, such as pollution and habitat destruction, are environmental and involve balancing the costs and benefits of different energy sources. But A.B. Lovins, et al. (1981) have shown how low-cost energy conservation strategies can increase energy security and be consistent with other ecological and political security concerns.

Rapid industrialization, often accompanying oil and energy development, has been associated with environmental risks and degradation in Mexico (Barkin 1988). Chronic, low-level exposure to industrial pollutants is likely to result in increases in cancer, pulmonary disease, and other severe health problems around major centers such as Mexico City, Monterrey, Ciudad Cárdenas, Coatzalocoacos, and the northern border cities (Vizcaíno Murray 1975). The sugar and paper industries have also been sources of chronic contamination in many rural areas. Major industrial accidents, such as the San Juan Ixhuatepec liquid natural gas explosion, have already occurred with significant loss of life and property (Arturson 1987; Johnson 1985). Previous accidents included a leak of hydrogen sulfide gas in Poza Rica in 1955 (twenty-two deaths) and arsenic contamination in Torreon in 1962 (Toledo 1985).

Degradation of Atmosphere and Oceans

M exican security may also be threatened by global environmental problems associated with pollution of the atmosphere and oceans. In addition to local pollution from oil, industry, tourism, and cities, Mexico's oceans are also contaminated by biological, chemical, and radioactive wastes from neighboring countries (Hatch 1978; Martín del Campo 1987; Merino 1987). Such contamination could affect the nutritional, health, and economic security of those who eat or sell marine resources or who rely on the prosperity of Mexico's coastal-based tourist industry. Ocean contamination, especially any cases involving medical waste washing up on beaches, such as recently occurred in the United States and the Mediterranean, could create financial problems for Mexico if it affected tourism, a major source of foreign exchange (*Mexican-American Review* 1980).

Among the wide range of global atmospheric pollutants, the "greenhouse gases" may be the most significant for Mexico. The recent predictions of a global warming associated with increases in atmospheric carbon dioxide and other greenhouse gases in the atmosphere have serious consequences for Mexico and other parts of Latin America. Fossil fuel burning and deforestation have led to increasing concentrations of atmospheric carbon dioxide, and the expansion of agricultural activities, such as livestock and paddy rice production, has led to increases in atmospheric methane. Mexico and Latin America have clearly contributed to such increases in carbon dioxide and methane. These, as well as other gases like nitrogen dioxide, trap outgoing terrestrial radiation and warm the atmosphere (EPA 1989). Mexico has so far made only a small contribution to such increases in carbon dioxide and methane, but future expansion of population, industry, and agriculture could bring much greater responsibility. In the last fifteen years, Mexican oil use has gone up 800 percent, motor vehicle ownership has tripled, and the cattle population has doubled (Ortiz 1987).

For hundreds of years, stable concentrations of greenhouse gases have maintained the average earth temperature at about 15°C. Most of the computer models that have been used to predict the climatic impact of a doubling of greenhouse gases, specifically carbon dioxide, suggest a global average temperature increase of 1.5°C to 4.5°C by the year 2030 (Schneider 1988). This will alter regional patterns of temperature and rainfall and, through a variety of mechanisms including thermal expansion and polar ice melting, may lead to a rise in sea level of up to two meters (Hekstra 1989).

These predictions, supported by some evidence of temperature and sea level rise already occurring, and fueled by dramatic weather events in 1988 (including drought in North America and severe storms in the tropics), have gained the attention of many politicians and international organizations (Jager 1988). In the United States, the Environmental Protection Agency is just one of the groups that are doing major assessments of the impact of global warming on the United States (EPA 1989). They have reported that global warming may result in reductions of water in the Colorado and Rio Bravo/Grande rivers of over 40 percent but have not addressed what this means for U.S.-

Mexico agreements and relations. As a result of such studies, the United States is beginning to push for agreements to control greenhouse gases and for collective action to deal with the impacts of global warming.

In Mexico — perhaps, because specific impacts have not been assessed or, more likely, because of other more urgent problems — little attention has been paid to the issue of climate change. It will be difficult for countries like Mexico to take a position on these actions unless they know how impacts are likely to affect them. In addition, it is important for any country to understand the regional impacts of warming on agriculture around the world in order to assess its future trade and food security situation (Crosson 1989).

D.M. Liverman and K. O'Brien (1989) have provided preliminary estimates of the possible impacts of the greenhouse effect on Mexico. They demonstrate that computer model estimates for Mexican climatic conditions, given a doubling of atmospheric carbon dioxide, show some disagreement. Four of the major models predict temperature increases in northern Mexico ranging from 2.4°C to 4.4°C. For central Mexico, the predicted temperature increase is from 2.3°C to 4.2°C. In northern Mexico, the predicted rainfall change varies by model from -24 percent to +4 percent, and in central Mexico, the predicted changes are from -7 percent to +5 percent. These discrepancies among the models, and between the predicted and observed current climate, emphasize the uncertainty associated with global warming studies.

Despite the differences in models, we find that the effect of various temperature increases, combined with both increases or decreases in precipitation, points to the same general conclusions. The increases in temperature result in significant increases in evaporation which outweigh the effects of any increase in rainfall and severely exacerbate any decreases. Generally, warmer, drier conditions are likely.

The implications of these predictions for Mexican agriculture, food security, human comfort, and coastal development are worrisome. For example, in Sonora, where summer temperatures are already uncomfortable for many people, we find that temperature rises of 3°C to 5°C bring June through September mean monthly temperatures of over 35°C. This temperature increase, which also occurs in the cooler winter months, counterbalances the value of the predicted rainfall increases so as to produce even more severe water deficits in the already arid climate of Sonora. These changes imply increased demand on already stressed irrigation systems and more stress on certain crops such as wheat, which prefer cooler temperatures. Sonoran agriculture is also threatened by any sea level rise. Irrigation systems and coastal agriculture, already experiencing salinization and poor drainage, will be further degraded by rising sea level and associated intrusions of salt water.

In Mexico City, increasing temperatures would bring much higher year-round temperatures, with a complex set of implications for pollution and human comfort. And these higher temperatures, combined with significantly lower rainfall in several months, will mean greater water deficits for the already overused regional water supply system (Farquarson 1988a). In other regions of Mexico, sea level rise may affect coastal developments and cities, including the Laguna Verde nuclear plant, oil facilities on the Gulf Coast, low-lying urban areas, and tourist developments. Although the average sea level rise is of concern, the implications of this rise for the frequency and magnitude of extreme flooding are even more significant. Some scientists also suggest that a warmer world might mean more intense tropical hurricanes. Overall, it may be a rise in the number and severity of natural disasters, such as floods, hurricanes, and droughts, which may pose the greatest risks to Mexico's food and economic security in a changed climate.

Despite the urgency of other problems in Mexico, the possible impacts of climate change merit more attention. Hydroelectric energy, irrigation systems, and limited urban water resources could be threatened by any decline in water supplies in major river basins. Sea level rise could threaten coastal agriculture, industry, and tourist developments, and higher temperatures could directly affect human comfort and labor productivity. Climatic changes could alter natural ecosystems, affect biosphere reserves, important species, and pests and disease. Changes in resources along borders with the United States and Central America could create political tensions, and any change in Mexican agricultural production will have some impacts on regional and global trade in key products, such as maize, wheat, cotton, winter fruit and vegetables, and beef. In planning irrigation, energy, and other developments, in thinking about food security, and in joining the planned international negotiations to control global warming, Mexico needs to be fully aware of the implications of climate change for national security. For, in addition to the direct impacts of climate change on agricultural production and other sectors, global climate change may be accompanied by major shifts in Mexico's and other nations' comparative agricultural advantage and population movements. The contributions of Mexico to greenhouse gas concentrations also need to be assessed, and the feasibility of limiting fossil fuel burning and deforestation discussed, so that Mexico can decide its position in any international negotiations.

There are other risks to Mexico from global atmospheric contamination. The depletion of the ozone layer, apparently due to the use of certain chemicals in aerosol propellants, refrigeration, air conditioning, and foam manufacture, may cause worldwide increases in skin cancer. Mexico is, however, a signatory to the recent Montreal protocol to control the use of ozone-damaging chemicals. Another concern would be the possible impacts on Mexico from a nuclear war. Scientists have suggested that the smoke and dust from nuclear explosions could prevent the sun's rays from reaching the surface and create cold "nuclear winter-type" conditions (Crutzen 1985). Mexico might suffer cooling effects directly and would also be affected by disruptions in the U.S. agricultural economy.

Urbanization and Environment

Journalists in many countries now use Mexico City as the environmental horror story of the century (Rother 1988; Voss 1986). The image of unbreathable air, mountains of garbage, overcrowding, and rampant disease do little to help Mexico's international business or conservation reputation. Obviously, much that has been written is exaggerated, stereotyped, and sensationalistic and can be set in context through a careful examination of facts and causes. But there are few careful and comprehensive studies of Mexico City's ecological situation because of a lack of data, because of bureaucratic problems, because conditions change daily, and because of the sheer size of the city. However, an important set of studies reported in V. Ibarra, et al. (1987) and S. Puente and J. Legoretta (n.d.) documents living conditions and environmental problems in certain areas of the city. Certainly, pollution and crowding in Mexico City are affecting the health and productivity of its citizens and, hence, the economy and administration of the country. Problems of waste disposal and water supply are particularly acute, and air pollution has reached dangerous levels in recent winters (*Excelsior* 1983; Marco del Pont 1986; Outerbridge 1987; Puente and Legoretta n.d.; Rivera, et al. 1987).

Of the several major environmental threats to the city, one, a major earthquake, occurred in 1985 and had widespread effects on the national economy and political situation. An acute air pollution episode that, like the earthquake, could paralyze the city and kill several thousands of its citizens is feared but has not yet occurred.

The centralization of government, banking, and many economic sectors in Mexico City increases the vulnerability of the nation to its capital's ecological problems. Yet, in some ways, the recovery from the 1985 earthquake suggests considerable resilience of the capital in the face of catastrophe. Perhaps the greatest security issue raised by the environmental problems of Mexico City (and other urban areas) is the frustration felt by large numbers of people with their living conditions and the lack of government response (Barkin 1988; Sternberg 1987). This dissatisfaction is evident in mass demonstrations focused on ecological and pollution issues and in the large opposition vote in recent elections.

Population Pressure, Resources, Environment, and Security

Although population growth is clearly a factor which can increase pressure on the environment and, hence, affect security, demographic explanations for global and Mexican problems are controversial and complex. Simplistic Malthusian explanations for global environmental problems were heavily criticized in the 1960s by authors, such as F.M. Lappé and J. Collins (1979), J. de Castro (1977) and M. Mamdani (1973), who claimed that the unequal distribution of resources was the major force behind poverty and environmental degradation and that overpopulation was a symptom rather than a cause of social problems. In addition, statements by representatives of more developed nations that less developed countries should control population growth were seen as hypocritical and culturally insensitive.

Several Mexican scholars have, nevertheless, included population growth as one of Mexico's major problems and population control as one of the major challenges (Alisky 1977, 1981; Beltran 1979; Urquidi and Morelos 1979). The role of population growth, given a fixed spatial and social distribution of resources, is clearly significant. At population growth rates of 2 to 4 percent, the pressure of local populations on resources in many regions of Mexico doubles every twenty years. This increases competition for land, water, and employment and exacerbates poverty and social unrest (Alisky 1977, 1981). Population growth is also a factor in the rapid urban growth of Mexico City and border communities, with associated resource demands and waste disposal problems. In southern Mexico, refugees from Central America are a concern (Aguayo 1985).

Although there are many researchers working on population questions and policy in Mexico, there are few studies which attempt to document systematically how Mexico's changing demography interacts with other factors to change pressure on resources. Such studies would be possible, and increasingly efficient, with the computerization of land and geographic information in Mexico. Such analyses could be powerful lobbying and educational tools for both ecological and population activists.

Environmental Policies and Security

A s in many other countries, most of Mexico's legislation relating to the environment stems from the 1970s (Leonard 1987). A wide range of laws and institutions have some responsibility for environmental management and protection (Branes 1987; DuMars and Beltran del Rio 1988; Mumme, Bath, and Assetto 1988). In 1988, a major new law, the Ley Ecológica, was passed to address a number of environmental problems, such as pollution and nature protection. The law decentralizes responsibility for enforcement and protection and contains proposals for penalties against polluters and for discussions with public interest groups. However, Mexico's environmental laws and government institutions, such as SEDUE (Secretaría de Desarrollo Urbano y Ecología), have been strongly criticized for their weak powers, lack of enforcement, or narrow vision (Barkin 1988; Toledo 1985a). Many of the current problems in environmental protection in Mexico can be related to the economic crisis and lack of government resources.

Mexico has been a signatory to most of the major international environmental agreements, such as the Law of the Sea (1982) and the Montreal Ozone Convention (1985). In 1974, Mexico led the way to the Cocoyoc declaration of a new international economic order, which elaborated the positions of the developing countries and included a discussion of environmental protection. As noted in the section of this chapter on the border, Mexico has signed a host of agreements with the United States on environmental management along the border and has recently signed an agreement with Guatemala dealing with ecological issues. Mexican environmentalists lament the fact that Mexico has not signed the CITES agreement (Convention on International Trade in Endangered Species). Mexico is thought to be one of the key gateways for trade in endangered animals and birds (Gómez-Pompa 1983).

It is important to restate that, apparently, local or national environmental issues actually have origins and impacts beyond Mexico's borders. For example, much of the ecological degradation and pollution from agriculture can be traced to the internationalization of the Mexican food system and the associated intensification of land and water use, application of fertilizers and pesticides, and expansion of the livestock industry (Sanderson 1986). Similarly, industrial pollution has been linked to multinational enterprises and export-oriented production. In both agriculture and industry, environmental problems have been indirectly linked to the imperatives of capital expansion into Mexico and the need to expand the export sector to obtain foreign exchange and service foreign debt (Barkin 1988). Pollution and accidents have been traced to inappropriate or costly technologies introduced into Mexico by alliances of foreign and Mexican investors or governments.

Economic crisis and foreign debt have led to increased pressure on environment and resources in many Latin American countries and to less active conservation and protection efforts. The search for foreign exchange to service debt and purchase imports has stimulated a push for expanded production in export sectors. This has been linked to deforestation, soil erosion, and increased use of chemicals in agriculture and to lax safety standards in industry. Government cutbacks have meant a lack of enforcement of existing environmental legislation and lower priorities for other conservation activities, such as pollution cleanup and park establishment. Individual citizens cannot afford to repair automobiles or contribute to civic conservation activities, which, in turn, hastens the decline of local air and landscape quality. Poor rural dwellers, faced with soaring food costs, are forced to clear forests, overuse their land, or migrate to the cities and borders in a desperate bid for survival.

There has been little documentation of these links between debt, economic crisis, and environment in Mexico. Several studies have been done in Brazil, where international lending agencies are more deeply implicated in the ecological crisis (*The Ecologist* 1987). In Bolivia and several other countries, the concept of "swapping debt for nature" has been initiated (Lovejoy 1984). In these programs, international conservation groups have helped to arrange for banks to forgive portions of debt in exchange for assurances of forest and wildlife conservation programs in debtor nations and tax benefits in their own countries (Bramble 1987). Discussions about similar programs have occurred in Mexico and, at first glance, seem a creative way to resolve the problems of debt and ecology. Yet, in many ways, these programs ignore the fundamental structural problems that are forcing local people to degrade their environment and, because they are frequently proposed by North American environmentalists, can seem paternalistic or elitist. There are also many other competing proposals for debt swap, including tourist and industrial development (Weinert 1986-87). The links between debt and environment could be studied in much greater depth in Mexico and alternative strategies for debt-for-nature exchanges sensitively explored.

The role of the United States in Mexican environmental problems and the growing interest and concern in the United States regarding the Mexican environment are important considerations. The United States seems particularly concerned with the role that environmental degradation may play in border migration, the drug trade, and political stability (Caldwell 1985; Ehrlich et. al. 1981; Keeley 1982; Maguire and Welsh Brown 1986; Myers 1988; Pastor and Castañeda 1988). The traditional suspicions and tensions about U.S. interests or intervention in Mexico (Bailey and Cohen 1987; Lowenthal 1987; Reynolds and Tello 1983; Sanders 1986) could easily be fueled by inappropriate statements and responses from the United States concerning the Mexican environment. Fortunately, there are a number of sensitive bilateral arrangements and discussions between academics and nongovernmental organizations regarding environmental cooperation.

Political action and social movements organized on the basis of environmental issues are growing relatively rapidly in Mexico. Some groups, such as the Grupo de Cien, the Movimiento Ecologista Mexicano, Fundación Domeq, and Grupo Monterrey, are led by intellectuals and the wealthier, urban populations (Toledo, V.M., 1983,

1985a). Others are based on grass roots social organizations, such as those in Michoacán, Tabasco, and Chiapas (Barkin 1988; Redclift 1987). The burgeoning environmental movement in Mexico now produces several magazines and journals, such as *Ecología, Movimiento Ecologista* (from the Movimiento Ecologista Mexicano), and *Desarrollo y Medio Ambiente* (from the Instituto Mexicano de Tecnologías Apropiadas). These publications are evidence of an important new popular and political awareness of the ecological crisis in Mexico.

When these groups form coalitions for specific issues such as urban pollution, deforestation, or nuclear risks, they can marshal thousands of people and gain media and international attention. Coalitions to fight development and environmental degradation around Lake Pátzcuaro and Laguna Verde have been particularly visible (Barkin 1988; Weinberg 1987). Members of these groups have also been active in political parties opposed to the governing PRI because both right and left opposition parties have seen ecological issues as powerful political themes. In the 1988 elections in Mexico, environmental issues were an important part of the agenda.

This emergence of an environmentally oriented political movement in Mexico has interesting parallels to the development of similar "Green" movements in Europe, North America, and Japan. In West Germany, in particular, the Greens have aligned with the peace and feminist movements, as well as new leftist groups, to become a powerful political force within and outside the government system (Hulsberg 1987). In other countries, ecological activists, such as Earth First and Greenpeace, have employed both violent and nonviolent tactics to apply political pressure and gain media attention. Some authorities view such ecoactivism, particularly when directed against nuclear facilities, as a serious security threat.

Environmental issues in Mexico are serious enough and raise such strong emotions that similar environmental activism is likely to emerge. The state's response to such pressures has already been indicated in the heavy police and military presence at demonstrations against Laguna Verde. Leaders on both sides of confrontations on environmental issues will need to recognize the ways in which such movements can be seen as security threats to the state. Repressive responses to ecological groups may be less acceptable than the repression of other political activists.

Conclusion

The emphasis of this chapter has been on the negative ways in which environmental problems can alter Mexican security. It is possible, however, to take a more positive view on how environmental issues can contribute to peace and security in Mexico and other countries. For example, environmental cooperation can be the first step in negotiation and agreements between otherwise opposed countries or social groups. Shared threats and shared resources can be important incentives to international cooperation, especially when environmental protection is seen as a nonthreatening or face-saving activity (Mathews 1989). Cooperative river basin management or park management has been suggested as a potential step en route to a more peaceful world (Thorsell 1985).

Similarly, within Mexico, ecological issues can be seen as legitimate and nonthreatening bases for social movements as long as they do not threaten the existing power structures. Concern for the environment can broaden the number of people who actively participate in political debate and organization. The government may see response to environmental problems as an easier way to gain popular support.

This positive contribution of environment and resource issues to Mexican national security is one of many themes that could be explored and researched more fully in the future. This chapter has highlighted several other important topics for further research, including the possible impacts of climate change, the pollution problems of Mexico City, and the protection of biodiversity. Other possible research questions relate to the impact of the military activities of Mexico and her neighbors on environmental and living conditions and the effects of nuclear war, the drug industry, and migration on ecological degradation.

Although general theoretical frameworks and overviews such as this may be useful, they need to be backed up by, or followed with, detailed empirical studies in specific local contexts. There are dozens of problems and places in Mexico that merit detailed case studies of relations between political economy, environmental degradation, and security, similar to those undertaken by the Centro de Ecodesarrollo in the oil regions of the Gulf coast and by other people in agricultural communities.

This essay has examined in a number of ways the relevance of environment and resources to Mexico's security. Using a broad definition of security, it is clear that the future of Mexico and the Mexican people is closely linked to the future of the global and Mexican environments. The international nature of many environmental issues requires concerted action and sensitive negotiation with respect to questions of national sovereignty. Although Mexico has taken a number of steps to protect the environment, many economic, political, and demographic factors are acting to increase environmental insecurity. Making Mexico more environmentally secure is a challenging, complex, and urgent task that should be given a prominent place on the national and international security agenda.

References

Aguayo, S. 1985. *El Exodo Centroamericano.* Mexico: SEP-FORO 2000.

Aguayo, S. 1987. *Chiapas: Las amenazas a la seguridad nacional.*

Mexico: Centro Latinoamericano de Estudios Estratégicos.

Aguilar Zinser, A. 1986. *Aún Tiembla: Sociedad política y cambio social: el terremoto del 19 de septiembre de 1985.* Mexico: Grijalba.

Albert, L. 1980. "Organochlorine Pesticide Residues in Human Adipose Tissues in Mexico: Results of a Preliminary Survey in Three Mexican Cities." *Archives of Environmental Health* (September-October).

Alisky, M. 1977. "Mexico's Population Pressures." *Current History* 72.

Alisky, M. 1981. "Population and Migration Problems in Mexico." *Current History.*

Almeida, M.O. de, W. Beckerman, L. Sachs, and G. Corea. 1972. "Environment and Development: the FOUNEX Report." *International Conciliation* no. 586.

Altieri, M.A., and J. Trujillo. 1987. "The Agroecology of Corn Production in Mexico." *Human Ecology* 15(2).

Amerlinck, M.C. 1986. *Relación histórica de movimientos sísmicos en la ciudad de Mexico 1300-1900.* Mexico: SOCIOCULTUR.

Applegate, H.G. 1982. "Transboundary Air Quality." *Natural Resources Journal* 22(4).

Applegate, H.G., and R.C. Bath. 1978. "Air Pollution Along the U.S.-Mexican Border." *Natural Resources Journal* 18.

Arad, R.W., ed. 1979. *Sharing Global Resources.* New York: McGraw-Hill.

Arias J., and L. Barquera, eds. 1988. *Laguna Verde nuclear? No gracias!* Mexico: Claves Latinoamericanas.

Armstrong, N.E. 1983. "Anticipating Transboundary Needs and Issues." *Natural Resources Journal.*

Arturson, G. 1987. "The Tragedy of San Juanico: The Most Severe LPG Disaster in History." *Burns* 13(2).

Austin, J.E., and G. Esteva. 1987. *Food Policy in Mexico: The Search for Self-Sufficiency.* Ithaca, N.Y.: Cornell University Press.

Bailey, N.A., and R. Cohen. 1987. *The Mexican Timebomb.* New York: Priority Press.

Barkin, D. 1978. *Desarrollo regional y reorganización campesino: La Chontalpa como reflejo del problema agropecuario mexicano.* Mexico: Nueva Imagen.

Barkin, D. 1988. "Environmental Degradation and Productive Transformation in Mexico." Paper presented at Latin American Studies Association, New Orleans.

Barkin, D., and T. King. 1970. *Regional Economic Development: The River Basin Approach in Mexico.* Cambridge: Cambridge University Press.

Barkin, D., and B. Suárez. 1982. *El fin de autosuficiencia alimentaria.* Mexico: Nueva Imagen.

Barkin, D. and B. Suárez. 1983. *El fin de principio: las semillas y la seguridad alimentaria.* Mexico: Océano.

Barnaby, F., ed. 1988. *The Gaia Peace Atlas.* New York: Doubleday.

Bassols Batalla, A. 1983. *Recursos naturales de México.* Mexico: Nuestro Tiempo.

Bataillon, C. 1969. *Las regiones geográficas en México.* Mexico: Siglo XXI.

Bath, R.C. 1979. "U.S.-Mexico Experience in Managing Transboundary Air Resources." *Natural Resources Journal* 22(4).

Beltran, E. 1979. *Los recursos naturales de México y el crecimiento demográfico.* Mexico: Fundación para estudios de la población.

Behar, N. 1985. "Non-military Aspects of Mutual Security: Regional and Global Issues." *Bulletin of Peace Proposals* 16.

Boyer, R.E. 1975. *La gran inundación: Vida y sociedad en la ciudad de México 1629-1638.* Mexico: Sep Setentas.

Bramble, B.J. 1987. "The Debt Crisis: The Opportunities." *The Ecologist* 17(4/5).

Branes, R. 1987. *Derecho ambiental mexicano*. Mexico: Universo Veintiuno.

Brown, L.R. 1977. "Redefining National Security." *Worldwatch Paper* 14. Washington: Worldwatch Institute.

Brown, L.R., ed. 1987. *The State of the World*. New York: W.W. Norton.

Bull, D. 1982. *A Growing Problem: Pesticides and the Third World*. Oxford: Oxfam.

Byers, D.S., ed. 1967. *The Prehistory of the Aehuacan Valley: Volume 1 - Environment and Subsistence*. Austin: University of Texas Press.

Caldwell, L.K. 1985. *U.S. Interests and the Global Environment*. Iowa: Stanley Foundation.

Castañeda, J.G. 1986. "Mexico's Coming Challenges." *Foreign Policy* 64.

Castro, J. de. 1977. *The Geopolitics of Hunger*. New York: Monthly Review Press.

CEPAL. 1980. Report on Environment and Economic Development. *CEPAL Review* 12(December).

Choucri, N., ed. 1984. *Multidisciplinary Perspectives on Population and Conflict*. Syracuse, N.Y.: Syracuse University Press.

Clark, W.C. 1987. National Security and the Environment." *Environment* 29(5).

Claxton, R.H. 1986. *Investigating Natural Hazards in Latin American History*. Carrollton, Georgia: West Georgia College.

Cooley, J. K. 1984. "War Over Water." *Foreign Policy* 54.

Crosby, A.W. 1976. *The Columbian Exchange: Biological and Cultural Consequences of 1492*. Westport, Conn.: Doubleday.

Crosson, P. 1989. "Greenhouse Warming and Climate Change: Why Should We Care?" *Food Policy* (May).

Crutzen, P.J. 1985. "The Global Environment After Nuclear War." *Environment* 27(8)(October).

Day, J.C. 1970. *Managing the Rio Grande: An Experience in International River Development*. Chicago: University of Chicago.

DuMars, C.T., and S.M. Beltran del Rio. 1988. "A Survey of the Air and Water Quality Laws of Mexico." *Natural Resources Journal* 28(4).

Dupuy, R.J., ed. 1983. *Settlement of Disputes on the New Natural Resources.* Hague: Martinus Nijhoff.

Ecologist, The. 1986. "Special Issue on Chernobyl." *The Ecologist* 16(4/5).

Ecologist, The. 1987. "Special Issue on Deforestation and Debt." *The Ecologist* 17(4/5).

Editorial Research Reports. 1985. *Troubled Mexico.* Washington, D.C.: Congressional Quarterly.

Edwards, C.R. 1986. "The Human Impact on the Forest in Quintano Roo, Mexico." *Journal of Forestry History* 30.

Ehrlich, P.R., L. Bilderback, and A.H. Ehrlich. 1981. *The Golden Door: International Migration, Mexico, and the United States.* New York: Wildeview Books.

Ehrlich, P.R., and A.H. Ehrlich. 1981. *Extinction: The Causes and Consequences of the Disappearance of Species.* New York: Random House.

EPA (Environmental Protection Agency). 1989. "Draft Report on the Impacts of Global Warming in the United States." Washington, D.C.: EPA.

Esteva, G. 1983. *The Struggle for Rural Mexico.* South Hadley, Mass.: Bergin and Garvey.

Ewell, P.T., and T. Poleman. 1980. *Readjustment and Agricultural Development in the Mexican Tropics.* Mexico: Instituto Nacional de Investigaciones sobre Recursos Bióticos.

Excelsior. 1983. (Series on environmental issues in Mexico City).

Excelsior (18-23 January).

Farquarson, Mary. 1988. "The Cost of Ecology." *Business Mexico.* 5(3).

Farquarson, Mary. 1988a. "Mexico's Wells Running Dry." *Business Mexico* 5(2).

Feder, E. 1977. *Strawberry Imperialism.* Hague: Institute for Social Studies.

Fernández-Kelly, M. 1983. *For We Are Sold: I and My People: Women and Industry in Mexico's Frontier.* Albany, N.Y.: SUNY Press.

Florescano, E. 1969. *Precios de maíz y crisis agrícola en México.* Mexico: Colegio de Mexico.

Florescano, E. 1980. "Una historia olvidada: la sequía en Mexico." *Nexos* 32.

Galtung, J. 1982. *Environment, Development, and Military Activity: Towards Alternative Security Doctrines.* Oslo: Universitetsforlaget.

García, E. de Miranda, and Z. de Gyves Falcon. 1972. *Nuevo Atlas Porrua de la República Mexicana.* Mexico: Editorial Porrua.

Gentleman, J. 1984. *Mexican Oil and Dependent Development.* New York: Peter Lang.

Gleick, P.H. 1988. "The Effects of Future Climatic Changes on International Water Resources: The Colorado River, the United States, and Mexico." *Policy Sciences* 21.

Gliessman, S.R., R.E. Garcia, and M.A. Amador. 1981. "The Ecological Basis for the Application of Traditional Technology in the Management of Tropical Ecosystems." *Agroecosystems* 7.

Gómez-Pompa, A., ed. 1976. *Regeneración de selvas.* Jalapa, Mexico: INIREB.

Gómez-Pompa, A. 1983. "Entrevista - La larga marcha de los ecológicos mexicanos." *Nexos.*

Gómez-Pompa, A., ed. 1985. *Los recursos bióticos de México.* Mexico: INIREB.

González Casanova, P., and P. Aguilar Camin. 1985. *México ante la crisis.* Mexico: Siglo XXI.

González, Pacheco C. 1983. *Capital extranjero en la selva de Chiapas 1863-1982.* Mexico: Instituto de Investigaciones Económicas.

Guzmán, S.A., et al. 1986. "The Impact of the Ixtoc-1 Oil Spill on Zooplankton." *Journal of Plankton Research* 8(3).

Halffter, G. 1977. *Colonización y conservación de recursos bióticos en el trópico.* Mexico: Instituto de Ecología.

Hansen, N. 1981. *The Border Economy: Regional Development in the South West.* Austin: University of Texas Press.

Hatch, Katherine. 1978. "California's Industrial Wastes Foul Mexico's Coastal Waters." *World Environment Report* 4(1).

Hekstra, G.P. 1989. "Global Warming and Rising Sea Level." *The Ecologist* 19(1).

Herzog, L.A., ed. 1986. *Planning the International Border Metropolis: Transboundary Options for the San Diego-Tijuana Region:* San Diego: Center for U.S.-Mexican Studies, Monograph no. 19.

Hewitt de Alcántara, C. 1976. *Modernizing Mexican Agriculture.* Geneva: UNRISD.

Hoberman, L. 1974. "Bureaucracy and Disaster: Mexico City and the Flood of 1629." *Journal of Latin American Studies* 6(2).

House, J.W. 1982. *Frontier on the Rio Grande.* Oxford: Clarendon Press.

Hulsberg, W. 1987. *The German Greens.* New York: Verso.

Humboldt, A. von. 1966. *Political Essays on the Kingdom of New Spain.* Translated from the French by J. Black. New York: AMS Press.

Ibarra, V., S. Puente, V. Saavedra, and M. Schteingart. 1987. *La ciudad y el medio ambiente en América Latina: seis estudios de caso.* Mexico: Colegio de Mexico.

Iltis, H.H. 1980. "Background, Preliminary Results and Commentary on Nature Preservation in Mexico." Madison: Department of Botany, University of Wisconsin.

Ingram, H.M. 1988. "State Government Officials' Role in U.S.- Mexico Transboundary Issues." *Natural Resources Journal* 28(3).

IUCN (International Union for the Conservation of Nature). 1980. *World Conservation Strategy.* Gland, Switzerland: IUCN.

Jager, J. 1988. "Anticipating Climate Change." *Environment* 30(7).

Jamail, M.H., and S.P. Mumme. 1982. "The International Boundary and Water Commission as a Conflict Management Agency in the U.S.-Mexico Borderlands." *Social Science Journal* 19(1).

Johnson, K. 1985. "State and Community During the Aftermath of Mexico City's November 19, 1984 Gas Explosion." Boulder, Colo.: Natural Hazards Center.

Juffer, Jane. 1988. "Dump and the Border." *The Progressive* 52(10).

Kandell, J. 1988. *La Capital: The Biography of Mexico City*. New York: Random House.

Keeley, C.B. 1982. "Illegal Migration." *Scientific American* 246(March).

Lappé, F.M., and J. Collins. 1979. *Food First: Beyond the Myth of Scarcity*. New York: Ballantine.

Lee, S. 1976. "Oaxaca's Spiraling Race for Water." *The Ecologist* 6.

Leonard, J.H. 1987. *Natural Resources and Economic Development in Central America: a Regional Environmental Profile*. New Brunswick, N.J.: Transaction Books.

Liverman, D.M., and K. O'Brien. 1989. "The Possible Impacts of Global Warming on Mexico." Paper presented at Conference of Latin American Geographers Meeting. Querétaro, Mexico (May).

Lobato, R. 1980. "Social Stratification and Destruction of the Lacandona Forest in Chiapas." *Ciencia Forestal* 5.

Looney, R., and W.T. Fredericksen. 1981. "The Regional Impacts of Infrastructural Investment in Mexico." *Regional Studies* 15(4).

Lovejoy, T.E., III. 1984. "Aid and Debtor Nation's Ecology." *New York Times* (October 4).

Lovins, A.B., L.H. Lovins, F. Krause, and W. Bach. 1981. *Least- Cost Energy: Solving the CO2 Problem*. Andover, N.H.: University of New Hampshire.

Lowenthal, A.F. 1987. *Partners in Conflict: The United States and Latin America*. Baltimore, Md.: Johns Hopkins University Press.

Maas, J.M., et al. 1988. "Soil Erosion and Nutrient Losses in Seasonal Tropical Agroecosystems under Various Management Techniques." *Journal of Applied Ecology* 25(2).

Maguire, A., and J. Welsh Brown. 1986. *Bordering on Trouble*. Bethesda, Md.: Adler and Adler.

Mamdani, M. 1973. *The Myth of Population Control*. New York: Monthly Review Press.

"Maquiladoras Turn U.S.-Mexican Border into a Toxic Wasteland." 1988. *Latin American Press* (8 December).

Marco del Pont, L. 1986. *El crimen de la contaminación*. Mexico: Villacana.

Mares, D.R. 1987. *Penetrating the International Market: Theoretical Considerations and a Mexican Case Study.* New York: Columbia University Press.

Martín del Campo, D. 1987. *Los mares de México: Crónicas de la tercera frontera.* Mexico: Era.

Martíncz, O. 1988. *Troublesome Border: U.S.-Mexico Borderlands Issues Through Time.* Tucson: University of Arizona Press.

Mathews, J.T. 1989. "Redefining Security." *Foreign Affairs* (Spring).

Merino, M. 1987. "The Coastal Zone of Mexico." *Coastal Management* 15(1).

Mexican-American Review. 1980. "Tourism and Development." *Mexican-American Review* 48(3)(March).

"Mexico: Chimalapas Forest Falls to Loggers, Oil Pipelines, Poppy, and Marijuana Fields." 1988. *Latin American Press* (21 July).

Mondragon, J. 1986. "The Change in Land Use as a Factor in the Desertification Process in Pueblo Valley." *Agrociencia* 0(64).

Mumme, S. 1984. "The Cananea Copper Controversy." *Inter-American Economic Affairs* 38(1).

Mumme, S. 1986. "Complex Interdependence and Hazardous Waste Management Along the U.S.-Mexico Border." In *Dimensions of Hazardous Waste Politics and Policy,* eds. C.E. Davis and J.P. Lester. Westport, Conn.: Greenwood Press.

Mumme, S. 1987. "Progress and Problems in Managing the order Environment." *Mexico Policy News* (2)(Spring).

Mumme, S. 1988. *Apportioning Groundwater Beneath the U.S.-Mexican Border: Obstacles and Alternatives.* La Jolla, Calif.: Center for U.S.-Mexican Studies, University of California, San Diego.

Mumme S., R.C. Bath, and V.J. Assetto. 1988. "Political Development and Mexican Environmental Policy." *Latin American Research Review.*

Musacchio, H. 1986. *Ciudad Quebrada.* Mexico: Océano.

Myers, N. 1984. *The Primary Source: Tropical Forests and Our Future.* New York: W.W. Norton.

Myers, N. 1988. "Environment and Security." *Foreign Policy* 74.

Nahmad, S., A. González, and M. Rees. 1988. *Tecnologías indígenas y medio ambiente.* Mexico: Centro de Ecodesarrollo.

Nalven, J. 1986. "Transboundary Environmental Problem Solving: Social Process, Cultural Perceptions." *Natural Resources Journal* 26.

National Academy of Sciences (NAS). 1972. *The Genetic Vulnerability of Major Food Crops.* Washington, D.C.: National Academy of Sciences.

Natural Resources Journal. 1982. "Special Issue on the U.S.-Mexico Border." *Natural Resources Journal* 22.

Nye, J.S., Jr., and S.M. Lynn-Jones. 1988. "International Security Studies: A Report on a Conference on the State of the Field." *International Security* 12(4).

Ortiz, F. 1947. *El huracán.* Mexico: Fondo de Cultura Económica.

Ortiz, Monasterio F. 1987. *Tierra profanada: historia ambiental de México.* Mexico: INAH/SEDUE.

Outerbridge, J. 1987. "The Disappearing Chinampas of Xochimilco. *The Ecologist* 17(2).

Pastor, R.A., and J.G. Castañeda. 1988. *The Limits to Friendship: The United States and Mexico.* New York: A.A. Knopf.

Pearse, A. 1980. *Seeds of Plenty, Seeds of Change.* Oxford: Clarendon Press.

Pérez, Zapata, A.J. 1983. "La contaminación por plomo en Coatzacoalcos." *Ciencia y Desarrollo* 52.

Puente, S., and J. Legorreta, eds. n.d. *Medio ambiente y calidad de vida.* Mexico: Plaza y Valdes.

Redclift, Michael. 1982. *Sustainable Development: Exploring the Contradictions.* London: Methuen.

Redclift, Michael. 1987. "Mexico's Green Movement." *The Ecologist* 17(1).

Repetto, R. 1985. *The Global Possible.* New Haven, Conn.: Yale University Press.

Restrepo, I. 1986. *El paraíso fraccionado: de cuestiones agrarias y ambientes.* Jalapa, Mexico: Universidad Veracruzana.

Restrepo, I. 1988. *Naturaleza muerta: Los plaguicidas en México*. Mexico: Océano.

Reyes, Carmen, et al. 1979. "Impact of Petroleum Industry Activities in the State of Tabasco." *Ciencia Forestal* 4.

Reynolds, C., and C. Tello, eds. 1983. *U.S.-Mexico Relations, Social and Economic Aspects*. Stanford, Calif.: Stanford University Press.

Rivera, F., et. al. 1987. "Amoebae Isolated from the Atmosphere of Mexico City and Environs." *Environmental Research* 42(1).

Romero, F.J. 1987. "The Volcano Rabbit — A Shrinking Distribution and a Threatened Habitat." *Oryx* 21(2).

Ross, S.R., ed. 1977. *Views Across the Border*. Albuquerque: University of New Mexico Press.

Ross, S.R. 1983. *Ecology and Development of the Border Region*. Mexico: ANUIES.

Rother, L. 1988. "Makesicko City." *New York Times* (16 January).

Salinas de Gortari, C. 1989. "Speech in Commemoration of UN Environment Day." (5 June). Press manuscript.

Sanders, S. 1986. *Mexico: on Our Doorstep*. Lanham, Mass.: Madison Books.

Sanders, W.T., J.R. Parsons, and R.S. Santley. 1979. *The Basin of Mexico: Ecological Processes in the Evolution of a Civilization*. New York: Academic Press.

Sanderson, S. 1986. *The Transformation of Mexican Agriculture: International Structure and the Politics of Rural Change*. Princeton, N.J.: Princeton University Press.

Sauer, C.O. 1952. *Agricultural Origins and Dispersals*. New York: American Geographical Society.

Secretaría de Desarrollo Urbano y Ecología (SEDUE). 1986. *El Estado del Medio Ambiente en México*. Mexico: SEDUE.

Schneider, S.H. 1988. "The Greenhouse Effect: Science and Policy." *Science* 243.

Schoultz, L. 1987. *National Security and United States Policy Towards Latin America*. Princeton, N.J.: Princeton University Press.

Sheridan, T.E. 1988. *Where the Dove Calls: The Political Ecology of a Peasant Corporate Community in Northwestern Mexico.* Tucson: University of Arizona Press.

Simonian, Lane. 1988. "Pesticide Use in Mexico: Decades of Abuse." *The Ecologist* 18(2).

Sparks, S. 1988. "Pesticides in Mexico." *Multinational Monitor.* 9 (10)(October).

Sternberg, R. 1987. "Mexico City: The Politics of Pollution." *In These Times* (7-13 October).

Székely, M. 1978. *El medio ambiente en México y América Latina.* Mexico: Nueva Imagen.

Székely, M., and I. Restrepo. 1988. *Frontera agrícola y colonización.* Mexico: Centro de Ecodesarrollo.

Thorsell, J. 1985. "Parks That Promote Peace." *WWF News* 38.

Tickell, C. 1977. *Climatic Change and World Affairs.* Harvard Studies in International Affairs, 37. Cambridge, Mass.: Harvard University, Center for International Affairs.

Toledo, A., ed. 1982. *Petróleo y ecodesarrollo en el sureste de México.* Mexico: Centro de Ecodesarrollo.

Toledo, A. 1988. *Energía, ambiente y desarrollo.* Mexico: Centro de Ecodesarrollo.

Toledo, A., A. Núñez, and H. Ferreira. 1983. *Cómo destruir el paraíso: El desastre ecológico del sureste.* Mexico: Océano.

Toledo, V.M. 1983. "Ecologismo y ecología política." *Nexos* 69.

Toledo, V.M. 1985. *Ecología y autosuficiencia alimentaria.* Mexico: Siglo XXI.

Toledo, V.M. 1985a. "La crisis ecológica." In eds., P. González Casanova and P. Aguilar Camin, *Mexico ante la crisis.* Mexico: Siglo XXI.

UCLA. 1983. "Bioresources and Environmental Hazards of the U.S.-Mexico Borderlands." Symposium at UCLA (September 11-13).

Ullman, R.H. 1983. "Redefining Security." *Población y desarrollo en América Latina.* Mexico: Colegio de Mexico.

Urquidi, V.L., and J.B. Morelos, eds. 1979. *Población y desarrollo en América Latina.* Mexico: Colegio de Mexico.

Usher, P. 1989. "World Conference on the Changing Atmosphere: Implications for Global Security." *Environment* 31(1).

Utton, A.E., ed. 1973. *Pollution and International Boundaries: U.S.-Mexican Environmental Problems.* Albuquerque, N.M.: University of New Mexico Press.

Utton, A.E. 1982. "Overview." *Natural Resources Journal* 22(4).

Vargas Márquez, F. 1984. *Parques Nacionales de México.* Mexico: Instituto de Investigaciones Económicas.

Vizcaíno Murray, F. 1975. *La Contaminación en México.* Mexico: Fondo de Cultura Económica.

Voss, D. de. 1986. "Mexico City's Limits." In *Bordering on Trouble,* eds. A. Maguire and J. Welsh Brown. Bethesda, Md.: Adler and Adler.

Vovides, A.P. 1981. "Lista Preliminar de Plantas Mexicanas Raras o en Peligro de Extinción." *Biótica* 6(2).

Warman, A. 1982. *El cultivo de maíz en México.* Mexico: Centro Ecodesarrollo.

Weinberg, Bill. 1987. "Laguna Verde: The Nuclear Debate in Mexico." *The Ecologist* 17(6).

Weinert, R.S. 1986-87. "Swapping Third World Debt." *Foreign Policy* 65.

Weir, D., and M. Shapiro. 1981. *Circle of Poison: Pesticides and People in a Hungry World.* San Francisco: IFDP.

Westing, A.H. 1986. *Global Resources and International Conflict.* New York: Oxford University Press.

Wilken, G.C. 1987. *The Good Farmers: Traditional Agricultural Resource Management in Mexico and Central America.* Berkeley: University of California Press.

World Commission on Environment and Development. 1987. *Our Common Future.* Oxford: Oxford University Press.

World Resources Institute/IIED. 1986-87; 1988-89. *World Resources Reports.* New York: Basic Books.

Wright, Angus. 1986. "Rethinking the Circle of Poison: The Politics of Pesticide Poisoning Among Mexican Farm Workers." *Latin American Perspectives* 13(4).

Yates, P. Lamartine. 1981. *Mexico's Agricultural Dilemma.* Tucson: University of Arizona Press.

Mexico's Environment: Securing the Future

Richard A. Nuccio and Angelina M. Ornelas,
with contributions by Iván Restrepo

Introduction

Mexico is experiencing some of the most far-reaching upheavals of its political and economic system in decades. The death knell of Mexico's oil-fed economic boom came in August 1982, when external financing of the economy collapsed and what has come to be known as the Latin American debt crisis spread from Mexico to the major economic powers in South America. Since then, Mexico has been engaged in a series of heroic holding operations to stabilize its stricken economy, satisfy the insistent demands for major restructuring of the Mexican economy by external lending institutions such as the International Monetary Fund (IMF) and the money-center banks, and negotiate new loans that go only to pay the interest on past debt — payments that amounted to $60 billion over the past six years and consume 50 percent of Mexico's foreign earnings.

Mexico has made progress on each of these fronts but at enormous social cost. Per capita income fell by some 7 percent between 1980 and 1986; real wages declined by at least 20 percent during the same period. This is in a country with few social "safety nets," where the wealthiest 10 percent of the population receives 41 percent of total income and the poorest one-fifth, less than 3 percent.

Politically, Mexico has had the dubious privilege of occupying more U.S. news column attention than at any point in recent memory. A pattern of fraudulently conducted elections has characterized Mexican politics for decades and has helped to solidify the hold of the ruling Partido Revolucionario Institucional (PRI) on national power. These fraudulent practices became the object of organized protest and greater international scrutiny as the economic crisis of the 1980s deepened. The economic crisis encouraged the party of traditional middle-class protest, the PAN or National Action Party, to question its role as a local party of meek and perpetual semi-loyal opposition and to debate whether it should attempt to acquire real national power. The PRI's imposition of orthodox stabilization policies that so pleased international bankers splintered the party's nationalist left wing and helped to forge the most successful challenge from the left in modern Mexican history. In July 1988 Cuauhtémoc Cárdenas, son of a legendary PRI president, led a coalition of left-of-center parties to an electoral victory second only to that of the PRI. By the PRI's own contested count, the Democratic Front won 30 percent of the popular vote, and challenges continued months after the election.

The origins of Mexico's acute contemporary political and economic crises lie in the 1960s. It was during that decade that the economic model of import-substitution industrialization followed by Mexico gave early indications of having exhausted its usefulness. As discussed more fully below, part of the inadequacy of the model lay in its neglect of the rural areas — where the majority of Mexicans, at one point, lived and where productive activities might have helped feed Mexico's increasing numbers and slow the rush of population to the cities.

Another shortcoming lay in an intrinsic failure of the model everywhere it was applied in Latin America: the creation of an inefficient industrial structure that produced low-quality goods competitive only in an internal market protected by high tariffs. This model led to the dead end in Mexico, as in many countries, of substituting imports of even more expensive capital goods — and at times, raw materials — for the earlier imports of finished and intermediate goods. Poor-quality products, desirable only in the protected domestic market, never earned the foreign exchange as exports necessary to pay for the imports of capital goods. Foreign borrowing became the only way to fill the resulting foreign exchange gap.

Moreover, only the relatively privileged upper and middle classes could afford Mexican-produced, high-priced luxuries such as stoves, washers and dryers, and refrigerators. This small market of wealthier Mexicans, constituting perhaps 15 percent of the population, was to be found in the major cities. A vicious cycle began. Protected industries located close to their major markets in the cities drew labor from the countryside into increasingly crowded urban centers. Government policies kept agricultural prices low to supply inexpensive foodstuffs to the urban working class. Low agricultural prices drove even more peasants into urban areas and producers out of basic commodities, such as beans and corn, and into cash crops for exports.

The environmental consequences were equally grave. Guadalajara, Monterrey, Puebla, and above all, Mexico City became the primary poles of economic growth and of environmental deterioration. A macrocephalic development that outstripped urban services of housing, potable water, sewage, and other waste disposal became the rule. Industrial discharges and the proliferation of residential areas in dangerous, but previously isolated, sites of chemical production and energy distribution contributed to truly horrific environmental conditions. It is this pattern of development that Mexico must now, in the midst of severe austerity, try to reorient.

The environmental and resource consequences of Mexico's development did not happen by accident. They flowed from a pattern of economic growth that was presented as being technically sound at the time — perhaps because it was politically acceptable to a growing middle class. But that model of development has already seriously eroded the human and material base upon which the future of Mexico will be built. In response to the economic and environmental failures of this import-substitution model, a new model of export-led growth has been adopted by Mexico.[1] But the resumption of growth in Mexico without an examination of the style of development followed in the past and its environmental consequences may leave Mexico less equipped in the future to deal with the powerful social, economic, and political challenges it will face in the next century, less than a decade away.

This chapter examines those key issues that are, at once, the most crucial for Mexico's future and, therefore, most likely to affect its national security if not addressed effectively. It then focuses on Mexico's responses to its environmental dilemmas and draws some policy conclusions about how the United States and Mexico can work more effectively together and separately to lift the unbearable burdens that environmental deterioration is likely to impose on Mexico's future generations. It does not pretend to be a comprehensive review of all the environmental challenges facing Mexico nor, necessarily, to reflect the priorities that Mexicans would establish in dealing with them.

The Utility of the National Security Concept

It is not self-evident to all Mexicans that the parlance of national security is the appropriate way to address political, economic, or environmental issues. Indeed, a sub-theme of the conference upon which this book is based was the view of several Mexican scholars that the concept of nationalism, rather than national security, is the proper way for Mexicans to organize their thinking about challenges to Mexico.[2] This is due, in part, to the association for most Mexicans of national security with the U.S. national security state and its virulent form of anti-communism. Moreover, this concept was adopted by several military regimes in Latin America in the 1960s and 1970s to justify their particularly harsh forms of dictatorial rule.

There is an interesting parallel between this rejection of the national security concept by some Mexicans and the experience of the left in the United States in the 1960s and 1970s. Here, too, intellectuals opposed to the Vietnam War saw that war as the logical extension of the national security state. They viewed the concept as one invented in the postwar period to justify extra-constitutional activities by the U.S. government, such as domestic political spying, assassinations of foreign leaders, and other nefarious acts. And they sought to build an alternative vision of U.S. foreign and military policy.[3]

Whether for good reasons or bad, this attempt has largely been abandoned in the 1980s. Groups and individuals critical of U.S. foreign policy have sought rather to change the content of national security by expanding it to include concerns for human welfare. In a reversal of the previous approach, those concerned about environmental issues, for example, have argued that the importance of these issues requires that they be made a matter of national security, presumably obtaining for them consideration at the highest levels of government.[4] This amounts to an attempt to redefine national security to include broader and "softer" elements of national and international concerns.[5]

However Mexicans decide to conceptualize their national interests, this paper argues that the preservation of Mexico's natural resource base is a matter of the highest national importance. Because of the severe pressures on Mexico's land, air, and water, the country's long-term viability, as well as the short-term welfare of significant numbers of its people, depend on prompt attention to its resource base. From either a national security or a nationalist perspective, the environment has leapt to the top of the agenda in Mexico.

The State of the Mexican Environment

This section focuses on those environmental and resource issues that are the most basic to the structure of production in industry and the rural sector and to the provision of food and essential services to the poor majority of Mexicans. It begins with Mexico's natural resource endowment and the way it has been used and abused, particularly in the tropical zones. Part of the reason for abuse of natural resources is population pressure. While Mexico has made great strides recently in controlling population, the weight of past growth strains Mexico's ability to provide a decent standard of living for the majority of its people. Agriculture and industry are the sectors that must provide the employment and food to improve living standards, and the environmental consequences of past and present policies in those sectors are examined next. Finally, the situation in Mexico City is described as an extreme example of the consequences of overcentralization as pursued in Mexico's past development policies.

Natural Resources

Mexico has a rich natural endowment but not necessarily one fully suited to the patterns of settlement and economic activity undertaken by modernizing Mexico. From the location of its principal rivers to the availability of land for distribution to landless peasants, Mexico faces a series of resource challenges that require wise management.

The distribution, availability, and quality of Mexico's water supply remains at the top of the country's resource dilemmas, despite the fact that this precious liquid is renewable. Surface waters in Mexico are scarce. Those that do exist are far from the areas of major water demand or are located at elevations that require significant transport and/or pumping costs. All five of Mexico's major rivers — totaling more than 50 percent of the mean annual flow of all Mexican rivers — are located in the tropical, southeastern part of the country. Eighty-five percent of Mexico's water resources are located in areas of less than five hundred meters in elevation, yet 70 percent of the population and 80 percent of the country's industry are in areas above that level. A disproportionate 55 percent of industrial activity is located in the Valley of Mexico at elevations of between seventeen hundred and twenty-three hundred meters (Cummings 1988, 30-32).

As in most developing countries, this relatively poor geographic endowment is aggravated by an accelerated development process that has increased the extraction and consumption of water and produced discharges that are often dumped untreated into water supplies. This problem is particularly grave in Mexico City and the surrounding valley of Mexico and is discussed more fully in the section on Mexico City.

Mexico is experiencing conflicts over water usage on regional and local levels. In Baja California, international agreements with the United States divert nearly two billion cubic meters of water annually to Mexico from the Colorado River. Mexico City, in turn, draws supplies from more and more distant points. Conflicts over water supplies or problems with water quality have led to calls for the diversion of water from agricultural production to urban use in cities such as Tampico, Coatzalcoalcos, Merida, Torreon, Nogales, and Guadalajara (Secretaría de Agricultura y Recursos Hidráulicos 1981).

The pressures noted on Mexico's inland water supplies are, unfortunately, equally true for coastal zones. Mexico possesses some ten thousand kilometers of coastline, a wide continental shelf, and several hundred thousand acres of estuaries that are an unrealized source of food and economic activity. Rich and complex coastal ecosystems are in constant danger from the discharge of waste waters from urban and industrial centers and ships and from pesticide and fertilizer runoff. The impact of oil extraction and refining in the southeast (Mexico) and Gulf has been documented as particularly alarming (Toledo 1982).

Each year nearly a million acres of Mexican forests are lost due to human exploitation.[6] Figures vary as to the exact amount of forested land that remains (at least 100 million acres) and the degree of desertification.[7] But there is agreement that the overexploitation of renewable resources, the extension of cattle grazing to vast new areas of the country, and the inappropriate application in tropical zones of techniques suited to temperate climates are producing grave losses in the quantity and quality of Mexico's land and forest resources.

The tropical areas of southeast Mexico have been particularly hard hit by "modern" techniques of land exploitation. Tropical silviculture requires a careful application of land-use techniques based on extensive studies of the existing flora and fauna. Yet these detailed investigations of field conditions in the southeast do not yet exist.[8]

Development projects in the southeast have too often ignored the special needs of the tropical areas. They have followed a pattern of razing the jungle with heavy earth-moving equipment and either planting monoculture crops, such as sugar cane or rice that are not well suited to the climate and soil conditions of the region, or establishing cattle-raising operations that damage the fragile ecosystem and actually increase unemployment in the area.[9] This has been the case in the ambitious development projects in the region of Uxpanapa in the state of Veracruz; those of Candelaria and Valle de Edzna in Campeche; and, in the state of Tabasco, those of Balancan-Tenosique and La Chontalpa.

As one of the Mexican government's oldest development projects for the tropics, La Chontalpa merits special mention. Conceived in 1963, the Plan Chontalpa was designed to be a model of modern agricultural methods. It covers nearly one hundred thousand acres, includes almost six thousand households, and represents an investment by the Mexican government and the Inter-American Development Bank of more than 3 billion pesos (or more than $120 million at exchange rates prevailing during the years of the plan).[10]

Intended to focus the benefits of agricultural development on the local region, the Plan Chontalpa has suffered during its existence from political and technical confusion and has produced mixed results. A backward and economically and culturally isolated region has become integrated into the national and even international market. But the clearing of large tracts of land for cattle raising and for sugar cane production has created new problems for La Chontalpa.

The tropical environment has been dramatically altered by the new agricultural and cattle-raising activities in ways not foreseen by the original developers of the plan. The clearing of jungle forests and construction of dams to control floods and channel water has lowered the water table and reduced the soil's productivity by eliminating the nutrient-rich sediment that accompanied the floods. This has created a growing necessity for expensive artificial fertilizers to maintain an adequate return on investment. A dramatic decline has been noted in the number of species of plants and animals that traditionally served as an important component of local inhabitants' diets. Families eat more "modern" foods, such as wheat bread and processed products, but their relatively high cost has actually led to a reduction in nutritional levels. The destruction of forest cover has increased winds that damage crops and accelerate soil erosion. The relocation of peasant families to urban centers has given them greater access to health care facilities, and certain diseases such as tuberculosis and malaria have decreased.

But gastrointestinal parasites are more common among children living under the plan.

The contradictions of modernization as revealed in the costs and benefits for the local population of the Chontalpa Plan are a warning sign of problems intrinsic to the current models of development being followed in the Mexican tropics. It is an example of massive investment being insufficient to raise diet and nutrition consistently in the countryside because of the plan's unforeseen effects on the environment and on patterns of consumption and production.

Population

Until very recently, Mexico was not overly concerned about population growth at the national level. As late as 1970, Mexico's President Luis Echeverría endorsed a pro-nationalist view with such comments as "To govern is to populate" and "I do not know whether Mexican mothers understand the effectiveness of the contraceptive pill. What I do know is that we need to populate our country.... We do not want to control our population" (Nagel 1987, 18).

In the late 1970s, the inability to meet rising economic demands, despite impressive rates of economic advancement, led the Mexican government to recognize that uncontrolled population growth threatened the Mexican economic "miracle" which had been central to the success of the PRI's dominance of the country. Consequently, a revised General Law of Population was passed in 1973 and implemented in early 1974. Its key provision was Article 3, Part II, which stated the government's intention was to carry out programs of family planning through the educational and public health services of the public sector and to take care that these programs and those of private organizations be carried out with absolute respect for the fundamental rights of man and that they preserve the dignity of families, with the object of regulating rationally and stabilizing the growth of population, so as to achieve the best utilization of the human and natural resources of the country (Nagel 1987, 20).

In 1974, Article 4 of the 1917 Constitution was revised to guarantee equal rights for women, to bring about responsible parenthood, and to enable women to decide "in a free, responsible, and informed manner" on the size and spacing of their families (Nagel 1987, 20, 31). Mexico thus became, with Yugoslavia and China, one of only three countries in the world to guarantee family planning as a constitutional right. Under the banner of slogans such as *"Vámonos haciendo menos"* ("Let's become less"), the government mobilized considerable resources in its attempt to change public attitudes toward parenthood. In the field of the mass media, the government orchestrated planned population messages through radio and television stations, newspapers, and magazines. From a population growth rate as high as 3.5 percent as recently as 1973, Mexico decreased its rate of increase to 2.6 percent by 1986 (Nagel 1987, 34; Brown, Wolf, and Starke 1987, 23). This dramatic turnaround is credited by population specialists to the effective measures taken by the government's often-criticized bureaucracy (Alba and Potter 1986).

But the damage had already been done. The base on which these lower rates will grow is already large. By the year 2010, Mexico's current population of 85 million is projected to reach nearly 200 million. Because of past population growth, Mexico is now a very youthful country. United Nations world population estimates show that every year seven hundred thousand to eight hundred thousand young men and women enter the labor force. To reduce just the rate of open unemployment from its present level of 13 to 14 percent to 6 percent, Mexico will have to generate about a million new jobs per year through the end of this century.[11]

Unfortunately, forces have been set in motion that could reverse the important gains in controlling population made by Mexico in the last decades. A growing consensus among experts argues that three ingredients in modern developing economies produce declining birth rates: a growing degree of security in the society, based on security of land tenure or employment; a "rising opportunity cost for children" that encourages families to forgo additional children in favor of expenditures on goods and services; and the availability of easy and effective means of contraception (Wright 1988, 9). The virtual abandonment of Mexico's fitful land reform programs, the transformation of the agricultural sector to export crops (detailed below), and the rapid decline of purchasing power for most Mexicans are putting pressure on the first two of these factors, affecting attitudes toward the costs and benefits of additional children. Indeed, as Angus Wright has pointed out:

> All of those things that provided a measure of security and
> rising opportunity costs for children during the high growth
> and relatively high social spending years of the seventies

are being lost. The average Mexican is beginning to experience an increasingly insecure world in which the institutions of society other than the family are failing badly. If such trends continue long enough to constitute the main learning experience of a generation, there is every reason to believe that the rate of population growth will not decline further and that it might even begin to rise again (Wright 1988, 13).

Mexico, like many developing countries, finds itself in the middle stage of a demographic transition marked by high fertility and low mortality that cannot continue indefinitely without exhausting Mexico's resource base. Yet Mexico has been trapped in this middle stage for nearly four decades. To exit from it, Mexico must be encouraged to develop a combination of economic policies and family planning programs capable of further reducing birth rates and increasing living standards. Otherwise, the logic of the ecological transition — rapid population growth overwhelming natural support systems and environmental deterioration reducing per capita food production and income — takes over (Brown et al. 1987, 36).

Agriculture and Industry

In 1942, after President Lázaro Cárdenas's successful land and agricultural reform of the 1930s, President Avila Camacho initiated the restructuring of Mexico's agricultural sector to "serve as a basis for the founding of industrial greatness" (Lappé and Collins 1978, 125).

Steven Sanderson, in his book, *The Transformation of Mexican Agriculture,* argues public infrastructure investment centered on huge dams, irrigation canals, and federal districts for water control, while private sector investment sought to modernize agricultural support industries such as fertilizer, farm machinery, seeds, and pesticides (Sanderson 1986, 38).

Furthermore, continues Sanderson, "as the economy shifted from a rural to an urban setting and from agriculture to industry after World War II," the role of agriculture in the Mexican economy shifted to become the "adjunct of industrialization" (Sanderson 1986, 38, 29). Industrialization was intensified through public capital investments in industry and infrastructure programs and projects such as roads, electrification, telecommunications, and irrigation. These investments, combined with the Mexican government's ability to maintain political stability, increased confidence among the Mexican private sector and foreign (mainly U.S.) investors, promoting important infusions of private capital.

Under Mexico's import-substitution industrialization, the modernization of agriculture was sought through the investment of public funds in capital-intensive technologies suitable for good farmland or areas brought under cultivation by large irrigation projects. During 1941-52, "18 percent of Mexico's federal budget and 92 percent of its agricultural budget were spent on irrigation projects that created vast new stretches of rich farmland in the north of Mexico" (Lappé and Collins 1978, 126). A pattern of inequality was established early in the irrigation programs that endures to the present day: of the more than 7 million acres of land that benefited from these public investments, only four hundred thousand belonged to small farmers or were part of the communal farm system known in Mexico as *ejidos*.

The End of Food Self-Sufficiency

By the 1970s, a new pattern of agricultural production in Mexico had emerged. As technology facilitated the exportation of manufacturing and of advanced labor processes worldwide, a "globalization" of production occurred. For Mexican agriculture, this meant a new mode of production characterized by the commercial contracting and technological packaging of whole-crops industries such as strawberries, asparagus, cucumbers, and tomatoes. Agribusiness giants like Del Monte, General Foods, and Campbell's, other "food brokers," and contracting supermarket chains such as Safeway brought Mexico into the "global supermarket." The shift in cultivation from local consumption to production for the U.S. market was dramatic.

For example:

- From 1960 to 1974, onion exports from Mexico to the United States increased over five times, to 95 million pounds.
- During the same period, cucumber exports soared from under 9 million to over 196 million pounds.
- Between 1960 and 1972, eggplant exports multiplied ten times, and squash exports, forty-three times.
- By the late 1970s, frozen strawberries and cantaloupe from Mexico supplied more than a third of U.S. annual consumption.

- About half of all tomatoes sold in the wintertime in the United States (some two-thirds of a billion pounds by 1976) came from Mexico, or more precisely, from fifty growers in the state of Sinaloa, who in 1976 sold $100 million of tomatoes in the West and Midwest (Lappé and Collins 1978, 281, 282).

The reduction of agriculture to the "adjunct of industry" and the internationalization of agribusiness to the production of exportable fruits, vegetables, and feed grains have contributed to Mexico's crisis of the 1980s. Despite the supposed benefits of comparative advantage theory, Mexico's agricultural exports have not kept pace with the costs of increasing imports of other agricultural commodities made necessary by this very model of agricultural development. In a pattern not unlike that of manufactures, the prices of crops sold predominantly by industrial countries, crops like grains and soybeans, have risen faster than the prices of commodities exported by developing countries. In addition, agribusiness has failed to absorb rural labor displaced by modernization and industrialization and to improve the nutritional standards of the mass of the population (Sanderson 1986, 40).

The Catch-22 of Mexico's current agricultural dilemma is well illustrated by the $5 billion program to spur food production announced in mid-1985 by President Miguel de la Madrid. The impetus for the program was a food import bill for 1985 of $1.5 billion — to be paid with scarce foreign exchange — to import corn and other daily dietary staples once grown in sufficient quantities in Mexico. In making agriculture the "adjunct of industry," the Mexican government held down the price of tortillas to feed the thousands of people from the countryside drawn to industrial jobs in the cities. This depressed prices for corn, driving even more rural inhabitants off the land and into the cities, where industrial employment could not keep up with expanding demand for work.

While the government controlled the corn market, a private sorghum market sprouted. Land planted to sorghum (primarily used as feed grain for dairy cattle raised in Mexico) rose to 3.7 million acres from 2.5 million acres between 1970 and 1980. Corn cultivation, on the other hand, declined to 17 million acres from 18 million. From 1958 to 1980, the production of sorghum grew 2,772 percent, and the amount of land sown in sorghum climbed 1,300 percent.

At a time of heavy indebtedness, the last thing Mexico needs is a $5 billion program that will add to the public deficit because its product — corn — will be sold at controlled prices to lower the cost of tortillas. But any attempt to raise tortilla prices to provide greater incentives for corn producers could provoke urban protests of a kind Mexico must also seek to avoid.

Pesticides

Each year hundreds of millions of pounds of pesticides are used in developing countries. Unwise or unrestricted use of pesticides in Mexico has had truly disastrous consequences. In the Rio Grande Valley of Mexico, cotton production virtually disappeared in 1970. Some seven hundred thousand acres were abandoned. Cotton gins, compresses, and oil mills went out of business, and farm workers sought work elsewhere. A once-prosperous community was plunged into social and economic depression (Bull 1982, 16).

This disaster occurred when the tobacco budworm, an important cotton pest, became resistant to a wide range of pesticides. When the budworm's natural enemies were wiped out by pesticides, even higher levels of these chemicals — often making farm workers ill — were insufficient to defeat the budworm. In northwestern Mexico alone, the budworm almost totally wiped out cotton crops worth $135 million a year.

Unfortunately, crops are not the only casualties of indiscriminate pesticide use. The *Los Angeles Times,* as part of a 1980 investigative report on pesticides in Mexico, found that in Culiacan, Sinaloa, a state in northern Mexico, government doctors saw two or three pesticide poisonings every week on large plantations where tomatoes for American supermarkets are grown. Since they lacked sick leave, stricken workers often returned to the fields immediately. The report also charged that some farm workers died from aplastic anemia, a blood disease linked to organochlorine pesticides used in the area (cited in Wier and Shapiro 1981, 12).

Los Angeles Times reporters Laurie Becklund and Ron Taylor found that workers lived on small plots of land between the crops and irrigation canals that collected the pesticide runoff. In addition to washing their children, dishes, and clothes in the canals, the workers would fill discarded insecticide tubs with contaminated water from the canals for drinking purposes. Nearby, modern greenhouses were supplied with purified water to nurture tomato seedlings (Wier and Shapiro 1981, 12).

Angus Wright has reported from his field experience in the Culiacan Valley that farmers apply toxic pesticides to their crops twenty-five to fifty times a season "in almost total disregard for elementary rules of human health protection and environmental safety." The result is that

> with the new emphasis on and success of the winter vegetable crops sold in the United States, there are nearly a quarter of a million migrant farm workers who live and work in an environment constantly sprayed with substances known to cause, in addition to immediate poisoning symptoms ranging from dermatitis to death, severe respiratory disease, long-term nerve damage, blindness, mental disturbances, birth defects, abortions, leukemia, aplastic anemia, liver cancer, kidney cancer, and a variety of other serious disease syndromes. Leukemia rates, for example, are three times as high in the agricultural areas of the state of Sinaloa as in nonagricultural areas (Wright 1988, 14).

Although farmers, handlers, and field workers suffer the most from pesticide exposure, consumers of fruits and vegetables on which pesticides are used are also potentially threatened. In the United States, shipments of imported raw agricultural commodities are regularly monitored, but authority for the control of pesticide residue in imported foodstuffs is divided between the Food and Drug Administration (FDA) and the Environmental Protection Agency (EPA). Critics charge that the monitoring program allows chemically contaminated food products to be sold to U.S. consumers.[12]

There have been consistent problems with monitoring programs directed toward Mexico, the largest exporter of fresh fruits and vegetables to the United States. The EPA and FDA argue, for example, that because of climatic and biological differences between the United States and Mexico, pesticides permitted for use in Mexico may not always be approved for use in the United States. Residues of pesticides remaining on products grown in one country for export to the other are said to pose "legal" rather than "health" problems for consumers. U.S. government agencies have, therefore, granted Mexico numerous "emergency" exemptions to permit the importation of fruits and vegetables into the United States without established residue standards, examinations of dietary exposures, or regard for toxicological considerations.

In 1979, a special program of surveillance exclusively for Mexican produce imports was instituted by the FDA. Monitoring was stepped up by increasing the amount of "spot-check" sampling by 20 percent, so that by 1983 the Government Accounting Office found that the number of Mexican shipments sampled in monitoring programs equaled the total number of shipments sampled from all other countries combined.

But stepped-up monitoring has not actually prevented the entry of adulterated products into the United States. Almost one-third of the violated imports from Mexico are still sold in the United States as a result of the FDA's policy of allowing perishable goods to be marketed before completion of their analysis, if the product has no previous history of residue violations.

Cooperative efforts between the United States and Mexico to reduce the misuse of pesticides apparently have been successful in the past. In 1981 an educational program on pesticide application and usage led to significant decreases in the percentage of contaminated samples. Yet because of Mexico's financial crisis and the lack of U.S. congressional funding, this cooperative program to prevent chemically contaminated foods from entering the United States was phased out.

Mexican growers have responded to these concerns about pesticide residues on their exports and the lobbying efforts of ever-watchful Florida growers to restrict Mexican imports on health grounds by changing the types of pesticides they use (Wright 1986, 15, 18). They have largely abandoned so-called persistent compounds banned in the United States (such as DDT) that have relatively low toxicity for workers applying them but persist for long periods in the environment. Instead, they now employ nonpersistents (such as parathion) that deteriorate rapidly and do not concentrate in animal and human tissue but pose grave toxic risks to workers applying them, especially under the lax safety standards practiced in Mexico. Consumers and migrant workers who will suffer the illness and potential cancers associated with the use of these pesticides are arguably the most important interests at stake, and yet they are the least protected by the way in which Mexico and the United States are addressing this environmental problem.[13]

The Border and the Environment

In 1965, the Mexican government instituted the Border Industrialization Program — known as the *maquiladora* or in-bond industry in Mexico — to stimulate industrial development and provide employment on the Mexican side of the border and to help reduce illegal immigration to the United States. Taxed only on the value added to goods produced in the *maquiladora* program, numerous U.S. firms have been attracted to invest in border operations.

Particularly well-suited for the *maquiladora* program have been industries that combine three features: high labor intensity within an easily separable portion of the productive process; moderate transportation costs and easily transportable goods; and a need for fast turnover and rapid delivery to U.S. markets (Leonard n.d.). These include industries such as electronic and electric goods, machinery and transportation equipment, shoes and apparel, furniture, and nonelectric equipment.

Concern that flight from stricter pollution controls in the United States motivated some of these industries to participate in the *maquiladora* program was initially diminished by the fact that, for many of the participating industries, pollution control was not a major factor of production costs. However, because of the labor-intensive nature of their industrial processes, "There has been a growing focus in recent years on the work place health dangers associated with some of the *maquiladora* industries."[14]

Because the electronic and electric industries represent close to half the *maquila* sector, recent pilot studies suggesting work place hazards in their processes — once considered "clean" — are a special area for attention (Pastides 1986). The manufacture and assembly of high-tech equipment and components requires the storage, use, and disposal of a wide range of hazardous materials. Accidents, faulty equipment, inadequate procedures, and routine releases all have the potential to expose substantial numbers of people in adjacent communities to chemical risks (Sherry 1985, 2).

Studies documenting injury to workers in the electronic in-bond industries do not yet offer conclusive proof. But the indications of pilot studies in the United States that pregnant women (and their fetuses) may be especially susceptible to the health effects of solvents and chemicals used in these industries give cause for great caution. In 1983, Mexican women in the prime childbearing age made up more than 60 percent of the blue-collar jobs in the *maquila* sector.

Illegal Dumping and Transborder Flows

Despite the fact that there are few fully documented cases of illegal transboundary movement of toxic and hazardous waste from the United States and Mexico, the suspicion is that such movement is a growing problem with both national and international implications. Fear of an environmental and public health catastrophe caused by waste from the United States reportedly helped to bring about a bilateral agreement between the United States and Mexico on the transboundary movement of hazardous waste and hazardous substances.

On November 12, 1986, the EPA and the Ministry of Urban Development and Ecology (SEDUE) agreed to take steps to regulate the export and import of hazardous substances in order to reduce or prevent risks to public health, property, and environmental quality. The agreement provides for "notification, and, in the case of hazardous waste, for prior written consent from a receiving country for a proposed export." Improperly shipped materials can be returned to their country of origin under the agreement. Finally, under its guidelines, it establishes "a program for the exchange of data and criteria regarding imminent and substantial endangerment and emergency responses" (EPA and SEDUE 1986, 1).

To encourage coordination between EPA and SEDUE in a number of areas, including hazardous wastes, air quality, and water quality, this agreement was incorporated into an early framework agreement between the United States and Mexico, signed by Presidents Ronald Reagan and Miguel de la Madrid in 1983. At a time of generally poor relations between the two countries, the negotiation of this agreement was a significant step forward in addressing bilateral environmental dangers.

The enactment in March 1988 of the General Law of Ecological Balance and Environmental Protection establishes much higher penalties for violations of Mexican environmental laws and devolves enforcement onto Mexican state and local governments. Environmentalists concerned about the lax enforcement of current laws believe that this new law may lead to stronger prosecution of violators and a cleaner *maquila* industry (Pinkerton 1988).

Mexico City: Contamination Central

The Metropolitan Zone of Mexico City (MZMC) is the center of Mexico's most important economic, political, and cultural activities.[15] A product of unplanned urban growth, the city contains almost 25 percent of the national population, provides 42 percent of all jobs, generates 53 percent of wages and salaries in the country, includes 38 percent of the total value of industrial plants, accounts for 49 percent of sales of durable goods, and receives 55 percent of public investment in social welfare. According to the Instituto Nacional de Estadística, the city and the metropolitan area consume 40 percent of the total food production, buy 90 percent of all electrical appliances, use 66 percent of the country's energy and telephones, and purchase 58 percent of the automobiles on the country's highways. Between 1970 and 1980, while the Federal District grew at a 2.54 percent annual rate, surrounding metropolitan municipalities grew at a rate of 10 percent. Over the last ten years, two hundred seventy thousand people arrived in the city annually, attracted by the hope of economic opportunity and driven from the countryside by declining employment in the agricultural sector. This population increase and natural growth have combined to produce one of the largest cities on earth: 18 million inhabitants by 1988 (10.3 million in the Federal District and another 7.7 million in the state of Mexico) in an area of approximately fifteen hundred square kilometers (or nine hundred square miles).

The outcome of a policy of centralized growth, Mexico City has become the place in which the majority of the natural and artificial sources of contamination are concentrated: erosion; exposed trash and feces; entry into the subsoil of untreated water; emissions from factories, workshops, thermoelectric plants, refineries, petrochemical plants, cement and fertilizer plants, iron and steel foundries, and a large quantity of industrial and domestic incinerators; and millions of internal combustion vehicles and airplanes. Together, these sources spew approximately six thousand tons of contaminants into the atmosphere daily.

Indiscriminate dumping of domestic and industrial liquid waste into lakes and rivers and along shorelines has led to a significant contamination of aboveground and subterranean waters. Approximately fifty cubic meters per second of residual waters are dumped, and only 70 percent is filtered by the sewage system. In the past few years, the degradation of important ecosystems has worsened. For example, Lake Guadalupe (the closest lake to the Federal District) has become extremely polluted. Surrounded a few years ago by more than seven thousand acres of farmland, today this lake is considered the "world's biggest septic tank." It receives nearly 30 million cubic meters of residual waters annually, which come principally from industrial and residential areas close to the dam. These discharges contain garbage, grease, detergents, and phosphates. Almost all the waste waters generated in neighboring residential areas enter the lake without any treatment (Gobierno Federal 1985, 12, 13).

Excessive water consumption in the MZMC has already produced serious ecological imbalances in the water table of the region. Overuse of water has caused terrain in various zones of the Mexico Valley to sink. In Xochimilco-Tulyehualco, the land has sunk thirteen feet in less than twenty years (Gobierno Federal 1985, 12).

To compensate for the indiscriminate extraction of drinkable water, one of the policies followed by the authorities is the substitution of treated residual water. Recycling of this water has been the only available alternative for area farmers to maintain the use of their lands. Unfortunately, studies have shown that the utilization of treated waste water for cultivation eventually causes sterility of the soil because of the high concentration in the treated water of salts and heavy metals. In addition, some agricultural products grown with this treated water are highly noxious because they contain toxic elements affecting human health. Several studies have confirmed that residual waters in the Mexico Valley contain some forty pathogenic microorganisms that are very resistant to water treatment and to drugs taken by humans infected by them.[16]

The costs of expanding Mexico City's water supplies are becoming prohibitive. By the 1990s, increasing the supply will require bringing water from sources some 120 miles away and 6,500 feet lower than the altitude of the city. Such a feat would take nearly 125 trillion kilojoules of electrical energy each year and require construction of six 1,000-megawatt power plants, at a cost of some $6 billion. Thus, the city is faced with three rising costs in obtaining water: increasing distance of water transport, increasing height of water lift, and rising energy costs (Brown et al. 1987, 52). The new power plants, like all those run on fossil fuels, will contribute to the greenhouse warming effect and, depending on the technology, to other environmental effects downwind.

Atmospheric pollution in Mexico City is another grave problem. According to the Ecology Commission of the Federal District, industry contributes 20 percent of the annual total of atmospheric contaminants to the MZMC: approximately 393,000 tons of sulfur dioxide; 130,000 tons of hydrocarbons; 114,000 tons of carbon monoxide; 91,000 tons of nitric oxide; and 383,000 tons of diverse particulate matter. Of the total number of industries located in the MZMC, only 30 percent have antipollution equipment, equipment that, in many cases, is insufficient or inoperative.

Automotive vehicles are, however, the main polluters. In 1983, the state-run oil company PEMEX, based on its own studies, classified motor vehicles as the principal source of pollution, producing 85 percent of the tonnage emitted daily.[17]

The search for solutions is complicated by the explosive growth in the number of vehicles, the types of technology and fuels used in them, the lack of strict controls over the maintenance of motors, and the atmospheric conditions prevailing in the Valley of Mexico.

Between 1940 and 1980, the number of automotive vehicles in the Federal District grew six times as fast as the population.[18] This predominance of private over public transportation and the higher fuel consumption of private vehicles has increased atmospheric pollution. About 33 percent of the total annual national fuel consumption — some 3 million cubic meters of gasoline and 400,000 cubic meters of diesel fuel — is attributed to vehicles in the MZMC. Yet, according to *La Jornada*, of the almost 3 million motor vehicles that operate, 97 percent are private cars that provide only 19 percent of the trips per person per day. It is calculated that this private transportation consumes fifteen times more fuel per person transported than the mass transit system.

Poor motor maintenance and the advanced age of the vehicles also contribute to pollution. Devaluation and inflation, and the subsequent loss of buying power, have increased the number of rundown vehicles on the road and impeded government efforts to replace older, polluting buses (Sternberg 1987, 13).

The relationship between vehicle speed and air pollution contributes to the city's pollution dilemma. As the number of vehicles increases and average speeds decline on the Federal District's principal roadways, the situation becomes more grave. During peak hours (7 to 9 a.m., 2 to 4 p.m., and 6 to 9 p.m.), when 60 percent of the vehicles are in transit, the use of gasoline increases 1.5 times and exhaust emissions double the average (*Gobierno Federal* 1985, 51).

The geographic location of the MZMC further complicates the pollution problems of vehicles. At Mexico City's altitude (7,800 feet above sea level), internal combustion engines produce more contaminants than at lower elevations. Calculations indicate that altitude-induced inefficiencies mean the 2.5 million vehicles in the MZMC produce as much pollution as 6.3 million vehicles operating at sea level. A second disadvantage of the MZMC's location is its low wind velocity. The high mountains surrounding the city effectively reduce ventilation of the city's polluted atmosphere. This lack of wind turbulence combines with seasonal drops in temperature to produce thermic inversions that trap life-threatening levels of pollution in the city.

Of all the particles suspended in the atmosphere, sulfur dioxide and sulfates are considered the most dangerous pollutants because of their effects on the environment. They form part of what is called "acid rain," and, together with formaldehyde, contribute to photochemical smog in the city and adjacent areas. Photochemical smog is now a normal component of the atmospheric pollution in the Mexican capital. High levels of sulfur dioxide have been detected in the MZMC, emitted principally by diesel traffic and industry, even in apparently uncontaminated zones, such as the south of the city, where it is blown by the wind.

In spite of the efforts of PEMEX to reduce contaminant particles in fuel, almost all private automotive transport continues to use gasoline with high tetraethyl lead compound content, and only a minimal proportion of public transportation (between 1.2 and 1.5 percent) employs diesel fuel with low sulfur content. Leaded gasoline is a particular concern because of recent studies documenting high levels of lead in newborns. In a sample of Mexican newborns conducted by Dr. Stephen Rothenberg, 70 percent of those studied had lead levels above the 10 microgram per deciliter (mcg/dl) standard established as the point at which children will suffer retarded development during the first two years of life. Half had blood levels above 13 mcg/dl.[19]

Contamination by motor vehicles is not limited to smoke and gases. Noise pollution is also a significant danger for humans. In Mexico City, standards established by the United Nations and the World Health Organization as the acceptable limit for humans are exceeded on a daily basis: The Ministry of Urban Development and Ecology has determined that 80 percent of the noise pollution in Mexico City comes from urban buses and that the city is the third noisiest in the world after Tokyo and Los Angeles.[20]

The Government Response

D evelopments in the last few years have placed increasing pressure on the federal government to take more direct and immediate action against environmental dangers, especially in Mexico City. A series of thermal inversions in the winters of 1985, 1986, and 1987 dramatically increased pollution levels in the metropolitan area.[21] The catastrophic explosion in November 1984 of the PEMEX gas distribution facility at San Juan Ixhuatepec, a Mexico City suburb, killed more than five hundred people, injured some five thousand, and forced the evacuation of one hundred thousand, provoking public and media outcries for government action.[22]

Numerous government programs and agencies are attempting to address environmental problems in Mexico. At the federal level, the agency charged with prevention and control of atmospheric as well as soil and water pollution is the Ministry of Urban Development and Ecology, and, more specifically, the Subsecretariat of Ecology.[23] Within the federal government, there is the Ecology Commission, which also has lower-level offices charged with responsibility for the state of Mexico. In addition, the Senate and Chamber of Deputies have several committees concerned with environmental problems, including a National Ecology Commission.

One significant response of the de la Madrid government to increasing public concern for the environment was the issuing of the so-called "21 Points" in February 1986 — a series of decrees that included reforestation projects, regulation of automotive pollution, relocation of especially dangerous or toxic industries in residential areas, innovative pilot projects to use gas and energy sources more efficiently, water purification projects, and public education programs promoting environmental awareness. Significantly, the government promised (and delivered) a report on its progress in implementing each of these points eight months after they were issued.

The increasing gravity of the pollution situation in the capital and continuing public protests led to a new series of "100 Actions" by the federal government. Announced in a January 13, 1987 meeting of the National Ecology Commission (created in 1986 and chaired by President de la Madrid), the "Program of 100 Necessary Ecological Actions" includes a number of emergency provisions for responding to grave pollution levels in the capital. These include forced closing of schools and of selected, highly polluting industries during severe thermic inversions, compulsory inspection of motor vehicles, relocation of polluting and/or dangerous industries, prohibition of parking on important arteries in the city, and reforms of the laws regulating forests.

The 100 Actions were put into force during 1987 and 1988 and have a special focus on air pollution generated by automobiles and industry, both because of the gravity of the air-quality situation in Mexico City and because of the visible nature of the pollution. They will encourage relocation of schoolchildren and teachers and of industrial workers to avoid long commutes, prohibit the location of new factories in areas that already suffer high pollution levels and water shortages, and subsidize the installation of pollution control equipment in existing factories. Although the program has a particular focus on the metropolitan area, there are steps planned for a number of Mexico's most threatened rivers, reservoirs, and shorelines.

It is too early to judge the effectiveness of the "100 Actions." Skepticism among Mexican environmentalists runs high, however. Manuel Fernández, president of the Mexican Conservationist Federation, has criticized the program as having "no timetable, no system of accountability, no enforcement mechanism." Others pointed out the lack of a specific budget for the program, estimated to cost $100 million (Sternberg 1987).

On March 1, 1988, a new General Law of Ecological Balance and Environmental Protection (*Ley General del Equilibrio Ecológico y la Protección al Ambiente*) was enacted. Among the main features of the new law are regulation of natural resource use as well as of pollution; decentralization of a wide range of policy development, regulations, and enforcement to the level of state and municipal authorities; a focus on the causes of pollution rather than merely its effects; and encouragement of the participation of nongovernmental actors in the environmental policy process (*Ley General de Equilibrio Ecológico y Protección Ambiental* 1998, Chap. 2, Art. 6). Because of the new law's emphasis on enforcement and decentralization of important powers to local authorities, initial reactions to the new law by environmentalists have been positive.

Environmental Policy Making in Mexico

As recently as the mid-1970s, environmental problems in Mexico, as in much of the rest of the world, commanded only limited public attention. Under Presidents Luis Echeverría (1970-76) and José López Portillo (1976-82), concerns about environmental issues had a low priority. When the environment did reach the president's policy agenda, it came as the result of agitation by middle-level government planners, university researchers, and professional organizations, generally located in Mexico City. Even though it was included in the global planning documents favored by the López Portillo administration, "environmental policy as such was never mentioned in the president's major policy speeches, nor actively promoted as a major policy initiative at the national level" (Mumme 1984, 17).

This changed with the beginning of de la Madrid's presidential campaign in 1982. De la Madrid pursued a three-pronged strategy to push environmental issues up the agenda of Mexican politics: a program of popular mobilization, a strengthening of environmental statutes, better coordination of administrative responsibilities in the environmental area, and improved regulatory performance.

In a searching evaluation of environmental policy making in Mexico, Stephen Mumme gives de la Madrid's administration the highest marks for its program of popular mobilization. Perhaps spurred by the PRI's assessment of the likelihood of a Green Party-like movement emerging in Mexico (Leonard 1985, 799), de la Madrid's government set up a series of impressive "consultative mechanisms" to arouse and channel awareness of environmental issues among the population. State and regional conferences brought together local political leaders from the PRI's sectors, government officials, scholars in the state universities, and citizen groups to discuss a new environmental program being proposed by the government and to identify environmental problems. These efforts appear to have succeeded in placing the issue of the environment permanently on Mexico's domestic political agenda and in uniting urban and rural, middle and lower classes in common cause (Mumme 1984, 18, 35).

With his "consultative mechanisms" to arouse and channel popular concern for the environment, Miguel de la Madrid made a clear contribution to the focusing of greater attention on the need for government action on the environment. But Mumme's assessment of two other areas — statutory reform and regulatory performance — is less sanguine. Despite SEDUE officials' protest that de la Madrid's measures are more than symbolic reform and represent a serious commitment to environmental improvement in the long run, Mumme concludes, "Unfortunately, the government's record fails to bear them out" (Mumme 1984, 26). Mumme attributes this weak performance to both what he calls "circumstantial problems" and "actual priorities." Mexico's economic crisis and the crushing burden of the foreign debt are among the principal "circumstantial problems" hindering the fulfillment of commitments to environmental programs.

"Actual priorities" refer, however, to aspects of environmental policy making that are intrinsic to the nature of the Mexican political system. Mumme points out that rather than relying on sanctions and making the initial investments in costly abatement programs, the government has opted for an approach to abatement that stresses moral suasion, planning, bargaining, education, data collection, and incentives. The activities of environmental interest groups are dealt with in the classic petitionary pattern of supplication and persuasion that often characterizes legitimate interest articulation in Mexico (Mumme 1984, 29, 32).

It may seem, at first glance, that this is precisely the kind of strategy that Mexico should pursue under the prevailing conditions of extreme fiscal austerity. By relying on the traditional mechanisms employed by the state to encourage compliance by the private sector and interest groups, the government avoids difficult political confrontations and costly expenditures that would be necessary strictly to enforce regulations and punish violators. But as Mumme points out, this approach rests on plans underway for conversion and decentralization of industrial activities that will require decades to take full effect. In response to increasingly grave environmental deterioration, the Mexican government appears to have retreated into more of a hortatory and less of an enforcement role with regard to pollution.

Moreover, the success of any decentralization strategy will require that new areas of industrial growth be under the same environmental restrictions as those mandated in the capital in order to prevent pollution problems from merely being transferred elsewhere. Although the evidence so far is anecdotal, some observers of Mexican environmental policy are concerned that in some officials' desire to stimulate growth outside Mexico City, they may loosen environmental standards in the new industrial growth areas. One senior U.S. business executive was quoted as saying that government officials "don't care [about pollution] so long as a plant is going to be built away from Mexico City and will create a lot of jobs."[24]

A hortatory approach to environmental enforcement may, in the long run, strain Mexico's limited financial resources more rather than less. The explosion of the PEMEX gas plant in November 1984 may ultimately cost the government dozens of times the entire 1983 environmental budget. Yet, according to Mumme, only this "planning by disaster" was sufficient to spur the government to begin to relocate hazardous industries outside the immediate metropolitan area (Mumme 1984, 31).

Clearly, Mexico cannot do everything at once. It cannot open its political system, dramatically restructure the economy, and spend unlimited sums of political and financial capital on environmental enforcement. Yet it is important to heed the judgments of experts such as Mumme who believe that the Mexican government's approach to environmental policy regulation has sought to defer high costs by responding to demands primarily through symbolic reform and by opting for low-cost, future-oriented solutions (Mumme 1984, 32-33).

The steps taken by the de la Madrid government were obviously welcome. Focus on the environment will continue. Carlos Salinas de Gortari, the winner of the 1988 elections, is a brilliant and technically sophisticated leader who counted the minister of SEDUE among his closest personal advisers. The environmental law of March 1988 gave important new powers to the federal government and to local authorities, which, if exercised, could break with the hortatory tradition of Mexico's regulatory past. But any meaningful assessment of the status of the environment as a policy concern in Mexico must also confront the fact that decades of neglect have brought the nation to the brink of environmental disaster in key areas, such as the urban problems of Mexico City and land use in the tropical areas, of the southeast. The scale of these problems and the difficulties Mexico's authoritarian political system will have in addressing them caution against easy optimism that an environmental corner has been turned in Mexico.

Perhaps, the most sobering aspect of Mexico's economic and environmental dilemma is that the strain on the country's urban services, the destruction of forests and rural habitat, and the pollution of crucial water resources are the unintended, but nevertheless inevitable, consequences of a style of development pursued by Mexico since World War II. This import-substitution model of development no longer serves Mexico as an engine of growth, and an alternative path of export promotion is being sought. But the model's heritage of overcentralized production, protected and polluting industries, and distortions between the rural and urban sectors will be the central concerns of Mexico's economic and environmental actions in the coming decades.

Powerful alliances of political and economic groups were forged in the creation of the import-substitution model. Those alliances are already being challenged in Mexico's search for a new model of economic development capable of overcoming the external financial constraints and excessive dependence on foreign capital and technology that ended Mexico's unprecedented growth since World War II. The journey to a new and less environmentally damaging pattern of development has barely begun. Tragically, this search comes at a time of economic travail, when public sector spending is being slashed, when wages cannot keep up with triple-digit inflation, and when businesses are being driven into bankruptcy.

A strong but perceptive critic of the official approaches to environmental protection in Mexico ended a recent review of the prospects for environmental improvement on this somber note:

The present development model, which privileges large-scale export manufacture at the expense of all else, provides no effective means to reverse the tendency toward environmental decay. Industry will not, unless obliged by government regulation, integrate a social conscience into its calculus of profit and loss. In Mexico, the state has shown itself unwilling to impose the costs of environmental controls on production, lest the drive for successful export promotion be thwarted. Some people argue that small-scale industry and agricultural production may be more consistent with an environmentally sound pattern of development, but such considerations seem beside the point at a moment when macroeconomic policy has decimated small industrial firms and converted the country into a net importer of food, leaving millions of hectares of land and millions of people idle. Official policy offers no solace in this regard: In place of a concrete set of policies to deal with the impending environmental crisis, the candidate of the ruling party for the presidency only implores the "civil society" to raise its level of collective conscience. And what shall we ask of the producers? (Barkin 1988, 12).

How Can the United States Help?

G iven the political and economic constraints under which Mexico must operate and the importance of Mexico's decisions on the management of its resource base for both the United States and Mexico, it is vital to ask whether the United States can play a positive role in helping Mexico meet its environmental challenges. The first point to be made is that there is virtually unanimous agreement among those who have studied Mexico that expressions of concern by the United States about conditions there are often interpreted as intervention in Mexico's internal affairs and that actual attempts at pressure will be totally counterproductive.[25]

A recent interaction between these two neighbors gives a negative example of how environmental issues work themselves out in the bilateral relationship. The debate over regulation of the use of the fumigant ethylene dibromide (EDB) on mangos exported from Mexico is a classic study in bureaucratic politics and of the blurred lines between international and domestic politics in U.S.-Mexican relations.

In the wake of a 1983 court decision, the Environmental Protection Agency banned EDB, commonly used as a fumigant on mangos grown worldwide, because of its cancer-causing potential. State Department concern with efforts to encourage export agriculture through President Reagan's Caribbean Basin Initiative and protests from growers in the producing countries led EPA to give Mexico, Haiti, Belize, and Guatemala a two-year grace period. That deadline has since been extended, protested, reversed in law suits, and extended again in a mixture of interagency disputes, foreign policy, and domestic politics.

Three competing interests clash in the case. The State Department, the Mexican government, and Mexican growers have as their primary interest the maintenance of an export market for Mexican goods and the flow of foreign exchange to Mexico at a time when it is sorely needed. Environmental groups and some officials at EPA see the protection of U.S. consumers as the highest priority. Domestic suppliers of mangos, such as those in Florida, see the pesticide issue as a way to combat foreign competition, and they have joined with environmental groups in suits to guard the health of consumers, which not coincidentally have the effect of protecting their markets from Mexican competition. Two other interests are not as well represented in this regulatory merry-go-round. One is the Mexican workers exposed to the hazardous chemicals used on the produce. The second is U.S. consumers, who are blithely unaware that their well-being is a bargaining chip in bilateral relations.

Addressing conflicts between the United States and Mexico in the largely uncoordinated fashion that characterizes current relations can have its successes and failures. In the case of the series of border agreements signed by the United States and Mexico since 1983 on hazardous wastes, sewage, and air quality, negotiations at relatively high levels on each side — mostly uncomplicated by local politics — produced success at a time when other Mexican-American relations were acrimonious. On the issue of pesticides, enmeshed as it is in a web of foreign policy concerns and domestic politics, agreement has been elusive and the environmental consequences more damaging.

Abraham Lowenthal has described this issue-by-issue, "muddling through" approach to U.S.-Mexican relations as but one of four ways in which contacts between the two countries could be organized. Others include a unilateralist and nationalist stance on the part of the United States that attempts to subordinate Mexican to U.S. interests; a "special relationship" approach that seeks to build the two countries' mutual dependence into preferential policies and procedures on energy, tourism, migration, markets, capital, and technology; and Lowenthal's own preferred proposal for a more generalized positive response by the United States to Third World concerns that is to the advantage of Mexico because of the especially close ties between the two countries (Lowenthal 1987, 96-102).

Mexico's Environment

Which of these approaches to Mexico will contribute most to protecting the resource base upon which future development and stability depend? The most severe environmental threats facing Mexico today flow from the style of development pursued since World War II. That Mexico must now reorient its developmental approach is plain from the exhaustion of the prior model and its inability to provide a future engine of growth for the economy. Government proposals to relocate and decentralize productive activities and the modest steps taken so far to implement these proposals indicate recognition in official circles of the connection between environmental deterioration and the economic patterns established in the country over the last several decades.

It would be foolish, however, to underestimate the immensity of the task facing Mexico. The current economy and environment are the results of complex political arrangements worked out between powerful actors such as business, labor, the peasantry, foreign investors, the state, and the party apparatus. These arrangements and the economic benefits created by them have favored a relatively small group within Mexican society, referred to repeatedly here as the middle class or middle sector. Those advantaged by this distribution of burdens and benefits will be reluctant to see them changed significantly. Nothing less than the consensus underlying Mexican stability for the last 60 years is at stake.

Of the four options for approaching U.S.-Mexican relations just outlined, it is easy to reject two as being inadequate to the enormous challenge before Mexico. A unilateral, nationalist approach on the part of the United States that tries to bully Mexico into "recognizing" that its interests are best served by subordinating them to those of the United States is bound to increase the already formidable pressures on Mexico to the point of explosion. The issue-by-issue "muddling through" that has mostly prevailed in U.S.-Mexican relations can perhaps patch up oil spills, salinity problems, and pesticide dangers, but it will not produce the positive context needed for the system-wide changes required.

What Mexico needs from the United States are actions that help to depressurize the situation, to open up more political and economic space, and to encourage the use of this breathing room to take some difficult decisions. U.S. initiatives in three interrelated areas are vital.

First, strong efforts are needed to relieve Mexico's debt burden. Analysts have argued for some time that this would include combinations of measures to limit interest payments; convert some part of the debt to long-term, fixed rate securities; and confer greater accounting flexibility on creditors (Bailey and Cohen 1987, 48). The agreement to a partial write-down of Mexico's debt through the issuance of Mexican bonds backed by U.S. Treasury paper is an important first step in this direction.[26] Innovative proposals by private organizations to swap outstanding debt for the establishment of conservation preserves, sites of "ecological tourism," and transfers of pollution control technology need to be explored with Mexico. Reduction of the public sector deficit in the United States would also help to reduce pressures on real interest rates.

A second priority is increased development funding, to come primarily from international financial institutions, such as the regional development banks, the International Monetary Fund, and the World Bank. This will help to end the dangerous anomaly of Mexico's exporting of capital to the United States when it needs to be importing funds for future growth. The increased sensitivity of these international institutions to criticism of the environmental impacts of past projects may allow the targeting of new capital flows on environmental problems.

A third area for U.S. action is the avoidance of protectionist legislation that affects Mexican exports. Demands for trade reciprocity between industrialized countries such as Japan and the United States are understandable and necessary, but the same standards will not be productive if applied to Mexico. The removal of existing barriers to trade between Mexico and the United States and the prevention of new forms of protection can, however, be part of a bilateral process of negotiation (Bailey and Cohen 1987, 50). The planned North American Free Trade Agreement (NAFTA) looks promising in this regard.

Steps such as these, difficult as they will be to take, could help to open up political and economic space in Mexico and avoid immediate disasters or the adoption of extreme solutions. A more subtle dilemma for U.S. policy is how to encourage Mexico to use this space to make hard decisions on the reorientation of its development strategy, the revival of the agricultural sector, and the enforcement of environmental regulations. As a Mexican analyst has pointed out with regard to pressures for greater democratization in Mexico, there are trade-offs between economic breathing space and political change:

Concessions are easier when cushioned by prosperity; the country's rulers will not loosen their grip on power unless they can make the process relatively painless through economic growth. Yet, if such growth were possible, the need for political change would not be so acute (Castañeda 1985/1986, 294).

How to lessen economic pressure on Mexico, while encouraging the government to use the political space created to protect that country's environment and resource base, brings us back to a consideration of Lowenthal's last two approaches: whether the United States should seek a "special relationship" with Mexico or address Mexico as a component of a more general policy toward Latin America and the Third World.

Each approach has its advantages and disadvantages, as judged from the perspective of what will best support positive change in Mexico. The "special relationship" has much to recommend it because it offers the possibility of rallying the U.S. domestic support necessary for such an initiative. Constituencies in both Mexico and the United States have long argued for greater recognition of the unique relationship between the two countries.[27]

The "special relationship" would, however, require an immense amount of coordination among the myriad agencies concerned and would contravene some of the U.S. broader international commitments. Most importantly, such a direct focus would raise Mexican fears of being overwhelmed culturally, economically, and politically by the United States.

Because it avoids a direct focus on Mexico and, hence, may lessen such concerns about U.S. interference, Lowenthal believes that a more general set of policies designed to address Latin America's problems of debt and development is the most desirable approach. Because of its close ties to the United States, Mexico would benefit differentially from this overall policy initiative toward the developing world. Specific issues, such as migration, the border, energy, and the environment, could be the subject of special bilateral arrangements and procedures (Lowenthal 1987, 101). The central defect in this proposal is precisely its advantage. By deflecting attention from the bilateral relationship, it mutes Mexican sensitivities, but it also loses a coherence and immediacy that would allow the policy to be explained and justified to a U.S. public already skeptical of the value of foreign aid programs.

This analysis of the problems Mexico faces and the approaches by the United States that are most likely to be effective in encouraging Mexico to take the hard decisions necessary to address them ends with a dilemma. The United States must proceed with the day-to-day business of the bilateral relationship with Mexico and utilize the mechanisms already in place as a result of border agreements on environmental cooperation. By protecting its own environment, policing the export of hazardous substance and industrial processes to Mexico, and making available training and technical assistance, the United States will contribute to the solution of the current problems produced by the style of development pursued by Mexico.

The larger challenge the United States must face, however, is that these kinds of efforts will ultimately be inadequate to the task that

Mexico must undertake. That task is no less than a fundamental restructuring of the prevailing development model and the acceptance of the political changes required to support such a restructuring by a majority of Mexicans. The emergence of strong challenges to the PRI from Cárdenas on the left and the PAN on the right will force a public dialogue about the different directions that Mexico's future might take. Contrasting proposals on a range of issues, from debt repayment to the agricultural sector, will be offered by opposition parties whose combined votes (by official count) nearly equaled those of the PRI in the recent election.

If the United States is to be more than a mere bystander in this process of debate and change, it must develop both an even more sophisticated approach to Mexico than it now has and a greatly strengthened political will to ease Mexico's unbearable burden.

Notes

1.   Mauricio de María y Campos, "Mexico's New Industrial Development Strategy," in *The United States and Mexico: Face to Face with New Technology*, ed. Cathryn L. Thorup. (Washington, D.C.: Overseas Development Council, 1987), 67-81.

2.   See especially the contributions to this volume by Clark W. Reynolds and Lt. Col. Stephen J. Wager, "U.S.-Mexican Economic Integration: Implications for the Security of Mexico and the United States," and Roger Bartra, "Revolutionary Nationalism and Security in Mexico."

3.   An organization, recently disbanded, called the Coalition for a New Foreign and Military Policy, was founded to promote such an alternative.

4.   See Jessica Tuchman Matthews, "Redefining Security." *Foreign Affairs* 68(2)(1989): 162-177 and Michael Renner, "National Security: The Economic and Environmental Dimensions," *Worldwatch Paper* 89(May 1989). Changes in the general public's perceptions of national security parallel this evolution. In the Americans Talk Security project and in the Roosevelt Center for American Policy Studies report, *Old Doctrines vs. New Threats, Citizens Look at Defense Spending and National Security* (April 1989), opinion findings confirm the inclusion of issues such as the environment, nuclear proliferation, and economic competition with Japan as among the principal threats to U.S. national security. They also ranked traditional threats such as nuclear war with the Soviet Union and the spread of communism as among their lowest concerns.

5.   Some have urged caution in defining national security in a too broad and all-inclusive way, believing that a narrower definition is less subject to abuse. See the "Comments" by Gene Sharp in this volume.

6.   Figure cited by José Sarukhan Kermes, president of the Academy of Scientific Research, in a speech given at El Colegio de Mexico, June 26, 1987.

7.   For estimates on desertification, see Comisión Nacional de Zonas Aridas, diverse documents, 1976-1984; A. Bassols Batalla, *Geografía Económica de México* (Mexico: Editorial Trillas, 1984); Consejo Nacional de Ciencia y Tecnología (CONACYT), *Programa Nacional de Desarrollo Agropecuario y Forestal* (Mexico: CONACYT, 1981). Estimates on forested lands come from Iván Restrepo of the Centro Ecodesarrollo and are based on studies from the Subsecretaría Forestal of the SAHR and from the Instituto Nacional de Investigaciones sobre Recursos Bióticos (INIREB).

8.   For indictments of the lack of adequate research on the tropical ecosystem, see Alejandro Toledo, *Petróleo y ecodesarrollo (1982)*; David Barkin, *Desarrollo regional y reorganización campesina* (Mexico: Centro de Ecodesarrollo/Nueva Imagen, 1978); and Iván Restrepo, "El estado del medio ambiente en México: una visión de conjunto" (Mexico: Centro de Ecodesarrollo, 1986), 37.

9. Discussions of the dangers of planting crops such as rice in areas with tropical conditions of thin topsoil can be found in Ana María Ortiz, *El cultivo del arroz en el sureste de Mexico* (Mexico: Centro de Ecodesarrollo, 1987). The environmental and employment effects of cattle-raising are discussed in Barkin, *Desarrollo regional y reorganización campesina*.

10. This section on the Plan Chontalpa is drawn from Barkin, *Desarrollo regional y reorganización campesina*, 131, 134, and 135.

11. Víctor Urquidi, "Population and Employment at the End of the Century," speech presented at the First Seminar on "Projections on Mexico's Population," Colegio de Mexico, no date, 6-7. By way of comparison, the U.S. economy during the Reagan administration generated less than 2 million new jobs per year.

12. Cited in David Wier and Mark Shapiro, *Circle of Poison: Pesticides and People in a Hungry World* (San Francisco: Institute for Food and Development Policy, 1981), 12.

13. A recent study by the Board of Agriculture of the National Research Council concluded that up to twenty thousand cancer tumors may be caused annually in the United States by insecticide residues on imported and domestic fruits and vegetables. See Department of Agriculture, National Research Council, *Regulating Pesticides in Food, The Delaney Paradox* (Washington, D.C.: National Academy Press, 1987).

14. Leonard, *Pollution and the Struggle for the World Product*. Certain firms do appear to have been attracted to Mexico for reasons related to environmental issues such as the production of hazardous chemicals (lead, zinc, and arsenic trioxide) for export to the United States, smelting of copper (a potential source of "acid rain" problems for the United States), and the production of banned or highly regulated chemicals such as pesticides. A more recent study produced by the AFL-CIO asserts that "one of the big attractions that the *maquiladoras* hold for American industry is the Mexican government's hands-off attitude toward environmental protection and worker health and safety laws." Source: Leslie Kochan, *The Maquiladoras and Toxics, The Hidden Costs of Production South of the Border* Publication No. 186(February 1989), 2.

15. The MZMC includes the Federal District of Mexico City and the surrounding metropolitan area of the state of Mexico.

16. Studies by Dr. Armando Báez of the Centro de Ciencias de la Atmósfera of the National Autonomous University and Professor Eduardo Rodríguez Mestre of the Autonomous Metropolitan University have identified various contaminants and heavy metals in the treated water of Mexico City. Because these materials combine with sulfuric acid also present in the waste waters to form insoluble compounds, the metals do not present a danger to human health in the concentrations and forms in which they arrive in the fields. The microorganisms carried by the waters, however, are very dangerous for humans consuming irrigated crops. *Unomásuno*, April 2, 1985.

17. Figures provided by the Cámara Nacional de Comercio (CANACO), *Punto*, November 12, 1984.

18. Statement by engineer Gerardo Cruickshank, spokesperson of the Comisión del Lago de Texcoco, *Unomásuno*, 13 January 1985.

19. See the studies by Dr. Lilia Albert of the Instituto Nacional de Investigaciones sobre Recursos Bióticos (INIREB) and by Dr. Stephen Rothenberg of the Instituto Nacional de Psiquiatría.

20. Armando Báez, "Situación actual del problema ambiential en México," paper presented in the Regional Meeting on Environmental Legislation, Monterrey, Mexico, August 18-19, 1983. See also Instituto Nacional del Consumidor,"¡Sscht! Que el ruido también contamina," *Revista del Consumidor* 98, Mexico, April 1985.

21. In the thermal inversion of January 1987, songbirds literally dropped from the trees because of pollution levels. In the inversions of 1989, visits of a few days by those unaccustomed to the pollution levels produced bleeding in nasal passages.

22. Jonathan Kandell, *La Capital, The Biography of Mexico City* (New York: Random House, 1988), 565. Sixty-six acres were razed by the explosions and fire.

23. The predecessors of this agency are from 1972 to 1976, the Subsecretariat of Environmental Improvement, Department of the Secretariat of Public Health and Assistance; and from 1977 to 1982, the Directorate of Ecology, a Department of the Secretariat of Human Settlements and Public Works.

24. Interview with Edward Wyegard, director, Arthur D. Little (Mexico), quoted in Leonard, "Confronting Industrial Pollution," 791.

25. This is the conclusion of experts with such disparate viewpoints as Bailey and Cohen 1987, *Mexican Timebomb*, New York: Priority Press; Jorge G. Castañeda, "Mexico at the Brink," *Foreign Affairs* 64(2) (Winter 1985/1986); Lowenthal 1987, *Partners in Conflict*; and Sol Sanders, *Mexico: Chaos on Our Doorstep* (Lanham, Md.: Madison Books, 1986).

26. This proposal by Mexico and J.P. Morgan & Company was announced in late December 1987. Details of the plan are discussed in Peter Truell and Alan Murray, "Debt Breakthrough," *Wall Street Journal*, December 30, 1987. The plan has proved to be far less than a breakthrough for Mexico on debt reduction.

27. President Reagan raised this idea explicitly in his 1980 presidential campaign but did not pursue it while in office. Henry Kissinger has also suggested that some form of association of Mexico with the U.S.-Canada free trade area, spaced over a period of years, would be a desirable element of future U.S.-Mexican negotiations. See Henry Kissinger, "The Rise of Mexico," *The Washington Post* (August 17, 1988).

References

Alba, Francisco, and Joseph E. Potter. 1986. "Population and Development in Mexico Since 1940: An Interpretation." *Population and Development Review* 12 (1)(March).

Báez, Armando. 1983. "Situación actual del problema ambiental en México." Paper presented at the Regional Meeting for Environmental Legislation. Monterrey, Mexico (18-19 August).

Bailey, Norman A., and Richard Cohen. 1987. *Mexican Timebomb.* New York: Priority Press.

Barkin, David. 1978. *Desarrollo regional y reorganización campesina.* Mexico: Centro de Ecodesarrollo/Nueva Imagen.

Barkin, David. 1988. "Environmental Degradation and Productive Transformation in Mexico: The Contradictions of Crisis Management." Paper presented in the XIV International Congress of the Latin American Studies Association. New Orleans (17-19 March).

Bassols Batalla, A. 1984. *Geografía Económica de México.* Mexico: Editorial Trillas.

Brown, Lester, Edward Wolf, and Linda Starke. 1987. *State of the World 1987.* New York: W.W. Norton & Co.

Bull, David. 1982. *A Growing Problem: Pesticides and the Third World.* Oxford: OXFAM.

Cámara Nacional de Comercio (CANACO). *Punto.* 12 November 1984.

Castañeda, Jorge G. 1985/1986. "Mexico at the Brink." *Foreign Affairs* 64(2)(Winter).

Comisión Nacional de Zonas Aridas. 1976-1984. Diverse documents.

Consejo Nacional de Ciencia y Tecnología. 1981. *Programa Nacional de Desarrollo Agropecuario y Forestal.* Mexico: CONACYT.

Cummings, Ronald G., Víctor Brajer, James W. McFarland, José Trava, Mohamed T. El-Ashry, and Manuel Puebla. 1988. *Improving Water Management in Mexico's Irrigated Agricultural Sector.* Washington, D.C.: World Resources Institute.

De María y Campos, Mauricio. 1987. "Mexico's New Industrial Development Strategy." In *The United States and Mexico: Face to Face with New Technology*, ed. Cathryn L. Thorup. Washington, D.C.: Overseas Development Council.

Department of Agriculture, National Research Council. 1987. *Regulating Pesticides in Food. The Delaney Paradox.* Washington, D.C.: National Academy Press.

EPA (Environmental Protection Agency), International Division, and SEDUE (Ministry of Urban Development and Ecology). 1986. Joint press release (12 November).

Gobierno Federal. 1985. *Programa de Desarrollo de la Zona Metropolitana de la Ciudad de México y de la Región Centro.*

Instituto Nacional del Consumidor. 1985. "¡Sscht! que el ruido también contamina." *Revista del Consumidor.* Mexico: INC (98) (April).

Kandell, Jonathan. 1988. *La Capital, The Biography of Mexico City.* New York: Random House.

Kissinger, Henry. 1988. "The Rise of Mexico." *The Washington Post* (17 August).

Kochan, Leslie. 1989. *The Maquiladoras and Toxics, The Hidden Costs of Production South of the Border,* 186 (February).

Lappe, Frances Moore, and Joseph Collins. 1978. *Food First: Beyond the Myth of Scarcity.* Canada: Houghton Mifflin Co.

Leonard, Jeffrey. 1985. "Confronting Industrial Pollution in Rapidly Industrializing Countries: Myths, Pitfalls and Opportunities." *Ecology Law Quarterly* 12(4).

Leonard, Jeffrey. n.d. *Pollution and the Struggle for the World Product, Multinational Corporations, Environment and International Comparative Advantage.* London: Cambridge University Press. In press.

Ley General del Equilibrio Ecológico y Protección Ambiental. 1988. Mexico: Chap. II, Art. 6.

Lowenthal, Abraham. 1987. *Partners in Conflict.* Baltimore, Md.: Johns Hopkins University Press.

Matthews, Jessica Tuchman. 1989. "Redefining Security." *Foreign Affairs* 68(2)(Spring).

Mumme, Stephen. 1984. "The Evolution of Mexican Environmental Policy." Presented in the XII International Congress of the Latin American Studies Association. Albuquerque, N.M. (18-20 April).

Nagel, John. 1987. "Mexico's Population Policy Turnaround." *Population Bulletin* 33 (5)(December).

Ortiz, Ana María. 1987. *El cultivo del arroz en el sureste de México.* Mexico: Centro de Ecodesarrollo.

Pastides, Harris. 1986. "Digital Equipment Corporation Pilot Study." Unpublished article. University of Massachusetts, Amherst, School of Public Health.

Pinkerton, James. 1988. "Chemicals Catastrophe Lurking Behind Border." *Austin American Statesman* (27 March).

Renner, Michael. 1989. "National Security: The Economic and Environmental Dimensions." *Worldwatch Paper 89* (May).

Restrepo, Iván. 1986. "El estado del medio ambiente en México: una visión de conjunto." Mexico: Centro de Ecodesarrollo.

Sanders, Sol. 1986. *Mexico: Chaos on Our Doorstep.* Lanham, Md.: Madison Books.

Sanderson, Steven. 1986. *The Transformation of Mexican Agriculture: International Structure and the Politics of Rural Change.* Princeton, N.J.: Princeton University Press.

Sarukhan Kermes, José. 1987. President of Academia de Investigación Científica, speech delivered in El Colegio de México (26 June)

Secretaría de Agricultura y Recursos Hidráulicos (SARH). 1981. *Plan nacional hidráulico* (March).

Sherry, Susan. 1985. *High Tech and Toxics: A Guide for Local Communities.* Sacramento, Calif.: Golden Empire Planning Center.

Sternberg, Rachel. 1987. "Mexico City: The Politics of Pollution." *In These Times* (7-13 October).

Toledo, Alejandro. 1982. *Petróleo y ecodesarrollo en el sureste de México.* Mexico: Centro de Ecodesarrollo.

Truell, Peter, and Alan Murray. 1987. "Debt Breakthrough." *Wall Street Journal* (30 December).

Unomásuno, 2 April 1985.

Urquidi, Víctor. n.d. "Population and Employment at the End of the Century." Paper presented in the first seminar on Projections of the Population in Mexico. El Colegio de Mexico.

Wier, David, and Mark Shapiro. 1981. *Circle of Poison: Pesticides and People in a Hungry World.* San Francisco: Institute for Food and Development Policy.

Wright, Angus. 1988. "Agriculture Policy and the Future of the Mesoamerican Environment." Paper prepared for the XIV International Congress of the Latin American Studies Association. New Orleans (17-19 March).

Wright, Angus. 1986. "Pesticides in Mexico: The Culiacan Valley Farmers." *Catholic Rural Life* 35 (February).

Part Four

Bilateral Issues and National Security

Undocumented Migration and National Security

Jorge A. Bustamante

Introduction

This essay offers an analytical framework for predicting some trends in the future evolution of Mexican-U.S. relations. Although at times it may seem to be an exercise in imagination, the framework is based on a series of well-founded assumptions, from which the connection between two important aspects of Mexican-U.S. relations — undocumented migration and national security — can be analyzed.

The first assumption is that undocumented migration between the two countries is basically an economic phenomenon that corresponds to the international labor market. This market adjusts itself according to the interaction between Mexican supply and U.S. demand.

To understand this assumption, it is necessary to understand that the interaction between the Mexican and U.S. economies, as a determinant of undocumented migration, is more apparent than real. There is a belief, as widespread as it is erroneous, that the Mexican economy, expressed in terms of poverty and unemployment, causes Mexican workers to go to the United States.[1] Various independent studies have demonstrated that undocumented migrants do not come from the poorest regions or sectors of Mexico and that the majority of them were employed in Mexico before crossing the U.S. border.[2]

Therefore, the way the behaviors of both countries are tied together in the fashioning of the labor migration phenomenon is grounded in the issue of salary differences (Reynolds 1979) — the greater the salary differential, the greater the incentive to look for work in the United States.

However, salary difference is neither the only nor the most important factor in determining the volume of migratory flow between the two countries. If it were so, the majority of the migrant workers would be from the regions and sectors of the Mexican economy with the lowest salaries. This has not been the case, especially since 1977, as shown by the National Survey of Northern Border Emigrants (ENEFNEU) conducted by the Mexican Labor Secretariat (Secretaría de Trabajo y Previsión Social 1979).

Were there some relation between poverty and emigration, there would be an observable predominance of border or northern Mexican cities in the volume of migrants — the lower the distance between place of origin and the U.S. border, the lower the cost of migration. But almost all the empirical studies done on migration in the past twenty years indicate that the mid-western part of the country is where most migrants come from.[3]

A second assumption is that variations in the demand for foreign labor in the United States will principally depend, in the near future, on two factors: 1) growth of the U.S. economy, particularly within the state of California,[4] where 60 percent of all undocumented migrants are found in the United States (Consejo Nacional de Población 1986); and 2) the rate of aging for the U.S. working population, which will create growing deficits in the labor force for the lowest-paying jobs in the United States (Fullerton 1987).

Therefore, the future of migration will depend — to a greater extent than is produced by the explicit immigration policy of the United States or economic changes in Mexico — on first, the behavior of U.S. regional and national economies, especially in Texas and California, and second, changes in age distribution for the working population.

The third assumption has to do with the operational definition of the concept of "national security," which thusfar has not gained consensus. For the purposes of this study, an issue will be considered a national security problem when the state defines it as such. The basis for this is as follows:

The definition of national security is related to theoretical elements of the definition of sovereignty. Since the French Revolution, it has been universally accepted that the sovereignty of a nation resides in its people, but it is the legitimate representation of the people, as reflected in institutions and on a constitutional basis, that exercises that sovereignty. This legitimate representation of the people is called the "state of law." The exercise of sovereignty under a state of law is expressed in the principle of self-determination of peoples. If this premise is accepted, it leads to the conclusion that there is a national security problem when self-determination is threatened. This would seem to leave open the identification of "who" and "how" in the operational definition of a situation involving national security. This tension is resolved if the basic principle of the general theory of the state is accepted, that the state is the only legitimate source to express the sovereignty of a nation. That is to say, the people express their self-determination through the state, making the state the only legitimate source for defining when there is a national security problem.

If one accepts the military's raison d'être as that of protecting national sovereignty, the order for mobilization in response to a problem is an empirical indication that the state has decided it is facing an issue of national security. Understood in this way, the mobilization of the army to combat drug trafficking would correspond to the definition of a national security problem on the part of the Mexican state. The degree to which such a definition is or could be objected to by a part or a majority of the people the state represents is determined by the institutionalized forms through which voters correct the decisions of their representatives in the institutions of state where such decisions are made. However, the political or legal vulnerability of a definition of a situation as a problem of national security, as made by governmental authority, should not be confused with a theoretical weakness of the conceptualization of national security.

A fourth assumption is that the most important consideration for Mexican national security is internal political stability. That implies that political stability gives the state a greater capacity to respond to the pressures or threats to national sovereignty, whether originating from inside or outside the country. When there is a situation of internal political instability, the organs of state lose a certain amount of legitimacy in defining a situation as one of national security. Internal political instability also weakens the state's capacity to make those decisions necessary to define and respond to a threat to national security that comes from the outside.

For the purpose of this essay, the relation between undocumented migration to the United States and national security comes from a fifth assumption: The future of the migration phenomenon will be determined by the interaction between the economic stability of the United States and the political stability of Mexico.

A sixth and final assumption is that the relations between Mexico and the United States are characterized by an asymmetry of power (Ojeda Gómez 1982), which extends from macrodimensional levels in state-to-state relations to the microdimensional levels of individual interactions.

The Basic Framework of the Proposed Analysis

An analytical framework can be proposed that attempts to operationalize the preceding assumptions, going from the most abstract to the most concrete. Through this framework, a process of interaction between two variables is suggested: the state of the U.S. economy and the Mexican political situation. Both variables have been divided into two categories to facilitate the analysis: stability and instability. The intention is to predict, given the available data, the possible scenarios from the interactions of the variables, operationalized through a division into opposing categories. The four scenarios are derived from the intersection of the variables, with their respective dichotomies.

The interaction of the variables allows four possible scenarios. In each one of them, situations will be analyzed according to the contextual explanations presented below that seek to define what is understood by undocumented migration and by national security. Obviously, this framework does not set out to prove anything. It is presented only as an analytical tool that allows a discussion of the possible future of relations between the two countries from the perspective of national security and the migratory phenomenon.

The Migration of Workers as an International Interaction

First, a conceptual premise for the understanding of the phenomenon of migration from Mexico to the United States: There is a growing consensus in the international academic community that the phenomenon occurs in the context of an international labor market in which the conditions of U.S. labor demand are causally linked to the conditions of Mexican labor supply (Sobel 1982; Reynolds 1979; Greenwood and McDowell 1986).

This consensus refers to the fact that the migration phenomenon is produced by the interaction of factors that occur on both sides of the border, creating a characteristic of bilaterality that feeds the phenomenon. This is a view shared by authors of the most recent studies whose field work with migratory workers has been done in Mexico as well as in the United States (Cárdenas 1983).

This view contradicts that of some authors whose studies and analyses were done with pre-1980 data (Ray Marshall and Vernon Briggs, for example). In their time, these authors held that the presence of undocumented immigrants in the United States was a phenomenon of exogenous causes, in which the United States was an innocent victim (Marshall 1978). Although fewer authors now maintain the absence of responsibility on the part of the U.S. economy in the configuration of undocumented immigration, some analysts of solid credentials did hold the position (Reubens 1979).

For purposes of this study, at the macrodimensional level, reference will be made to the interaction between labor supply and demand in a way that should not be understood in the context of neoclassical economics as a market relation which tends toward balance, but rather in the theoretical context in which Max Weber (1965) referred to market relations. In other words, it can be seen as a web of social relations that constitute certain recurrent, consensual patterns and a structure in which there are actors who occupy different positions of power from which they act toward others in a way that is understood by them, and who respond with their own behavior, which is within the cultural expectations that initiated the relations.[5]

At a microdimensional level, we are referring to the relations that occur between the migrant worker and those who contract for their work in the United States. At another level, it would be the social, economic, political, and cultural conditions that have historically allowed these relations.

There is a parallel between the asymmetry of power that characterizes relations between Mexico and the United States at the macrodimensional level and the asymmetry of power that characterizes the relations between migratory workers and U.S. employers. That asymmetry is no accident but rather springs from the inequality of power between the two nations and the historical processes involved in the exercise of that inequality by the citizens of one country over the citizens of the other. In those historical processes, we can show that inequality extends from the macrodimensional level, between the two nations, to the microdimensional, between individuals. We find the inequality in its most dramatic expression among individuals because the undocumented migratory workers are in a state of maximum vulnerability in their interactions with U.S. employers in the international labor market.[6]

This is not a spontaneous vulnerability or one mechanically resulting from the free play of supply and demand. It is a vulnerability that was constructed in a historical process that led the United States to be the only country in the world where employers were expressly permitted to contract foreigners who had entered the country in violation of immigration laws. This juridical aberration was the foundation of the asymmetry in the relationship between the undocumented worker and the employer. The migrant does not have the power to exercise options other than accepting the work under conditions imposed by the employer, or risking being exposed by that same employer and being expelled from the country.[7]

This legislative example of brutal asymmetry was in effect from 1952, when the famous "Texas Amendment" was approved, to 1986, when its repeal was implicitly approved in the Simpson-Rodino legislation (Immigration Reform and Control Act of 1986 (IRCA) (Bustamante 1987a).

However, it would be an error to think that the reforms brought about by this legislation eliminated the asymmetry of the traditional relation between the employer and undocumented migrant worker. This law contains a loophole by which employers do not have to retain copies of the foreign worker's documentation proving his right to work in the United States. This allows employers to continue hiring undocumented workers with impunity, aided by the proviso contained in the new legislation that the undocumented worker in question may have presented a document that appeared authentic at the moment of hire — whether or not there was such a document, or whether or not the one shown had actually been falsified. This loophole in the law has indirectly resulted in the flourishing of massive false document production, since the employer has no obligation to keep document copies but rather only to have seen them at the time of hire. This loophole has also indirectly produced a cheapening of undocumented migrant labor among those who use falsified documents with the knowledge of the employer, who now holds an even more effective "sword of Damocles" over the worker's head. Before the IRCA, the employer dissatisfied with the performance of an undocumented worker had recourse to exposing him as an illegal alien in the United States. Now, he can indict the worker for something worse: being in the country illegally and using false documentation.

In practice, this represents enhanced criminalization of the undocumented worker without significant alteration of the employer's power to contract the labor despite employer sanctions established by the IRCA. In practice, the employer has the last word in whether or not there was or was not a document with which the worker established his right to work in the United States (Bustamante 1988).

This loophole is not as clear as the "Texas Amendment" in excluding employers from responsibility for hiring undocumented workers, but legally it can produce the same effect. Over time, this will be the principal reason that the Simpson-Rodino legislation is ineffective in stopping the hire of undocumented workers, allowing another debate and another new legislative reform to occur as soon as there is another economic recession in the country. At that time, following a historical pattern, one can suppose that the legislators will think of some new way to protect the interests of employers who do not want to lose their source of cheap labor.

The comments above summarize the structural situation of social relations between Mexican migrants and those members of U.S. society with whom they most frequently interact. It is a situation characterized by inequality of power between the principal actors: the undocumented migrant and the U.S. employer. This inequality is a microlevel representation of the power asymmetry that characterizes relations between Mexico and the United States. At both levels, the macro and the micro, the conditions in which they occur are not static, and although they do not change in ways that substantially alter the structural position of the principal actors, they are subject to variations that can cause very contrasting relations. The analytical utility of the formerly proposed framework can be seen here. It includes variations hypothetically represented in scenarios whose probability of occurrence decreases with extreme situations. There is a need to distinguish, however, between structural changes and relational changes.

Aging of the U.S. Population

It is paradoxical that such restrictive legislation as the IRCA was approved the same year in which there was a noticeable increase in the demand for foreign labor due to changes in U.S. demographic patterns. Indeed, in 1986, the year the IRCA legislation was approved, what could be seen as a watershed in the population dynamic of the United States took place. That year a deficit began in the entry of young males into the labor force. The U.S. Department of Labor predicts that by the year 2000, there will be a 6 percent decrease in the number of men between the ages of 16 and 24, and a 15 percent decrease in the group between 24 and 36. The proportion of the labor market occupied by young men was 23 percent in 1972, 20 percent in 1986, and is projected to decrease to 16 percent by the year 2000. By then, the proportion of workers in the over-35 age group will have increased from 51 percent in 1986 to 61 percent (Fullerton 1987).

If these data on the relations between demographic changes and the increase in the demand for undocumented migrant workers are not convincing enough, add to them the most recent projections of the U.S. labor force composition (Silvestri and Lukasiewics 1987). Silvestri and Lukasiewics, from the Office of Labor Statistics of the U.S. Department of Labor, have found that among the twelve occupations with the highest demand between 1986 and 2000 are waiters, clerks in food stores, office and house cleaners, messengers, kitchen helpers and cooks, bartenders, errand boys, private club attendants, and security guards.

As will be discussed later, more than half the undocumented workers occupy such positions. The cited authors add that the service sector, where those jobs fall, will grow more rapidly from now to the end of the century. The growth will be from 17.5 million in 1986 to almost 30 million in the year 2000. Given the patterns of growth of the age groups that will be working from now to the end of the century, there is no way that the available work force in the United States can fill the demand for the more than five million vacancies that will open in the lowest salary and skill levels. Unless a robot is invented in the next few years that can perform the aforementioned tasks for the wages paid undocumented workers, the U.S. economy will be threatened by a decrease in the rhythm of economic growth — if it does not in some way import the foreign labor force that can cover the deficit produced by the aging of the working population.

This information points to a greater U.S. dependence on foreign labor dating precisely from 1986, when a law was passed that drastically restricted undocumented immigration. However, this growing dependency can be significantly altered by conditions of economic recession and critical increases in unemployment. Given these conditions, which for our purposes can be termed those of economic instability in the United States, the most likely result is that the Simpson-Rodino legislative sanctions would be strictly implemented. This possibility suggests two scenarios: one in conditions of expansion, or of U.S. economic stability, and the other in conditions of recession or economic instability.

Mexican National Security

A s noted previously, for purposes of this study, national security is understood as that which is defined as such, implicitly or explicitly, by the organs of the state. The proposed definition for Mexican national security is derived from that which would be legal justification for the mobilization of the country's armed forces as an instrument of the state for the defense of national security in the face of internal or external threats.

This, in effect, proposes that a threat to national security would be any action whose predicted direction or concrete effects might impede the effectiveness and force of constitutional precepts. This idea must be understood in relative terms. It is evident that the Mexican constitution is not, in reality, respected in an unambiguous sense. It is likely that no constitution anywhere is respected in absolute terms. However, the constitution is not only the maximum normative law from which the notion of "public order" is derived, but also that which in theory has been conceptualized as the "social contract" between the society and the state.

Starting from this operational definition, any problem of internal origin defined by the state as "national security" has implications for both the maintenance of constitutional guarantees and the fundamental normative framework on which the legality of state actions and institutional security functions hinge. From these same concepts, it can be said that the constitution represents the legitimate basis of the defense of society and of individuals against an arbitrary definition of "national insecurity" by the state. Therefore, the constitution is a reference point for any definition of national security, be it legitimate or arbitrary.

One could argue that Article 29 of the Constitution of Mexico is too narrow to define when there is a national security problem since it speaks of conditions of "invasion" or "serious disturbance of the public peace" as those for which the president can partially or totally suspend the individual guarantees assured by the Constitution. It is conceivable that a problem conventionally defined as one of "national security" could arise without meriting the "suspension of guarantees" described in Article 29. That would perhaps be the case with drug trafficking at its current levels. This phenomenon of organized crime is threatening the constitutional regime of other countries, such as Colombia. In Mexico, evidence has appeared of drug trafficking involvement by public security officials at the highest levels. The president himself recently characterized drug trafficking as a serious national security problem.

To date, no one has suggested that the problem of drug trafficking merits the application of Article 29 of the constitution in terms of a suspension of guarantees; however, there is a possibility of consensus that it is a national security problem in the sense that it threatens to alter the constitutional bases that support and justify the function of the Mexican government. It is in this same theoretical context that the migration from Mexico to the United States could become a national security problem — not because it is one now, but because it has the potential to become one.

It is clear that the proposed definition of national security is not the one conventionally employed in U.S. political discourse. In general, there the concept of national security has been used to justify internal as well as external actions, generally tied to the notion of strategic interests related to the exercise of power around the world. The definition proposed here has a more internal than external sense to it.

In the proposed analytical framework, national security would not be considered threatened in those scenarios that envision political stability, although it could be seen as threatened from the outside. On the other hand, in the conditions of political instability proposed by the framework, national security could be seen as threatened both from the inside and outside.

Given the independence of the phenomenon of undocumented migration from Mexico to the United States and the key role played by the government in the U.S. economy, the analytical model presented above is useful for analyzing the future in the short and medium term, in terms of four hypothetical scenarios derived from a theoretical interaction or intersection of economic variables originating in the United States and political variables originating in Mexico.

The analysis of each scenario will be done by focusing sequentially on the following: 1) the economic aspects of the United States that correspond to the assumptions of the case in terms of the interaction of the variables; 2) the Mexican political aspects that correspond to the case assumptions; 3) the repercussions for migration resulting from the interaction of 1 and 2; and finally, 4) the repercussions for national security resulting from the interaction of 1 and 2.

Case 1

The U.S. Economy

In this scenario, the U.S. economy maintains an annual growth rate of at least 3 percent and California of at least 4 percent.[8] Under these conditions, the demographic trends (aging of the work force and the decrease in the percentage of young people in the age groups for the employed population) will produce the highest level of foreign labor force demand (Reynolds 1979).

In such circumstances, one could foresee a relaxation in the application of the migration laws (IRCA), despite the pressures of restrictionist groups — for example, the Federation for American Immigration Reform (FAIR)— and of Immigration and Naturalization Service (INS) officials in favor of new measures to staunch the flow of undocumented migration. The demand for foreign labor would provoke the constant appearance of programs for new means of legalizing undocumented workers, as in variations on the Special Agricultural Worker (SAW) regulations. The hiring of undocumented workers would become more and more open, contracting any undocumented worker with only the presentation of any document similar to those accepted for proof of legal residence in the United States, independent of whether the document had been falsified.

A generalized and well-understood complicity between employers and undocumented workers concerning the presentation of documentation at the time of hire would be akin to the laxity of some U.S. bars where young people are asked for identification to prove they are older than 21 as a legal requirement for alcoholic beverage consumption, but where the providers of the beverages accept any type of documentation, independent of its authenticity. With the demand generated from the United States by an expanding economy and an aging population, U.S. employers would pay more attention to the laws of the labor market than to immigration laws.

Under these conditions, the Simpson-Rodino legislation would become obsolete. However, not everything would be rosy even under conditions of U.S. economic expansion. It is likely that a phenomenon would appear that is more common to bureaucracies than to individuals. The Border Patrol, in particular, and the Immigration and Naturalization Service, in general, would see the importance of their function threatened in the eyes of the public in a context of generalized indifference to immigration laws. If it is valid to say that there have been times when the Border Patrol has achieved the image of a group of heroic guardians of the borders, saving the country from the "silent invasion," the laxity in immigration law enforcement produced by an economy in expansion and the aging of the national labor force could threaten the bureaucracy of the Border Patrol. This effect could translate in practice to artificial provocation of border incidents to maintain the image of "protectors of the country" against invented dangers, such as associating undocumented immigration with some publicly recognized calamity such as drug trafficking or "violent aggression" on the part of undocumented migrants. It would not be the first time that undocumented migrants were used as the scapegoats for disasters. In the past, they have been blamed for unemployment, burdens on public assistance, and even the pollution of Los Angeles, independent of whether such an association could be faithfully shown.

The Political Situation in Mexico

This scenario assumes that President Carlos Salinas de Gortari achieves consolidation of his presidential leadership with measures that produce a broad consensus. For example, let us assume that the political parties approve reforms to the Federal Electoral Law, notwithstanding disagreements with the final law on the part of some opposition parties; the principal effect of the renegotiation of the debt is a resurgence in the confidence of investors, manifested in a return of capital and an increase in foreign investment; there is a spectacular increase in Japanese investment, which does not pass unnoticed in the United States; and as a result, critical voices are heard in the United States which, charged with ideological overtones, allude to the Monroe Doctrine to pressure Mexico into slowing or refusing Japanese investment.

In this scenario, the return of capital, the increase in foreign investment, and the return of petroleum prices to more than $25 per barrel become the most important factors in the new growth of the national economy. With the lowering of unemployment and improvement in real salaries, there is a resurgence in government credibility, which favors the official party. The favorable moment is taken advantage of to change the name of the PRI (the Institutional Revolutionary Party), which begins with a restructuring in which other sectors are added to the traditional three, with the apparent purpose of giving more influence to the middle class and the private sector. The fruits of this strategy are reflected with most immediacy in electoral victories by the government party in the Federal District.

Let us go on to assume the growth of the national economy at 6 percent to 8 percent annually is not equal across regions. The petroleum region is benefitted by renewed investment in PEMEX. Migration toward the petroleum cities of the Gulf is renewed to satisfy growing demands for labor, especially skilled and semi-skilled labor. The growth rate makes the lack of progress in training and technical and advanced education over the years quite visible.

In regional terms, the greatest economic growth is seen in northeastern Mexico, above all in Baja California. This area benefits from foreign investment that seeks to bring the manufacturing areas of California involved in new technologies in biotechnology and electronics as close as possible to the sources of cheap labor in Baja California. International service industries proliferate, first based in Tijuana, then expanding into Ciudad Juárez and the main border cities. Daily, thousands of workers commute from these cities to do cleaning jobs in the southwestern United States, under service contracts with transnational companies whose workers reside in Mexican border cities that absorb the major part of the migratory workers who arrive at the northern border with intentions of working in the United States.

This growth of the regional economy on the northern border, principally in the northeast, generates an urgent need for renovation of urban infrastructure, which includes the construction of subways in

Tijuana and Ciudad Juárez, as well as housing, paved roads, and sewers, which generate new employment in competition with the *maquiladora* industries that begin to complain about the rising cost of labor. The political consequence of this economic growth is the recovery of the governorship of Baja California by the candidates of the new party which supports the federal government.

Consequences for Undocumented Migration

Under the conditions outlined above, the migration phenomenon to the United States would appear to follow the trends observed in 1989. Until that year, the Simpson-Rodino legislation had not had significant impact on the flow of undocumented migrants into the United States (Bustamante 1988).

The main trends that would be seen are 1) a higher percentage of women in the flows, 2) more migrants from urban areas, 3) bigger differences between national levels of education and the levels of the migrant workers, 4) increases in the costs of migration, 5) increases in police extortion in Mexican border cities, 6) a decrease in the numbers of migrant workers, and 7) an increase in the demand for migrant workers in the United States.

In this scenario of economic expansion in the United States and political stability in Mexico, the most promising conditions would arise for achieving a bilateral accord on migrant workers. However, the degree of politicization that the topic of "illegal aliens" has reached in the United States would make it difficult to garner the support of the general population for the idea of a bilateral agreement between the two governments. The Mexican government would be encouraged, at least for a time, by the approval of a multilateral agreement on the rights of migrant workers that would be finally approved by the Organization of American States after almost a decade of debate. The United States would vote against the agreement. However, this would be the best time to attempt such a bilateral accord.

For its part, the government would have better information sources and knowledge about the United States, particularly about the interaction between the economy and politics at regional and sectoral levels, in relation to the conditions of demand for Mexican labor. Using this information, the Mexican government could create more favorable conditions for a bilateral negotiation strategy, beginning with a political consensus in Mexico for the following negotiation objectives: decreasing the flight of human capital otherwise needed for regional (northern Mexico) and national development, starting from the premise that the emigration of the labor force is contrary to long-term national interests; given the impossibility of stopping the labor flight to the United States, the Mexican government would propose short-term objectives, looking for an agreement with the United States that would provide operative mechanisms to protect the human and labor rights of the migrant workers while living in the United States, thereby stimulating their return; and finally, including authentic labor representation in the bilateral discussion and negotiation process.

Though the probability of achieving an agreement on migrant workers on the aforementioned terms is slim, new ways should be tried, such as using as a theme the idea of including migrant workers in the service area. In this type of agreement, the Mexican workers would enter the United States hired by a service company that would be responsible for their entry and exit from the country, where they would stay only to render the contracted service under a non-immigrant visa. The advantage for the workers would be in obtaining better salaries than are available in Mexico for the same work, and receiving government benefits appropriate to the international conditions for that work.

In the most advanced stages of this international labor practice of contracting service workers, the following scenario could be considered: 1) a corporation could be established with U.S., Canadian, and Mexican capital, headquartered in Dallas, Texas, with the objective of providing cleaning and maintenance services; 2) to realize this objective, the company could create a permanent training program in different central Mexican cities (Guadalajara, Leon, Morelia, San Luis Potosí, Zacatecas) to provide cleaning and maintenance for large buildings in important cities of the United States on weekend shifts; 3) the company might offer the graduates of its highest training levels a four-day contract, which could be renewed each week; the work would begin on Friday, when the contracted workers, already dressed in their uniforms, would arrive at the airport nearest their permanent home; 4) hundreds of uniformed workers could be seen lining up ready to board jumbo jets hired by the service company destined for major U.S. cities; 5) in route to their destinations, the workers would be instructed on the buildings in which they would be working that weekend. They would also be informed of the location of company facilities where they would stay and which they would use from Friday to Sunday; 6) the company would have already negotiated H-2 visas for the workers' entry into the United States under terms previously agreed to by the governments of the United States and Mexico to guarantee the arrival and departure of the workers; 7) on Friday evenings between 6 p.m. and 8 p.m., the workers would arrive at the building installations to set up the company stores; 8) the workers would complete their work following the instructions given on board the airplane, including a videotape of building interiors; 9) the work would be finished by dawn Monday, at which time the stores would be packed up and the workers returned to respective airports for the trip home, during which they would be paid in national currency for the four-day contract; 10) on Monday morning the uniformed workers could be seen leaving their respective jumbo jets, and arriving at their homes in time to change and get to their regular weekly jobs, or perhaps make do with the salary earned during the weekend, which is higher than they could have earned during the week in their own cities.

It is important to note that if this scenario sounds like science fiction, it is totally feasible under current conditions. The GATT agreement, to which Mexico is a party, permits international trade in services. Given that, what is now seen as a problem of undocumented immigration could be converted into an international trade activity. Further, H-2 visas could be used under the terms suggested by the scenario. Of course, there are serious obstacles. They are, however, of a more ideological than practical nature.

Independent of whether such scenarios are enacted, the conditions determined by the expansion of the U.S. economy, plus the interaction of the conditions of labor demand from the United States and the conditions of supply in Mexico, would result in a growing scarcity of labor in the United States, where there would be a growing demand for Mexican labor. On the other hand, the growing costs of migration to the United States from the traditional places in Mexico would create a downward trend in the volume of migratory workers crossing the northern border without documents. These conditions would favor the pursuit of a bilateral negotiation initiative by the Mexican government.

Implications for National Security

Under the assumptions above, the implications for Mexican or U.S. national security would be minimal. From the Mexican perspective, the most serious implications would be tied to the continuation of extortionist practices by Mexican police toward undocumented Mexican and Central American migrants in the northern cities of Mexico. However, under conditions of political stability, it is likely that the practice of extortion would become more visible and the political costs to the government would increase if they did nothing to combat it. Under the conditions of this scenario, the president himself would propose severe measures against police extortionists, such as mechanisms to prevent extortion through greater citizen participation in the evaluation of border police forces.

Case 2

U.S. Economic Situation

This scenario assumes that at the beginning of the 1990s, the U.S. economy begins to show signs of recession. The state of California would be the last to feel the effects of a national recession, almost a year after the rest of the country. Soon, unemployment would begin to grow, reaching 8 percent at the national level and 7 percent in California. Interest rates would increase, as would protectionism, particularly affecting imports from Mexico.

Given the recession and the growth of unemployment, diverse political actors in the United States would again utilize undocumented immigration as the scapegoat for the problems of the recession, particularly unemployment. Xenophobic rhetoric would enjoy a general resurgence — against Mexicans in particular — among officials of the Immigration and Naturalization Service and politicians seeking election or reelection. Violent border incidents would increase. There would be full implementation of the Simpson-Rodino Act, including massive deportation of undocumented migrants.

Mexican Political Situation

On the Mexican side, we assume the electoral reforms to have been consolidated with greater competition between the political parties. Under these conditions, there would be a very conspicuous reaction to U.S. events. A political phenomenon would be generated beginning with a national consensus among all the political parties against the verbal aggression of the United States. This would have repercussions on the Mexican side, above all in Tijuana, where the irritation might be expressed in protests at the U.S. consulate. The massive expulsions predicted in this scenario would coincide with frequent incidents of violence on the border between border police and migrants and would prompt various Mexican political parties to seek and receive the support of Mexican workers and chicano organizations in the United States in defense of the migrants. Under the conditions of this scenario, there would be an upsurge of ethno-political activity in the border cities of both countries that would bring together the interests of U.S. organizations of Mexican origin and Mexican political organizations.

In response to the massive deportations that had produced a sudden excess of unemployed workers in the border cities, a general anti-U.S. sentiment would be generated in the larger northern border cities that Mexican political organizations might try to take advantage of to ignite a general protest strike by border *maquiladora* industry workers. The organizers might try to connect their action with a series of strikes in the United States where there are concentrations of Mexican workers or workers of Mexican origin. In this context, a new leader could appear in the United States using the symbol of César Chávez successfully to organize a major strike by California and Oregon agricultural workers that would threaten to decrease U.S. agricultural production by more than 25 percent.

Consequences for the Migration Situation

Despite U.S. economic conditions, the undocumented migrant flow would continue. The problem of the migrant workers would become the biggest issue in bilateral relations. Mexico would win the support of international public opinion in its denunciations of violations of the human rights of Mexicans in the United States. This would further propel a new United Nations Convention on the Rights of Migrant Workers. The tensions and incidences of violence generated by the conditions of this scenario could lead to the organization of citizen solidarity brigades in Mexican border cities to assist those deported in returning to their cities of origin, and the Mexican federal government might create an emergency employment plan to respond to the crisis.

Consequences for National Security

In this scenario, U.S. pressure on Mexico would increase significantly to force a bilateral convention of political cooperation that would close the border to undocumented migration and drug trafficking. It would be suggested in the United States that Mexico should use its army to patrol the border and impede the crossing of migrants and drugs. Pressure would grow from conservative groups inside the United States to militarize its borders. One might well see the reinforcement of a wire fence the length of the border with Mexico, as well as the construction of walls and observation towers.

Case 3

The U.S. Economic Situation

Besides the economic conditions proposed in the scenario for Case 1, in this instance, the United States would try to take advantage of the problems of Mexican political instability, offering economic assistance in exchange for unprecedented concessions such as the participation of U.S. investment in Pemex. Pressures mount for the idea of a North American common market, as well as more and more exceptions to Articles 27 and 123 of the Constitution of Mexico in regard to foreign investment. The U.S. government could use the occasion to create conditions that translate into an unprecedented cheapening of Mexican labor in the border *maquiladora* industry and in the United States. The loans that the Mexican government obtains under conditions of political instability could lead them to accept conditions damaging to national sovereignty.

The Mexican Political Situation

The political instability of the country would be more clearly manifested in the Federal District, where protest demonstrations could culminate in violent repression. We could imagine a scenario in which political instability provokes capital flight, which this time is accompanied by a human exodus, particularly by people of the middle and upper classes. The "*antichilanguista*" sentiment in the north is intensified, and new separatist talk arises, fueled by powerful groups in the United States. The government might decide to return the banks to the private sector as a gesture to help obtain additional loans required to curb the wave of violence in the country.

Consequences for the Migration Situation

The disturbances in Mexico City would produce, among other things, a massive exodus of capital city residents toward the border cities and the United States. A greater proportion of people from the capital in the overall flow of migrants to the United States produces various immediate effects: 1) the educational level of the migrants rises; 2) the proportion of women rises; 3) competition among the migrants for work in the United States increases, with those from the capital tending to win; 4) the excess of labor supply tends to bring down migrant worker salaries in the United States; 5) there is an exponential increase in the number of people in the informal economic sector from border cities; and cumulatively, 6) the frustrations resulting from being expelled from the United States, running out of money before finding work in the United States, and the effect known as 'relative deprivation' resulting from finding positions only in occupations that required lower skills than did the last job the migrant held, would provoke an accelerated increase in crime and violence in the border cities, similar to the phenomenon of criminalization in South American cities such as Bogotá, Medellín, Rio de Janeiro, and Lima.

With the massive exodus to the United States, the brutality of repression against those who tried to cross would grow. The violence against Mexicans who entered U.S. territory would generate a very strong reaction from the Mexican population and those of Mexican origin. Repression with racial overtones might arise against groups and individuals of Mexican origin in a way similar to that at the end of the 1960s against blacks.

Consequences for National Sovereignty

The political instability and the growing vulnerability of Mexico to the United States would lead to practices driven by the weakness of the government in the face of the crisis. For example, the government would give in to the pressures of the Mexican right that would translate to the loss of efficacy of some articles of the Mexican Constitution — for example, the 3rd (education and church/state separation); the 11th ("Everyone has the right to enter and leave the republic, travel its territory and change residence..."); the 14th ("No one can be deprived of life, liberty, property, possessions, or rights..."); the 16th ("No one can be violated in their person, family, papers, or possessions..."); the 27th ("The ownership of the land and water contained within national territory pertains by origin to the nation.... The nation will at all times have the right to impose on private property the rules that serve the public interest..."); the 123rd ("Everyone has the right to dignified, socially useful work..."); and the 130th ("The law does not recognize any special rights to religious groupings called churches").

Case 4

The U.S. Economy

This scenario has as its point of departure a recession in the 1990s. To that can be added that the long process of U.S. consumer indebtedness initiated in the 1970s reaches its limit, and consumers have to reduce their levels of consumption drastically. Companies have been investing more in the stock market than in the renovation of their industrial plants and equipment. Productivity has been decaying throughout the 1980s. Public spending for research and development has decreased drastically, and the United States has lost the technology race to Europe and Japan. In 1992, a new economic power arises with the political and economic unification of the European Economic Community, aided by the transformation of Eastern Europe, which generates a trade war in which the United States is disadvantaged because its manufactured exports are not competitive in price or quality. In sum, the U.S. economy stops growing and begins a new recession.

In as much as the income and utility of businesses begin to decline, the already enormous U.S. government deficit gets even larger because of the decrease of fiscal income tied to the overall slump. The U.S. Federal Reserve decides to increase interest rates to stimulate loans to the government, necessary to cover a gigantic deficit of more than $300 billion. The high interest rates brake the growth of the economy, creating a vicious cycle of not being able to prod growth with an increase of public spending, which implies an increase in the government deficit. The U.S. government would be forced to maintain high interest rates to obtain the money necessary to service the debt, which would represent a larger and larger proportion of the federal budget.

As the U.S. economy entered a recession, all the countries that export to the United States would be affected by the decrease in its buying power. The countries that depend most on exports to the United States would be, obviously, the most affected, creating as a consequence an economic recession and rise in unemployment levels.

Because of the growing practice of buying more imported than domestic goods, the United States would deluge with dollars those countries exporting the most, causing a fall in U.S. foreign exchange. The high interest rates the country would be maintaining to keep attracting the capital required to cover the huge external debt would make the cost of capital so high that investment would be virtually prohibitive, which would aggravate the recession further.

Finally all the debts would accumulate, causing a collapse of the economy. The U.S. foreign debt, along with consumer and business debt, would be so great and interest rates so high that the debtors would stop meeting obligations. In a domino effect, farmers, with the oldest debt, would be the first to go bankrupt. The small banks that had made loans to the farmers would follow. Then the larger banks would go. The most indebted countries would also stop payments, accelerating the demise of the even larger banks. The stock market crash might be more profound than that of 1929.

As an effect of the most profound economic recession in history, the United States would return to unusually aggressive protectionist strategies. Xenophobic sentiments would be heightened in the country, exacerbated by those who look for outside scapegoats to explain the crisis. It would not be the first time in the history of U.S. economic recessions that the victim of this economic and socio-psychological phenomenon would be foreign migrants, particularly undocumented Mexican migrants. The xenophobic environment created by the crisis would make it possible for organizations such as the Federation for American Immigration Reform finally to be successful in proposals to build a moated wall several meters high along the U.S.-Mexican border, financed by fines imposed on detained undocumented immigrants and a fee on those Mexicans who wanted to enter the country.

Such a wall would substantially change the nature of social, economic, and cultural relations that characterize the border region between the United States and Mexico. Transborder interactions would rapidly disappear, making the border appear more and more like that of China and the Soviet Union.

That would be a new phenomenon in Mexican border cities. The depth of the U.S. economic recession would immediately impact the northern border region of Mexico, causing accelerated unemployment. It would, at the same time, spur a massive exodus of border Mexicans to the United States, at which point the Border Patrol might even declare a state of alert with sorties of paramilitary swat teams whose actions would be well publicized through the U.S. mass media. To this border exodus would be added a migratory flow from the interior of the country. The more the U.S. recession penetrated the Mexican economy, the more the flow would increase.

This phenomenon of Mexican border cities would culminate in a "sandwich" syndrome: the accumulation of the unemployed local population, plus the migrant population expelled to those cities by more and more drastic and massive actions by the Immigration and Naturalization Service, as well as a migrant population that would arrive in the border towns with more frustrated intentions to enter the United States. The buildup of these three populations would be unprecedented in number and could reach the point of provoking collective attacks on shopping centers, similar to those seen in Caracas recently and in Brazilian cities in past years.

The rest of the scenario described in Case 2 would be virtually duplicated in its manifestations inside the United States.

The Mexican Political Situation

It would be difficult to distinguish which disturbances and violence in Mexico City — and other cities in the country — corresponded to desperation, political militancy, or simple crime. Acts of terrorism and kidnappings might occur. The Mexican border cities could turn into powder kegs with sporadic explosions, leading to repressive action, followed by greater proliferation of violence. At the maximum level of political instability, one could see the constitutional government fall and a military junta take power, suspending constitutional guarantees. Then the United States would truly lose control of its borders, faced with the largest human exodus in the history of the continent.

Consequences for the Migration Situation

Under the political conditions described above for Mexico, what was once only a political exaggeration for domestic consumption occurs: The United States truly loses control of its southern border, in the face of a mass exodus.

Consequences on National Security

Individual rights would be lost, and a state of siege, under military control, might be declared in Mexico.

Summary

The hypothetical scenarios presented here start from the premise that the interaction between Mexico and the United States at the macrodimensional level has historically been different for each country. Independent of the intentionality of U.S. policy toward Mexico, actions of an economic character have predominated in the fashioning of bilateral relations whose effects south of the border are determined by the structural conditions of the asymmetry of power. From these premises the analysis divides the different predominant features of the actions of one country and their effects on the other. The criteria are "stable-unstable" with respect to Mexican politics and "expansion-recession" with respect to the U.S. economy.

This, then, provides an analytical instrument useful in the study of the future bilateral relations between Mexico and the United States. There is, obviously, no effort to make any real prediction. The purpose of the construction of scenarios is to analyze even the remotely possible to plan and evaluate for avoiding undesired results. It tries to analyze to what degree we are prepared for some opportunity that now seems remote or for some disaster that now seems improbable. The most certain outcome of the previous exercise is that the interactions between the U.S. economy and Mexican political stability will affect and be affected by the migratory phenomenon from south to north, which will have implications for the national security of both countries.

Notes

1. A theoretical focus on the migration of Mexican workers to the United States as a result of the international labor market was initially developed by Bustamante (1975). For a follow-up on this focus, see Bustamante 1975a, 1975b, 1979, 1979a, and 1979b. For a revision of this type of focus, see Sobel 1982. Also see Reynolds 1979.

2. This view was very characteristic of Ray Marshall, who temporarily left academia to become U.S. labor secretary in the Jimmy Carter administration. His ideas on the exogenous character of the "causes" of undocumented migration became very influential; see Marshall 1978.

3. Since Samora in 1969, no study has contradicted these findings.

4. The annual GNP growth rate for California in the past decade has generally been higher than that for the entire United States. However, in 1988, GNP for California was 3.7 percent, while for the United States it was 3.8 percent; see State of California 1989.

5. I refer, in particular, to the notion of the social relations, to the notion of economic relations, and to the notion of markets analyzed by Weber (1965).

6. For an analysis of the process in which this vulnerability developed, see Bustamante 1972.

7. For a broader analysis of this process, see Bustamante 1972.

8. These are levels below those that characterized the respective economies in 1988, for example.

References

Bustamante, Jorge A. 1972. "The Wetback as Deviant: an Application of Labeling Theory." *American Journal of Sociology* (University of Chicago Press) 77(4)(January).

Bustamante, Jorge A. 1975. "Mexican Immigration to the United States and the Social Relations of Capitalism." Ph.D. thesis. Sociology Department, Notre Dame University.

Bustamante, Jorge A. 1975a. "Espaldas mojadas: migración mercancía." *Cahier des Ameriques Latines*, 12. Paris.

Bustamante, Jorge A. 1975b. "Commodity Migrants: the Structural Analysis of Mexican Immigration." In *Views Across the Border: The United States and Mexico*, comp. Stanley Ross. Albuquerque, N.M.: New Mexico University Press.

Bustamante, Jorge A. 1979. "Migración indocumentada." *Foro Internacional* 18(74). Mexico: El Colegio de Mexico.

Bustamante, Jorge A. 1979a. "Las mercancías migratorias, indocumentados y capitalismo: un enfoque." *Nexos* 14(February). Mexico.

Bustamante, Jorge A. 1979b. "Undocumented Immigration from Mexico: Beyond Borders but Within Systems." *Journal of International Affairs* (New York: Columbia University) 33(2).

Bustamante, Jorge A. 1987. "La migración de los indocumentados." *El Cotidiano*. Mexico: Universidad Autónoma Metropolitana, Unidad Atzcapotzalco, special no. 1.

Bustamante, Jorge A. 1987a. "La migración indocumentada de México a Estados Unidos." In *Visión histórica de la frontera norte de México*, comp. David Piñera. Mexicali, Baja California: Universidad Autónoma de Baja California.

Bustamante, Jorge A. 1988. "Research Findings and Policy Options." In *Mexico and the United States. Managing the Relationship*, ed., Riordan Roett. Boulder, Colo.: Westview Press.

Cárdenas, Gilbert. 1983. "Research on Mexican Immigration." In *The State of Chicano Research on Family, Labor, and Migration: Proceedings of the First Stanford Symposium on Chicano Research and Public Policy*, comps. Armando Valdez et al. Palo Alto, Calif.: Center for Chicano Research, Stanford University.

Consejo Nacional de Población. 1986. "Encuesta en la Frontera Norte a Trabajadores Indocumentados Devueltos por las Autoridades de Estados Unidos de América." *Resultados Estadísticos* (ETIDEU). December 1984. Mexico: Consejo Nacional de Población.

Fullerton, Howard N., Jr. 1987. "Labor Force Projections: 1986 to 2000." *Monthly Labor Review*, 110(9).

Greenwood, Michael, and John M. McDowell. 1986. "The Factor Market Consequences of U.S. Immigration." *Journal of Economic Literature* XXIV(December).

Marshall, Ray. 1978. "Economic Factors Influencing the International Migration of Workers." In *Views Across the Border: The United States and Mexico*, comp. Stanley R. Ross. Albuquerque, N.M.: University of New Mexico Press.

Ojeda Gómez, Mario. 1982. "The Structural Context of U.S.-Mexican Relations." In *Mexico Today*, comp. Tommie Sue Montgomery. Philadelphia: Institute for the Study of Human Issues.

Reubens, Edwin P. 1979. *Temporary Admission of Foreign Workers: Dimensions and Policies*. Washington, D.C.: National Commission for Manpower Policy.

Reynolds, Clark W. 1979. "Labor Market Projections for the United States and Mexico and Their Relevance to Current Migration Controversies." *Food Research Institute Studies* (Standford University) 17(2).

Samora, Julián. 1971. *Los Mojados: The Wetback Story*. Notre Dame, Ind.: University of Notre Dame Press.

Secretaría de Trabajo y Previsión Social, Centro Nacional de Información y Estadísticas del Trabajo. 1979. *Análisis de algunos resultados de la primera encuesta a trabajadores mexicanos no documentados devueltos de los Estados Unidos, CENIET, octubre 23 a noviembre 13 de 1977*. Mexico: CENIET.

Silvestri, George T., and John M. Lukasiewics. 1987. "A Look at Occupational Employment Trends to the Year 2000." *Monthly Labor Review* 110(9).

Sobel, Irving. 1982. "Human Capital and Institutional Fearing of the Labor Market: Rival and Complement?" *Journal of Economic Issues* (March).

State of California. 1989. *California Economic Indicators*. Department of Finance (January).

Weber, Max. 1965. *Economía y sociedad.* Trans. by Medina Echavarría. Mexico: Fondo de Cultura Económica.

Drug Trafficking
From a National Security
Perspective

María Celia Toro

Arnold Wolfers has argued that "when political formulas such as 'national interest' or 'national security' gain popularity, they need to be scrutinized with special care. They may not mean the same thing to people. In fact, they may not have any precise meaning at all" (Wolfers 1962, 147).

From the beginning of the 1980s, both Mexican and U.S. political leaders have presented their strategies for reducing drug trafficking under the auspices of national security policy. However, few studies have addressed drug trafficking as a national security issue in either the United States or Mexico. One reason for this may be the lack of a clear, operational definition of national security; another may be that few analysts really believe that drug trafficking poses a threat for either country's security. These issues pose various questions: What do politicians from both sides of the border mean when they say that drug trafficking is a threat to national security? What threats are posed by drug trafficking? Can anti-drug trafficking policies guarantee the national security of both countries?

Answering these questions requires clarification of the concept of national security and an evaluation of whether government policies designed to stop drug trafficking increase or decrease threats to national security.

It is my opinion that the challenges presented by drug trafficking are often mistakenly characterized as national security problems. In those cases where one can accept the link between the two in either

317

country, policies and perspectives, at times, bring worrisome consequences. There occurs what students of the arms race have called a "security paradox" — a vicious circle in which the security of one leads to the insecurity of the other.

Preliminary Considerations

There are at least two ways to deal with the ambiguous nature of the concept of "national security." One is historical interpretation, that is to say, to trace what policy-makers have understood at different times as constituting threats to their nations.[1] Another is simply to use the concept in a traditional sense — national security as the ability of a nation to protect internal values from external threats. Both approaches conceptualize "security" as the "absence of threats to acquired values," and coincide with Walter Lippman's definition that "a nation is secure to the extent that it is not in danger of having to sacrifice core values" (Wolfers 1962, 150). On the other hand, it is important to keep in mind that since the Second World War, "national security" as a concept and area of study has been closely identified with U.S. defense needs.[2]

Including the term "value" runs the risk of stretching an already elusive concept to the point where it becomes meaningless (or even politically dangerous); nevertheless, it allows us to keep in mind that "national security" as a concept is neither absolute nor unchanging but, rather, politically defined. For purposes of this analysis, we will say that, to be taken seriously, a so-called national security policy must fulfill two requirements. First, the policy must be supported by assigned resources sufficient to avoid the potential threat. Second, the threat must be of an external nature. In this way, the term is not limited to its strictly military use, and the risks of expanding it unnecessarily are somewhat diminished.

From this perspective, external threats could range from military operations leading to combat, to more subtle threats such as covert operations, military mobilizations, incidental incursions, and exchange of fire across borders between police or military units. There are potential forms of external interference that do not necessarily carry the risk of war but which governments have traditionally considered disadvantageous to their security (Tillema 1989, 419-420).

States consider legitimate the use of any instrument of power to guarantee their security, which they frequently identify with autonomy (the capacity to keep the state free of political pressure or economic coercion and to reduce foreign intervention in internal policy). In these cases, power is utilized defensively, with the majority of countries willing to resort to the use of force when so endangered. In other words, when national security is at stake, governments are willing to sacrifice other less important interests.

It is important to note that I am starting from the premise that national security is the same as state security.[3] Except in those cases where the interests of the state are in open conflict with those of the society, it can be said that national security includes the security of the majority of the population. (Otherwise, the state may be hiding behind a false definition of national security to repress certain sectors of the population.) Thus, *internal* threats or attacks against established governments — as from guerrillas, coups, or drug traffickers — cannot be considered as national security risks, although it is possible to classify them as "internal security threats," which may or may not become national security risks, in line with Moss and Rockwell's categories. With this analytical framework, which takes only *external* threats as national security risks, I will evaluate whether or not drug trafficking can, in any meaningful way, be considered as a national security risk for Mexico or the United States. Additionally, I will examine whether these countries are taking adequate steps to counter the perceived threats.

Drug-Related Threats

Cocaine, marijuana, and heroin production and use have become a cause for grave concern for the U.S. government as well as a source of international discord. The preponderance of these three drugs enters the United States via illegal importation. The belief of the U.S. government, now shared by many other governments, that drug consumption can be eliminated by reducing availability, has led to the internationalization of efforts to prohibit drug production and trade. With the idea of raising prices to deter drug users, current anti-drug strategies concentrate on crop eradication in source countries[4] and the breakup of drug trafficking organizations.

This anti-narcotics policy lumps together three very different types of issues: 1) national production and distribution, 2) international drug trafficking, and 3) drug consumption. The policy assumes a causal linkage — the greater the production and illegal transit, the greater the consumption. However, the relation among the three issues is not as simple as the current anti-drug policy would indicate, and it affects the United States and Mexico in quite different ways.

As far as consumption is concerned, the objective of a "drug-free" society has become a core value in the United States. Both the government and the society at large have decided that drug use has reached such a magnitude as to undermine the social fabric and a future generation of productive Americans. Consumption statistics in the United States are well known: 20 million people admit to using marijuana; 4.5 million, cocaine; and 0.5 million, heroin.

Although there has been some rise in consumption in Mexico, particularly of marijuana, the use of the three target drugs does not represent a serious public health problem. Preliminary results of a 1989 national drug survey in Mexico show that 2.52 percent of the population has used marijuana at least once; 0.28 percent has tried cocaine, and 0.09 percent, heroin (Secretaría de Salud 1989). Regular use of any of these drugs is obviously lower; the survey did not report even one active heroin user. Of course, it is impossible to determine general consumption trends on the basis of one national survey.

Unfortunately, we know very little about the reasons for drug consumption and demand in some countries and the lack of it in others. One of the reasons for this ignorance is the deeply held belief that the demand for drugs merely depends on supply, which the Mexican case disproves.

Almost all the marijuana and heroin produced in Mexico is destined for the U.S. market. South American cocaine traffickers use Mexico to transport the drug to U.S. and European markets. From the perspective of internal consumption, the Mexican government can only hope that the drugs transit the country on the way to somewhere else and do not intensify domestic consumption. The Mexican government takes responsibility for destroying the drugs before they leave Mexican territory, in an attempt to curb the growth of local and U.S. consumption as well as to insure a positive assessment by U.S. officials of Mexican interdiction efforts.

On the other hand, it should be understood that the clandestine nature of the market is independent of the dimensions of drug demand. The phenomena of illegal production and distribution are better explained by their prohibition than by demand. Smuggling occurs because the international narcotics trade is illegal; the causal relation is clear. However, there is not such a strong relation between the levels of consumption and the institutional framework of production and distribution. Ethan Nadelmann states, for example, that it "is possible to consider the period between the end of the nineteenth and beginning of the twentieth centuries as a time when it was more or less legal to buy the majority of substances that are today classified as illegal.... During that era, drug consumption in the United States came close to today's levels" (Nadelmann 1988, 98).

More is known about the influence of illegal markets on political institutions. The contraband "can affect the internal structure of a society by creating new actors, power bases, and consumption patterns. It is possible that smuggling is an extreme example of loss of control by the state" (Domínguez 1975, 87). Drug traffickers who form sophisticated organizations represent the greatest threat; they come to have the greatest influence on the market and the state.

The major distributors and traffickers are the biggest problem in Mexico and, perhaps, in the United States as well. It is a question of organizations that control distribution, affect supply, and manipulate producers and consumers. The power they acquire allows them to challenge state authority openly (as in Colombia) and weaken — through their corrupting influence — governmental capacity to enforce law and order. This is the type of drug trafficker able to buy protection and willing to intimidate producers, the police, and others.

Although small producers, traffickers, or sellers who cross the border with small quantities of narcotics can offer bribes to the police who discover them, they lack the means to incorporate the police into an efficient trafficking organization. However, independent producers and small dealers also are part of an unacceptable spread of clandestine activities, both inside and outside their respective countries. One of the consequences of this small-time growth in trade is the need for the greater assignment of resources to combat it on both sides of the border. This results in fewer resources available for more serious crimes, including other "crimes against health." The continued cost is often justified with the argument that it is necessary to "maintain the norm of prohibition" to remind future users and traffickers that it is, in fact, an illegal business.[5]

We do not know very much about how the drug market is organized in either country. The levels of corruption — a consequence of dedicating police forces to drug work — are a source of scandal and speculation but not of study. The corruption that drug trafficking has spawned among the military has not been documented either, although it is known that some members of the Mexican army have not escaped it. The problem has also penetrated the judicial and prison systems.

Regardless, drug traffickers have not been able legitimately to enter political life. Up to now, the main drug traffickers in Mexico have been content (or have only been able) to garner money and fame. With the exception of some old families whose fortunes originated in the narcotics trade, such as the Herreras of Durango, traffickers do not occupy positions of prominence in the society, nor are they recognized as participants within political debate.

It is thought that marijuana trafficking is in the hands of hundreds of small groups and individuals with few opportunities to form a Mafia-type criminal organization. Heroin trafficking has been the most stable in past decades, and its associated groups have a well-deserved reputation for violence. Cocaine trafficking tends to be controlled by a few international networks, the majority of which are headquartered in Colombia, with important branches in Mexico, the Caribbean, and the United States.

On the other hand, no studies exist on the profits generated by the drug trade in Mexico nor on their impact on the Mexican economy. In spite of this, one can presume that the overall size of the economy reduces "narco-dollar" importance at the national level. Moreover, exportation is not the source of greatest profits, and the majority of those generated are "laundered" outside the country. If we accept that in 1987, cocaine and marijuana exports generated $2 billion in foreign exchange for all Latin America,[6] we can estimate that, including heroin, almost one billion dollars entered Mexico — close to 15 percent of annual interest payments on the external debt. Of course, it is entirely possible that the political and economic influence of drug trafficking at the local level is far greater than that on the national scene.

In relation to smuggling, the capacity to decide who crosses borders is usually considered by governments to be a necessary condition for guaranteeing national security and sovereignty. Consequently, the Mexican and U.S. governments have designed strategies — albeit, ineffective — to prevent smugglers from entering their territories. If the price of narcotics and conditions of cultivation were similar in both countries, the governments would continue having problems with a clandestine market to serve internal demand, but geographic distribution would be entirely different, and smuggling would be drastically reduced. However, the characteristics of the current market offer such disproportionate economic incentives that traffickers are willing to get involved in a broad spectrum of transnational operations, ranging from drug transport to distribution networks to money laundering.

From the perspective of bilateral relations, there are two aspects of the U.S. anti-drug policy that affect only Mexico. The first is the possibility of economic and political sanctions exercised by the U.S. government against countries that do not "cooperate" in the struggle against drug trafficking. Mexico is particularly vulnerable to this type of diplomatic coercion, although it is unlikely that the U.S. government would impose economic sanctions against Mexico for drug-related reasons. The second and more important aspect of U.S. policy is the presence of DEA (Drug Enforcement Administration) agents on Mexican territory (Nadelmann 1987). The fundamental problem, as the history of U.S. and Mexican police forces shows, is the tendency of U.S. police to cross the Mexican border in pursuit of offenders (Walker 1981), an unacceptable violation of territorial integrity and a threat to national sovereignty.

Anti-Drug Policies

How do the two governments deal with various drug-related problems? Mexican government programs date back to the beginning of the century, when trade in marijuana and heroin was declared illegal. These programs have never been unrelated to changes in the Mexican drug market and U.S. policy. Despite the fact that drug-related crimes in Mexico are classified as "crimes against health," administrations have been more concerned with the political and legal ramifications of production and trafficking than with consumption.

The Mexican government has chosen to increase resources to fight drug trafficking when it has deemed it necessary. Judging by changes in Mexican anti-drug policy, "necessity" has been linked to undesirable developments in the domestic market (be it the quantity or type of drugs trafficked, the market organization, or smuggling routes) or when more aggressive U.S. behavior is feared, possibly leading to extraterritorial application of U.S. laws.

In the mid-1970s, the Luis Echevarría administration intensified its fight against drugs through an aerial eradication campaign to destroy marijuana and poppy fields and the creation of special anti-narcotics police forces (Craig 1978, 110-111). The decision sought to avoid the risk of organized violence against police and military forces in the countryside and to fight the power of the traffickers, especially in the states of Durango and Sinaloa (Lupsha 1981, 99).

The programs were also intended to ward off greater U.S. interference in anti-drug campaigns. By then, Mexico had become the largest supplier of marijuana and heroin to the U.S. market. A special Domestic Council Drug Abuse Task Force Paper (1975) recommended a more active role in Mexico for U.S. anti-narcotics authorities. It stressed the need to take on joint law enforcement activities for the sake of greater effectiveness, particularly along the border. The Mexican government preferred instead to strengthen its own narcotics control capabilities (Toro 1990).

Ten years later, in 1987, President Miguel de la Madrid characterized drug trafficking as a national security issue and described it as "an affair of state" for the first time. From the beginning of his administration, President Carlos Salinas de Gortari emphasized these same aspects of the problem, backing up his statements with significant drug policy changes. The 1985 assassination of Enrique Camarena had already forced Mexican officials to see how tenuous the success of their policies during the second half of the 1970s had been and to realize how vulnerable Mexico was in relation to the United States on the drug control matters.

Part of the problem was that the narcotics market had been reorganized along more sophisticated and aggressive lines (and, occasionally, with the collusion of government officials), and the cocaine routes from the south had been diverted to Mexico. Colombian measures adopted against marijuana and the U.S. program begun in 1986 to staunch the flow of cocaine smuggling through South Florida forced traffickers to look for safer routes and territories. Mexico, with its U.S. border, thus became the point of entry for the tenacious traffickers. Moreover, the cocaine smugglers were better organized and more powerful than their predecessors in the heroin and marijuana trades. With this new pressure, in combination with U.S. rhetoric indicating a willingness to go to any length in the drug fight, Mexico saw the need once again to redefine its policy. Mexican strategies began to be oriented toward the "immobilization" of criminal organizations (as suggested by the U.S. experts) and, although eradication efforts were still budgeted, drug confiscations and the capture of principal players (such as Felix Gallardo in 1989) were the focus.

The term "national security" is seldom used in Mexican political vocabulary. Mexico's relative weakness in the international system explains why the country has not assigned resources to defense issues outside its own borders. The national security of countries with little capacity to mount a war in defense of their own interests depends largely on the stability of the international scene. Weak countries have "little possibility of resolving their security problems by either military means or diplomatic pressures that carry any threats behind them" (Holsti 1986, 647).

To refer to drug trafficking, then, as a national security problem, is noteworthy in the Mexican context. In the recent past, Mexican politicians have spoken of national security in only two cases, both related to defense of the nation's borders. One was the protection of the southern border from military or guerrilla incursions from Central America; the other involved the anti-drug campaigns.

But the connection between national security and drug trafficking has not been fully established in the nation's political discourse; it has simply been asserted. It is, nevertheless, apparent that if the classical definitions of national security and the practices of Mexican narcotics policy serve as a guide to interpretation, we have to conclude that in the case of drug trafficking, the Mexican government has perceived two types of threats to its territorial integrity and sovereignty: the clandestine entry of drug traffickers from other countries (in possible association with Mexican traffickers) and the active (and, at times, unauthorized) involvement of DEA agents on Mexican soil.

This interpretation would coincide with traditional Mexican fears about police activities such as "hot pursuit" or, in more recent times, with fears created by the new North American strategies in the "war on drugs" — for example, the presence of troops in Bolivia in 1986 or the recent capture and "American-style" trial of Mexicans involved in drug trafficking.

Thus, one can understand why Salinas would have embarked upon an open "policy of dissuasion" to warn foreign drug traffickers and politicians of the importance the Mexico state places on two essential prerogatives: preservation of law and order within its territory and control of the dispensation of justice in the country. The resources dedicated to this policy also show the importance given to it. It is clear how much importance the Salinas government has given the issue. It both created a new undersecretariat in charge of the anti-drug trafficking campaign and organized a new force, with twelve hundred agents, for the apprehension of traffickers. Patrols of both borders have also been intensified. In 1988, the attorney general's office invested approximately $50 million (60 percent of its budget) in anti-drug programs, up from $20 million in 1987.

These expenditures do not include those made by the Mexican army, which assigned more than twenty-five thousand soldiers to the campaign. According to some sources, a third of the nation's defense budget went to these efforts (Treverton 1988, 215). To this would have to be added the largest air force of its kind on the continent (basically, helicopters and light aircraft for spraying and transport) (García Ramírez 1988, 141). These statistics indicate the magnitude of the problem and the attention given it, especially when compared to efforts in the 1970s, when only five thousand soldiers and some three hundred fifty members of the Federal Judicial Police were involved in fighting the illegal drug trade (Craig 1978, 116, 119).

U.S. politicians have not been as constrained as their Mexican counterparts in their use of the term "national security." Indeed, they often speak of "national interest" and "national security" as if they were interchangeable. The concept is historically linked to the policy of containment, as applied to communism, and has proved to be politically effective. At least three presidents — Richard Nixon, Ronald Reagan, and George Bush — have declared "wars on drugs" to fight what they have seen as a threat to U.S. national security. A variation on this position comes from those groups who hold that U.S. military forces should get involved in the drug fight, both at home and abroad, and who believe that narcotics control strategies should be cast as national security policies.

The 1986 report of the President's Commission on Organized Crime offered a long list of recommendations to stop drug smuggling. Among others, it called for a national security approach on the basis of the definition of "national security" now employed by the U.S. Joint Chiefs of Staff: a "hostile or destructive action from within or without, overt or covert" which should include the "airborne, amphibious, and overland invasion" of the United States by drug smugglers (President's Commission on Organized Crime 1986, 473).

In spite of adherence to the same policy principles, U.S. anti-drug policies have also changed over time in terms of type of enforcement and resources committed. The U.S. international policy to stop the entry of drugs has been one of enlisting the cooperation of other countries in drug control efforts. Building drug fighting capabilities in other drug producing and transiting countries through police training and technical assistance programs has been at the core of U.S. international strategy since the beginning of the 1970s. DEA agents have been sent abroad to promote the development of similar agencies and to gather drug-related intelligence.

The Reagan administration decided to take on a more preponderant role in drug interdiction both at home and abroad. It was what Bruce Bagley called the "Americanization" of enforcement in Latin America, a policy that proved unwise (Bagley 1988). Between 1981 and 1990, the federal budget targeted at reducing the availability of drugs on U.S. streets progressively increased. More recently, funds for education and treatment of actual or potential users have grown, but they still only account for 25 percent of the drug control budget (Perl 1988, 44). Punitive programs for users and domestic and foreign traffickers consume the major part of these resources, reaching some $8 billion dollars in 1990.[7]

The principal focus is on the interception of drugs in transit to the United States and the capture of traffickers at points of entry (Reuter 1988, 56). And within interdiction efforts, Mexico is considered a key country. In past decades, the Mexican government has received more State Department money for drug fighting efforts than any other country; Mexico is host to the largest number of DEA agents abroad — about forty, officially — and is the principal source of drugs for U.S. consumption (taking into account the production and transit of the three principal drugs). The country offers unparalleled advantages for drug traffickers: proximity to consumers and an enormous and relatively open border.

Given that transportation costs, including protection, represent the biggest expense for traffickers, it is thought that confiscation on the high seas or at the borders drives up the price of the drugs that manage to get through. Even Peter Reuter, while pointing out the difficulty of raising consumer prices through interception policies, asserts that the best way to reduce availability of drugs in the United States is by more efficient control of contraband on the U.S.-Mexican border (Reuter 1988). This explains the increase in border surveillance over the last few years, especially after the "success" of the Florida programs.

Consequences

In light of these observations, it is important to ask whether drug-related threats have diminished as a result of anti-drug policies. The answer, apparently, is no. The policies have not managed to resolve the problems they sought to address nor diminish the threats identified as national security issues. The "threats" from the outside (traffickers and police) are more serious today than a decade ago, despite the fact that the policies of both countries are frequently presented as being based on international cooperation.

Returning to the problem of consumption, the sheer number, resourcefulness, and adaptability of producers, traffickers, and smugglers to different types of law enforcement undermine almost any attempt to reduce consumption by stopping the flow of drugs. Despite that, there has been notable "success" in drug confiscation. In the case of cocaine, the drug that most concerns the two governments, U.S. policy managed the confiscation of more than ninety tons in 1989, and Mexico the confiscation of forty tons in the same year. Clearly, the business today has become riskier for both buyers and sellers but not enough to impact the millions of drug users and thousands of dealers.

It is impossible to know if the norm of prohibition has discouraged people from trying drugs, as is hoped by those in enforcement. In the case of Mexico, if we start from the assumption that cheap narcotics are a strong consumption incentive, then the illegal market and the acquisitive power of American consumers have protected potential Mexican consumers from cocaine and heroin by keeping prices too high for the average citizen.

Little information exists about drug prices in Mexico, but we know that they are high enough to spur production. According to former Mexican attorney general Sergio García Ramírez, the price of a ton of corn is equivalent to a kilo of marijuana (García Ramírez 1988, 146, 148), the cheapest drug with the highest potential of mass consumption in Mexico.

On the other hand, eradication campaigns in Mexico have not managed to destroy marijuana and poppies in sufficient quantities to affect the U.S. market. Mexican and U.S. interdiction policies have not been able to reduce the trafficking of drugs nor U.S. consumption and could even prove counterproductive for Mexican consumption in obliging traffickers to warehouse their products (while "weathering the storm" or finding safer ways to move their merchandise) and to adopt a strategy of selling their wares at low prices on the local market.

Though more expensive than tobacco and alcohol in the United States, drugs are within the reach of many people, and Mexican government actions cannot affect retail prices on the U.S. market. With cocaine, for example, some "99 percent of the sale price on U.S. streets goes to the distributors" (Reuter, Crawford, and Cave 1988, 56). As such, strategies to reduce Mexican supply have not had, nor will have, a significant impact on drug consumption in the United States.

As for domestic and international trafficking, the Mexican government has finally recognized its vulnerability to enforcement programs in other countries, such as Turkey, Colombia, and the United States, as well as its inability to lessen the disparity between Mexican and U.S. drug prices. The success of the United States, or any other country for that matter, in disrupting established trafficking routes will always affect Mexico. In 1982-83, for example, the Mexican government reported seizures of three hundred kilos of cocaine, while in 1989 it confiscated more than thirty tons in a few months (albeit, with the use of increased government resources) (García Ramírez 1988, 584).

The Mexican government eradicated crops to avoid even greater growth of the clandestine market. For the same reason, and to guarantee that changes in transshipment routes would not affect the country, Mexico has adopted measures to stop the entry of traffickers and block transshipment. Unfortunately, these strategies have led to more violent and perverse forms of market organization, with the principal cost being police and judicial corruption. Despite the fact that this represents a serious problem for the Mexican justice system, it is hard to see it as a security threat to the United States.

Currently, the United States and Mexico are concentrating an important part of their efforts on the "immobilization" of key traffickers. This is, perhaps, the most fruitful approach to achieve a temporary drug shortage on the U.S. market (which is all current policies can hope for) and fight the most serious social and political consequences of drug trafficking in Mexico. Although, up to now, drug traffickers in Mexico have not turned to violence for political ends, their existence has negative political repercussions. But attacking this end of the problem leads both countries onto the terrain of criminal prosecution and opens the door to juridical conflicts between the governments, precisely those the Mexican government has sought to avoid. It is also possible that stopping wholesale trade multiplies the number of people interested in taking advantage of the temporary scarcity. As a result, crossing the border with smaller shipments (given that the possibilities of being detained are very slim) (Reuter, Crawford, and Cave 1988) increases the "aerial, amphibious, and overland" invasion the Americans consider to be a security threat.

With all these limitations — and despite the fact that the policies of one country might negatively affect the interests of the other — Mexican policies have slowed the development and consolidation of alternate power bases of drug trafficking. However, these same policies have not prevented the U.S. government from exerting discreet or open pressure on Mexico. After all, a principal objective of the Mexican strategy has been to avoid stronger bilateral cooperative ties in the enforcement arena, at just the time when U.S. officials are saying that joint policy actions could be the best solution. For example, the President's Commission on Organized Crime recommended "facilitation of Customs pursuit of suspected drug traffickers into Mexican air space" and encouraged "joint enforcement and intelligence operations in countries of origin and transshipment" with the participation of U.S. personnel (President's Commission on Organized Crime 1986, 467).

Drug control costs in the United States have been frequently cited by those who advocate legalization (Ostrowski 1989; Nadelmann 1988a). What is clear is that both governments have put resources and important values on the line to deal with the different drug-related problems, without resolving any of them. The assigning of resources (which are already quite limited in Mexico) originally destined for other problems of public order is a good example of these sorts of expenditures. In 1987-1988, one-third of U.S. federal prison inmates were drug law violators (Nadelmann 1988, 99); in Mexico that same year, 60 percent of all criminal prosecutions were drug-related, with 17.6 percent for illegal possession of arms (García Ramírez 1988, 581).

Conclusions

A ppeals to national security are meant to create a broad consensus in favor of anti-drug policies and increase their importance. This is also a way of sending strong messages to traffickers and enforcers alike. However, classifying drug control problems and policies as national security issues and strategies paves the way to unacceptable costs and consequences (such as military solutions to public health problems) and creates false notions about "allied" or "enemy" countries. It also creates antagonism between countries and, from the analytical point of view, obscures the real nature and interrelationships of the problem.

The U.S. government has decided to give priority to the reduction of drug consumption. A public health issue can occupy a position of importance in policy when the society and government so deem, but that does not make it a national security threat. If the fear is of drug consumption — as distinct from an imported disease — the problem lies with the consumers and will continue to be a domestic problem, regardless of international cooperation. No government can effectively win the battle in the face of such a lucrative market.

The resilience of the market within the prohibition framework forces the Mexican state — or any other, for that matter — to attack production and trade. Unable to modify demand, the Mexican government must react against changes in trafficking. Its policy mandate is to prevent the development of criminal organizations capable of taking over parts of national territory or corrupting military and police forces. As such, the threat to Mexico is also internal, if we discard the possibility of full-scale invasion by U.S. forces. From this perspective, drug trafficking represents a problem of public order and an affair of state but not a national security threat. This is in line with the traditional interpretation of national security presented in the first part of this essay.

Successfully meeting the challenges posed by the illegal market in the judicial and political realms does not necessarily affect Mexican or U.S. consumption levels, although it affects the drug lords and smuggling routes. For example, an "effective" operation against international cocaine trafficking rings operating through Mexico might simply force them to move to other parts of the country, or continent, and look for other ways to enter the U.S. market. (Canada has recently become an attractive entry point for more than one trafficker.)

Additionally, if dismantling major organizations creates short-term scarcity, it may benefit smaller operators. The number of illegal border crossings could increase rather than decrease. Inevitable unexpected consequences of this nature would create greater U.S. pressure on Mexico to intensify its interdiction programs and create greater border vigilance. However, if the classical definition and the resources assigned to drug control programs constitute a good guide for determining national security threats, one could characterize the proliferation of drug traffickers and the imposition of laws across national borders as national security threats.

The United States is most affected in terms of the number of smugglers entering its territory. For institutional and geographical reasons, Mexico is more likely to suffer the illegal immigration of drug-trafficking organizations (and, frequently, of arms-trafficking networks). The problem of national jurisdiction only affects Mexico.

The anti-drug policies in use do not appear to protect national security as defined by the governments of both countries. It is possible to argue that such threats do not represent prime security issues, even though the governments sometimes act as if they do. That does not mean that they do not have legitimate interests to defend against drug-created problems. However, it means, for one thing, that the lack of an adequate solution leads to a spiral of mutual distrust that places the Mexican government in a position of growing vulnerability. The Mexican strategies are oriented by national security considerations, which are defined as the need to maintain control over the application of law within national territory and to protect the Mexican state from external pressure, intervention, blackmail, and ultimatums.

The United States does not face this type of threat, but it considers "control of its borders" as indispensable to national security. From this vantage point, neither government can protect its own national security. Under current conditions, Mexico cannot be free of pressure, and the United States cannot stop the entrance of traffickers. In this situation, appealing to national security could be politically expedient for the United States, but it does not assist in the honest evaluation of domestic and international costs and benefits of the so-called "war on drugs."

More disturbing, the worst-case scenarios for both countries are nearer today than ten or fifteen years ago. For the United States, the national security logic leads to "militarization" of drug policy, despite the fact that the U.S. army would have little success in containing drug trafficking (Reuter, Crawford, and Cave 1988). For Mexico, whether or not the problems posed by the drug trade become national security risks will depend on two variables: the U.S. decision to assign a greater role to the army (or more permissive role to the police) at home and abroad and the capacity of the Mexican government to stop trafficking groups from acting with impunity.

In conclusion, the anti-drug policies of both countries, as policies of dissuasion, are caught in a "security dilemma." The policies frequently have consequences contrary to those desired and negatively influence national security considerations for both countries. Policies that directly attack the causes and effects of drug consumption would bring better results. The objective of indirectly influencing levels of use and abuse in the United States through programs designed to attack heroin, cocaine, and marijuana exports to the U.S. market is not only unfeasible but also increasingly costly.

Up to now, policies of prevention and treatment have not had the opportunity to demonstrate their effectiveness in modifying consumption patterns. These programs require financing, time, and patience that a rhetoric based on national security cannot offer. The budget for a more ambitious educational program would have to come from a reduction in the anti-drug enforcement efforts. This type of reallocation (Kleiman 1985) would have positive effects on at least two drug-related problems: organized crime (as much in Mexico as in the United States) and efforts at enforcement beyond national borders (which adversely affect Mexico and do not benefit the United States). Official corruption and levels of violence would also decrease. At the same time, the risk of encouraging drug use through its possible legalization would not present itself in the same way.

Under these changed circumstances, both countries would abandon their national security rhetoric and concentrate on finding solutions to a public health problem without using methods that provoke serious complications in national policies and the administration of justice, nor would they launch "wars" where the enemies and objectives are unclear.

Notes

1. A good example of this type of study is that of Shoultz (1987).

2. For a history of national security doctrine in the United States, see the work of Daniel Yergin.

3. See the chapter by Richard Rockwell and Richard Moss in this volume.

4. The best analysis of the effects of crop eradication on U.S. street prices can be found in Peter Reuter (1985).

5. This argument was developed by Philip Heymann and Mark Moore (1988).

6. This is Ethan Nadelmann's estimate (1987, 86).

7. These statistics do not include municipal and state budgets or private anti-drug education and rehabilitation programs.

References

Bagley, Bruce. 1988. "Colombia and the War on Drugs." *Foreign Affairs* 67(1)(Autumn).

Craig, Richard. 1978. "La Campaña Permanente: Mexico's Anti-drug Campaign." *Journal of Interamerican Studies and World Affairs* (May).

Domestic Council Drug Abuse Task Force. 1975. *White Paper on Drug Abuse*. Report to the President. Washington, D.C.: GPO (September).

Domínguez, Jorge I. 1975. "Smuggling." *Foreign Policy* 20(Autumn).

García Ramírez, Sergio. 1988. *El narcotráfico: un punto de vista mexicano*. Mexico: Porrúa.

Heymann, Philip, and Mark Moore. 1988. "Conferencia El Colegio de México-Harvard sobre un nuevo enfoque a la estrategia antinarcóticos México-Estados Unidos." Mexico: El Colegio de Mexico (28-29 April).

Holsti, Kal J. 1986. "Politics in Command: Foreign Trade as National Security Policy." *International Organization* 40(3) (Summer).

Kleiman, Mark. 1985. "Allocating Federal Drug Enforcement Resources: The Case of Marihuana," Ph.D. thesis. Cambridge, Mass.: Harvard University.

Lupsha, Peter. 1981. "Drug Trafficking: Mexico and Colombia in Comparative Perspective." *Journal of International Affairs* 35(1).

Moss, Richard H., and Richard C. Rockwell. 1993. "Reconceptualizing Security: A Note about Research," in this volume.

Nadelmann, Ethan. 1987. "Cops Across Borders: Transnational Crime and International Law Enforcement," Ph.D. thesis. Cambridge, Mass.: Harvard University (June).

Nadelmann, Ethan. 1988. "Unintended Victims: The Consequences of Drug Prohibition Policies." Princeton: Woodrow Wilson School (July). Unpublished.

Nadelmann, Ethan. 1988a. "U.S. Drug Policy: A Bad Export." *Foreign Policy* 70(Spring).

Ostrowski, James. 1989. "Thinking about Drug Legalization." *CATO Policy Analysis* 121(May).

Perl, Francis Raphael. 1988. "Congress, International Narcotics Policy, and the Anti-Drug Abuse Act of 1988." *Journal of Interamerican Studies and World Affairs* 30(2/3)(Summer/Winter); special edition.

President's Commission on Organized Crime. 1986. Report to the President and the Attorney General. *America's Habit: Drug Abuse, Drug Trafficking and Organized Crime*. Washington, D.C.: GPO.

Reuter, Peter. 1985. "Eternal Hope: America's Quest for Narcotics Control." *The Public Interest* 79.

Reuter, Peter. 1988. "Can the Borders be Sealed?" *The Public Interest* (Summer).

Reuter, Peter, Gordon Crawford, and Jonathan Cave. 1988. "Sealing the Borders: The Effects of Increased Military Participation in Drug Interdiction." National Defense Research Institute. Santa Mónica, Calif.: The Rand Corporation.

Secretaría de Salud. Sistema Nacional de Encuestas de Salud. 1989. "Encuesta nacional de adicciones." Mexico. Mimeo.

Shoultz, Lars. 1987. *National Security and the United States Policy Toward Latin America*. Princeton, N.J.: Princeton University Press.

Tillema, Herbert K. 1989. "Foreign Overt Military Prevention in the Nuclear Age: A Clarification." *Journal of Peace Research* 26(4).

Toro, María Celia. 1990. "El control del narcotráfico: ¿podemos cooperar?" In *La interdependencia ¿un enfoque útil para el análisis de las relaciones entre México y Estados Unidos?*, coordinated by Blanca Torres. Mexico: El Colegio de Mexico.

Treverton, Gregory F. 1988. "Narcotics in U.S.-Mexican Relations." In *Mexico and the United States: Managing the Relationship*, ed., Riordan Roett. Boulder, Colo.: Westview Special Studies on Latin America and the Caribbean.

Walker, William O., III. 1981. *Drug Control in the Americas*. Albuquerque, N.M.: University of New Mexico Press.

Wolfers, Arnold. 1962. "National Security as an Ambiguous Symbol." *Discord and Collaboration: Essays on International Politics*. Baltimore, Md.: The Johns Hopkins University Press.

Part Five

Rethinking Mexican National Security

Reflections on the Use of the Concept of National Security in Mexico

Luis Herrera-Lasso M.
Guadalupe González G.

Introduction

After five decades during which the concept of national security was practically absent from Mexican political life, the last few years have seen its growing use. This is due to the fact that fundamental challenges to national security now seem to go beyond the limits of the traditional concepts of sovereignty and independence, insofar as there also exist threats deriving from failures of Mexican national development creating potential areas of vulnerability that, if poorly handled in relation to foreign policy, might negatively impact national goals and objectives. Among the areas of concern are possible manifestations of political and social instability, problems and shortcomings of the economic system, the loss of natural resources, an accelerated deterioration of the environment, and, in more general terms, institutional structures that may prove incapable of peacefully and effectively realizing the great changes that are before present-day Mexico.

The concept of sovereignty can continue to function as the principal frame of reference for conceptualizing and managing the threats arising from external forces that intrude upon internal matters of national concern. This is the case with pressures applied by the U.S. government or with the recent instability in Central America as well as the problems of drug trafficking, border difficulties, and refugees. Nevertheless, it is apparent that traditional concepts are not capable of producing the more sophisticated strategies needed to confront contemporary situations that are, undoubtedly, more complex than those faced by Mexico a decade ago.

As a tentative approximation, we define national security as the entirety of conditions — political, economic, military, social, and cultural — necessary to guarantee sovereignty and independence and to promote national interests, while strengthening components of the nation's objectives and reducing the weaknesses or inconsistencies that might translate into windows of vulnerability in external relations.

As indicated in some of the contributions to this volume, the debate in its present state still contains serious doubts concerning the necessity of using the concept of national security, whether out of fear that it might bring about situations by no means favorable to democracy — as in the recent history of South America — or because other concepts are considered to be sufficient. Arguments both pro and con are numerous. In this chapter, we do not seek to exhaust the debate but simply attempt to develop a framework for the discussion of specific subjects that allows us to proceed more systematically.

In the opening section of this essay, we will review how the use of the concept of national security has changed in Mexico. In the following three sections, we will propose some basic criteria for defining the concept. Using these criteria as a point of departure, in the final sections we will outline elements of a tentative agenda for Mexican national security. We do not seek to develop a blueprint for the political and operative conceptualization of national security but, rather, to suggest those areas of research that we feel must be tackled at this point in order to make real contributions toward Mexican national security.

The Evolution of the Use of the Concept of National Security in Mexico

Until a few years ago, the concept of national security was not central in Mexico as either a conceptual or operative political term. It seems that this was due not to careless oversight but to clear political purposes, motivated by the following circumstances.

On the one hand, it had not been considered especially necessary to speak of "national security," given that the concepts of sovereignty and national independence had responded, politically and operatively, to the principal challenges of national security as understood in terms of the endangerment of national integrity from abroad. Faced with situations of instability in Mexico, the U.S. government, historically, has felt it has the authority to intervene in order to preserve conditions it believes compatible with its overall strategic interests — as evidenced during the Mexican Revolution and in subsequent years. This explains why the means adopted for defending Mexican sovereignty in relations with the United States was the development of solid and stable political institutions rather than a military deterrent. This was possible thanks to the civil character of the political regime and as a result of the interests of the group in power toward the end of the 1920s, who wished to put an end to the factionalism of the revolutionary generals and the hegemony of the military in the country's political life.

It is interesting to note that the same revolutionary generals — Alvaro Obregón and, later, Lázaro Cárdenas — themselves made reference to a concept of national security that, in principle, discarded the use of force as the main component of Mexico's external relations, while emphasizing the need to strengthen the country's political institutions.

On the other hand, the handling of the concept of national security elsewhere also helps to explain the fact that in Mexico it has not been similarly employed. In the United States, national security has been used in relation to global considerations. While in some Latin American countries, authoritarian military governments have sacrificed the security of the nation and the rule of law in the name of an alleged "national security" that conflates the term with the security of the regime or government.

The traditional concept of Mexican national security takes the defense of sovereignty as its point of departure. In its broadest definition, the defense of sovereignty includes a range of items, from territorial integrity to those objectives that comprise the national interest and give form and content to national aspirations.

However, in recent years, official circles have begun to use the concept of national security — apparently, as a reflection of both the insufficiency of the operative reach of the concept of sovereignty as a means to encompass all possible threats to national security and a lessening of the fear associated with the use of a term previously considered taboo. The concept of national security has been in use by Mexican officials responsible for domestic and international policies since 1983, when it was defined in the National Development Plan

(PND). In the armed forces as well, a deeper analysis of the problem has also begun. In parallel fashion, academics are tackling the problem and are beginning to exchange ideas with their counterparts in official circles, thereby initiating an informal debate. These developments — as indicated in the chapter by Sergio Aguayo — have continued under the government of President Carlos Salinas de Gortari.

It is clear that the growing use of the national security concept is far from being the product of individual thought, whether that of academics or a few members of officialdom. Thus, the obligatory question is why, after five decades of living without this concept, has its use acquired — in just a few years — an importance such that it is incorporated into the organic law of the Mexican state. This question is necessarily speculative, since in the Mexican system it is difficult to gather information on how such changes occur, given that governmental initiatives and decisions do not pass through Congress, to say nothing of civil society. However, we will try to suggest a few hypotheses:

1. The concepts of sovereignty and national independence today provide insufficient responses to potential threats to national security.

2. The discovery of enormous oil deposits in areas near the southern border is a catalyst leading to a heightened awareness of national security concerns.

3. Recent events involving Mexico's borders — such as Central American political turmoil, drug trafficking, and attempts at controlling the border with the United States — demand a reassessment of existing schemes with respect to both the definition of threats and the appropriate strategies for coping with them.

4. The potential for internal political and social destabilization resulting from a transformation of the nation's political economy has implications for national security.

5. Some officials within the armed forces feel the need for a better explanation of the military's functions in relation to new conceptions of national security.

6. The increased importance given to some issues within the United States has a bearing on Mexican national security. Here again,

examples include political stability, drug trafficking, and developments in Central America.

State Security, Government Security, and National Security

To put the security of the government or the state before that of the nation — or to treat them as equivalents — is to create the potential for the gravest political consequences. The problem of definitional distinctions is obviously not merely methodological but fundamentally political.

Nation, state, and government are concepts that are frequently confused in political practice. We use the concept "nation-state" to distinguish the political entity par excellence in the international political system. However, in many instances the state does not correspond to the nation, as can be seen in Africa as well as in the recent vivid examples of the Soviet Union and Eastern Europe. Mexico does not present a problem in this sense. Today, the Mexican nation is easily identifiable as a unitary entity, with the added caveat that the normal sorts of regional differences found nearly everywhere do not invalidate "nation" as a basic concept. As a result, the concept of national unity is imbued with great power.

The state gives political, governmental, and institutional content to the nation. The organs of the state must respond to the intentions and purposes of the nation, integrating all Mexicans into the same political entity from which, in the last instance, sovereignty derives. The government is the operative part of the state. Its actions and foundational guidelines are framed in the constitution and, ultimately, must respond to the interests of the nation.

Therefore, when we speak of national security, we are referring in principle to the security of the nation in its entirety and not only to that of the state or government — although it is surely the latter two who hold the greatest responsibility for the security of the nation under any representative political system. The security of the nation is based on the protection and strengthening of national objectives in the face of external threats, whether they explicitly originate from abroad or result as a consequence of internal vulnerabilities.

A strong state has greater capacity to confront internal and external threats to national security. This brings us to the problem of the relation between the state and the government. In Mexico, it is usually assumed that the strength of the state is tied to that of the government. This supposition leads to the idea that the government may make use of the resources of the state in whatever manner necessary to guarantee the security of the nation.

To put the security of the government before that of the state, and the state before the nation, distorts the relationship between state, government, and nation, contravening the concept of the government and the state at the service of the nation. To justify governmental actions toward the population for "reasons of state" is to contradict the broadest definition of national security, granting to the government a margin for maneuver that can easily surpass the boundaries of its constitutional mandate.

An example of this was the arrest of the oil union boss, "La Quina" (Joaquín Hernández Galicia), during which the government used state resources, including the armed forces. The government argued that the offense of stockpiling arms constituted a threat to the institutions of the state and, therefore, the state was entitled to resort to the legitimate use of one of its own resources — the armed forces — to preserve those institutions. In reality, the oil union leader was not threatening an armed uprising — at least, the nation was never so informed. Instead, his strength within the political system was of such magnitude that, at a delicate political moment, the government saw the need to limit the scope of his political influence within key sectors of Mexican society.

Were the actions taken in order to protect the nation, the state, or the government? It is evident that the political motives for the arrest were linked to the threat La Quina represented to the government. However, this did not justify the use of state resources, including the armed forces, since it was unclear that the alleged offense was really a threat to the nation.

The fact that in Mexico the differences between security of the government, security of the state, and security of the nation are not clearly recognized in political practice corresponds to the nearly total lack of checks and balances within the political system. In fact, the existence of a strong executive, a congress under the control of the majority party, and a judiciary subordinate to the executive leaves considerable room for the exercise of authority with virtual impunity. This lack of real counterweights allows for the exercise of authority often beyond the bounds of the law.

Beyond this problem, the Mexican judicial system suffers from an insufficiency of human and material resources, creating quantitative and qualitative deficiencies in the administration of justice. Since those responsible for the administration of justice are part of the government and the state, the law all too often responds to their interests, leaving the nation and the citizenry as residual considerations.

A similar situation exists throughout the system; from the coast guard police to the employee issuing government permits, the citizen is seen as an adversary. If one were to conduct a poll concerning the manner in which providers of public services exercise their responsibilities — especially those having to do with internal security and the law — the overall opinion would hardly be favorable.

An examination of the boundaries between government, state, and nation will permit us, then, to establish with greater clarity the authority of the state and the government with respect to national security, bringing us, in turn, to a more precise definition of the concept of national security itself.

Internal Security and National Security

The distinction between national security and internal security is highly political and is subject to frequent distortions, since the close ties between them make difficult the process of delimiting their boundaries. To say that internal threats fall within the realm internal security, and external threats within that of national security, proves to be inadequate, because it is sometimes the case that internal threats are relevant to national security in the context of broader circumstances.

Matters having to do with the security of the government or state due to internal factors are threats to national security only when they are likely to produce internal instability, threaten the survival of state institutions, or, in the extreme case, produce possible civil war. Such instances would include the following:

1. Treasonous actions on the part of internal actors — such as citizens or public officials who provide assistance to foreign governments

2. Violent actions against the state — such as military coups — that attempt to bring about significant changes in the structure of power in clear violation of constitutional arrangements

3. Criminal activity that reaches the level of generalized vandalism and disorder — such as has been seen in the recent past in some South American countries, where the armed forces have been called upon to restore order.

Actions undertaken as an expression of opposition, protest, or dissent are matters of a strictly internal political nature, as long as they fall within the scope of those rights granted by law to citizens and social organizations. Public demands should be channeled through state mechanisms and, in principle, should not result in any use of the armed forces and should not be considered part of the national security agenda.

When such actions go beyond legal limits, the state has the right to use its resources to maintain order, while also strictly adhering to the law. In any event, governmental responses to revolts, unauthorized demonstrations, guerrilla movements, and so on relate to internal security — as long as such discontent is not the product of the support or participation of external actors and does not threaten or make vulnerable the existence of the state. In those extreme cases where the state is so threatened, the Mexican constitution provides for the use of the armed forces. All this notwithstanding — as Sergio Aguayo's contribution to this volume shows — the use of the concept of national security in Mexico has, until now, conceptually and operatively subsumed the distinguishably different category of internal security.

The lamentable events that took place at the Plaza de las Tres Culturas in October 1968 serve to illustrate this fact. On that occasion, the Mexican army and state paramilitary forces were used to control a demonstration that began as a student protest. Several hundred persons died, the majority of them students. At that time, the official discourse spoke of the "interventions of external agents" and raised the conflict to the level of "national security." Thus, that which began as an internal political conflict was transformed into a confrontation between military and paramilitary forces and a defenseless civil population. With the bloody events concluded, however, the Mexican people were never satisfactorily apprised of the nature of the supposed external meddling that had justified such extreme actions on the part of the state.

Another area of security that frequently meets with some confusion is that having to do with natural disasters. In principle, any phenomenon that affects the entire nation can become a matter of national security. However, in the case of natural disasters, it is not easy to identify the moment or magnitude at which a catastrophe becomes a matter of national security. Whether or not to declare a state of emergency is ultimately a decision that can only be made by the head of state.

The earthquake that struck Mexico City in September 1985 was of a magnitude sufficient to unleash the prospect of public disorder and, therefore, a state of emergency was declared. However, within the government, there was a lack of clarity with respect to what means the executive should use to manage the situation. According to the National Development Plan III in effect at the time, the task fell under the purview of the armed forces. However, the president apparently decided that the first responsible official was the minister of the interior, followed by the elected official in charge of the Federal District. The armed forces were to serve these officials in a supporting role.

In large measure, the rapid and positive response of the population was that which, in the first few hours, prevented the tragedy from leading to chaos, thus obviating the need to invoke national security measures. In the end, cooperation between citizens and the authorities (who were somewhat tardy in their response) proved to be adequate to control the situation. Improvisation, an innate quality of the Mexican people, in this instance yielded positive results. But a corollary issuing from this experience is that the state apparatus was unprepared for an emergency of this magnitude, not only with respect to resources but in the realm of decision making as well.

The protection of the person of the president — chief of state, leader of the government, and in charge of a highly sophisticated security apparatus comprised of military, police, and civilian elements — is directly related to the security of the state and the government. In the case of Mexico, as a matter of fact, the merging of the powers of the government and the state in just one person creates an organic fusion of the security of the state and that of the government. Strictly speaking, the security of the president, governors, and high state officials should be handled in rigorous accordance with the law — although in practice the freedom for action allotted to the security apparatus frequently eclipses the rights and security of the citizens themselves. This is one of the elements that continues to reflect the enormous weight of the presidency in the Mexican political system.

In Latin America, the dangerous fusion of internal security and national security has given the concept of national security a negative connotation. Placing the security of the government before that of the state or nation has even led to changes in the law giving special powers to the executive, thus attempting to legitimate the situation. In such cases, the supposition that enemies of the government are, by definition, enemies of the state and nation has served to justify decades of military government, repression, the loss of individual rights, and the overall absence of a democratic life.

However, the process of democratization that has taken place in various South American countries over the past decade has had an important impact on strategic thinking. Some sectors of the armed forces — discredited before civil society — have once again adopted the concept of national security as security in the face of external threats and not a struggle against internal insurgency.

In sum, the clarification of what is meant in Mexico by internal security and security of the government appears today as worthy of further research and reflection — not least for the sake of a better political and operative definition of national security.

National Security and National Defense

In order to examine the difference between national security and national defense, it is useful to begin by reviewing the concept of national defense, identifying the functions assigned to the armed forces in relation to national security.

For reasons having to do with the history and geopolitics of Mexico, it is difficult to understand the Mexican concept of national security in terms of the military defense of sovereignty and national interest. With the exception of a very short period in the first years of its independence, Mexico has never been a country with an expansionist policy. And given its geopolitical position as neighbor to the preeminent world power, its international position has not rested with the capacity for the use of force. Since the last century, the United States presence to the north and on the seas has been a determining factor, not only because it has made any possibility of a strategy of national defense based on military capacity ineffective but also because it has limited the possibility of Mexico's consolidating its regional position through the use of force as an instrument of foreign policy. This is due to the fact that, in any regional scenario in which there was the possibility of economic, political, or territorial dispute, Mexico always found itself in a position of clear inferiority in relation to the resources available to the United States in the pursuit of its objectives.

As a result of these factors, Mexican governments have set aside military defense as a possible foundation for their national security plans and have, instead, elaborated ever more sophisticated schemes to promote independence and sovereignty in a manner more in accordance with the nation's real capabilities in the international system. Thus, the definition of national security goes beyond the idea of national defense understood solely in terms of the use of the armed forces.

But not only is the concept of national security not synonymous with national defense, the mission of the armed forces is not exclusively restricted to the realm of national defense. The 1983-1988 National Development Plan defines the objectives of the functions of the armed forces as "defense of the territorial integrity, independence, and sovereignty of the nation" — although it goes on to say, "In view of the fact that circumstances have changed, the armed forces have been transformed so that their strictly military original role has been recast to include growing activities related to the well-being of the community." Hence, in addition to providing for the defense of territorial integrity, the armed forces "undertake complementary tasks in regard to national development, with great impact in the areas of the country with the greatest social problems."

The 1989-1994 National Development Plan repeats the aforementioned duties of the military, as well as adding such tasks as countering drug trafficking, assisting with the recovery from national disasters, and protecting the ecosystem. Within the plan there is also an explicit mention of the modernization of the army; however, it seems to refer not to any changes in the army's mission, but simply to improvements in its professionalism and efficiency, as well as in the standard of living of personnel and their families.

National Defense and Threats to Territorial Integrity

The armed forces respond to assaults on the nation's territorial integrity. Since actual military incursions are hardly likely, we mean by this the following possible threats, which correspond more closely to contemporary realities: the illegal use of territorial waters, the unauthorized use of the exclusive economic zone or airspace, and the illegal crossing of borders by foreigners for political or military ends.

An example of the last threat was seen during the 1980s when Guatemalan armed forces engaged in sporadic incursions into Mexican territory in the pursuit of refugees or guerrilla forces that had crossed over the border in search of a sanctuary. In all of these areas, then, the army, navy, and air force have fundamental responsibility for the defense of territorial sovereignty. The accomplishment of these tasks requires constant vigilance and control of coastal areas, airspace, and the land borders.

In recent years, the duties of the armed forces along the southern frontier have intensified due to the conflicts in Central America. This has meant the creation of a new military zone, both for physical surveillance of the border and in order to protect strategic oil and hydroelectric installations from possible attacks from abroad.

Similarly, there has been growing participation on the part of the armed forces in the fight against drug trafficking, which, while not falling within the area of national defense in the strictest sense, does fall, in general terms, within the area of national security. The participation of the armed forces in such efforts — which, in principle, fall under the purview of the attorney general's office — brings with it new elements that bear upon their structure and functions. Among these new elements are the increasing use of defense budget funds and human resources to counter drug trafficking, without the allocation of additional resources to replace them; the difficulties of inter-institutional coordination; the inherent problems that derive from exposing the army to a multimillion-dollar business that buys protection through corruption; and finally, the growing contact between some sectors of the armed forces and their counterparts in the U.S. military.

It is interesting to note that in the majority of cases in which the armed forces have engaged in operations related to internal security during the last few decades, explicit or implicit reference has been made to national security. Such was the case during actions taken against guerrilla groups in the 1970s, during efforts to control demonstrations protesting the political system's shortcomings, and most recently during the campaign against drug trafficking (the legal vacuum in this area, notwithstanding).

In the field of national defense, there are threats that, curiously, are not handled by the armed forces. This is the case with any possible military confrontation between the superpowers, which could have catastrophic effects along Mexico's northern border were there to be nuclear explosions in the southern regions of the United States. In the face of such a threat, it is quite clear that national security cannot be based on the traditional concept of military defense.

This serves to remind us that, in the Mexican case, there is a tight linkage between national security and politico-diplomatic activities. Since Mexico is a country not given to the use of force as a means of international influence, and since it lacks any nuclear deterrent, its politico-diplomatic efforts necessarily play an important role in the defense of its territorial integrity. Based upon this logic, Mexico's efforts have centered on the international campaign for nuclear disarmament — in particular, the pursuit and enactment of a treaty proscribing nuclear arms in Latin America. Mexico has participated in the Group of Six since its creation and is continually active in multilateral discussions pertaining to disarmament. Looking ahead, Mexico is likely to take on an active role in discussions concerning the prevention of nuclear accidents in the southern United States and the disposal of nuclear wastes in that neighboring country.

Finally, there exists today an enormous potential for the exploration of links between Mexican national security, regional security in Latin America, and hemispheric security. This area, which also falls in the politico-diplomatic arena, requires further significant research efforts and political attention as well as ongoing dialogue with the military.

Instability and the Armed Forces

In any country with the potential for political and social instability, the possibility of a military coup is frequently discussed. But under the conditions prevailing in Mexico, such a scenario is unlikely.

First, even though there may be those within the military whose pretensions go beyond their assigned responsibilities, the nationalistic, institutional character of the armed forces is such that the possibility of the military acting outside the bounds of existing constitutional arrangements is limited. Second, civilian authorities have, over the last fifty years, developed sophisticated means of controlling the armed forces, defeating all those who have attempted to change the political path of the country by force of arms. Third, the lack of experience of most elements of the military in the exercise of political power over the last few decades limits the capacity of the armed forces to take power and maintain it. Fourth, the institutional character of the armed forces has been such that there have been few linkages to powerful sectors outside of the state. While the ascendance to power of the military in other countries has been frequently facilitated by alliances with groups possessing private economic power, in Mexico the institutional spirit and essentially popular origin of the armed forces has made such alliances improbable. Finally, the Mexican political culture is not conducive to military political power. In a system like that found in Mexico, where a complex mosaic exists among ethnicities, social groups, classes, and subcultures, a radical change in the arrangements of coexistence would prove an almost unachievable task.

Unfortunately, these observations are essentially speculative, since the closed nature of the military with respect to how officials perceive the country impedes the study of its relation to society. However, the unprecedented vote of the armed forces in favor of Cuauhtémoc Cárdenas, opposition candidate of the left, in the 1988 elections provides us one fact that points to future areas open for investigation.

Drug Trafficking

If the problem of the production and illicit sale of drugs has a long history in relations between Mexico and the United States — from 1945 to 1989 there were forty-eight bilateral accords signed concerning such matters — it was in the decade of the 1970s that the problem acquired unprecedented dimensions. In the United States, its definition as a matter of national security has, for the first time, brought the direct participation of the U.S. military on its own territory in the fight against drugs.

For Mexico, this problem leads to distinct threats: internal and external, traditional and nontraditional. First, the availability and, therefore, the consumption of drugs has grown by virtue of the increase in the production and trafficking of drugs within the national territory — although the problem has not remotely approached the dimensions of the drug problem in the United States. Second, there has been a notable increase within Mexico in the involvement of individuals, both foreign and national, in the production and distribution of narcotics. Within this group one finds a range from peasants, who find it economically more advantageous to grow illegal products on their land, to multimillionaire heads of drug networks who produce, refine, and market drugs and who have succeeded in placing themselves among the top rank of drug kingpins. The latter are also tied to foreigners within Mexico who engage in operations related to either the production or transshipment of drugs.

The battle against drug trafficking in Mexico is a problem complicated by the large number of agencies involved: the attorney general's office, state prosecutors' offices, state judicial police, all supported by the growing participation of the armed forces. Moreover, the attorney general's office and the intelligence bodies, especially the Mexican Interpol, not only have to coordinate with domestic agencies but also have the responsibility of increasingly working collaboratively with foreign — principally, U.S. — agencies so as to conduct international operations against drug traffickers.

In the area of politics and diplomacy, drug trafficking has indisputable consequences for the bilateral agenda of Mexico and the United States. Pressures from the U.S. government during the 1980s have contributed to decisions to increase the human resources and equipment used by Mexico to counter drug trafficking and have resulted in additional programs of binational cooperation. Within such programs, the U.S. government has pressed for greater direct participation in Mexico of U.S. agencies. However, necessary international collaboration can complicate matters; here, it is sufficient to recall the consequences of the killing of Drug Enforcement Administration (DEA) agent Enrique Camarena in Mexico in 1985. And to all of these difficulties should be added the problems that exist among the various U.S. agencies.

While the drug problem advances more rapidly than solutions — especially in the United States — pressures, such as the annual certification process and the continual attacks by groups within the United States who believe Mexico is making insufficient anti-drug efforts, continue to make the drug issue one of the most difficult in U.S.Mexican relations. Despite the fact that the president of Mexico himself has identified drug trafficking as the principal problem for national security, the reasoning behind such an assessment is still far from being clear and precise. And within scholarly circles, studies of the drug problem have gone from a trickle to a torrent.

External Threats to Internal Stability

Acts of international terrorism by foreign groups or governments do not really pose a significant threat to Mexico. In fact, even the sort of outside intervention that historically came from the United States has fallen into disuse as a consequence of the stability of the nation's political institutions and the deeply rooted nature of Mexican nationalism. Further, the traditional pluralism of Mexican foreign policy has kept the country from serving as either sanctuary or fertile soil for terrorist actions. The establishment of tighter immigration controls upon the entry of foreign nationals — itself a product of proximity to the United States — has made even more difficult any such activities.

There are, however, possible external threats to internal stability that could come about through spillover effects related to Mexico's geopolitical position. The Central American crisis during the 1980s was the example par excellence of this possibility. On the one hand, the geography of the region lent itself to the passage of large numbers of refugees to or through Mexico, engendering the various border difficulties with Guatemala mentioned earlier. On the other hand, a generalized war in Central America would have posed a threat with unpredictable consequences. This consideration contributed greatly to the course taken in Mexico's foreign policy toward the region in recent years. Had the position of the United States toward Central America shifted sharply toward a military solution — an approach which seemed within the realm of possibility on more than one occasion — Mexico would undoubtedly have come under pressure to integrate itself within U.S. defense schemes aimed at protecting the northern neighbor's southern border. Here, then, one sees with considerable clarity the link between foreign policy and national security, although its incorporation into political and strategic thinking remains inadequate.

Internal Threats to National Security

One of the most complex subjects for analysis is, undoubtedly, that of internal threats to national security. We have suggested thinking about national security in relation to areas of vulnerability deriving from weaknesses or inconsistencies in the nation's chosen political course, which may, thereby, invite the interference or intervention of external actors in the nation's political life, altering or blocking its development. The problem of internal threats should be seen in this broader context and is a poorly explored area ripe for further investigation. For purposes of this essay, we will limit ourselves to a brief survey of some of these threats and sketch out their significance.

Political Aspects

Although one can hardly speak of a crisis in Mexico's governmental institutions or the state, it is true that it is increasingly difficult to resolve the economic problems of large sectors of the population, democratize political life, remedy accumulated social ills, determine Mexico's proper role in a changing international system, and grapple with such day-to-day problems as crime and pollution without the support and involvement of a majority of the population. Faced with such difficulties, it becomes increasingly problematic for a highly centralized government — with limited economic resources — to proceed effectively while lacking credibility among many sectors of the population.

Toward the end of 1987 and throughout 1988, as a result of the apparent loss of power of labor and the lack of working class support for then-candidate Salinas, there was considerable discussion of the end of corporatism. However, the manner in which the Salinas government put into place the Pact for Stability and Economic Growth in December 1988 (and renewed it in June 1989) not only contradicted any such conclusion but also revealed a more sophisticated corporatism that formally included business groups.

Growing demands for democracy, which were expressed in overwhelming fashion during the federal elections of 1988, indicate that real democratization is increasingly necessary for the country's political and social stability. It will be most difficult for the government to confront Mexico's enormous challenges successfully unless a majority of the population identifies with its national goals and objectives. A nation without cohesion or national unity, without a credible or trustworthy political leadership, becomes vulnerable, by definition.

If the government and the state maintain power by means of concentration and centralization, with limited genuine participation, it becomes necessary to expend a considerable amount of scant resources for the maintenance and strengthening of legitimacy, which, at the same time, diminishes the resources available for the pursuit of national interests. The distorted functioning of some of the key institutions of the government and the state, particularly those having to do with internal security and the administration of justice, combined with lukewarm or embryonic political reforms, could lead over time to potentially explosive social and political circumstances. In such a situation, the temptation to muddle and mingle national security with internal security, governmental security, and state security becomes ever greater. This dilemma will be a topic of central concern in Mexico over the next few years, and it further advances the argument that both the state and civil society need to deepen the discussion and analysis of national security.

Food Production and Supply

National sovereignty and autonomy do not imply only territorial sovereignty and the management of problems related to it. Of equal concern is the maintenance of those conditions that ensure the viability of national objectives and aspirations over the medium to long term. A country with critical deficiencies in the material well-being of its inhabitants is clearly vulnerable to external forces. In this context, there arise considerations that touch upon national security but which have, traditionally, not received attention.

An inadequate food supply is one such factor. Here it is sufficient to recall the history over the last few decades of various African and Asian countries that have had to resort to "international charity" so as to provide for the mere physical survival of their populations. In more than a few cases, this assistance has resulted in modifications of the beneficiary country's national plans and has led to changes whose real benefits were far from evident.

Financial Aspects

The emergence of a global economy today places old challenges in distinctly new conditions. However, today more than ever, any program of modernization aimed at addressing these changes must give priority to bringing about a model of economic development that benefits a clear majority of the Mexican people. A decade into the debt crisis, the programs of structural adjustment "suggested" by the international financial institutions — whose seal of approval is indispensable for the acquisition of further resources from the commercial banks — have not yet been the solution to the pressing development problems of indebted Latin American nations. At the same time, foreign investment presents a problem in those instances when its contribution to national needs is less than the "decapitalization" that results from the exploitation of nonrenewable resources, the degradation of the environment, and above all, the net transfer of resources abroad rather than reinvestment within the host country. These negative outcomes represent, in effect, a loss of the national patrimony, and such a systematic loss of assets is especially serious under conditions of low internal savings and a stifling debt.

The external debt is intimately related, in fact, to many dimensions of Mexican national development. As a result, the scope of negotiations must be sufficient to take into consideration such factors as foreign investment, economic liberalization, the freeing of exchange controls, and plans for economic integration.

Insufficient attention to these areas could bring economic concerns into the realm of national security. This could happen, for example, were coveted foreign investment to take place indiscriminately, leading to the growing influence of foreign actors with respect to the distribution of the national product and the overall goals and means pursued in the name of national development. Economic modernization is a solution to all of these problems only if it is coherently responsive to an integrated conception of national goals and objectives. Thus, the area of the economy today also demands greater study in relation to national security.

The Institutional Expression of Mexican National Security

The analysis of the political management of national security is still definitionally imprecise with respect to the relative powers of governmental branches and is skewed toward the powers of the executive. The seriousness of this difficulty is to be found in the fact that it is precisely the shortcomings in the institutional and operative translation of the concept that frequently distort the concept itself.

The concentration of functions related to national security in the executive is to the benefit of the government but not necessarily to the benefit of the nation. For cxample, as we have seen, it was evident at the time of the 1985 earthquake that in some areas there did not exist a sufficiently solid, coherent, and functional framework to confront crisis situations. The absence of a more precise and coherent framework is linked to the fragmentation of managerial duties and complicates the effective handling of delicate state responsibilities. In fact, for the citizenry — including researchers — it is unclear in certain instances who has authority in the conduct of national security.

It is for this reason that the legislative definition and codification of national security tasks takes on such significance, with respect to both fundamental statutes and secondary laws. The more effective conduct of national security activities is enhanced by an appropriate institutional and operative translation of the concept of national security that results from a recognition of 1) the role of the legislative branch in the definition and framing of the legal limits operationally associated with the concept, 2) the role of the judicial branch in operational oversight, and 3) the role of civil society with respect to both the definition and assessment of national security. This also increases the capacity of the system to modify its course, whether this is called for by changes in the nature of various threats or required by distortions in the system's operative performance.

The recently created National Security Research Center is, at least potentially, the appropriate, nonoperative institutional site to undertake the important task of the definition of duties, while both the National Defense College and the Advanced Center for National Studies are engaged in systematic analysis of issues related to national security. With the recently established National Security Cabinet, there is an attempt — at least in some measure — to create a solid framework for crisis management.

However, it is certain that this debate will have to involve other sectors of society not engaged in operational tasks, which not only will contribute to the legal and conceptual development of Mexican national security but also will lead to a greater state-society sharing of responsibilities — an inevitable product of the healthy practice of pluralism and democracy.

Contributors

Sergio Aguayo Quezada. Professor, Center for International Studies, El Colegio de México; President, Mexican Human Rights Academy

Bruce Michael Bagley. Professor of International Studies and Associate Dean, Graduate School of International Studies of the University of Miami

Roger Bartra. Professor and Researcher, Institute for Social Research, Universidad Nacional Autónoma de México (UNAM)

Jorge A. Bustamante. President, El Colegio de la Frontera Norte

Matthew Edel. Until his death, Professor of Urban Studies, Queens College; Co-Director of the Project on U.S.-Mexico Relations at the Bildner Center for Western Hemisphere Studies, the Graduate School and University Center of the City University of New York

Candace Kim Edel. Lecturer, Department of Urban Studies, Queens College; Research Associate, Bildner Center for Western Hemisphere Studies of the Graduate School and University Center of the City University of New York

Javier A. Elguea. Professor, Center for Sociological Studies, El Colegio de México

359

Guadalupe González G. Researcher, Division of International Studies, Centro de Investigación y Docencia Económicas, A.C (CIDE)

Luis Herrera-Lasso M. Principal Advisor, Under-Secretariat of Foreign Affairs, Mexico

Diana M. Liverman. Associate Professor of Geography and Earth Systems Science, Pennsylvania State University

Lorenzo Meyer. Professor, Center for International Studies, El Colegio de México

Richard H. Moss. Deputy Executive Director, Dimensions of Global Environmental Change Program, Royal Swedish Academy of Science

Richard A. Nuccio. Staff Consultant, Subcommittee on Western Hemisphere Affairs, Foreign Affairs Committee, U.S. House of Representatives

Angelina M. Ornelas. Media Relations Specialist

Iván Restrepo. Director, *La Jornada Ecológica*

Richard C. Rockwell. Executive Director, Inter-University Consortium for Political and Social Research, Institute for Social Research, University of Michigan

Gene Sharp. Senior Scholar-in-Residence, Albert Einstein Institution, Cambridge, Massachusetts

Jeffrey Stark. Research Associate and Managing Editor of *North-South ISSUES* and *North-South FOCUS*, North-South Center of the University of Miami

Cathryn L. Thorup. Director of Studies and Programs, Center for U.S.-Mexican Studies, University of California at San Diego

María Celia Toro. Professor, Center for International Studies, El Colegio de México

About the Editors

B ruce Michael Bagley is associate dean and professor of international studies at the Graduate School of International Studies of the University of Miami. He formerly taught at the Universidad de Los Andes in Bogotá, Colombia, and at the School of Advanced International Studies at Johns Hopkins University in Washington, D.C. He is the author of many articles, monographs, and books, including most recently, *Development Postponed: The Political Economy of Central America, Contadora and the Diplomacy of Peace in Central America*, and *The State and the Peasantry in Contemporary Colombia*.

S ergio Aguayo Quezada is a prominent Mexican academic, journalist, and human rights activist. He is a former Social Science Research Council-MacArthur Foundation Fellow and is professor of international relations at the Colegio de México. He also is a regular columnist for the newspaper *La Jornada* and serves as editor for the monthly magazine *Este País*. Professor Aguayo is president of the Mexican Academy of Human Rights and is co-author of *Escape from Violence: Refugees and Social Violence in the Third World*.

About the Publisher

THE NORTH-SOUTH CENTER promotes better relations among the United States, Canada, and the nations of Latin America and the Caribbean. The Center provides a disciplined, intellectual focus for improved relations, commerce, and understanding in the hemisphere, wherein major political, social, and economic issues are seen in a global perspective. The Center conducts programs of education, training, cooperative study, public outreach, and research and engages in an active program of publication and dissemination of information on the Americas. The North-South Center fosters linkages among academic and research institutions throughout the Americas and acts as an agent of change in the region.

Ambler H. Moss, Jr
Director, North-South Center

Richard Downes
Communications Director

Kathleen A. Hamman
Editorial Director

Mary M. Mapes
Publications Director

Jayne M. Weisblatt
Editor

Production Notes

This book was printed on 60 lb. Glatfelter Natural, text stock with a 10 point CIS cover stock.

The text of this volume was set in Garamond for the North-South Center's Publication Department, using Aldus Pagemaker 4.2, on a Macintosh Centris 650 computer. It was designed and formatted by Stephanie True Moss.

The cover was created by Mary M. Mapes using Adobe Photoshop 2.5 for the tritone photograph and Quark XPress 3.2 for the composition and color separation.

Cover photo by AP/Wide World Photos, featuring a view of Mexico City from Cerro de la Estrella.

This book was edited by Jeffrey Stark and Jayne M. Weisblatt.

This publication was printed by Thomson-Shore, Inc. of Dexter, Michigan, U.S.A.